An American Girl
in the
Hawaiian Islands

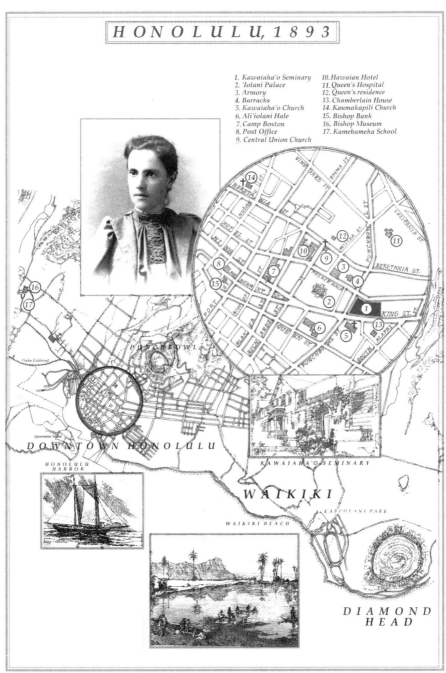

HONOLULU, 1893

1. Kawaiahaʻo Seminary
2. ʻIolani Palace
3. Armory
4. Barracks
5. Kawaiahaʻo Church
6. Aliʻiolani Hale
7. Camp Boston
8. Post Office
9. Central Union Church
10. Hawaian Hotel
11. Queen's Hospital
12. Queen's residence
13. Chamberlain House
14. Kaumakapili Church
15. Bishop Bank
16. Bishop Museum
17. Kamehameha School

DOWNTOWN HONOLULU

HONOLULU HARBOR

KAWAIAHAʻO SEMINARY

WAIKIKI

WAIKIKI BEACH

DIAMOND HEAD

Honolulu, 1893, montage by Barron Storey. Incorporates a map of the lower part of the city of Honolulu by Loebenstein, Library of Congress; a portrait of Carrie P. Winter; and sketches of Kawaiahaʻo Female Seminary, the missionary vessel *Hiram Bingham,* and Diamond Head.

An American Girl
in the Hawaiian Islands

Letters of Carrie Prudence Winter
1890–1893

Selected and Edited by
Sandra Bonura and Deborah Day

Foreword by
C. Kalani Beyer

University of Hawai'i Press
Honolulu

Library of Congress Cataloging-in-Publication Data

Winter, Carrie Prudence, 1866–1942.
An American girl in the Hawaiian Islands: letters of Carrie Prudence Winter, 1890–1893 /
selected and edited by Sandra Bonura and Deborah Day; foreword by C. Kalani Beyer.
p. cm.
Includes bibliographical references and index.
ISBN 978-0-8248-3627-6 (hardcover: alk. paper)
1. Winter, Carrie Prudence, 1866-1942—Correspondence. 2. Women missionaries—Hawaii—
Correspondence. 3. Missions—Educational work—Hawaii. 4. Hawaii—History—To 1893.
I. Bonura, Sandra, 1954– II. Day, Deborah, 1951– III. Title.
BV3680.H4W566 2012
996.9'027092—dc23 [B]   2012003454

University of Hawai`i Press books are printed on acid-free paper
and meet the guidelines for permanence and durability
of the Council on Library Resources.

Design and production services provided by
Peak Services (peakservices.squarespace.com)

Printed by Sheridan Books, Inc.

Contents ⫸

Acknowledgments ⑊

First and foremost, our special appreciation must go to our husbands, Carl Bonura and Robert Day, who deserve much credit for their practical and emotional support as well as their patience throughout this long process.

It is impossible to mention all the dedicated scholars and family members of Carrie Winter's students in Hawai'i who not only showed us true *aloha* spirit but went over and above the call of duty to assist us in our efforts to track sources. During the entire research process, we were met with the delightful courtesy and warmth that we now know defines the people of Hawai'i.

Our great appreciation goes to Janet Zisk and Candace Lee of the Kamehameha School Archives for warmly inviting us into their domain multiple times to use their collection, providing valuable support, and offering advice on sources documenting the education of Hawaiian children in the nineteenth-century. We acknowledge the very capable staff of the Hawai'i State Archives, the Hawai'i State Library, and the Kaua'i Historical Society. The experts at the Hawaiian Mission Children's Society Library and the Hawaiian Historical Society were great resources, especially Barbara Dunn, who identified the first royal figure we found in a photograph and who encouraged us to send a book proposal to the University of Hawai'i Press. Our warm thanks go to Masako Ikeda, acquisitions editor, who fell in love with this book from the beginning. Ultimately, our greatest appreciation goes to UHP director William Hamilton for his unwavering support. We could not have finished this book without his steady guidance. His selected reviewers helped us shape and mold the book in rich ways, and we are most grateful for the time these scholars spent reading our manuscript and providing thoughtful and critical evaluation.

We are exceptionally grateful to C. Kalani Beyer, who provided the foreword. His scholarly work on the history of nineteenth-century missionary education in Hawai'i was foundational reading for us at the beginning of this project. Our discussions with him were invaluable as he helped us to see new meanings in the letters and to better understand his Hawaiian heritage.

We thank the incredible staff of the Scripps Institution of Oceanography Archives and Library at the University of California, San Diego, especially Peter Brueggeman, Carolyn Rainey, and Rebecca Smith, who made the collection accessible to us and always made us feel "at home." Tracking down the background of the Oberlin missionary teachers could not have been accomplished without the help of archivist Ken Grossi at Oberlin College Archives, his staff, and Lindsay Fusfeld, our research assistant. Michael J. Paulus and his staff at Whitman College and Northwest Archives also assisted us in tracking down teachers. Many thanks to Jack von Euw and David Kessler of The Bancroft Library, University of California–Berkeley, who helped us access their rich Hawaiian collections, and to the staff at Houghton Library, Harvard, for assistance with using the American Board of Commissioners for Foreign Missions collection. We thank the Huntington Library and its staff for access to its rich collections.

We acknowledge with gratitude the assistance of the families of the Kawaiahaʻo Female Seminary students, who aided us in the identification of Carrie's pupils and inspired us with their knowledge of Hawaiian history and genealogy. Their enthusiasm added buoyancy to the project and continually reminded us why this story should be told.

With heartfelt gratitude, we thank the families of Lilla Estelle Appleton and Ida May Pope who offered diaries, correspondence, and priceless photographs for this book. Mary Lois Ivey, Ida Pope's grand niece, has been an unwavering supporter of this project from the beginning. We considered it an honor and a privilege to hear stories from the past, and we thank each family member for this generous gift.

If the Michener family members had not safeguarded Carrie's correspondence after the death of their Uncle Charlie, this book would never have been realized. Our gratefulness also extends to Marlon Maus for his gracious permission to visit Carrie's home, where the 1892 mat purchased from Molokaʻi still remains on the ceiling, and for the opportunity to climb up into the attic where the old trunks, once hidden behind a false wall, began the adventure of this book. The Pacific School of Religion and the University of California graciously granted us permission to publish Carrie's letters, and we thank them very much.

The creative frontispiece by the renowned artist Barron Storey delightfully captures Carrie's 1893 Honolulu. We are so very grateful for the time he and his research partner and wife, Petra Davis, took out of their busy schedules to provide this beautiful and lasting record of the original Kawaiahaʻo Female Seminary location.

This book could not have been finished without the selfless contribution of all these people—archivists, librarians, genealogists, historians, editors, artists, and families. We thank you and hope you see the benefit of your work in *An American Girl in the Hawaiian Islands*.

Foreword ⫸

Providing a Context for
An American Girl in the Hawaiian Islands

C. Kalani Beyer

*A*n American Girl in the Hawaiian Islands *provides a means for the reader to understand the history of Hawai'i from the perspective of a teacher who was born in the United States who moved to the Islands to teach Hawaiian girls for three years. Contextualizing this history helps the reader understand the experiences Carrie Winter shares, including her work with Hawaiian girls, the political atmosphere, and her social outings with other prominent citizens of Hawai'i. More successfully than most non-western societies during the nineteenth century, Hawai'i was transformed into a modern nation and education played a primary role in this outcome.

The Hawaiian Islands were brought into the Western orbit in 1778, when James Cook made contact with the archipelago. Between 1778 and 1820, when the missionaries arrived, Hawaiian society was already being transformed by the collision of external and internal forces. The most important change was precipitated by the death of Kamehameha, the figure who united the Islands into one kingdom, leading to the entire religious system rapidly dissolving. Even before the dissolution of the ancient religious system, the American Board of Commissioners for Foreign Missions (ABCFM), an interdenominational religious body whose membership was predominately Presbyterian and Congregational, had sent the first company of missionaries to Hawai'i. Upon their arrival on March 30, 1820, the missionaries learned of the downfall of the ancient religious system and were convinced that they had received God's grace, preparing the way for their "laboring in the field" of Hawai'i.

In 1810, the ABCFM was established according to the principles of cooperation and non-sectarianism, self-governing missions, and evangelism. The Board was organized to assign missionaries, individuals who were determined to become missionaries and individuals who had declared their willingness to prepare themselves for mission work (Anderson 1862). In 1860, Rufus

Anderson, ABCFM's senior secretary, stated that there were two essential qualifications for a missionary: consecration and common sense.

Patricia Grimshaw (1989) stated that both the men and women who were sent as missionaries to Hawai'i were prepared by their education, work experience, sense of calling, and adherence to American values. The men were well-educated graduates of a variety of institutions predominant in New England. Congregationalists and Presbyterians by affiliation, they usually came from areas in which farming was the principal livelihood. They were from the middle class and their lives were marked by familiarity with a variety of skills and by hard work, self-denial, thrift, and initiative. The women of the mission were efficient and versatile. From rural middle class backgrounds, they were adaptable, skilled and willing to work to fund their own education, and were unaccustomed to leisure or comfort. A substantial number of these women received their training from the female seminaries emerging during the first half of the nineteenth century. When the daughters of these missionaries or new recruits from the United States took over the education of Hawaiian females during the last forty years of the nineteenth century, many more were trained in female seminaries. As Miss Winter's letters indicate, many of her colleagues at Kawaiaha'o Female Seminary were graduates of Oberlin College. While Oberlin College was not a female seminary, its curriculum included manual labor and manual training with a strong Christian education, so the Hawaiian Mission eagerly sought its graduates.

The Hawaiian community was in a vulnerable stage of transition when the missionaries arrived in 1820. The missionaries believed that they could win "the spiritual allegiance, the hearts and minds, of the inhabitants" (Grimshaw 1989, xviii). Between 1820 and 1844, twelve companies of missionaries were sent to Hawai'i, 71 women and 66 men for a total of 137 members. Thirty-seven were ordained ministers; 59 were wives of the men; 24 were teachers (12 were single women and the other 12 were spouses chosen for their ability to teach), 4 were administrators, 1 was a farmer, 2 were mechanics, and 4 were printers. Between 1854 and 1894, the ABCFM sent 5 additional ministers as the need arose.[1] The ABCFM ended the Sandwich Islands Mission (SIM) in 1863 and the Hawaiian Evangelical Association (HEA) took over its labors. Those missionaries who remained, along with their children continued to convert Hawaiians to Christianity and also to an American culture.

Thirty-five missionary couples stayed their entire lives in Hawai'i and among them, raised 225 children.[2] In 1853, as the number of second-generation missionaries grew substantially, the Hawaiian Mission Children's Society (HMCS) was formed. Many of these second-generation missionaries would enter fields not related to mission activities, but through the HMCS, they were always able to participate.

Western education arrived in Hawai'i with the missionaries by the ABCFM in 1820. From the beginning, the obstacles appeared insurmountable. Missionaries were confronted by either Hawaiians clinging to their ancient religion or anti-religious whites, who included sailors, adventurers, merchants, and anyone who disagreed with Christian teaching. The history of the missionaries in Hawai'i was thus one of a battle waged on two fronts: carrying out a mission that required converting Hawaiians to Christianity, and fighting the immoral institutions and values of their irreligious white brothers, who threatened to undo all the good works they attempted.

The missionaries represented the best of the Calvinist faith. In the short run, they were successful. But the accomplishments of their mission were not achieved without the help of Hawaiians, especially the *ali'i* (chiefs). From the time of the missionaries' arrival, the *ali'i* held the power to decide if they would be allowed to proceed with their labors. Thus, with the support and aid of the *ali'i*, many schools were established including Lāhaināluna Seminary, Hilo Boys' Boarding Schools, and Waialua, Kohala, and Waioli Boys' Schools; a public education system for both genders; The Royal School which educated the High Chiefs (sixteen children, five of which became the last rulers of the Hawaiian Kingdom); Punahou School, which educated the missionary children (renamed Oahu College); and boarding schools for Hawaiian females which educated future wives for the Hawaiian students at the boys' schools (Alexander 1902; Alexander and Atkinson 1888; Westervelt 1911).

Beginning in the 1860s, four female seminaries were established: Wai'alua and Kawaiaha'o on the island of O'ahu, Kohala on the island of Hawai'i, and Mauna'olu on the island of Maui. These female seminaries were promoted based upon the model being used in the United States. The instruction at these American female seminaries tended to focus on performing the practical arts of running a household. Very often the schools included manual labor as a means to inculcate industriousness and to help defray expenses. By the time the Hawaiian female seminaries were founded, American female seminaries were utilizing manual training in their curriculum as well (Beyer 2003).

Initially, education for Hawaiian females was based upon the "cult of true womanhood." According to this belief, the home was the female's only sphere of influence. Women were considered morally superior to men, and the role of the mother was idealized in terms of her attention to and sacrifice for her husband and children (McClelland 1892).

Through the creation of seminaries for Hawaiian girls, there was a common thread of preparing the students to be ethical models in their own homes. Hawaiian female education was primarily a tool developed by the missionaries to convert Hawaiian girls to Christianity and to acculturate them to the values and lifestyle of Americans. This meant that education for Hawaiian girls was mostly directed at changing their values, attitudes, and behaviors. Moreover, throughout the nineteenth century, educators were concerned with what they saw as the sexual depravity of Hawaiian females (Grimshaw 1989). While at many points in Miss Winter's letters, she remarks on the severe discipline used to educate the Hawaiian girls, the reader should realize that during the nineteenth century this was a common practice, especially for non-Western children. From the establishment of the very first seminary to educate Hawaiian girls, the educators felt that strict discipline was necessary.

All four of the Hawaiian female seminaries begun after 1860 had a great deal in common. When one reads the reports of the principals of these seminaries, it becomes clear that they highlighted the successes and/or failures they were having in training their students to become good Christian housewives and models for other Hawaiian women. The principals exhibited pride in the marriages of their students, especially if their husbands were Hawaiian pastors or missionaries. Towards the last twenty years of the nineteenth century, female seminaries like Kawaiahaʻo, expanded their enrollment. Most likely this was due to the success the seminaries were having in preparing their students for paid employment, which coincided with the growth of industrial departments and the acquisition of industrial skills by the students.

During the second half of the nineteenth century, it became increasingly clear to the second generation of missionaries that as the Hawaiian economy modernized, the future of Hawaiians depended on their developing the work ethic and industrial skills necessary for success in an international economy. Thus, altering the curriculum at all their schools to include instruction in English and manual training was done to educate Hawaiians in skills they needed to become productive members of society. This goal required the collaboration of the Hawaiian leadership. However, by the early 1880s, it was apparent to the second-generation missionaries that there was resistance to their plans.

King Kalākaua was licensing *kahuna* (the ancient priesthood), legalizing the sale of opium, considering not renewing the lease of Pearl Harbor as a naval base to the United States, and threatening to throw all whites out of governmental positions. These actions by the King appeared to the missionaries to be moving the Kingdom backward, not forward. In 1887, the reaction was swift. American marines stormed ashore to support the missionaries who forced a new constitution on Kalākaua. This new constitution lessened the power of Hawaiians and increased the power of non-Hawaiians. Later, when the King died and his sister, Liliʻuokalani, became Queen, her attempt to return to the pre-1887 constitution, precipitated the revolution that ended the Hawaiian Kingdom.

Education in Hawaiʻi had always been a collaborative effort between the missionaries and the Native Hawaiian leadership. Even during the 1890s, when missionaries and Hawaiians were often in conflict over political issues, education remained a joint venture between the two groups. Even the business community supported the missionary schools. Thus, while Hawaiians, the missionary faction, and the business community (particularly the planters) often disagreed on the actions of the monarchy, importing foreign labor, and annexation to the United States, they all agreed on the value of the missionary schools for Hawaiians.

An American Girl in the Hawaiian Islands provides a personal means for the reader to understand both the history of Hawaiʻi during the early years of the 1890s and the education provided to Hawaiian students in a missionary school. As a scholar of the history of education in Hawaiʻi, I had read all the letters of the missionary principals and the reviews of schools by members of the Kingdom's department of education but I found that Carrie Winter's letters added a new perspective to my understanding. It is my hope that by providing this brief historical context, I have given the reader a better understanding of Miss Winter's letters. Having read numerous handwritten letters myself, I can appreciate the difficulty of having to read and understand the contents and then prepare them for publication in print. Sandra Bonura and Deborah Day have done an excellent job of selecting and editing these letters. I commend their efforts and I predict that you will enjoy this wonderful book.

NOTES

1. Inspecting the biographies provided in *Missionary Album* (1969) led to this breakdown of the 12 companies of missionaries.
2. These figures were obtained by using *Missionary Album* to determine who among the 12 companies spent the rest of their life in Hawai'i and then counting the number of children they had.

Notes on Transcription and Research ⫸

The Kofoid Papers are held at the Scripps Institution of Oceanography Archives, University of California–San Diego Libraries and include some forty cubic feet of correspondence dated from 1825 to 1947. Carrie Prudence Winter's Hawaiian material consists of some three cubic feet of letters, photographs, objects, published material. This includes both sides of her correspondence with Charles (Charlie) Kofoid, as well as her letters to her family, Oberlin College classmates, and letters from Kawaiaha'o Female Seminary students and teachers to her. Most letters and enclosures were found in their original postmarked envelopes.

This book focuses on the letters from Carrie to Charles during her years in Hawai'i (1890–1893). Once painstakingly transcribed, the material yielded twice the size expected. This quantity was too great for a single volume, and so this book presents just a selection of letters from Carrie to Charlie, edited to focus on her experiences in Hawai'i. It is not a documentary edition of her correspondence.

Every effort was made to accurately and faithfully represent the original documents in transcription and to preserve the chronology of the letters. To this end, we have not corrected the spelling, punctuation, or grammatical errors, but only names of people and places and a few other proper nouns. Carrie's handwriting is so closely spaced that it was sometimes difficult to identify paragraphs. For clarity, we have inserted paragraph breaks that do not exist in the originals. Every mention of the names, lives, and movements of Carrie's students and other Hawaiians, however trivial, has been preserved. We eliminated most passages of family news from Connecticut and gossip about classmates and events at Oberlin College. We also omitted substantial material discussing Charlie's life and studies and shortened Carrie's long passages of love and longing. After transcription, the word-processed pages were checked against the original manuscripts.

The most daunting task was the accurate transcription of names and the identification of individuals in endnotes and in the appendix. There are three broad groups of individuals mentioned in the letters. The first group is the white elite of Honolulu, including residents, professionals and business people, tourists, and missionaries and their descendants. Following nineteenth-century practice,

Kawaiahao Seminary

Sept. 9, 1890

My Darling:-

This is my first after-
noon off. It seemed ridiculous
because I did very little yesterday on account of my illness.
In a few minutes I am to go
down street and then I am to
mail my letter to you which
has not yet gone. I suppose it
will be about two weeks before
this can go on on the 20th But
before that time I shall have
a letter from you on the 19th
I want to describe the teachers to
you and tell you my estimate
of them. Perhaps I shall have a
different one after a while. I
1st Miss Pepoon in personal appearance tall, slender, light hair,
light complexion, blue eyes. I think
her young looking. Her face seems
to me like a child's. Her voice has
a harsh quality in it and is not
so pleasing as her face. I think she
is possessed with a strong sense
of justice. I have found her very
kind to me and considerate of
my tiredness from the journey
and ignorance of the work. She
is unsparing of herself and to
my mind has the right spirit
for the place. I have noticed of her
particularly that she does not
allow herself to speak evil of
anyone. I think you would be
surprised to find how young
she is - younger than Miss
Appleton and quite pretty.
No. 2. Miss Davis - assistant Principal

Carrie generally refers to adults in this group by last name only (e.g., Mrs. Coan). As many individuals in Honolulu shared the same last name, we tried to identify the people by the context and checked against other sources when possible. For instance, we consulted the lists of steamer passengers published in newspapers, which sometimes provided first names or initials.

The second group is foreign teachers and church workers, a group that largely consists of individuals from the United States. Many individuals in this group are associated with Oberlin College or other American colleges and seminaries. We checked names against college directories, biographical directories, membership lists of Christian organizations, genealogical sources and other sources in order to identify them. This work was easier, because Carrie often mentions the college, business, family and home towns of these individuals in her letters.

The third group includes students and teachers of Hawaiian nationality at Kawaiahaʻo Female Seminary, as well as other Hawaiians Carrie met in the islands. The Kawaiahaʻo students include many of Hawaiian ancestry, but also some of other or mixed ethnicities.

The strategies employed to identify individuals within these broad groups differed slightly. We began by compiling a list of all the individuals mentioned in Carrie's letters in letters she received from others, in newspaper clippings, in invitations, in programs, and in other printed material within her collection. We also looked at photographs and the lists she kept in her teaching notebook.

The task was more difficult than one would think. Most of the names were handwritten, and some were difficult to decipher. Sometimes different spellings were provided for the same people. While first names were usually supplied for students, some of these were spelled phonetically; at other times, diminutives were used (e.g., Konie for Konia). The full Hawaiian name of each student was rarely given. We have attempted to transcribe the names accurately and to list variations where they occurred.

While compiling this list, we read primary and secondary sources relevant to the period. We were able to find several corroborative sources. For example, a letter of Ida May Pope (May 3, 1891) in Huntington Library describes the 1891 trip on which she accompanied Queen Liliʻuokalani to Molokaʻi. This letter mentions her visit to Ella Bridges, a girl who had previously been a student at Kawaiahaʻo Female Seminary.

Names were also checked using printed reports of the Hawaiian Evangelical Association (HEA) and annual reports of the Hawaiian Mission Children's

Society (HMCS). These materials reported on activities at Kawaiahaʻo Female Seminary and other schools and sometimes included full names of students and other people. Reports of the HEA were also a source of information on the parentage for seminary students who were daughters of clergy. Materials on these organizations held at the HMCS Library in Honolulu included unpublished reports on the seminary, letters of thanks from individual students supported by the Cousin's Society, and photographs. Issues of *The Friend* and other periodicals often published accounts of events and memoirs of individuals affiliated with Kawaiahaʻo Female Seminary.

We also used the Library of Congress website *Chronicling America* to search for descriptions of seminary events in Honolulu newspapers and to check the spelling of names. These often mentioned the names of those present at events. Newspaper accounts of marriages and deaths were invaluable in the identification of individuals. City directories and annuals, such as *Thrum's* and *Polk*, listed residents and some students. Biographical sources including *Notable Women of Hawaii* and *Men of Hawaii*, were also essential sources.

We searched for each name in the index provided at the Ulukau Hawaiian Electronic Library website. This important site indexes genealogical records kept in the Hawaiʻi State Archives and provides access to such published sources as Hawaiian genealogies, books, and newspapers.

We also checked the names on our list against genealogical websites, including Ancestry.com, and contacted families who had individuals in their genealogies whose names matched or were very similar to those on our list. In some cases, these families responded and were able to verify that the individuals were or were not at Kawaiahaʻo Female Seminary. In other cases, they could not verify that their family members were associated with the seminary, but the biographical information they provided closely matched allowing us to conclude that the two were the same. In many cases, families who confirmed the identities of their relatives provided us with Hawaiian names and the correct spellings. Many of these families shared their own documents: information from family Bibles and genealogies, copies of marriage certificates, and reports of death. We are most grateful for their help. They were very generous both with their time and information.

In some cases, we traced and contacted families of the seminary faculty to verify identities and acquire additional biographical information. Oberlin College Archives yielded class files, photographs, and collections with abundant information. The Lilla Estelle Appleton Papers at Oberlin College Archives included a transcribed journal, which led us to her family and a treasure trove of historical photographs. The George and Caroline Babb Papers at Bancroft Library, University of California–Berkeley, was a rich source. The Kamehameha School Archives had Ida May Pope's *Memory Book I,* an important source for information on her life and the lives of teachers and students, many of whom were affiliated with both Kawaiahaʻo and Kamehameha.

Biographical research on the students at Kawaiahaʻo Female Seminary was the most challenging aspect of this work. Sources at the HMCS Library, Kamehameha School Archives, and the Hawaiian Historical Society proved critical. We found that some of the students at Kawaiahaʻo Female Seminary transferred to the Kamehameha School for Girls when it opened in 1894. Fortunately, Kamehameha School Archives preserved one volume, A–K, of the early admissions records for the school. When we checked the names of the Kawaiahaʻo Female Seminary students against that volume, we found some matches. It provided substantially more biographical information on each girl, such as names of parents, guardians, and tuition payees; age at entrance; nationality/heritage; island home; and date of matriculation/graduation. Alumnae records gave us the married names of some of these girls and information on their later lives.

The Mission Houses Museum Library had a *1882 Circular for Kawaiahaʻo Female Seminary* that listed the students of the institution and a photograph, taken about 1888, of the Kawaiahaʻo students. Each individual in the photograph was identified in a handwritten list. We checked our list against these sources and found several matches, which enabled us to obtain more complete names, as well as married names.

We did not ascribe ethnic identity to any person, but we did reproduce information on ethnicity if it was available from a reliable source. Some girls identified themselves in their autobiographical essays as Hawaiian or Chinese. The admissions ledger of Kamehameha Girls School lists ethnicity, and reports of public instruction authorities list the "nationality" of some teachers. Marriage records searched at the Hawaiʻi State Archives sometimes gave the ethnicity of the bride and groom, and census records occasionally indicated ethnicity. Obituaries searched at the Hawaiʻi State Library sometimes identified the ethnicity of the deceased. While the sources are authentic, we have no way of knowing if the information on ethnicity is true in every case, so readers must make their own evaluations.

We found that many of the girls at Kawaiahaʻo Female Seminary became teachers. This became apparent when we read and searched the reports of the education officers and authorities during the monarchy, provisional government, and territorial government at Hawaiʻi State Archives. These records were an invaluable source of information on teachers, yielding full names, teaching venues, information on when and how they acquired teaching credentials, and, in several cases, name changes upon marriage.

After all of these sources were checked, we were confident that we had fully identified many individuals. In other cases, such as that of Irene Dickson, we found information, but not enough to make the identification conclusive. For some students, we found no information whatsoever. Identification was ofttimes a judgment call by us, based on either three or more facts collected from credible sources or a chronology of events fitting what we knew of the individual. Some of the hardest work concerned the identification of Annie Wong, who is mentioned frequently in Carrie's letters. We found that there were three Annie Wongs in Honolulu at that time, two of whom were Christians. Census records persuaded us that of the two, the sister of Wong Ah Fook, the Harvard-educated banker in Honolulu, was likely the seminary student.

There are always more sources to check, and researchers can never be sure they checked them all. We tried to be as conscientious as possible, but we did not check church membership and cemetery records. More research along these lines will doubtless be fruitful, as many of the individuals mentioned by Carrie were members of Protestant churches in Hawaiʻi. We hope that readers will take up the search and that families will come forward to provide corrections, verification of identity, or additional biographical details.

Introduction ∭

Let love attend my letter over the sea to my darling.
 Carrie Prudence Winter, August 29, 1890

When an old house in Berkeley, California, passed from one generation to the next, it needed a new roof. That construction project revealed five old trunks in the attic that had been forgotten for more than a century. Four of the trunks contained valuable scientific research records, correspondence, photograph albums, old newspaper clippings, and more. The late professor who had owned the home had been an internationally known scientist, so University of California archivists sought the collection for its value to the history of science. When the last trunk was opened, it contained an unexpected gift, an *extraordinary surprise.*

The surprise was a young woman's handwritten love letters to her fiancé. These letters were postmarked between 1890 and 1893, when twenty-three-year-old Carrie Prudence Winter was a missionary teacher at Kawaiahaʻo Female Seminary in Honolulu. Carrie's letters to her beloved "Charlie" give the reader a private view into a nineteenth-century courtship. Carrie described teaching and living with Hawaiian girls, the often strict discipline she and her colleagues imposed, and her struggles with pedagogy, classroom management, and fellow teachers. She earnestly described her encounters with royalty as well as ordinary citizens in the Islands. She discussed profound health issues, such as leprosy, smallpox, and malaria, which irrevocably affected the lives of her students. She took a lively interest in writing about the turbulent politics that would ultimately lead to the revolution and to the annexation of the Hawaiian Islands by the United States.

Carrie Prudence Winter was born August 24, 1866, in South Coventry, Connecticut, one of six children of a Congregational minister, Alpheus Winter (1839–1903), and his wife, Flora Damaris Thompson Winter (1835–1918). Carrie's siblings were Alpheus IV, Mahlon Alpheus, Julia Flora, Eugene, and Horace. She was raised with strict Congregational principles that were old fashioned even at the time. For instance, her father sought to introduce her to mortality and consequently to encourage the development of her Christian faith when he urged her, as a very young child, to prepare a will.

(L) Carrie P. Winter, Hartford, c1883. Tintype. *(R)* Carrie P. Winter, 1890. Portrait by Theo Endean, Cleveland

Carrie's father was a staunch New Englander who trained at Rock River Seminary in Mount Morris, Illinois, and led churches in Massachusetts and Connecticut. Even though Reverend Winter rose in prominence from pulpit to pulpit, his salary rarely increased, and Mrs. Winter supplemented the family income by growing and selling flowers. Reverend Winter served on the Connecticut State Temperance Union while his children were growing up but resigned in order to pursue some business opportunities that never proved as successful as promised. By all accounts, the Winter family was blessed with strong family ties and even stronger faith, but little ready money.

Carrie was an exceptional student at Hartford Public High School, and one of her father's parishioners gifted her with a scholarship to Oberlin College, a rare educational opportunity for a woman in the nineteenth century. A hotbed of abolitionism, this Ohio college accepted Christian students of all races and was the first college to accept black women students. Carrie was away from home for the first time, but in this progressive environment, she flourished both academically and socially, with a particular interest in philosophy and in classmate, Charlie.

Charles Atwood Kofoid was born October 11, 1865, in Granville, Illinois, to Nelson Kofoid (1838–1908), a Danish-born carpenter and house builder, and Janette Blake (1844–1865), who died in childbirth. Charlie's father married a second time to Elizabeth Jane Ellis, and they had three additional surviving children. Charles entered Oberlin to study theology and then natural history and took on the duties of tutor. It was during those tutoring sessions that he fell in love with Carrie. In 1889, they became engaged, and both graduated in 1890 with bachelor's degrees.

After their college commencement, the engaged couple faced the problem of setting the wedding date. Charlie had a strong desire to further his education and obtain an advanced degree in science, an expensive and time-intensive endeavor. Scholarships, assistantships, and money made on the side would support him as a doctoral student at Harvard, but it wouldn't support a family. Carrie agreed with his practical decision to delay the wedding. With a lengthy four-year engagement ahead of her, she considered how best to use this time to its greatest advantage. Since childhood, she had yearned to do missionary work. She had heard that several alumni had gone to teach in the "Sandwich Islands," and as it "seemed particularly attractive," she resolutely pursued this opportunity through the American Board of Commissioners for Foreign Missions (ABCFM).[1]

Charles A. Kofoid, 1890. Portrait by Theo Endean, Cleveland.

Founded in 1810, ABCFM had recruited many missionary teachers from Oberlin College. However, in the early nineteenth century, ABCFM banned single women from being missionaries to the Hawaiian Islands, due to concerns about living amidst a vast number of males of "unknown sexual proclivities" who might undermine the women's reputations (Grimshaw 1989). There was also the issue of where to house single women. But educated young women like Carrie were in great demand in the late nineteenth century. The less well educated and exhausted wives of the missionaries needed relief, and boarding schools now afforded security and living space for the young women.

With the ABCFM's encouragement, Carrie confidently wrote to the trustees of Kawaiahaʻo Female Seminary and was quickly offered a position.

Once she accepted the offer, she was put in communication with another selected teacher, Ida May Pope, who became her traveling companion. Carrie then set about obtaining the "reluctant consent" of her family and fiancé. The chance to teach Hawaiian children, even at a meager salary, was a once-in-a-lifetime opportunity, and she would not be daunted. She humorously recounted in her story "American Girl in the Hawaiian Islands," published in 1892 by *Southern Magazine,* that accepting the position "was a wild thing to do," but she "had been guilty of strange things before."

The three-year teaching commitment wasn't an easy decision for Carrie's fiancé, and Charlie expressed his apprehension in a letter just prior to her departure: "I only hope that this separation will not take us far apart." Carrie's own trepidation was expressed when she recalled the August 15, 1890, parting: "I looked into the loved faces and thought with fear of the changes that might take place in the period of separation."

Ultimately convinced this was the best course for their future, Carrie went off on an exhilarating but arduous journey. She mailed her "heart" for more than three years, using every available steamship sailing towards Charlie. He found her letters so riveting that he suggested she publish some special-interest stories on Hawai'i in her hometown newspaper. Impressed by her writing ability, the *Hartford Courant* editor wrote her in 1893 to request articles. These were published under the byline "C. P. W." Carrie became a prolific contributor and a local celebrity in Connecticut and earned respect among her fellow teachers at Kawaiaha'o for her enterprise. Her articles vividly described the "glorious scenes on Hawaiian soil" as "landscapes for an artist's brush." She offered her readers, in poetic tour-guide style, a history of prominent Honolulu structures, charitable institutions, politics, and landscapes and provided an indepth look at how the natives lived. She was particularly eager for her American readers to think of Honolulu as a "cosmopolitan" destination, and she compared the "elegant homes of the foreigners" to those of the upper crust in New England.

Carrie depicted the busy nineteenth-century wharves as the "business tale of the islands." Thousands of baskets of sugar from the other islands were constantly being loaded and unloaded onto sailing vessels. She described Honolulu as a place where "most of the business of the city has to do with plantation supplies, or sugar, or vessel supplies or vessels themselves." As shipping increased in Honolulu, the city required more conveniences, and by the end of the 1880s, a transportation system of mule- and horse-drawn streetcars was installed, and Carrie, her fellow teachers, and their students, used them with great pleasure. Prior to 1889, the piped water that fed the city came from streams and springs, but many residents drilled wells on their property. This caused surface waters to dry up (Pratt 1939, 289), which created a serious drought that often affected the operations of the school. Another nineteenth century challenge was traversing the island since there were very few inland roads. Carrie quickly found it necessary to purchase a horse to have the freedom, adventure, and exercise she craved to relieve the stress of living around the clock in a seminary full of girls.

Carrie bemoaned the fact that the transoceanic telegraph cable had not yet reached Hawai'i: "For our size and civilization, we are the most isolated city in the world. When King Kalākaua died in San Francisco, Europe knew it, Asia knew it, and even Australia knew it before we did." Even though Hawai'i was one of the first places in the world to have electricity and an organized telephone system, service was scarce and unreliable. Kawaiaha'o Female Seminary was fortunate to have both conveniences in 1890. And when the phone rang with the news that a ship carrying mail had arrived in port, the telephone became a valuable commodity. Carrie, along with every other isolated foreigner, was anxious for fresh news of the world, so the arrival of a steamship at the dock in Honolulu was the most exciting and important event of the day.

Transoceanic mail delivery in the early nineteenth-century was accomplished by slow-sailing vessels, but during the latter part of the century, the efficiency of steam-powered ships improved the dispatch of mail. Carrie told her *Courant* readers that "only once a month does a steamer from the colonies give us a chance to send mail to the States." However, "steamers" did not keep to their posted schedules, and mail was frequently weeks to months behind. Ships also carried disease, and mandated quarantine periods delayed mail. Throughout her correspondence, Carrie's moods varied with the steamers' unreliable schedules: "Oh Charlie, I wish that steamer would come in. I've looked for it again and I am afraid it is not coming today." Joy always replaced gloom when letters arrived: "It has been a great comfort these last two weeks to have your letters coming regularly and to have none of the steamers fail to bring me my letter."

When Carrie arrived at Kawaiaha'o Female Seminary, it was flourishing as a boarding school and was guided by strict Congregational principles typical of the nineteenth century. The school had its beginnings in 1865, when Dr. Luther Gulick's temporary home, the Clark house on King Street, became an official, albeit ragged day school for eight girls (Chamberlain 1889). Dr. Gulick became the secretary of the newly reorganized Hawaiian Evangelical Association (HEA), and his wife, Charlotte, and their five children welcomed into their home the daughters of Hawaiian missionaries in Micronesia (Damon 1945). Charlotte needed a ministry, these girls needed an education, and thus, the school began in earnest.

In close proximity to the Gulick home, the imposing coral-stone Congregational Kawaiahaʻo Church was an integral part of seminary life. The church was located at what was known as Ka-Wai-a-Haʻo (the freshwater pool of Haʻo), a sacred bathing place of the chiefess Haʻo, Queen of Oʻahu, and was named after it (Damon 1945).

In 1867 Lydia Bingham, the daughter of Reverend Hiram Bingham, who dedicated Kawaiahaʻo Church in 1842, was recruited from the United States to take over the seminary. With an experienced educator and the daughter of a prominent clergyman now in charge, the school saw its reputation and student enrollment grow rapidly.

An increase in pupils required expansion, and this inspired Caroline Atherton to begin an intensive fund-raising campaign among missionary friends to purchase the Clark house in 1868 for the "good cause of female education" at a very charitable price. Adjacent to the Clark home on King Street was the abandoned Mission Press and Bindery, and it did not take much persuasion for the Hawaiian Mission Children's Society (HMCS), a supporter of the seminary from its inception, to offer this building for further school expansion. In the dreary basement filled with the tiniest fleas tormenting the first pupils (Chamberlain 1889), the school began in earnest.

Early in 1869, the school was flourishing with forty-six students, and another daughter of Reverend Bingham was recruited to provide support for both sister and school. For four years, Elizabeth "Lizzie" Bingham worked closely with Lydia until her sister left to marry missionary Titus Coan. To support further expansion of buildings and more students, the monarchy offered government support, and in 1878, the seminary's first board of trustees was appointed by the HEA to oversee finances. These first trustees were influential men and included such prominent people as William R. Castle. Under them, the school steadily increased in stature, size, and enrollment. However, the increase in responsibilities took a toll, and in 1880, Lizzie Bingham resigned. Pupil Margaret "Maggie" Powers wrote in her charming 1891 essay, included in this book, the history of the seminary from Miss Bingham's tenure to the time Misses Winter and Pope arrived on the doorsteps in the late summer of 1890.

Ida May Pope was unquestionably the most influential person in Carrie's life at the school and "Miss Pope" is mentioned throughout her correspondence. In one of Carrie's first letters to Charlie, she offered this description: "[Miss Pope] is short, but has the appearance of being tall, very fair, wears glasses, is older, I think, than I, is not pretty but has something, and I don't know what yet, which saves her from being common-place. She is a little talkative."[2]

Ida May Pope during her college years.

Kawaiahaʻo Female Seminary's student records have not survived. During Carrie's era, 100 to 144 girls, aged five to twenty, were enrolled. Carrie's letters provide readers with an opportunity to learn more about the character of the student body and the lives of young Hawaiian women of this turbulent era. Many of the students had identical last names, and there were ten sets of sisters and four sets of cousins among them. Carrie noted that in comparison to American girls, her students suffered many deaths in their families. Research revealed that 18 of the 97 girls had lost one or both parents, 12 died before their thirtieth birthday, and 4 suffered chronic ill health, including mental illness, leprosy, consumption, and blindness. Some students boarded for only a few years, but others, lived their entire childhood under missionary teachers like Carrie and Ida Pope. While the school included girls from every island, 28 were from Oʻahu and 17 from Kauaʻi. Most of the girls were from Christian families; 10 were daughters of Hawaiian clergymen, many of whom were actively working as missionaries in the islands of the South Pacific. Marriage records showed that 52 girls married. The industrial education offered by Kawaiahaʻo Female Seminary benefitted many students, providing them with skills that allowed them to earn wages and achieve some measure of independence. Of those students who lived to maturity, 18 became teachers. Others worked as seamstresses, musicians, midwives, court officers, telegraph operators, bookkeepers, and farmers. Sadly, while some of Carrie's students lived long and productive lives, her records confirm the irreversible decline of a population caused by complex economic, political, health, and social forces. These would forever change the character of Hawai'i.

Carrie's fellow teacher, Lilla Appleton, profiled some of the prospective students as "bright interested girls," "girls who are anxious to learn and whose expenses the parents are willing to pay," and "others who have no homes or worse... some bad girls, too, whose parents bring them in from the

Anna Rice (Opunui), Kawaiaha'o Female Seminary, November 10, 1891. Portrait by J. A. Gonsalves.

streets and beg that they be shielded from ruin" (Appleton 1888). Carrie boasted to Charlie that some of the students were attached to the royal court. Queen Lili'uokalani's namesake and only *hānai* daughter, Lydia Ka'onohiponiponiokalani Aholo, was enrolled in the school at age five, and was kept "under the loving ministrations of Ida Pope" for many years to follow (Allen 1982, 161). Lydia chronicled her school years until age fourteen in her essay (see page 41). According to Miss Appleton's journal, half of the students in the school were supported by their families. The HEA, the HMCS, and the Women's Board of the Pacific each supported several students at the school and a substantial number were supported by the Lili'uokalani Education Society.

The Lili'uokalani Education Society was created in 1886 "to interest the Hawaiian ladies in the proper training of young girls of their own race whose parents would be unable to give them advantages by which they would be prepared for the duties of life" (Lili'uokalani 1964). During Carrie's time, funds were drawn from this charity to support twenty-seven students (Appleton 1893) and an additional five students were directly supported with funds from the "modest Dominis Fund" (Allen 1982, 263).

The Queen, in her 1898 biography, *Hawai'i's Story by Hawai'i's Queen*, (Lili'uokalani 1898, 117) recorded a seminary visit prior to leaving for London in April 1887:

But I could not think of leaving without saying farewell to some little girls, five in number, the charge of whose education I had assumed, and who were at Kawaiahaʻo Female Seminary. So on the day of departure, at about eleven o'clock I stopped at the schoolhouse. At my coming all the pupils were gathered together into the large room, where I made them an impromptu address, telling them…to be faithful to their duty to their teachers, and warning them that it would distress me more than could be expressed should I ever hear that any of them had done other than right during my absence.

The royal family of Hawaiʻi was not merely a patron and benefactor, but also an active participant in leadership at Kawaiahaʻo Female Seminary. Portraits and the royal crest were displayed prominently in the seminary buildings. There was a well-beaten path between the school and ʻIolani Palace. Carrie and her fellow teachers appreciated the privileged relationship the school had with the monarchy and never missed a royal opportunity to visit the palace. The frequent participation in Kawaiahaʻo exhibitions by the monarchs is documented by school programs and newspaper articles. Many in the close-knit Hawaiian community followed the example set by the royal family and contributed funds, supported students, volunteered as helpers, invited the students and teachers to their homes, attended the frequent school

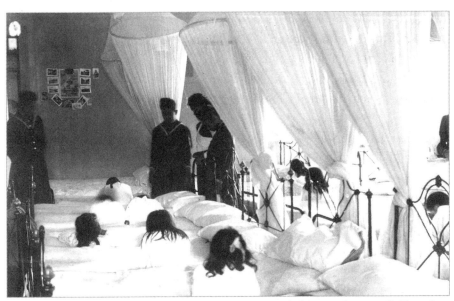

Bedtime prayers, Kawaiahaʻo Female Seminary. Note royal photographs on wall. Photo by Lilla Estelle Appleton.

fairs, academic exercises, and musicals. Most of these community events showcased student handiwork such as clothing and baked goods, which were sold to bring in needed revenue.

By 1890, the goals of Kawaiahaʻo Female Seminary had shifted from preparing girls to be Christian wives for missionaries to providing an industrial curriculum that would prepare students for practical work. With no formal teacher training, Carrie ethnocentrically mirrored the education that she received in New England. All instruction was in English, and the few textbooks in the classrooms were written for American schools. The core curriculum was devoted to general education in the morning hours; supplementary instruction including sewing, music, cooking, and housekeeping in the afternoons. Carrie's extracurricular area was sewing: "The students were so skilled on Mother Rice's donated sewing machines that they made uniforms for the entire school."

Carrie worked zealously to impart American values and strong principles of morality, industry, and frugality, but the trustees told the teachers that their most important purpose was to convert the Hawaiian girls to Christianity. The women were to be Christians first and teachers second: "Mr. Cooke said to me the other night the chief requisite in a teacher for this school was that she be a Christian for there are so many disappointments in the work that it is too much for anyone to carry it on in their own strength." Religious instruction for the girls included daily prayer and devotions, structured Bible studies, and Christian hymns. Sunday church attendance was most often at Kawaiahaʻo Church, which Carrie referred to as "our church." On special occasions, the students also attended Kaumakapili, the native church, and Central Union. Carrie and other missionary teachers joined Central Union, a Congregational church attended by many of the white families that dominated Hawaiʻi's economy.

Carrie fully supported the school's assimilationist policy and was dismissive of ancient Hawaiian values, customs, and beliefs inside and outside the seminary. She and other teachers spoke and behaved in a racist manner to Hawaiians including their own students. When she and her friends came upon a stone idol of Kaneʻaukai, an important fishing god, they destroyed it, "feeling like iconoclasts." Hawaiian historian David Malo (1793–1853) wrote about the bodies of *aliʻi* that were buried in caves, the skulls wrapped in tapa and the figures arranged in sitting positions on a shrine (Malo 1903, 137). Carrie confirmed what historians have long said about the looting of caves by nineteenth-century missionaries: she recounted an expedition by friends to examine mummies in caves and said they "brought away four bags of skulls and some fine tapa."

Like most novice teachers, Carrie struggled with discipline. She complained to Charlie: "Miss Pope seems to govern the girls with little trouble and it just cuts me to the quick to think I can't." Managing severe behavior problems sometimes required royal intervention as Carrie noted:

> The Queen told Miss Pope to tell all the girls that if [a student] or any other of her girls ran away from here she would have them arrested and put in the station house. I had Bible class last night and Miss Pope came in and gave the girls a talking to. And when she gave them the queen's command you should have seen the change in those girl's faces. All through the school now you can feel the change and the readiness to obey....We are delighted to have the support of the Queen.

Carrie inherited a strict system of schoolwide behavior management (Chamberlain 1889). When misbehavior arose, the first line of discipline was to assign additional work and place the girl's name on a "punish list." The next was for the teacher to admonish the student, first publicly and then privately to resolve the problem. Some behaviors sent girls into closets or corners for extended periods and often food was restricted.

Teachers were also allowed to whip students, and on several occasions, Carrie did so for such infractions as failure to do assigned tasks, cheating, speaking Hawaiian, or dancing the hula. For every infraction, students were required to acknowledge their actions and beg pardon after punishment had been applied. There are notations in Carrie's teaching notebook that suggest she implemented a demerit system, common at other missionary schools at the time (Mihesuah 1998), but this method of discipline is not mentioned in her correspondence. She instead wrote explicitly about the corporal punishments she administered. While her correspondence indicates that she was deeply conflicted by these punishments, she justified her actions to Charlie and her family because she anticipated their disapproval.

Like many nineteenth-century visitors to the Islands, Carrie set out to satisfy her wanderlust. Her letters vividly describe her trips during school vacations: to Maui in 1891 and to Kīlauea Volcano on the island of Hawaiʻi in 1892. She and her traveling companions took these rugged camping trips on horseback in a style that severely strained the standards of a lady from Connecticut. But as the daughter of an impoverished clergyman, she was unaccustomed to leisure, and as the hopeful wife of a botanist and biologist, she wanted practice in camping and mountain climbing. As a teacher connected with the HEA, Carrie enjoyed enormous privilege while on holiday. Before the revolution, Hawaiians opened their homes to the teachers, cooked for them, welcomed them to their churches, and shared the best camping, swimming, and fishing spots. And everywhere she went, from Hana to Hilo, Carrie called on the homes of her students.

The overthrow of Queen Liliʻuokalani in 1893 and the annexation of Hawaiʻi as a territory of the United States in 1898 remains a highly controversial and emotional subject to this day. Like everyone else, Carrie was deeply affected by the enormous economic and political tensions of this time, and she devoted much of her correspondence to the coup d'état that ended the monarchy. She could not have known when she stepped off the steamer a young and naïve preacher's daughter that she would witness the revolution for an American audience. Referring to her article on the revolution, the editor of the *Hartford Courant* wrote on January 18, 1893, "It is, we believe, the first letter of the sort published in the East from an American who actually witnessed the Honolulu revolutions." As an outright proponent of annexation, Carrie made no effort to guard her speech or to represent a neutral or balanced point of view, either as a journalist or as a teacher. In fact, she was surprised to find that her father and fiancé did not share her convictions. Charlie wrote to "My dear rebel girl" in 1893, gently admonishing her that he and his fellow students in the laboratory at Harvard had discussed "the Hawaiian Question" and were adamantly opposed to annexation. Carrie was socially placed in the very midst of the Missionary Party, which advocated annexation, and yet she lived amongst Hawaiian girls who were adamantly loyal to their Queen. As Carrie prepared to go home in 1893, she wrote, "I shall always have tales of that Revolution to tell."

Carrie did not personally witness every public event that led to the coup. She often repeated gossip and editorial opinions from the *Hawaiian Gazette* and referred to the Missionary Party as if it were a cohesive political party that spoke in one voice. However, historians have documented that opinions on the politics of this time diverged greatly. As a missionary teacher of Hawaiians, Carrie was in and out of the Honolulu homes of the infamous individuals who conspired to overthrow the Queen, as well as the homes of the Hawaiians who staunchly supported their Kingdom. An unyielding supporter of "Americanism," she was young and politically inexperienced, so her personal observations of the events of January 1893 may be less valuable to scholars than her observations of the educational and social environments of the Islands.

Many factors, most notably the loss of the Queen's support, led to the slow demise of the once prestigious Kawaiaha'o Female Seminary. Lili'uokalani, first as princess and later as Queen, had been a strong ally for both staff and students, as evidenced by Carrie's correspondence. Her support for the school survived the revolution, but ended in the fall of 1893 partly due to provocative comments by annexationists. In September 1893, S. E. Bishop, editor of *The Friend,* wrote that Kawaiaha'o Female Seminary would be improved due to the "removal of the corrupting influences of the Monarchy." Miss Ida Pope wrote to Carrie on October 7, 1893, that the article was written with malice and that "her late Majesty" was "incensed."[3]

Princess Bernice Pauahi Bishop had directed in her will that a portion of her estate be used to create and maintain two schools, one for boys (established in 1887) and one for girls, ultimately to be named the Kamehameha Schools. The Kamehameha Preparatory School (1888–1932), where Carrie's friend Iretta Hight taught, was a separate and distinct entity. Established by Charles Bishop for younger boys, this school prepared them for the rigors of the Kamehamaha School for Boys. It was these two institutions, located two miles west of Kawaiaha'o Female Seminary on the outskirts of Honolulu, that Carrie constantly visited. She described many combined school events that took place in the 1891 "new and elegant Bishop Hall." Now vacant and decaying, this historic building still stands adjacent to the Bishop Museum.

Carrie and others had speculated that Kawaiaha'o Female Seminary would cease to exist in name and instead transform into the planned Kamehameha Girls' School: "It has as large an endowment as Oberlin College and it is eventually to be opened to girls and will probably swallow up Kawaiaha'o which will be a good thing because of the better facilities possible. I should like to see the day myself." Carrie would learn later that a separate Kamehameha School for Girls was established in 1894, near the boys' Kalihi campus. The indefatigable Ida May Pope was recruited to assume leadership of the school and would remain there for the next twenty years. Many Kawaiaha'o students followed her to the new school, and the exodus of talented students and fatigued staff from the Kawaiaha'o Female Seminary would continue for the next several years.

Even though Charles R. Bishop and many others donated sums to keep the seminary running, its endowment income never equaled its operating expenditures. It is well documented that Kawaiaha'o was obliged to raise funds through concerts, fairs, and the work of its industrial departments. Those fundraising events appear throughout Carrie's correspondence as significant but exhausting affairs. Principal Christiana W. Paulding (1895–1902) fought the seminary's trustees over the fund-raising issue, claiming that the activities diverted both staff and students from the educational program. Principal Katheryn McLeod (1902–1908) led the students and teachers through another hard period, when repairs to the buildings on King Street were neglected in anticipation of the relocation of the school to the Mānoa Valley. Morale at this period was very low. McLeod wrote to the Board of Managers that the high attrition of her "faithful and hardworking faculty" supported the school's "established reputation as a woman-killer" (Pratt 1957, 27).

The HEA decided in 1905 to solve two overcrowding problems and merge Kawaiahaʻo with the Mills Institute for Boys and relocate them with the intention of combining them into a comprehensive educational organization in the Mānoa Valley (Pratt 1957, 26). Three years later, the "homelike group of buildings amidst a shady grove in King Street" (Logan 1903, 47), were sold to the Castle Estate, and the school finally moved.

In 1908, the first girls moved into their new homes and classrooms. While theoretically and logistically united under the name Mid-Pacific Institute, Mills and Kawaiahaʻo retained their names and operated independently for many years. In 1923, the names were dropped as a "partial step toward the creation of an integrated institution" (Pratt 1957, 108). The stately lava-rock building is forever memorialized as "Kawaiahaʻo" and remains a prominent feature on the Mid-Pacific campus in the Mānoa Valley.

As Carrie's teaching proficiency and confidence increased, so did her pride in her students: "I am just as proud as a peacock over them and you may always expect to hear me boasting of them. I do hate to have those girls have another teacher. Please may I bring them home with me? There are only 32." Though she didn't take any of her students home, she did carefully save for posterity many examples of their schoolwork.

As Carrie prepared to leave Kawaiahaʻo, she revealed the ultimate purpose of this adventure to Charlie:

> I want my last term to be my best. For one thing I am going to take a few minutes each morning for a little sermonet having them write the main proposition in their notebooks. The first series will be, "Why I should be a Christian," and the answer will be "That I may have a happy everlasting

life." I feel very seriously the amount of responsibility I have in this matter. Many of the girls never go beyond my room, life is very uncertain with them, my time here is short and I don't know what sort of a woman my successor may be and I don't know how practical for them the instruction is at their church.

Carrie saw herself as an author, rather than a missionary or teacher, and had often envisioned a future for herself as a writer. She hoped to someday write a book chronicling those exciting years at Kawaiahaʻo Female Seminary. Her first full-length feature article, penned on the job, is entitled "An American Girl in the Hawaiian Islands" and opens this book as chapter 1. Somewhere along the way, life's responsibilities intruded, and her book was never written. We united hearts and combined talents to bring this book, with Carrie's chosen title, to life. This lengthy project required us to explore both the beautiful and dark passages of the history of Hawaiʻi and has deeply enriched our historical understanding and increased our love for the Islands and its people. We hope the book will bring something of the same experience to the reader. *An American Girl in the Hawaiian Islands* is a century overdue, but is lovingly dedicated to the memory of Carrie Prudence Winter and her students.

NOTES

1. The principal American organization founded to support Protestant missions abroad, headquartered in Chicago.
2. Carrie Prudence Winter to Charles Atwood Kofoid, A.L.S. August 16, 1890. Kofoid Papers, Scripps Archives.
3. Ida May Pope to Carrie Prudence Winter, A.L.S. October 7, 1893. Kofoid Papers, Scripps Archives.

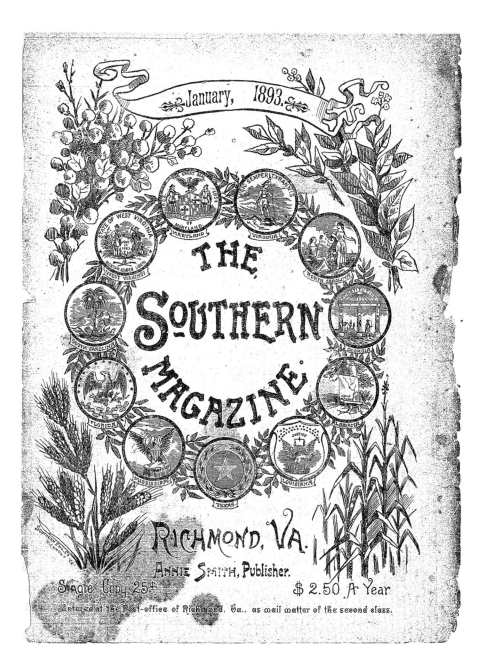

January, 1893.

THE SOUTHERN MAGAZINE

RICHMOND, VA.

ANNIE SMITH, Publisher.

Single Copy, 25¢ $2.50 A Year

Entered at the Post-office of Richmond, Va., as mail matter of the second class.

1

An American Girl in the Hawaiian Islands
August 15, 1890

Miss Winter wrote this article at the request of her brother, Mahlon Winter, for Southern Magazine, a new magazine edited by Mrs. Annie Smith of Raleigh, Virginia. It was published in the January 1893 issue, pages 7 to 16.

It did seem a wild thing to do, to hasten from one's great gala day, commencement to the Sandwich Islands.[1] But then I had been guilty of strange things before. This going five or six hundred miles to attend a co-educational college, in the day of it, had been counted strange. But that was long passed now and because I could not carry out my early wishes to be a missionary this teaching for a few years among the Sandwich Islands seemed particularly attractive. Several of our graduates had gone to the islands to teach and there were a few young people from Honolulu attending school in R—.

The necessary preliminaries were at last completed. I wrote to the trustees of Kawaiahao Seminary which name I thought I never could pronounce, in due time received a favorable answer, gained reluctant consent from all my relatives, wrote and telegraphed, hither and thither, was put in communication with the young lady in Columbus who was to accompany me[2] and, at last, the fact stood out bare and plain, I was going to Honolulu to teach in a school for native girls.

But where are the Sandwich or Hawaiian Islands which latter is the official name and the one to be preferred for many reasons? The idea of most people on this subject is very vague. We all know there are numerous groups of islands in the Pacific, and people are apt to locate them with others in the South Sea region. My own idea was that if one sailed straight out from San Francisco he would reach the islands. A glance at the map shows the error, for they are in a south-westerly direction from San Francisco and just within the tropics.

After my decision was made I found many bits of information coming to my attention. I availed myself of every opportunity to find out about the country so as to make intelligent preparations. Everything was very expensive in Honolulu so I must make ample provision of clothing, shoes, etc. The first week in July I was free to return to my Connecticut home and then only six short weeks before my departure! How the time flew! How hurried the preparations seemed! How pleasant the brief family reunions, the delightful family excursions, and how sad the parting when I looked into the loved faces and thought with fear of the changes that might take place in the period of separation. Friends went with me as far as Springfield, Mass., but when I boarded the noon express for Albany and the familiar faces quickly vanished, I felt that the new experience had indeed begun.

I was to meet Miss P. in Chicago and I felt that I knew the way there having been over that route a number of times. It was August 15, 1890, when I left home. That summer there was a strike on the New York Central and the train which I took was the first one that had gone through in many days. At every station crowds of idle men were to be seen and on the side-track numerous empty cars. In every one of the large towns, of which there are so many in central New York, policemen were stationed at regular intervals along the track. This was all interesting to me. It was a new sight in that beautiful Mohawk valley.

All the afternoon quite a pretty young girl occupied the seat with me and from commenting on the scenes through which we were passing we gradually engaged in a more personal conversation. She was well dressed and was evidently off on a vacation with a well filled purse. I found myself wondering what her social position was. She looked respectable, and I had about made up my mind that she was an orphan with money of her own who ruled it over on indulgent guardian, making her own friends, when she revealed the fact that she was head milliner in a large establishment in a Hudson town. I was filled with helpless astonishment. She was evidently several years younger than I, and yet for years she had been earning her own living quite independently, while I was starting out on my first independent venture. She told me of the regular millinery education she had received in New York, of the different steps in such an education from the simplest trimming to the "model" hat. I felt ashamed at last of extracting so much information from her without giving anything in return and so ventured on a few remarks in regard to myself and my journey. I couldn't have pleased her more. She turned and gazed upon me with delight. It was as if her adventures for the summer had begun already, for she had seen a very curious sight free of charge, a young lady on her way to the Sandwich Islands, which I doubt not were associated in her mind with nothing less than cannibalism.

Happy in our mutual discoveries and a chance to study a type so unfamiliar to each, we rode on for several hours together.

Saturday morning found me on the platform of the depot in Chicago with a somewhat faint heart, wondering if my description of myself had been sufficiently plain for Miss P. or her friends to recognize me. I had written they were to look for a young lady in a dark red dress, carrying a canvass bag, looking as if she came from Connecticut and were going to the Sandwich Islands. My fears were short-lived, however, for a young man stepped up to me at once and introduced himself as Miss P.'s brother. He explained that his sister was at the other end of town, that he was commissioned to take a room at a hotel as a basis of operations, see that I had a breakfast and then conduct me to her. Our experience in getting breakfast was amusing. Young Mr. P. was not very familiar with the city and took me into the first place that looked at all promising. I have never been able to decide just what the nationality and character of that restaurant was. It was certainly unique in its way. We sat down at one of the small tables, in the centre of which were grouped various articles, among other things a large waste paper basket full of rolls and a tall glass fruit dish full of butter. The man who came to wait on us was in keeping with the table. Across the top of his none too clean apron was written in large charcoal letters his name and number. Mr. P. was filled with chagrin and wanted to leave, but I prevailed upon him to stay in order that I might watch proceedings. As to the breakfast itself, one cares little for eating after a night in a sleeper.

A few hours later found us deep in the question of overland routes, tickets, lunch, and extra baggage. We only took time to visit one Chicago sight and that was the new auditorium, a magnificent building with a tower of eighteen stories. We mounted quite to the top of this and took a bird's-eye view of the city, or so much of it as the fog and smoke would permit. Only on one side could we see any limit to the city and that was where the blue waters of Lake Michigan, covered with shipping, reached to the north. On the other sides, in lines that seemed to radiate from us, stretched the blocks of stores and tenements into a near horizon of gray. At eleven o'clock that night the last familiar face for Miss P. had also vanished and we were speeding across Illinois. In the early morning, pulling the curtains aside, we saw that we were crossing the "Father of Waters." We were delighted with Iowa. As I look back upon the journey now I consider it the most beautiful country through which I passed. It was not monotonous. The knolls and ridges and gentle slopes of the rolling prairie saved it from that. The clusters of trees were frequent, and as we sped by them did not appear set or regular, but as if of natural growth. How I longed to get out and gather some of the beautiful wild flowers! Sunflowers seemed to be growing everywhere. We were paying the penalty for taking an "overland flyer." By two o'clock we had crossed Iowa and drawn into Omaha, and for the first time were able to leave our train for a few moments. In a short time we had crossed the brown waters of the Missouri, passed through Council Bluffs and were flying through Nebraska. The landscape was still green, but we were beyond the rolling prairie, the pretty villages and pleasant groves of Iowa. Here it was green but perfectly flat, and where we occasionally saw trees they were in long, straight rows. For the most part we saw no houses, no trees, no fences. When we closed our eyes it was upon this scene, but when we awoke we were in a new State—Wyoming. The greenness had all vanished and we seemed to be climbing up. The air became cool and thin. Great mountains rose on all sides, looking like immense ash heaps. We were passing through the Rockies. I was greatly disappointed that the portion we saw was so barren. Occasionally we caught a glimpse to the south of some snow covered mountains. There was a certain grandeur to the scenery throughout which we rode that day but I don't see how any wealth of mineral deposit could prevail on one to live in Wyoming. The people who go there must sometimes be disgusted, for we passed through more than one deserted village. We passed many dead cattle during the day. I saw no grass or water for cattle. We were not sorry to pass through the western part of Wyoming and the greater part of Utah in the night. Our route carefully avoided all points of especial interest, so in Utah we saw only sage bush and sand. That was the beginning of the never to be forgotten day in Nevada, through its alkaline plains. It was hot and every window and ventilator in the car had to be closed, while even then the sand seemed to sift in from every point.

It was hazy from one end of the car to the other. It filled all the pores. You tried to wash it off your hands and they became rough and chapped. The lips, the nose, the eyes all smarted. One could not read, the light was so trying. We could only sit and gasp the long hours of the day away with such patience as we could command. The only excitement of the day was a stop at a little village on the sand where a group of Indian women were playing cards and a young Indian mother with a papoose earned a good penny by exhibiting its puckered face to the passengers. Nothing less than a quarter would tempt her to uncover its face and then she managed to let only the one who had paid the fee see it.

Our dining car had left us back in Utah, and the majestic porter of our sleeper also managed the buffet service. We had dubbed him "Bismarck," and we caught him reading Tolstoi. It seemed an insult to offer him a smaller fee than fifty cents. Even the canned supplies of the buffet were giving out and we were glad that we were only one day from San Francisco.

How thankful we were when in the early evening we stopped at the foot of the Sierras. The air was cool and fresh, a fountain was playing in front of the little depot and we had a half hour or more to enjoy it. It was hard to go back into the stuffy sleeper. We missed all the beauties of the Sierras, but realized that we were nearing civilization again, for during the night there were sounds of people boarding and leaving the train. The early morning found us in Sacramento. We lost some pleasant fellow passengers there. A few hours later we rolled into Oakland, on the borders of San Francisco bay. I well remember the feeling the sight of those waters gave me. I think I had never really expected to look upon the Pacific ocean. It had always seemed the other side of the world, and now to really be beside it gave me a feeling of greater distance from home than I have ever had before or since. How glad we were to leave the car for good and be out on the bay.

Soon we were in San Francisco, had sought out the driver of the

Occidental and in a few minutes were able to rest our bodies on a bed that did not bounce up and down and this way and that. We soon realized that we were in California, for we were hardly in our room before the bell boy brought us a most exquisite basket of flowers, and half an hour later came a basket of fruit. Every day while we were there fresh fruit was brought to us. The Occidental is certainly one of the pleasantest of hotels. All that afternoon we sank into a long, dreamless sleep, roused ourselves while a young lady acquaintance of Miss P. called, and then slept again till dinner time. We woke to enjoy that and the attending concert, and after a long night's sleep were quite ourselves again.

We had made one acquaintance on our journey that had been very pleasant and was not likely to end as soon as the others. We had noticed in our car a lady, stately and white-haired, and had learned that she was on her way to Australia, and would probably go on the same steamer as ourselves. We hesitated about speaking to her, her manner was so imposing, but at last we decided we must do so, even if we were repulsed, as she was evidently alone and elderly. We were very glad we did, for we found her very gentle and glad to be with someone, and extremely childlike and dependent. She had come from Delaware and was on her way to Sydney to visit a son she had not seen for seventeen years.

On our second day in San Francisco we secured our tickets for the Zealandia. All the regular steamers that stop at Honolulu are owned by one company. There is one steamer, the Australia, that makes only the trip between San Francisco and Honolulu, remaining in each place a week and taking a week for each voyage, thus requiring a month for the round trip. Then there are three steamers that make the trip to Australia, stopping at Honolulu and Auckland, with time so arranged that one from the colonies and one from San Francisco meet, or rather just miss each other at Honolulu once every month. It was one of these through steamers that we were to take. The rates of travel are higher than on the Atlantic, as there is no competition. The fare to Honolulu is seventy-five dollars.

During the two remaining days of our stay in San Francisco we saw something of the city. Miss Clark and her father called for us this afternoon to show us something of Chinatown. Mr. Clark would not show us the worst part, the underground life. San Francisco is built on a series of very steep, high hills. On the slopes of one of the most central of these is Chinatown. One expects to "dive down into the slums," to go to the region of wharves or dirty river-side, but in San Francisco one enters a cable car, and as if by magic, "dives up" a long, steep hill to Chinatown. We first visited one of their curio stores. The sight of such exquisite china was enough to enrapture the feminine heart. Then the embroidered silks, the dainty fans, and at such low prices as compared with what one would have to pay East. From this store we went off into the side streets, where there were no side-walks and the buildings were swarming with humanity. The lower floors were given up to shops, chiefly fish and meat markets, from which came the most sickening odors. I saw one man buying the head of a fish. We passed through other streets not so revolting, but everywhere there was an indescribable odor. I could but think of that classmate who was going to China as a missionary, wishing she might have been set down in those streets for a few minutes before deciding to go. We visited one of their finest eating houses, passing through the cooking rooms on our entrance, and through various grades of eating rooms as we ascended, till we came out upon the roof, which was shaded by awnings and made beautiful by greenery. Here were beautiful inlaid tables and stools. If one had not had to see the lower regions a meal might have been taken there with pleasure. We also visited a joss house, looked at the hideous idols and bought some of the joss or prayer sticks. When lighted these had a pleasant odor.

On our way back to the hotel we went into the safe deposit bank and saw the vaults where are deposited the plate and valuables of the wealthy people of San Francisco. One notices at once the signs of lavish wealth, the superb public buildings and the fine private dwellings. In the jeweler's store at the corner of our hotel was displayed the city's gift to the new man-of-war, San Francisco. It was a massive service of plate, richly ornamented with gold.

As I have before said, it was the month of August when we were in the city, and we were surprised to see the ladies on the streets in the afternoon in heavy furs, seal-skin cloaks and capes. It seems that every afternoon a cold wind comes in from the ocean, very trying to tender throats and lungs, making warm clothing necessary.

The next morning we took an early start, Mr. Clark piloting us again and gliding up and down several of the long hills in the cable cars, and at length took a car drawn by a puffing little locomotive and so completed the journey to the Cliff House. This stands on a cliff jutting into the Pacific, and the great attraction is in watching the seals that gather on the rocks a short distance from the shore and keep up a constant barking and lively sporting as if for the special amusement of onlookers. Near at hand are the famous Sutro Heights, acres of land, cultivated to the highest degree. We can here see the reality of the stories so often told of the wonderful growth of flowers in California. Indeed, one cannot ride far in San Francisco without seeing a fuchsia climbing over a trellised door-way or a giant geranium in a front yard.

In returning from the Cliff we skirted the shore of the Bay, passing through a number of short tunnels and over long stretches of sandy wastes. We were told not to despise them for many such a tract, held worthless in former years, was now covered by fine buildings and the value of these very sand heaps was large.

I shall never forget the homesickness that came over me that evening as I wrote my last letter home before sailing. The next day at noon saw us on our way from the hotel to the wharf. The last attention of the hotel was a basket of fruit with a bouquet of roses atop.

We were anxious to explore the "Zealandia," to watch the people, to see everything that could be seen. In stories it is always taken for granted that every one has been on an ocean voyage, but now we were to see for ourselves what decks, and gangs, and companion-ways, and saloons were. In the shortest possible time we tossed our things into our state-room, found Mrs. Eccles, who already looked ill, and was making uncomplimentary comparisons between our steamer and Atlantic steamers. We found another young lady aboard with whom we had some previous acquaintance bound as teacher for Honolulu. We had met a number of teachers, new and old bound for the new year's work in the islands, and had learned that we should have to wait two hours for the English mail without any lunch. The time passed quickly in watching the throng of people who seemed constantly rushing on and off, and wondering which were to be our fellow-passengers. Then the small boy with the big gong began to rush around, once in five minutes making the most unearthly noise. With our new found friend, Ruth[3] we went to the upper deck to watch the departure. Slowly we parted from the land and I realized that I had looked my last on America for I knew not how long a time. There was a large crowd cheering us off, but no familiar face for us. We made a turn in the water and came in sight of the wharf again, and heard once more the cheering, but in a few moments were engrossed in the harbor sight. San Francisco has a wonderful Bay, so large that it seems as if it could hold the shipping of all the world and then narrowing down to the one opening, the Golden Gate. It takes an hour or more to get to the open sea.

A funny thing happened at the very beginning. A German Professor had been aboard to bid his friends farewell and they had become so engrossed in conversation that they did not hear or heed the warning gong, when he came to himself we were some distance from land. He went to the captain and besought him to turn back. "His friends did not know where he was, they would be dragging the harbor for him. He had to lecture at three that afternoon." The captain would not at all consent to turn back, but told him he might go off with the pilot. So when we had reached the rough water outside the Bay and the little row boat came along side for the pilot, he had the pleasure of climbing down the rope ladder and dropping into the rocking and tumbling boat. We were told that he would be taken to the pilot boat and there was no knowing when he would reach land as these pilot boats frequently stayed out for a week or ten days.

We did enjoy the ride down the Bay, but it kept getting colder, and we made one frightful trip to our state room for wraps. It was dreadful there. We turned pale, looked at each other, and hastened out. We were so hungry it seemed if the dinner hour would ever come our troubles would be over; but at the dinner hour our troubles had only begun. That never-to-be-forgotten night! The waves seemed to be pounding on the deck above us. We had to hang on to the sides of the berth to keep in, and yet were so sick we did not care whether we fell out or not. There was no opening through which we could get fresh air. I doubt if either of us had ever been so abjectly miserable before. The first night and day were one long misery. That day, too, happened to be my birthday, but I begged Miss P. not to wish me "returns" of it.[4] I felt better that evening and when the next morning I was awakened by the men on deck opening the air holes into our state-room it renewed my vigor to such an extent that I determined to make a break for freedom. Miss P. asked with consternation what I was about. Ruth called from the next state-room to know what the commotion was about. I told them they had best follow my example, and they did. Once on deck we soon felt almost as well as ever, though we did not at any time really enjoy the motion of the vessel.

We soon became greatly interested in our fellow-passengers and one would have thought us a country village afloat, from the amount of gossip around. There were a number of Island people aboard who were as pleasant company as one could wish. There were also a number of teachers and tourists for Honolulu.

There was also a United States Minister, with wife and niece bound for Melbourne.[5] The rest of us were not quite so respectable. There were a large number of young men on their way to Australia. They were Australian farmers who had been to the coast and were returning, clad in cinnamon colored clothes, broad brimmed hats and high boots. They were agents for various American farming implements and insurance companies and all of varying degrees of unattractiveness. There were some Australian "ladies" with very peculiar voices, manners and dresses. One of the teachers was unfortunate enough to be the room-mate of the one we called the "scarlet woman" from her fondness for a certain tea-gown, and she told us of the string of immense diamonds she wore about her neck and of the stimulants she had to take while performing the arduous work of dressing. The "stars" of a Wild West show were also among the cabin passengers, especially noticeable among them the golden-haired female contortionist. One of their riders was brought on board ill from a fall she had received. The stewardess and some of the lady passengers did all they could for the poor thing, and she was extremely grateful. The day we reached Honolulu she died and was buried there; but her husband was obliged by agreement to go on with his company at the end of the seven hours stay in Honolulu. It gave one a glimpse of the very dark side of such life.

It takes seven days to go from San Francisco to Honolulu, and during that time we saw not a sail or craft of any kind. It would not do to locate on the Pacific one of those tales of shipwreck or collision where the unfortunates are always picked up by the steamer near at hand. I talked with people who had made the trip many times and they had never seen a passing sail. For us every day dawned clear and beautiful and every evening saw the sun sink into the ocean in a blaze of glory, leaving its glow in the sky long afterwards, while every night the stars and moon seemed brighter.

Some of the young men, naturally taking Mrs. Eccles for our protector, devoted themselves to her comfort. She of course introduced her "charges," and we passed several merry evenings on the hurricane deck. A few of us were musical and all did their best, and the staid middle-aged people were kind enough to be delighted with our efforts and to encourage us by clustering around us. I must say the ship's officers paid far more attention to the "scarlet woman" and the contortionist than they did to us prosaic folk. I must make an exception, however, of the mail agent, who joined us every evening and sang the most delightful solos in a rich baritone voice. We asked a great deal of him and he was always ready to please us. I can feel the charm of the picture now. That southern moon, turning the sea to silver, the silent groups on the deck, the solitary figure in the moonlit spot with earnest, quiet face and rich, full voice pouring forth some sad, sweet song of the sea.

We planned to give two concerts in the saloon, but gave them up on account of the sick woman. We wrote and slept and ate in pretty constant rotation. I recommend a volume of Heine's poems to one upon the sea. Most of our moods and fancies at such a time are reflected in them.

On the morning of the seventh day land was in sight and we hastened on deck to see, in the far distance, a dim, brown mass which we were told was the island of Molokai, the home of the lepers. Soon another island to the north made its appearance which we carefully watched as we drew nearer. What had at first seemed brown gradually revealed shades of green. Next we could distinguish gorges in the mountains. We passed a point, Coco Head, and soon another, Diamond Head, and there before us lay the harbor, the city of Honolulu. I had never seen anything so beautiful. From the dull tint of the ocean we were suddenly transported into a world of color. Before us was a stretch of water of the deepest blue, broken only by long lines of white where the encircling coral reef broke the water into foam. Next came the tender green of the city's abundant foliage, and beyond rose the mountains, their summits lost in a mist of white, their sides varied with many a valley in which lurked vivid purple shadows. Where the land had been cut the soil showed red, where it was simply bared, all shades of brown. We were surprised and delighted. We had read of such scenes but they did not seem really possible till we saw this. Slowly we crept through the reef passage into the harbor and still more slowly neared the wharf where we could distinguish a crowd of people. Out in the harbor were brown-skinned natives, fishing in queer little boats. These boats were very narrow with huge outriders. We noticed that all had garlands of flowers about their hats. A thousand new impressions were crowding upon us! At last there was the rush aboard and we were hearing greetings on all sides and here was the sweet-faced principal of our school greeting us and introducing us to trustees[6] and making inquiries and hastening us to a two-wheeled "brake" and driving us through a maze of muddy streets and green foliage to a long, brown building with pretty grounds. Here we were greeted by more pleasant-faced teachers and conducted to our rooms, made fresh and beautiful for us by thoughtful hands, and adorned by beautiful roses. Then in a little while came more roses and an invitation to drive about the city from two young ladies who had been to the same college as myself.[7] I had never met them, though I knew them well by sight, but with true kindness they welcomed me as if they had always known me. But I was so bewildered with all the new sights of the different world in which I seemed to have dropped in the last half-hour that I begged to be excused from the ride and at last found myself alone in my room. I lay down and tried to make my room seem real to me, to feel at home there. I gazed at the mosquito netting above me, new in my experience, on the blue tinted walls, bare, painted floor and the roses. All this became clear and distinct in my mind. Everything else seemed a story, but I rested there and said over and over to myself, at last I am in Honolulu and this is my home.

NOTES

1. Miss Winter graduated from Oberlin College in June 1890.
2. Ida May Pope accompanied Miss Winter on the trip and was a fellow teacher at Kawaiahaʻo Female Seminary.
3. Ruth Hoppin, also from Oberlin College, was on her way to teach at Kamehameha Preparatory School.

4. Miss Winter's twenty-fourth birthday was on August 24, 1890.
5. George H. Wallace was U.S. Consul-General to Melbourne, Australia, and is listed as a through passenger to Australia on *Zealandia* in the *Hawaiian Gazette* (September 2, 1890, p. 1).
6. Kawaiaha'o Female Seminary principal Helen Pepoon and trustee Joseph B. Atherton were among those who greeted Miss Winter.
7. Mary (May) and Eleanor (Nellie) Waterhouse, sisters who had attended Oberlin College, were residents of Honolulu.

2

FIRST IMPRESSIONS
August 29–October 26, 1890

Kawaiahaʻo Female Seminary, 1893.

August 29, 1890, Kawaiahao Seminary

My Own Darling,

Let me see if I can begin to remember all the new things—the banana trees, every house has them, there are whole plantations of them out toward the ocean, some continue growing, year in and out, while others  simply spring up, bear a bunch, and die. The palms were the next most noticeable—some they say are 200 years old. They seem to have peculiar charm for me with their tall trunks and plumy tops. I learned to distinguish the coconut palm from the date palm, the royal, fan and wine palm. I know too the Algarroba tree, fine like smilax and the monkey pod tree. These last are very large and they go to sleep at night. There is a fine large one near my window. I saw the banyan tree, the fig tree and the famous traveler tree. Charlie, the hibiscus hedge is something wonderful, full you know of scarlet blossoms—then too the great trees with blossoms the color of nasturtiums. Oh darling, I am filled with despair, I am so afraid I shall never write it all to you as I want to—it is so wonderful.

Now you see I have taken you right into the middle and told you no "first impressions" of how we packed in a hurry and were out on deck. On one side were the mountains of Oahu and out the other, Molokai. It seemed well named "The Paradise of the Pacific" just on account of the color, a lovely sea-green.

There is only one narrow path way for vessels through the reef to the wharf. At last we were at the wharf and there was a rush both ways. We stood still and let ourselves be found, the Waterhouse girls were there and kissed me like old friends. Mr. Atherton got our baggage through without inspection, and soon we were in the carriage and started home.

My Own Darling:

It was after I had been here a while and had been shown to my room and had lain down awhile on my bed with eyes closed—trying to calm my excited nerves and adjust myself mentally to my new surroundings, that I opened your letter and read it. I want to tell you how much good it did me.

Wednesday night was prayer meeting and I attended. Friday morning I went out about two miles east to visit the Kamehameha School for Boys. I learned a great deal that I know will be helpful to me. We stayed to lunch and met all the teachers. Miss Hight is the only lady teacher though several of the men have their wives there. I think I prefer our school.

Waikīkī Beach and Diamond Head. Photo by Lilla Estelle Appleton.

In the afternoon I went down to Waikiki and took my first ocean bath. It was very invigorating and it seems to me now that I shall go there as often as I get a chance. Yesterday was a great day for the Waterhouse girls gave an Oberlin picnic in the park down toward Waikiki.

We had a good time but I was most too tired to enjoy it. I liked the guava jelly and luscious bananas, pickled pineapple and mangoes. How do you like to hear me speak of those things with such familiarity my Charlie?

When we started back, some of us stopped at Waikiki for a bath. I had more fun this time for all the girls sat in a row on the beach holding hands and then when the big waves came in such fun!! They would turn us right over a somersault almost and then on the way back drag us into the water again. You should have heard the screaming and laughing. I just thought of you and what fun if you were only there. Why, boy, I know I should die to see you. We would have a great time! I feel that I shall have plenty occasions to write about these places and you will soon be quite familiar with them.

Of course we have come to the end of the vacation and the idleness now. My work is to be teaching 3 hours a day and sewing class, 1 1/2 hours with the care of the dormitory and I begin today by having a large bunch of keys entrusted to me at 4:30. I am to unlock my dormitory and let certain girls out who get supper. The rest remain caged.

The school takes a daily Hawaiian paper, the Advance, Independent, a teacher's paper and the Youth's Companion. We are furnished ink for all uses and paper for school use. All the fine washing that the girls cannot do goes to a Chinaman and the school bears the expense. We have just as good board as we desire. They were not using much milk but because I like it they get it for me. We have meat of some kind three times a day. About mail—Be careful! All letters not stamped to their full value are tripled for me to pay. Only 1/2 oz. for 5¢. I have not got it quite clear but I think there is a new line of steamers established and that mail now comes in 3 times a month. It must have been done just for you and I, Carl.[1] As soon as I can get hold of a new time table you shall have it.

Tuesday, A.M.—Darling, my first day's teaching was not a brilliant success. We have about 100 girls to begin on and new ones coming in all the time. I must really stop writing but I shall begin another letter right away. Let love attend my letter over the sea to my darling.

Yours,
Carrie

Oceanic Steamship Company schedule, 1890.

Hawaiian Gazette

June 16, 1891

CHANGES AT THE KAWAIAHAO SEMINARY[2]

by Margaret Powers

When I first came to school at the age of five years—it was during the principalship of Miss Lizzie Bingham—the principal houses were adobe and stone. They were several feet apart, and in rainy weather, it was very inconvenient to go from our dormitories to our schoolrooms. The old chapel was very much too small to accommodate the pupils. We had old desks and chairs, and the children were seated all around the platform during devotions. The chapel was also used for school exercises of the highest class and for a sewing-room in the afternoon. Our dining room, which was the basement, was used for the recitation-room of the second class. The other three classes recited their lessons on the verandas.

We ate with spoons from tin-plates such as they now use in cooking and the tables, which were scrubbed snowy white, had no table cloths. In the morning, milk and bread served for breakfast. For dinner we had poi and meat or salmon, the poi bowls being such as are now used for mush bowls. At 5 o'clock, a bell was rung, and all the girls would run, as fast as their legs could carry them to the kitchen steps and there, in a pan, was our supper consisting of a cracker and a half or bread with molasses. Our food, though plain, was the best to be had as our school was very poor; and sometimes when we were sick and needed better food, a teacher would go without and let us have her share. This has happened many a time.

Our yard was not as large as it is now, but it was divided into three divisions, namely the front, middle and back yards. Our teachers usually came out and played with us, holding up our kites or playing catch. During Miss Bingham's principalship, the new kitchen, now used as a store room, was built, and the dining room, which is now the kitchen, was enlarged. After having served as our principal for many years, Miss Bingham retired, to the regret of us all, and the vacancy was filled by Miss Norton.

New dishes were purchased, and an addition to our building was made, thus giving a new parlor, sewing room and rooms for teachers and older girls. This part was called Sage Hall, from the donor Miss Sage of Mass.

After three and a half years, during which time there was much improvement in many ways, Miss Norton resigned yielding her position for the remainder of the year to Miss Chamberlain who acted as principal until a new one could be found. At the beginning of the next year, Miss Alexander became our principal. The number of pupils increased from about ninety to one hundred and twenty nine. Our yard was enlarged, and the adobe houses were torn down. Our present chapel, schoolrooms and Rice Hall dormitories were erected. The system of having a pupil teacher in the kitchen was adopted. The sewing department was enlarged, and since that time the majority of the older girls make their own clothes. During the past year, about seven hundred yards of cloth have been made up into clothing by the girls outside of school hours. After four years, Miss Alexander and all the other teachers but one resigned.

Miss Pepoon, our present principal, then took charge. The number of teachers increased from six to eight, so that we now have the opportunity of learning more than formerly.

In former days, when the girls were sick, there was no special place to put them, and a teacher would give up her room to be used as a sick room. To the joy of us all, we now have a cottage, which is used for that purpose only. It is comfortably furnished and well ventilated. I am glad to state that for a whole year there have been but two girls who had to be taken there. I think this shows that we have been well cared for.

I have heard many say, that we do not have enough to eat. This is not so. We have all we need or wish for.

We have nice dormitories also with iron bedsteads, which are a great improvement upon those days when we had to sleep in the attics, and were packed as close as sardines. We have comfortable school-rooms too, with nice seats, which have been greatly enjoyed by the one hundred and twenty-six girls who have attended school this year.

The drainage for the school buildings has been greatly improved, and just six months ago, our washing house was enlarged and repaired and ten new bathrooms were erected. Most of the girls do their own washing and ironing, and the work in this department has been better systematized than ever before. The music department has greatly improved, during the last five years, since Miss Morley and Miss Patch came to the seminary.

Changes have come too in the girls themselves. Of all the eighty girls who were here when I came there remains but one beside myself. Some have died, some have homes of their own and some are teachers.

Thus dear friends, you see the changes and the great improvements, which would not have been so great had you not given your money and time to make our school home as comfortable as possible. Those who, like myself, have lived here many years have proved it to be a very dear and pleasant home. Your kindness has also made the burdens of the teachers lighter, and it does not now require such sacrifices to teach in the seminary as it did in the early days of the school. We thank you all for what you have done for us.

We owe a large share of this advancement also to our teachers, who have been with us in rain as well as in sunshine; who have comforted and advised us in trouble and have given their precious time to us out of school as well as in school. Just now, as some of them are about to leave us, we wish to thank them heartily for all they have done for us, and hope that while at their homes in America their thoughts may sometimes return to "Hawaii nei" and in the picture which may rise before them of this "Paradise of the Pacific" may they see dear "Kawaiahao Seminary," where they have labored hard to educate us Hawaiian girls.

May God's blessing rest upon them, is the wish and prayer of us all.

September 9, 1890, Kawaiahao Seminary

My Darling,

I want to describe the teachers to you and tell you my estimate of them. Perhaps I shall have a different one after a while.

1st—Miss Pepoon in personal appearance—tall, slender, light hair, light complexion, blue eyes. I think her young looking. Her face seems to me like a child's. Her voice has a harsh quality in it and is not so pleasing as her face. I think she is possessed with a strong sense of justice. I have found her very kind to me and considerate of my tiredness from the journey and ignorance of the work. She is unsparing of herself and to my mind has the right spirit for the place. I have noticed of her particularly that she does not allow herself to speak evil of any one. I think you would be surprised to find how young she looks—younger than Miss Appleton and quite pretty.

No. 2—Miss Davis—assistant principal. Last year she had charge of the highest teaching department but this year has taken the place of matron and given her teaching to Miss Pope. Miss Pope is to learn gradually to be matron by taking Miss Davis's place when she is absent. I have taken a particular liking to Miss Davis and want you to know her. She is more nearly Louise Alcott's "Jo" than any one I ever saw—very tall and somewhat awkward with sharp features and bright brown eyes, rather pale complexion and a mass of dark red hair. She is somewhat blunt in her manner of speaking but full of wit. Her heart is in the right place I know. She is very energetic and capable and kind hearted—quick spoken and full of repentance for all sorts of imaginary sins— quite sure she wasn't born to be good—calls a spade a spade. She must be to- ward 30 yrs. old. Don't say she is a bad companion for me, Carlchen, for somehow I am attracted to her and she seems responsive to me.

3rd—Miss Hopper, the sewing teacher. She has been here the longest and is the oldest of the company. Her hair is quite gray but she is small and plump and good-looking and to all appearances always good natured. I had a delight- ful long chat with her the other night. She is fully in sympathy with the higher views of the work as are the two mentioned before. She was here in the days when the accommodations were very crude and has watched the improve- ments come in one by one through the unselfish labor of one and another. She has been here so long that she has many old friends.

4th Miss Brewer the teacher of the little ones—not very old, perhaps my age, rather short with a sweet, sunny face and rippling hair. She seems just the one for the children, all of whom she loves. She told me apologetically the other day that Miss Pepoon said her fault was not being stern enough. She seems unsuspicious of evil and loving in her ways.

5th is Miss Pope, whom I have already described to you to some extent. She and I run to each other I suppose because we feel better acquainted than with the others. We have many ideas in common but in some things I find her a little freer in thought than I care to be, i.e.—card playing, dancing and a few such things. These that I have described I like the best.

6th Miss Helen Hoppin, teacher of the grade below me. She is a very bright animated girl, wiry and lively who spends all her money and thinks everyone is stingy who doesn't. She is very popular among the town-people, confesses that she pushes herself everywhere, complains quite freely of our surroundings which I am sure must be more luxurious than her own home. She makes good company and I like her well enough for that.

7th is little Miss Patch, evidently fallen from some high estate and reduced to music-teaching. She is very vivacious and entertaining but makes all manner of fun of missions and missionaries and finds any work outside of her music irksome.

Well, Charlie, your picture is right before me. I know the girls are full of curiosity and I have heard them talk native about it but they have only got thus far, "Is he your brother?" and they all say he looks like the chief engineer of the *Morning Star.*

9pm—I have some insect powder burning here by my side and so I may be able to write. I have come to the end of my first school week and now must tell you all I can. Tuesday is my half day off. Miss Brewer has it with me and took me over to Mrs. Cooke's, across the street where we had a quiet nap. We three went down-town for a little shopping. I got my pictures framed and some steel pens. In the evening we called at the Atherton's. Charlie Atherton is quite ill now, malaria they say. The day was not over pleasant to me for I really wanted to be at work.

I think on Wednesday I had a typical day. At six, the rising bell, at 6:20, I go into my dormitory, wish my girls "good-morning" and give any particular directions. Then on their knees, they repeat the Lord's Prayer. My dormitory has about 30 in it and they are all the older girls from 15 to 20 yrs. old. They have little iron beds with mosquito netting over it. After the praying, I read or have one of my girls read till the next bell at 6:30.

Then all leave the dormitory except four girls whose work I superintend, two sweep out the dormitory, one tends to lavatory and stairs and one to the attic. These girls do their work pretty well but need coaxing up once in a while. At 7 comes breakfast and at about 7:30, I go to my dormitory again and see if the girls have made their beds well which each girl is supposed to do right after her breakfast. The chief things to look out for here is the tendency of every girl to pick up and destroy everything that comes in their way. I have rescued a pillow-case and some handkerchiefs from the dust-pan so far. Then again they are fond of making up their beds with but one sheet on, or if they have two they put the blanket on before the top sheet. At night they like to sleep in anything but the proper garment and are fond of other beds than their own. I get this work all seen to and have an eye too on the girl who does my room. By 8:30, I can go to my schoolroom and look over my work there.

At nine, we all file into the chapel or largest school room and have devotions. The teachers take turns in offering prayers. There are so many directions to be given to the girls that it is usually 9:30 before we get them into our several classes. There I have a problem—26 girls, 2 divisions of Arithmetic, one division each of Bible, geography, reading, spelling, writing English, in 2 1/2 hrs. Charlie, my mosquito poison has lost its power. They are returning to life, and I must get under my net.

It is around to Tuesday and you have not had a word since Saturday night. I have just returned from a drive up Punch Bowl with the Judds. A little after two, Judge Judd came for me and took me to their home. It is a rich place. Mrs. Judd had a sore foot and could not go on the ride with us but we visited for some time. She has a daughter who goes to Wellesley next year. Somehow I liked the home. There are nine children. When Judge Judd came in he kissed his wife and again when he started away. They told me it was the anniversary of their engagement day.

Love, I think you would like to have seen the little thing that happened just now. We have a poor little Chinese girl here who is sadly deformed but very gentle and good. She is in my class and has trouble in pronouncing the words in her Bible lesson. I told her to come to me every evening and I would help her. She has been here twice. Tonight I made a little bargain with her. She makes beautiful lace and she has agreed to make some for me and I will pay her and then she will have money for the church collection. The lace is suitable for table covers or pillow-cases. See? Don't it all work around well?

Wednesday—A little more about Punch Bowl. It is an old volcanoe just back of the city and there is a fine carriage road winding clear to the top. The air is cool and delicious and as you ascend you get wonderful views, of the rich valleys, of the mountains, then of the harbor and its shipping, Waikiki and its long sandy beach, the wonderful Diamond Head, and the blue, blue ocean as far as the eye can reach. The old crater is full of Algarroba trees and only in one place can you see the old lava, the tuff and the earth full of black ashes.

Now back to something about my work. I have my classes arranged like this

9:30–9:50	Bible
9:50–10:15	Division II Arithmetic
10:15–10:45	Division I Arithmetic
10:45–11	Geography

| 11–11:15 | Gymnastics |
| 11:15–11:25 | Reading, Spelling, English combined |

Friday, A.M.—I am listening all the time for the whistle which shall tell me my ship has come in bringing my first letters from you and home. The week has been hard for me and I have had to lie down and rest between every duty to prepare for the next. I think it will be better next week, especially when my foot is better. Isn't it ridiculous, Charlie, the mosquitoes have stung me so that one ankle is badly poisoned and I got so lame and it looked so bad yesterday I had the doctor. He had me poultice it right away and gave me powders to take. It is better this morning but walking around makes it worse. The worst of it is that I hate to sit around while others are doing my work or it goes undone.

We are all saddened because Miss Pope had news that her father is dead. He was buried last Friday. She was quite broken hearted.

> Very lovingly,
> Your Carrie

September 21, 1890, Kawaiahao Seminary

My Darling,

I am full of joy and peace today. I am really happy. Your letters have done much for making me so. I will be brave and good and loving for your sake. Then too, I find the work interesting, the girls interesting. I hope I can keep the same feeling right along.

I think some of the teachers are rather disposed to worry over everything and to consider the girls and themselves natural enemies. It has secretly grieved me to notice how some of them never speak to the girls except in a scolding or fretful way. I am really trying, darling, not to do so. A number of times already I have had to speak sternly and even severely, but inwardly I have not lost control of myself at all. The discipline is very strict—things that we would not mind at all in a family or even in our schools are here "tabu" but the days of constant whipping seem to be in the past—now the punishments consists of standing girls up in corners or putting them in closets to reflect or taking them to your own room for that purpose or depriving them of some pleasure, or most common of all, setting them at some extra task.

Work seems to be the greatest evil that can befall these girls. I am surprised at the docility with which these big girls will submit to punishment. Only Friday, two girls almost as large as myself and who had been half annoying me for some time added positive disobedience and I gave them the big flight of stairs belonging to my dormitory to scrub and they did it as meekly as I could desire. In my school room I have all the older girls on my side but there are a half dozen restless spirits that I shall have more or less trouble with.

Miss Davis took Miss Pope down to Waikiki for a quiet Sunday where she could be alone with her sorrow. It was Miss Patch's Sunday away also and we do each other's work when we are absent on our "off Saturday and Sunday." So yesterday morning I played the piano for the girl's singing, had an eye to the work Miss Patch sees to, and the cleaning of the parlors and front hall. Her girls are so competent that there was really nothing to do. In my own domain there was "plenty scrubbing" and I had the girls examine their bed nets where it is said bugs are wont to gather if there are any of them. Then to make sure, I went through them myself and found two curtains with bugs in it, the girls are ordered and down come the curtains and into the wash at once.

The afternoon was quite free only to be full in another way. It was Miss Davis' turn to have Bible Lesson in the evening and I offered to take that. The parents and families of the girls are all allowed to come then and she tries to meet them all and has to have an eye on everything that goes on. Ten or a dozen boys are allowed to come down from Kamehameha to play croquet with our older girls. Retta Hight was here to supper. I like her much better than I did at Oberlin. Perhaps I am more free from clique prejudice, etc.

The Bible class means to entertain the girls for an hour and a quarter. You cannot have 110 girls answer questions at their own sweet will. You must just give them the story of the lesson as simply as you can with as much illustration as possible. I had them sing some and then stood right out in front of the desk and talked to them. My society discipline helped me out. I could not have done it without that. Even here in this kind of school work, I am thankful for my Oberlin training.

I was the other morning at devotions. It was my morning to pray and we had visitors, the wife of the U.S. Consul and a Mrs. Wright who came down on the Zealandia[3] with us. She is one of these truly cultivated ladies who has read and traveled much and is in sympathy with all good things. Then this morning I had Miss Patch's task of going with all the girls to native church and teaching her class there. After dinner, came my own drilling of the girls in the Bible work for the past week. I read them a story and tonight I am going to take Miss Pope's task of going at one end of the procession down to the Central Union Church.

Yesterday I had a pleasant little happening. Judge Judd brought me a present of eight coconuts and two breadfruits. That makes you smile and realize where I am. We had one of the breadfruits today roasted for 2 hours with salt on one end. It looks on the outside like a big orange—orange rough green, but 5 times as big. Inside it turned out as pale yellow, mealy and much like sweet potato—to be eaten with butter, pepper and salt. It is very hearty eating and I liked it. The coconuts were not so agreeable to me for they were greener than we are accustomed to eat them and the white part was soft and like a piece of cheese, like heavy custard but lacking the real coconut taste which we like so much. The native oranges are wonderfully fine but do not seem to be much cheaper than at home.

Wages are high here not like Asiatic countries and so even the things that are plentiful and easy to get cost like everything. They raise beautiful white potatoes all the year around. I saw Miss Pepoon pay $2.25 for a bag. I should say eggs are 50 cents a dozen—butter 50¢ per lb. even fish is costly. I think though that we have the best of board here at the teacher's table. Sometime I am going to send you what we have for several meals. The warning bell for supper has rung and I must stop.

Monday—Dearest—Just from my schoolroom to Thee. Miss Davis and Miss Pope have come back and the latter is doing her accustomed work. It is very hard for her I can easily see. Miss Hopper received bad news too on the last steamer. Several of her nearest relatives are ill and have been for some time and she is going home by the first steamer if possible.

Charlie if you can get hold of any good story papers I wish you would send them to me. I will gladly pay postage. My girls are sadly in want of reading and I do not like the things I find in their hands. I propose to gradually establish a Reading Circle of my own.

Tuesday—I go to duties now which are becoming quite familiar but I am trying to learn more and more about my girls. God bless the ships and the winds that carry our letters and bless my boy over in the home-land.

Your loving girl

September 26, 1890, Kawaiahao Seminary

My Darling,

Last evening there was a reception given across the way
at Mrs. Cooke's for Miss Hopper. I was on duty all the
afternoon till seven o'clock in the evening but then I
dressed and went over. I did not expect to stay but an
hour but I did stay longer.

Two young men talked with me for a while. They were quite pleasant and
I have heard that they are good young men but in intelligence I should rank
them with our dry-goods clerks at home. They asked me if I could not go to
the bathing party at Waikiki on Friday evenings. I was rather glad to say "no"
because I don't feel like going in the water at night time when I can't swim.

What I enjoyed most last night was sitting beside Mr. Atherton (senior)
and Professor Alexander of Oahu College, and hearing them talk. Professor
Alexander is considered the most learned man in town. I could not join in
but I was interested and instructed. They were telling about the different trees
and talking about the tropical fruits. Professor Alexander experiments with
seeds from Africa and South America.

After going down town, we drove out to Mr. Beckwith's where I left my letters. We made one call on the teachers of the Industrial home and then went
on to Waikiki to Mrs. McCully's where we were invited to six o'clock dinner.
Our hostess is quite a handsome woman, quite robust and her husband is gray
headed. There is a little girl and two young ladies connected with the family.
Carrie Gilman's mother was out there too and the captain of the *Australia*
which bears this letter. First we went in bathing. It is a beautiful beach of the
finest sand with no undertow and a very gradual descent. The McCullys have
a house in town and a cottage at the sea. It is all very open—the dining room
being simply a large, square open verandah. There our dinner was served by
a Japanese boy while the captain beside me told sea stories and behind I could
hear the gentle murmur of the sea and watch the stars and moon come out
with wonderful distinctiveness—the outlines are perfect. The only thing to
mar it all was the mosquitoes which never leave me alone in the evening.

I must tell you a little more of my duties. I think I did not tell you of my afternoons at all. We get through dinner by 1:15 or 1:30 and at 2, I have a sewing
class that lasts till 3:30. This meets every day except Saturday and Friday. Generally I am free from that time till eight in the evening when the girls go to

their dormitories and then I am on duty till 8:30 the girls can talk as much as they wish in their own dormitories but by 8:45, they must be in bed and then only whispering is allowed till nine when all must be silent. Each day sees some variation in the regular program. Mondays Dr. Beckwith comes here and conducts prayers and drills the girls in Bible questions and in the afternoon Mrs. McCully conducts a prayer-meeting. This is a pleasant relief to the teachers as we do not attend. Miss Pope takes my sewing class and Miss Pepoon my dormitory. On Wednesday evening once in four weeks I have to go with the girls to a native prayer-meeting. On Thursday afternoon I am on duty in the play ground from 3:30 to 6:45.

Friday morning we get through our lessons at 11 a.m. and devote the next hour to cleaning heads. The girls are a very lousy set and this is the most trying of my duties. They have no sense of shame and try to deceive—but fortunately I know all about lice. I don't do the cleaning myself but inspect what the girl has done on another girl's head. I have some bad heads in my room but I mean to have them clean before long if I possibly can. When I am through with them I rustle to my room and give my own head the most vigorous kind of a combing. Don't you think this is missionary work?

> God keep you,
> Yours, Carrie

September 28, 1890, Kawaiahao Seminary

My Lover,

I wonder if you see, dearie that I am just now in a mixture of feelings, joy over you, and a little anxiety over home and now let me explain why I have certain feelings of disgrace. I think I have told you that the girls have lice but I don't think I have told you how abundant and copious they are how we devote part of Friday morning to head cleaning. I set the girls in my school room at one another's heads and then go around myself and see if the heads reported clean are clean. In most cases they are not. One girl has been so bad that I gave her a week to clean it out or have her long, heavy hair cut. She has done pretty well toward getting them out or more truly, I have, for three times a day I have followed her and used her as a means of punishment for other girls. They have no pride over the matter and told me the other day, to convince me that it was no disgrace that everyone had them and that God made them. I said "yes, he made them to punish the wicked Egyptians." They had nothing to say to that.

Now Charlie, don't ever breathe a word of this to anyone. I only tell you because I can't keep from telling you that I found three of these in my own head the other day. I don't think there are any more for I have combed and combed and am waiting as patiently as I can for the larkspur from home. They are different from the American variety, long and black. Charlie please pity me and love me still and believe that I am not going to keep any such things but comb morning noon and night—and I vow to you, Carl, that my girls have got to get rid of them too.

In spite of all this I mean to be well and happy. You must not worry about me, my darling, as Dr. Noble says it is a fine place for my health and think I can prove it to you. I have an appetite to match your own—everything tastes good—good meat, and tender, fresh young peas, beans and corn even here at the last of September and then the delicious fruit. My digestion is perfect. At breakfast we always have bananas or oranges or melons, at dinner we generally have fruit served up in some way and at supper there is strawberries or native pineapple or guavas or fresh figs—every meal is superb and just to my liking—the two or three times a month comes an ocean bath which is health in itself. We have good bath-tubs here in the home for the baths which must be necessary two or three times a week. Then the breezes fresh from the mountains, which have just come from way out on the sweet clean ocean. Just now it has been pretty warm,—up to 90° for two or three days together, but every night has been good for sleeping.

From now on I expect to be a marvel in the way of health—I think the month that has past has been the hardest that I shall know. There seemed a kind of slow fever in my veins, much of the time I felt physically bad—too tired to do anything when my work was done, arms and legs all swollen from bites, a languidness that I had to fight against and then the anxiety of getting the upper hand of my work—but every day I am feeling more calm and collected.

I think I have my school room in hand with the exception perhaps of three or four young girls, chock full of mischief who want to hold the governing. I recognize the situation with them and am preparing myself to meet them hour by hour this coming week and every time have them obey me. I am very anxious to have the best of order in my room without chance for a word from Miss Pepoon—I do not want to adopt the policy she believes in—that of constant scolding for everything. She is very sweet and good but to my mind, that is the chief fault of herself and assistants. I have heard my girls say among themselves "Miss Winter don't scold" and Miss Brewer told me yesterday that Emily Bartholomew my largest girl had said to her that she liked me because I didn't scold. I punish in various ways but I pray that I may be kept from scolding. I think with Dr. Drummond in "The Greatest Thing in the World" that it is the greatest evil in the world.[4] I know both you and I feel very strongly about it.

I think I told you of the special duties in my latest letter. Occasionally I must have a company of girls and clean the sick cottage. After thinking it over I proposed to Miss Pepoon to let me have the girls in two divisions in the chapel for gymnastics—a half hour each. She seemed glad to assent and Friday I had my first trial. They all took hold well and I think it is going to be popular with the girls. It is something of an undertaking for there are over 50 in each class. Friday evening, once in two weeks, I have charge of the study hour and conduct the evening devotions.

On Saturday there are no lessons but I see to the scrubbing of my entire domain. It is done by 10:30 and I look up other extra tasks that are want to accumulate during the week. In the afternoon the girls dress in their best and receive company from parents and brothers and cousins—recent visitation in the coming down of a dozen or so Kamehameha boys to play croquet.

In the evening once in 8 weeks I conduct the Bible Class. Once in four weeks on Saturday and Sunday I am at liberty to do as I please and once in four weeks I take Miss Patch's work which by the way is not very much, the hardest thing being the taking of the girls to Sunday school and teaching a class there. Once in eight weeks I go to Morning Service with the girls, once in four weeks to church with them in the evening. You see where there are two teachers in a duty it comes around once in four weeks, where there is one it comes once in eight weeks. Sunday evening before going to church, we have an exercise in our chapel. We sing and each class goes through the Bible work it has had during the week. The teachers rehearse them privately for this on Sunday afternoon. I think Sunday afternoon is a hard time as any because all the girls stay in their dormitory and have to be quiet all the afternoon. It means considerable watchfulness on my part as they are full of mischief and there is very little reading material. I mean to have a collection of stories in my own room for them on Sunday afternoons. With a little care I think I can make it profitable. The girls read some and I am surprised to find the worst kind of reading matter creeping into the school. Already I have put three paper stories in the stove without the owner's knowledge. I am taking my spare time now to look through the girls' trunks, marking clothes, looking for their mending and seeing if they have dirty clothes hidden away and then I have come across these books. It seems strange that I should have such rights over the girls but I think it is best from the more I learn of them.

October 15—Monday I taught, but I felt so badly I went to see the doctor in the afternoon. Then I went to bed and stayed there till Friday when Nellie Waterhouse came and took me to her home and I went to bed again and am now picking up. It has been better since I came here than at the seminary, for there, I saw all my work to be attended to and I had to be cared for by the teachers who had quite enough work to do without caring for me.

My fever has been gone for two days now and I am picking up. I am afraid I do not think much of Dr. McWayne as a medical man although he is very kind to me and I suppose will not charge me for all his attendance. Here is an example of his skill. On Sunday he wanted to have me perspire and gave me a powder. I have had to tell him again and again that I was sensitive to large doses of medicine and that he must not give me large doses. Well after the powder I began to sweat—it just poured out of me—four times they changed my clothing so wet you could wring it, and not only that but clear through the flannel blanket, the sheets, and deep into the pillow. I thought I was going to evaporate and it made me very weak and sick. I think that has made me slower about getting up—I was so completely flattened out. I have to take egg-nog twice a day and that means two teaspoons full of brandy [Don't tell, Charlie]. Once when I was feeling worst I cried a little while for you Charlie. It seemed as though I were so lonesome and so longing for you that I could not stand it but I said hopeful, cheerful things to myself and by-and-by I felt better. Good night, my darling.

Thursday, October 16—My dearest—I am downstairs today for the first time. By the time you are reading this letter I shall probably be all well and strong again. I cannot be too grateful to the Waterhouses for all they have done for me. I am surprised in this house. The grounds are very elegant and so is the furniture in the house but I do not think we would think the house itself anything extra. There is no pretty finishing anywhere in pretty woods, just common pine doors and finishings painted with pretty paper to make things nice. They have five servants, one an old native woman who has been with them 18 years and a Chinese cook who has been here 12 years.

Since I have been here the *Nipsic* has gone back to the U.S. She was one that was badly used up and repaired here. I saw her at the naval repair place when I came but no one explained about her. That makes me think to tell you about the *Charleston*. There is always a U.S. man-of-war in port and she had been here for a year and no one quite knew why she was ordered away but I think they felt better when she came back. There has been no revolution only politics are very muddled here. There seems to be the king's party and the good party. The king wants a new constitution giving him more power and he wants a standing army. I have read very childish and comical articles in the paper about the army. Most of the commotion is carried on by two politicians, Wilson and Bush who would undoubtedly like the bloodshed and revolution that they from time to time promise. But nothing happens and the people don't pay much attention to them now. The American papers rather overstated the matter. I was afraid you would think about it.

You wrote about Mr. Lyman. I was glad you met him. I have talked with his sister who teaches at Kamehameha preparatory. For the first time two Hawaiian boys have gone to Oberlin. The other one is John Wise from Kamehameha. He is sent by Missionary Society. Miss Hight is especially interested in John Wise. His first letters have come and the boys went to one of the teachers and asked if Oberlin were the largest city in America. The teacher was from Ann Arbor so you can fancy his disgust. It would be hard to tell what Mr. Lyman is, as is true in many cases, I am told that there is Hawaiian, Chinese, American and Indian blood in him and I don't know what else. Everyone speaks of the family very highly but because she is dark-skinned his sister has been approached with insults a number of times. That is the great evil here for all the native and half-white girls—the wicked white men. It is the practical danger that our girls at the seminary have to be guarded against.

Well, I have written a long time and will take a rest now. I love to write to you Charlie and could keep on all day.

> Your lover girl,
> Carrie

October 20, 1890, Kawaiahao Seminary

My Dear Charlie,

Now I will tell you of that luau as I promised if you would like to hear, right here, sweet in the chat between you and I. Luau (pronounce every letter for a long) is two things greens or a big native banquet. The greens  are made of taro leaves and are good. The tuber of taro you know is the main thing in poi, first that boiled and pounded up and water. Well the boys at Kamehameha gave a big luau on account of their base-ball victories and invited their parents and relatives, the King and his sister the princess Mrs. Dominis,[5] a large number of white people and thirty of our own girls with their teachers.

Miss Pepoon took half of the girls in the first car and Miss Brewer and I the rest in the tram car as they call them here. That school has very fine large grounds with a number of smallish buildings to serve their purposes. The boys only pay $40 a year and that includes board, and everything with fine instruction in the manual training department carpentering, printing or black-smith shop. After a half hour of greetings during which time I was introduced to the princess and much against my inclinations was sent to the dining room.

Lūʻau at Kamehameha School for Boys, October 1890. King Kalākaua is at the head of the third table from the bottom. The king's sister, Liliʻuokalani, is sitting on his left, in black with a light-colored feather lei.

Try to imagine yourself there, my dear. Contrary to the usual custom we sat in chairs at the table instead of squatting on the ground. On the tables were white tablecloths but they were covered with a large leaf call tea-leaf though it is not the China plant (supper). On each plate was either a baked fish or a funny greasy meat done up in tea-leaf which proved to be pork. These delicacies had been cooked under the ground wrapped up in tea-leaves. Scattered all around were big dishes of raw fish of which the natives are very fond, bowls of poi, dishes of coarse salt, funny little crabs, a mixture of coconut and sweet potato, big sweet potatoes, extra baked fish, watermelons and bottles of soda water, no bread or butter and not a knife, fork or spoon for anyone, even the King.

It was a little bit trying at first to see the natives eating their meal and fish till their hands were all smeared, then see two or three dip a couple of fingers into the same bowl of poi, give a graceful twist and raise a big gob of the sticky stuff to their mouths. Poi answers all the purposes of mucilage. I tried to do as the Romans do for my girls were watching me and I picked at my half-baked fish and at the pork and ate some watermelon. I did not try poi for I see too much of it here, though our girls have to eat it with spoons. They thought the whole repast delicious, but I do not recommend luaus for real pleasure. It was very interesting and I was glad I saw it.

Now here is my list, dear, which I have been wanting to give you for some time. Then I can tell you about my girls and you will know where to place them.

Division I

Victoria Ahoy*	Rose Anahu*
Louisa Kahili	Emma Akana*
Tamar Puni	Emily Bartholomew
Lilian Makaimoku	Emma Lahaina
Kathy Clarke	Mary Bridges
Nancy Ahia	Mikahala Apolo
Jessie Abraham	Harriet Lewis

Division II

Mary Kealoha	Lucia Kahai
Malie Kapali	Alice Meheula
Caroline David	Rachel Haina

Sarah Kapalehua	Tillie Previer
Miriam Keamuoku	Emma Hanaike
Emma Ai*	Eunice Puni
Maria Kaaumoa	Rose Kapalehua
Annie Wong	Maria Puuohau

There those are written from memory but at first I thought I should never learn the names. Those with the star are half Chinese and without exception nice girls.[6] Annie Wong is all Chinese and I have told you something of her before. I have given her the first 25 ¢ for lace.

> Your girl,
> Carrie

October 26, 1890, Kawaiahao Seminary

My Dearest Charlie,

My whole manner and mode of life had been turned upside down and yet instead of having time to adjust myself to it, I am put hard at work at what is utterly new to all my 24 years experience.

Tell me about John Wise, Charlie, I have caught a deep interest in him from Miss Hight. It seems it was a long and hard struggle for him to make up his mind to become a preacher to his people and go away to study for that purpose and he came to her in his difficulties. She has read me his letters which breathe the highest Christian spirit. I think they are dissatisfied here that he is not in the seminary. The idea is that he is to be gone only two years and then begin preaching at once. I fear you may love him as a pupil, perhaps not though, as Mr. Oleson the principal here, may not be able to dictate to Oberlin as he does here.

You ask some questions about school and such matters. I am fortunate in the housework that I oversee. My dormitory girls seem to be willing and efficient and not inclined to shirk. I do not have to stand over them but it is enough if I go afterward and see that it is well done and only once or twice have I had to call a girl back to do anything over. I have no teaching in the afternoon beside the sewing class and every day but Thursday is comparatively free. I find I must spend some time every day on preparing for sewing. I have some dormitory work that I am not up with yet that I can omit when I am too tired. I have 17 more trunks to examine and then a little better arrangement in the attic to work up, such as assigning and marking particular nails for particular girls and something of the same work in the lavatory.

I think you are right, dear, in the part love has in a woman's life, not that I would always have cared to say or think that it was more to her than to a man, but as you say, experience teaches me that it is so—that it is one of the differences and one that involves no question of superiority or inferiority but it is simply so—that is why a wicked woman is such a monstrosity as compared with a wicked man and that is why a man who does his whole duty by a woman and has the thought to comprehend her and respect her is universally respected and put in a higher place in all true hearts than a woman who respects her husband and does all for him.

I think I wrote you that I had joined Central Union. I am afraid it will be too late to ask you to send me a handsome autumn leaf next letter to show my girls. I wish I had thought of it before. No asters or golden-rod here. Another girl had to scrub my stairs this week for cheating.

Just one fact about Kamehameha. It has as large an endowment as Oberlin College and it is eventually to be opened to girls and will probably swallow up Kawaiahao which will be a good thing because of the better facilities possible. I should like to see the day myself. We are doing a good work though and perhaps the best possible under the circumstances. Take the love and kisses that are your due, Carl, or if you please I will give them to you which you will like better–

> Carrie.

Well, Charlie I am going to take up your second letter now. After all, it is ten o'clock—the dormitory work is all done, three of the girls were washing out their nets in which I found bed bugs. I have inspected the last girls head and I have a company of two in my room—one is sewing for me as a punishment for leaving her clothes around. I have them in my possession and she is working them out. The other girl is reading from a book I have drawn from the library an account of the Salem witchcraft on which she is to write a composition.

I have had my worst day so far in the schoolroom this last week and when I came to my room I did what you did on your birthday—knelt beside your picture for I felt very badly and sick at heart.

There was an Oberlin meeting last week on Mr. Bond's account at Dr. Whitney's. Charlie Atherton talked with me most of the evening. He seems like a young boy. He was quite confidential, showed me his wife's picture in his locket and talked of his year in Oberlin. He said he was always fond of ladies society and he was sent to Oberlin to get him away from some girl here and it was out of the frying pan into the fire. It was funny to hear him make his excuses. I guess he is rather weak in the "backbone." I learn from others that it was rather a bitter pill for his family—they did not know of his marriage till he drew on his father's banker for money to take his wife home. I understand too that she is not much of a success here. You see the Atherton's are really a very fine family, cultured and kindly and their son didn't quite come up to their expectation. He seems to be a good young man now, going regularly to church and prayer meeting. I enjoyed talking with him, he was so frank.

Retta Hight took me home with her. I quite like her now Charlie. She seems in the right place for she is the only lady teacher in Kamehameha proper and she is sisterly to all the big boys. Two of the young men at Kamehameha were pleasant to me—of course they all were, but three are married and one is a peculiar uncouth sort of a young man who doesn't count socially. Don't misunderstand darling, I am simply introducing you to people whom you would naturally like to know.

Last Sunday afternoon I had to have five girls in my room and three of them were here till supper time before they would learn their Bible verses. Since I wrote you last I have given my severest punishments. It is quite a come down to my vanity but I thought I should be a good disciplinarian at once when in reality I have to learn how to govern like most ordinary people I suppose. The girls got a strong impression that I was kind and never punished. Three or four got so they would not obey and were noisy in school and troublesome generally so to disabuse them of their idea, I have kept three girls all day long in a dark closet, with nothing to eat but bread water. It has had some effect but I shouldn't wonder if I had to repeat it in one case at least to convince the girls that I can punish every day if necessary.

On Monday afternoon, Miss Pope and I did a little exploring on our own account. We went down-town together and looked into some of the stores, particularly the Hawaiian curio stores. They have some nice things though not so great a variety as I supposed I should find. What I am particularly pleased with is the large fine mat that is like cloth in its suppleness and wears a life time. They cost $15, but I think when I go home I must take one for our house. Perhaps I can get one at a bargain sometime. The calabashes in the Koa wood are handsome too. It is a wood that is becoming scarce but has a wonderful grain and takes a fine polish.

Tuesday afternoon, Miss Brewer and I went down to Waikiki with our lunch. I am really getting so I trust myself more to the water and if someone will only hold me by the collar or the chin I kick out in great shape where as at first I would not trust my toes far from the ground. You see you never get chilled in this water or turn blue as I have seen so many people do in Long Island Sound.

This makes me think to tell you that every Friday evening there is a bathing party of ladies and gentlemen and I have often been asked to go but on account of my dormitory have never gone but a week ago Friday night I did go down just for the drive but did not go in and now I have definitely decided not to join that or any other evening mixed party. I am sure if you had been there and seen the extremely scanty attire of the gentlemen and their hearty and affectionate efforts to instruct the ladies in swimming you would prefer to have me stay away.

My favorite time is just at sunset, where the sun is just dropping into the water, and the whole sky is ablaze with color and speaking of color makes me think of a curious thing that takes place just at sunset and in the very few minutes before it is dark. The sun leaves a long column of red with clearly defined edges reaching way up into the sky which is intensely blue. At that moment all the trees outlined against the sky become an almost inky black and most strange of all the floating clouds are green—from a delicate sea-green to a deep, dark green.

Well, to go back to Waikiki. We did not eat our lunch there after all for Mrs. William R. Castle came from her cottage and invited us so urgently to dinner that we went in. They had roast duck. Miss Lowry is the sister-in-law and the young lady of the house. She came down on the steamer with us. She has the reputation of a flirt and of telling all she knows about every flirtation she indulges in.

Let's take a little intermission here in the course of events while I look at your picture and realize that there is a real man whom it represents who loves me and whom I love more than I can ever tell him, Oh beautiful boy, how wonderfully we have been blest. Few are as happy and content with their lot as we, who have such a beautiful future to look forward to and not only that but who are making that future now. I imagine myself often as old and telling the experiences of these days to others. I feel that I have a steadier purpose in being here than the others.

I am sorry to acknowledge it to you Charlie but it is a fact that not another teacher in this school pretends to be attached to this work. They all like individual girls but it is duty that keeps them at their work and they are ready to drop it all like hot cakes and I think the reason for it is that they have no future except of their own making and they cannot bear to think of a life alone here. Even Miss Pope is longing to go home next year but perhaps there is some excuse for her. That is one reason I like Retta Hight. She likes her work and is enthusiastic over it.

I am way off once more, for I was going to tell you about Wednesday. Nellie Waterhouse telephoned and asked me to dinner and as I had no duties after half-past three that day I was glad to go. It seemed like home to me there and Mrs. Waterhouse kissed me and was as kind as if she had a real liking for me. They had roast turkey for dinner. May and her father went down to prayer-meeting in the evening with me and I found some of our teachers there. Then that's not the end of the gayety for on Thursday there was a fair given for the benefit of a new Sailor's home and I was at liberty to go over for an hour in the evening. I didn't care very much about going but I notice that when I go out among people I feel better toward them while if I keep to myself, bitter feelings spring up against the other teachers who go. Miss Patch and Miss Hoppin went with me and we were hardly in the armory building before someone came up from behind and buried my face in yellow chrysanthemums. It was Nellie and her father. Mrs. Waterhouse marshaled all of us to the flower booth and had us pick out our own bouquet of roses—then he took Nellie and I to the tea garden to try the tea and then treated us to ice-cream. Nellie and I strolled about together looking at the booths and listening to the *Charleston* band. I bought two curios but I will not tell you what for fear I should want to send them to you for Christmas. Nellie took me to the candy stand to taste the coconut candy. We had chatted with a number of people. I thought it a very fine hour and went home quite happy over the kindness of people.

Well it is nine o'clock now and I am through with my study hour and my evening gymnastics, my girls are all abed and quiet except one little sinner who persisted in talking aloud after talking had been forbidden. She is standing in a corner with the mosquitoes for company to her bare legs. I feel sadly discouraged about discipline, Charlie, all the nice little theories about kindness and patience and gentleness don't work with these girls. They take advantage everywhere and insult and ride over a teacher rough-shod. I am thankful to say that I have got the upper hand of my sewing room work but not of my second division schoolroom work.

Dearest Charlie, I long to say some real heart things to you but I find that those heart things don't have many words. You are the most beautiful thing in my life and my very ideal of all that is good in a lover. It is after ten and I know you would send me off to bed in short meter if you were in authority.

NOTES

1. Miss Winter addresses her fiancé by his pet name, Carl.
2. This student composition was read at an exhibition at Kawaiahaʻo Female Seminary June 4, 1891, and appeared in the *Hawaiian Gazette* (June 16, 1891, p. 2). In later life, Margaret "Maggie" Powers would become a revered teacher memorialized as Mother Waldron and have a park in Honolulu named in her honor.
3. These were Mrs. George Wallace and Mrs. Edwin Wright.
4. Henry Drummond (1851–1897) was a Scots evangelist and author of the popular *The Greatest Thing in the World*, first published in 1884, which preached the teaching of Christian love in 1 Corinthians 13.
5. King David Kalākaua (1836–1891) reigned from 1874 until his death and was succeeded by his sister, Lydia Liliʻu Loloku Walania Wewehi Kamakeʻeha Paki-Dominis, who reigned as Queen Liliʻuokalani.
6. Odgers (1933) notes that a school for Chinese girls was founded in Honolulu in 1892 and the pupils proceeded from that school to Kawaiahaʻo Female Seminary.

Student Essay by Lydia Aholo

Lydia Aholo.   English.

I   My life as a school-girl

I am Lydia Aholo. I was brought in school when I was five years old. Her Majesty was not on the throne at that time. She was only a princess. One morning I was out in our yard playing the princess who is now her Majesty called me and I went up to her and she told me that she was going to put me in school. In the evening she told my grand-parents to bring me back to school. They brought me back to school that very evening. I remember at that time our dinning room was out in the front yard. And two other domitories were out there. We did not have very many trees at that time. I slept in one of the oldest domitories. In that domitory we had a lavatory where we wash our faces and comb our hair and besides that we had two closets where we hung our clothes. And the girls trunks were put in these closets. My bed stood near the makai closet and my trunk was put near my bed because the domitory was full at that time. And the first night that I slept in school I cried. When I was sleep that night I fell on the floor. And just as I was going turn on the other side I felt the floor it was so hard. When I woke up I couldn't do it because I was under my bed, then I began to cry. And when one of my teachers heard me crying she came out from and asked the girls who was crying. But of cause as you may all know I did not understand English at that time. Then my teacher came with a lantern in her

hand and she found me under my bed. She took
hold of me and put me on my bed again. Right
out of our dormitory we had a porch. One day our house
was set on fire because one of our girls had a box of
matches in the pocket of her dress and I think
the rat ate her pocket and it set our house on fire.
We were ready to go and have our dinner. In the morn.
at nine o'clock were all go in the chapel our
chapel in those days was not like our chapel
now. when we went in the chapel at nine
we had devotions and after devotions each class
went in their rooms. And on Sunday evening
we all were to go in the chapel. and each
class was to recite a chapter in the bible.
But we children instead of reciting bible restation
we were to sing songs and recite golden texts
It was one Saturday night all of us children
were in bed. But most of us were not asleep.
And just as I was going to sleep the older girls
that usually go to study began to scream and that
frightened us very much. We children did not
know where to go to. So we just got out from
our beds and ran in the other dormitory what
we call pauahi Hall. Some children when
they got up from their beds they got hurt
because they were very excited. We had our
night gowns on and mind you we were
all standing in the hall. One the older girls
was so frightened that cut her hand.

English Lesson.

But now we have new Domitories. We have three Domitories in all besides the teacher's rooms. One Domitory is New Rice Hall one Old Rice Hall and the other one is the Panahi Domitory. But I will not tell you very much about those old years. I will go on to the new years. In this new years we have had many pleasure. Every Saturday our parents come for our dirty cloth but some girls do their own washing. And the girls that are in the highest rooms they are allowed to go out in the front yard to play croquet. Before the Kamehameha boys use to come down and play croquet with our girls. And on Sunday Saturday morning each girl have to scrub the part of the house where she is responsible. Our girls cook our own food. We have tea bread and cracker in the morning and we have poi and meat in the after-noon. and sometimes we have poi and salmon And sometimes in the evening we have and sometimes potatoes and sugar and sometimes poi and meat sometimes we have rice and sugar. We wear uniform when we go to school. And any kind of dresses after school. When we go to prayer meeting on Wednesday nights we have to wear our uniform. Sunday mornings we have white dresses to go to church with and when it rains we have our uniform. We go to bed at half past eight. We give concerts many times. Every morning each girl

have to do her work. Sometimes we play base-ball
and sometimes we play other games. Kamehameha
boys usually invite us up there to spend the evening.
Sometimes we all go up Waikiki & have sea bath.
" " " " , down Ewa. And sometimes
we go down Kalia. Now I am 14 years old. I am one

II. fish = fishes &. the girls that take music lessons
    baby = babies The Queen is supporting for my tuition.
    boy = boys   Plural   Possessive Plural
    knife = knives   chairs   'chairs'
    potato = potatoes babies   ladies'
    piano = pianoes   boxes   boxes' 9
    goose = geese   men   men''
    ox = oxen   mice   mice's'
    child = children IV. Cash On Delivery
    plus = pluses   Rail road.
III. Possessive Sing. France
    chair's   District of Columbia
    lady's   After Christ.   9
    box's   Doctor of Medicine.
    man's   Reverent
    mouse's   Kentucky
                      Monday
                      Georgia

V. Another day its course has run,
And still O God Thy child is blest
for Thou hast been by day my sun
And Thou wilt be by night my res

3

Meeting Royalty
November 16–December 21, 1890

Iolani Palace. Photo by Lilla Estelle Appleton.

November 16, 1890, Kawaiahao Seminary

My dearest,

Charlie, I am a very exalted personage—this last week I have hobnobbed with royalty so you may expect this letter to have a very aristocratic flavor. There is a very handsome lady visiting here now from California and

Mrs. Dominis[1] has made considerable of her and last Monday told her to invite a party and she would show them over the palace. We were all invited and at 10:30 left our posts of duty. I think there must have been 40 or 50 people there.

Homage to the royal family in photographs and lei.

We paid our respects to Mrs. Dominis in the throne room in a long room carpeted in red, with its walls in white and gold. The principal object of interest here were the royal mantles and capes which were evidently out from lock and key for an airing. They are all made of beautiful yellow feathers, two little tufts coming from one bird and as this species is nearly or quite extinct, the mantles can never be replaced and therefore to the Hawaiians are much more valuable than diamonds. They are constructed in such a way as to be very pliable. One was very old and had belonged to Kamehameha, the grandest king the islands ever had, and the first in historic times to rule all the islands.

We passed from this room into the "blue room" and the pictures here were valuable fine paintings of the king and Queen—one of Louis Philippe, the king and Queen of Italy and a handsome large picture of Queen Victoria in her Jubilee robe. These are gifts from European countries, very interesting, and I suppose not to be found to any extent outside of royal hands. You would have been delighted with the great calabashes of Koa wood with gold finishings. I must get hold of that wood sometime to take home with me. I would want your advice before having it made up into anything.

Next was the Banqueting room with oak finishings and silver ornaments. There were more paintings here. I easily picked out Napoleon III and heard Mrs. Dominis telling someone that it was a Napoleon but she did not know which one. Blanche was one and a General Thomas who immortalized himself in Hawaiian history by being the first to rear the Hawaiian flag after the English flag was pulled down.[2] Thus I learned that the English had once tried to hold these islands. Back in the grand entrance hall we had to wait to sign our names and that gave us a chance to study the pictures there—Kamehameha I, in a red coat white shirt, no collars or cuff and yellow robe with a noble old face and a high forehead. His Queen had on a yellow gown with leg-of-mutton sleeves and a red scarf. There is all the togery of civilization in the next Kamehameha. He went to England and died there. His Queen has on a huge white turban with ostrich plumes and a gauzy dress. The Queen of Kamehameha the III is in white satin and Kamehameha IV in red velvet. She is the good Queen Emma. There is one more king and that is all the line.

They show their superiority in their faces. The present king was elected. There was one more Kamehameha who might have been Queen but she refused. She was Mrs. Bishop[3] whose husband owns the big bank here. At her death all the wealth of the Kamehameha's went into this Kamehameha School started only three years ago. What better memorial could there have been. When Mr. Bishop dies, his money is to go there also. The school certainly has a noble future. Mrs. Dominis who is by far the funniest appearing of the royal family was very affable and explained to the best of her ability.

Now for my next encounter with royalty or do you prefer to come down to common people first and have some kisses first. There—now I think I can go on. Well, the king was going to prorogue the legislature and I thought I would like to see such a big work put in action, so I went with Miss Pepoon, Miss Pope, and Miss Hoppin. Your precious letters were on the table but the legislature doesn't meet again for two years and I had the consolation of knowing they were there.

The foot-guards and the band were around the government building and with the arrival of every dignitary there was music. We got good seats and saw the royal mantles spread, the attendants take their stand with the Kahilis which look like big feather dusters. Then came in lots of gold lace on the officers of the men-of-war in the harbors—the diplomatic corps, the bishops and judges in their gowns and last with a big flourish, the King and Queen—she in a yellow satin gown with two footmen to carry the train. She was on the left of the king, which on the right was Mrs. Dominis in light blue. Her husband an Englishman, stood beside her while beside the Queen was Mr. Cleghorn, who was the husband of another sister of the king's, now dead. We all stood while the Bishop read a prayer in native. The king read a little speech in native and then in English to "The nobles and representatives before him." There was another short prayer and after royalty was once more ceremoniously gotten into their carriages, we all went home to dinner and our letters.

Wednesday—November 19—Sunday was the king's birthday and the public holiday was on Saturday. All our girls who have homes in town were allowed to go to them that day. The city was very gay with riding parties and flags and the races in the harbor. There was a reception at the palace and it said in the paper that ladies and gentlemen who desired to be presented should be on hand. So Miss Pope and I, bound to see all that was unique, dressed ourselves in fine apparel and bravely faced the unknown. It wasn't much after all. We were ushered in with much pomp by a big soldier, waited a while in the "blue room" with many others, then passed by their majesties with a bow and in a few moments left the room. We felt a little annoyed for we got in among a number of people who rather crowded matters and our names were not announced, but we went by in kind of a drove. Miss Pope and I intend now to go again sometime just for the sake of doing the thing in a more dignified manner.

Sunday, the king had appointed as a day of fasting and prayer for the lepers and went to church himself three times that day. He came to Kawaiahao church in the morning. I had to go with the girls to Sunday service that morning and saw the decorations. Something happened there too that was a little trying to me. The people from Kamehameha usually go to the better native church but that morning they all came down to our church. When I went in with our girls, I saw Mr. Oleson and Mr. Richards by the door. I bowed and in a few moments Mr. Richards came and asked if there was room to sit beside me. I made room for I supposed he had some errand—but no, he just wanted to chat and he stayed there through most of the opening exercises of Sunday Service while all the other Kamehameha teachers sat upstairs with their classes and his was there alone. Of course he talked and I had to reply although it is tabu for one of the girls to whisper in church. You can imagine my inward tumult for it was so very conspicuous and I feared that people would think I had made him come there in some way—and there the girls oh what wouldn't they say or do? Well, Charlie, you know what a queer girl I am—that little incident of his coming there stirred me all up for that day. I don't know why but I wanted you more than any time since I have been here. Perhaps it was because I have only been with ladies since I have been here. Is this a very sad muddle dearie? Some of that same feeling comes to me now and I wanted to be taken and feel your strength and tenderness and firm and gentle care for me, Oh my lover, my lover!

I went down to the Central Union church in the evening with some of our girls and Dr. Beckwith preached a fine sermon about Naaman the leper. Many of the girls wept for several of our girls have sisters in Molokai.

Monday was a holiday. Miss Pope and Miss Hoppin took off a riding-party of ten. You should see our girls on their Kanaka horses astride, with their garlands. The harnesses are all tricky but the more rearing and plunging they do the better the girls like it.

Friday 21 of November—Dearest, the steamer goes today and this must be finished before school time. As usual I hate to part with my letter to you for it does not tell the smallest fraction of my thought of you, my love for you and while I am writing I almost seem to be with you but when I see it go, I am farther away.

We had a disappointment yesterday. Miss Pepoon and Miss Davis have said for some time that Miss Pope and I were to go up to the Pali, a wonderful precipice up in the mountains. Well, yesterday we started with our fine new big strong horse, our lunch and one of the older girls. I took along some papers to put ferns in for I was told I would find some up there. On our way up the valley I marked several flowers I was going to gather as I came down.

By and by we were going up a little hill and without any warning Prince began to back and almost turned around. We stepped out of the break but we were bound we would not give in to him and lead him to the top of the hill and got on again. I held the whip and Miss Pope the lines and we went up several hills all right for whenever he showed any inclination to stop I laid on the whip to the best of my ability but when we were on quite a steep hill he again began to back straight down. We stayed in and whipped but he kept on bucking and we began to get out. The girl and I got out all right but the wheel turned a sharp angle with Miss Pope and she turned her ankle. There was nothing then to do but go home, but I was so angry with that big lazy horse. I wish he could have been made to go on up then and there. He ought not to have had his own way. I can't get over being angry with that horse. I whipped him much of the way home but he didn't seem to mind it.

A little about school now—we have a new little girl now.[4] She is German and comes from a very poor family where they were really suffering for food. She is about five but a real baby and so homesick. The first day she cried all the time and yesterday did not eat anything all the day till in the evening when she was alone in Miss Brewer's room. I got her to eat some "bread butter and sugar on it." She gets lots of petting from the girls who all feel very sorry for her.

Shall I tell you what we will do in school this morning? Hear them recite some verses they learned last evening—then there will be multiplication of fractions for the younger class and a talk with the older class on the history of New York. I prepare these talks once a week and it follows up their geography. Then the younger class will have a little Hawaiian history. Then I am going to read to them today for half an hour as a special treat.

Yours,
Carrie

November 23, 1890, Kawaiahao Seminary

My Dearest,

It is my Saturday and Sunday off and I am having a de-
lightful time. One of my eyes troubled me this morn-
ing so I did not go to church and am now enjoying the
luxuries of little Mrs. Hobron's dainty room. It is the
older Mrs. Hobron who owns the place I suppose and there seems to be a
sister of hers here in the family too. She has two children, Mrs. Smith, whose
home is right next to this, and "Tom" who is heir to this fine place and much
money beside I am told last July he married this dainty cousin of the Waterhouses. The whole house is more pretentious than any I have been in before with large, high rooms and beautiful furniture. In the dining-room,
plenty of silver, broad-winding steps leading up to the square piazza adorned
with elegant plants and inviting with its easy chairs. We stood out there this
morning and ate oranges fresh from the tree. The coffee was served on a
big silver platter and all the dainty china has a monogram on it. There is an
English flavor about things. I know Mrs. Hobron is American but I am wondering if her husband were not English.

Yesterday was full of pleasure for I went by invitation at ten o'clock in the
morning down to the Waterhouse's cottage at Waikiki. Nellie and May were

Horse car to Waikīkī. Photo by J. A. Gonsalves.

there, their two little brothers, Carrie Gilman, Miss Kinney and myself. Of course we were bathing and I always have to write about that because it is such delicious sport and because I am so proud now that I really can swim some. I had to keep an eye out at sea all the time for "my ship." I think it must be more trying to wait for mail here than at home—for here it is just one ship on which your hope hangs and you look for it to come up that horizon. I had to leave early, at two, and Mr. Waterhouse drove me down to the horse-car.

You see I was going on the *Charleston* with Miss Brewer. Her cousin Lieutenant Field had asked us aboard. A little boat met us at the wharf and soon we were aboard a man-of-war and we were shown carefully around it. The arming of the ship is $280.000. Lieutenant Field has this in charge and so he carefully explained all the big and little guns, the shells, the armory, etc. There are 10 big guns which carry 100 lbs shells as soon as they get to the coast they are to have two of the large guns replaced by one still larger, carrying a 250 lb. shell. He took us into his office and state room. The officers have a handsome dining room and staterooms. It is a big thing with 5 decks and over 300 men aboard. You could see rank everywhere. I don't know how to explain all the engines and things we saw. I haven't any vocabulary for that sort of thing although it was very interesting to me. The sailors were around taking naps in any shady corner, some of them reading and some playing checkers. I don't believe it is a very enviable life.

November 24—You ask about the girl's moral aptitude for religion. I hardly know what to say. They know well enough right and wrong and yet sometimes as a whole they seem better fitted to become Roman Catholics than Protestants. Some of them are good Christian girls. No matter how fiery they may be by nature they try to do right and to correct themselves. I think you can hardly realize how completely they give themselves up to the present emotion. As an example, I have seen a girl of 20 and a good girl, lose control of herself completely when she had made a slight mistake. They tell this story of a little girl last year. She was in Miss Jessie Hoppin's room and Miss Hoppin was on her bed and closed her eyes as if in sleep. The little tot knelt down and said her prayers and when she saw Miss Hoppin's eyes open exclaimed, "Oh, you can go to sleep, I said your prayers for you." I have talked with some of my older girls and find them very anxious for more religious life.

Today has been busy, with the regular work. After that, I did what I have long wanted to do and now for the first time had time to do—and that is getting the run of dormitory and attic. Each girl has a hook in the lavatory and a little bin like place in the attic but their places were all mixed up. Now their names are tied to the hooks. On her hook, each girl may have one dress, night-gown, towel and hat. She must hang her other things in the bin in the attic or keep them in her trunk. I had a "punish" girl to help me and she got quite interested in her "punish." Up in the attic I have a big box with a lock and key and whatever I find out of place, goes in there and does not come out again till it is paid for in work. I generally give them a seam to do for me. I hesitated over having them work on my things all the time but I have got over that now.

As usual, I hate to stop writing.

> Your love,
> Carrie

November 27, 1890, Kawaiahao Seminary, Thanksgiving

Dearest,

Some of the girls have been in my room this evening. One was fussing with your picture and the little standard slipped out of place. It was easy to adjust it back but Rose said, "Chee, he don't want us touch him." I be-lieve she really took it as a sign. The only exclamation I have heard the girls use are "Owee," "Chee" and "Ta."

I wrote some to mamma this morning and did some absolutely necessary sewing and then went down to Central Union with a few of the girls. I wore a white dress but it was very warm walking. We had rather poor singing and preaching and outside were all the busy signs and noises of city life. All the stores were open. Neither English nor Hawaiians celebrate the day. Some of them do to the extent of a fine dinner but is not as we mean it. The church was adorned with American and Hawaiian flags and beautiful roses. The singing of America was the best part of the service and it seemed to me the people sang it with peculiar fervor and feeling in their voices. I liked also the reading of the President's proclamation and that of Mr. Stevens, minister plenipotentiary.

At one, four of us teachers were at Mrs. Waterhouses for dinner. The center of the table was adorned with a basket of fruit, tipped to one side and showing its profusion gracefully on the cloth. There were eight courses—1st soup, 2nd fish and cucumbers, 3rd tongue, curry & minced green peas, 4th turkey, cranberry sauce, potato, string beans and almonds, 5th pumpkin pie and plum pudding, 6th strawberry ice-cream with real strawberries in it (The season is just beginning), 7th nuts and fruit, 8th coffee.

After all this, we all went outdoors and had a game of tennis. It was rather warm work. After having our pictures taken we came home. The girls were all tired from their holiday and have gone early to bed.

Sunday, Nov. 30—I am afraid the *Charleston* will not make the trip in a week but you will surely get that letter before this because they can use steam if they wish to. The king decided to go up to the coast with them. From what I heard I do not think he was over welcome. Friday was Independence Day for the Hawaiians. The anniversary of their freedom from England. Miss Pepoon hesitated about celebrating it but finally decided that it was politic to do so. The Hawaiians are quite touchy now days about foreign interference.

The day was full for me as you will see. There was a service at their church and I took all the girls who cared to go to that. I was glad I went. I was the only white person there and all was in Hawaiian but I could easily see what an earnest meeting it was. There were so many prayers by both men and women with such earnestness and the frequency of the word "Hawaii." One old white headed man made a very earnest talk and at one time all the people began to cry. Most of the girls with me wiped their eyes many times. When it was over I asked one of the girls what he said. It seems he was telling them of the earnest Christian life of the first converts of one Queen who became a Christian and traveled all around the islands in Christian work and that now he feared the people were not Christians only in name and he thought if they would arouse themselves and pray earnestly like the old Christians, the good God would take the leprosy from the nation. You know they are a light hearted people and don't often think serious thoughts of themselves. This was the most seriousness I have seen displayed among them before.

In the afternoon I took a party of girls who had been good in school out to see the ostriches.[5] It was the most satisfactory expedition I have made with them. There was none of that dissatisfaction which they so often express over everything.

Yesterday was a busy day also for me. I am trying all the time to systematize things in the dormitory and yesterday I tried to get the upper hand of towels. Clean ones were ordered under every pillow in the morning and the dirty ones up in the attic. There were many delinquents and I took all the names and then hunted each girl up and enquired into her towel state—five had none at all and no money to buy with—five more gave me money to buy some. I went down-town after dinner and got them and marked them with their names. Girls who had not unlocked their trunks for my Saturday inspection had to be looked up. Then I had a large box of clothing that I had picked up during the week that had to be redeemed and marked. It was quarter of twelve when I sat down to study my Bible lesson.

December 6—Oh Charlie dear, Charlie dear. I am so discouraged and as blue as indigo and with pretty good reason. I haven't heart to write except about what is in my heart so it will all have to come out to you. Here I have been "going on four months" and I seem to be almost a failure in the way of discipline. Perhaps that seems a little thing but it means real suffering to me and I have about resolved that if things don't straighten out before the year is over I shall give up and go home. Sometimes I think it grows out of an entirely weary system of governing and yet everyone seems to think it is the only way to govern these native girls—to have them in complete subjection and punish every slight deviation. I have asked questions of Katy Clarke about Jessie Hoppin's way. She had perfect order but every day she had long lists of girls to punish in one way or another. I asked if there ever came a time when she didn't punish "No, she was always punishing scrub, scrub, and scrub, for a word out loud, for a whisper, for a look out of place." I don't think you can realize Charlie, what work it is to punish a lot of girls. First you get the work laid out and the pails and brushes seen to, then they are always out of clothes and its run here and run there till you are all worn out and all this on top of your regular work.

Evening—Well, dear I have taken heart again during the day and see a little brighter side to things tonight. Perhaps it isn't so bad after all and there are some things to be thankful for. I was the bluest yesterday of any time since I have been here and the tears would keep coming to my eyes, again and again. I think I have got into a wrong habit of letting the girls see how much some of the things they do irritate me. I have scolded I am sorry to own. Miss Pope seems to govern the girls with little trouble and it just cuts me to the quick to think I can't. I sometimes think if she had the same set of lively girls in school sewing class and dormitory it would be harder for her but perhaps not. Today has gone pretty well. I don't know of any who have been impudent to me, at least without afterward giving in, in the proper way.

Yesterday was very hard indeed and I think I will tell you some about it. It lasted from six A.M. to 10 P.M. The girls were very noisy in school time and when I stopped proceedings to give them a good talking to—in the midst of my remarks I found one of my best girls talking about examples to another. I sent her off to our punishment closet as an example. Another girl who has given me much trouble scuffed her big, bare feet all the way. This is a favorite trick of the girls at all times to show their displeasure. Patience with her had ceased to be a virtue. I sent her to my room. At noon I went up and applied a pretty good bamboo rod to her feet. She struck out at me and I applied it to her big, fat body. She subsided but would not promise to keep her feet still so I switched them some more. Then she gave in and since then has been quiet and peaceable. It was the second cane in the week. Both the girls are cowards and though much stronger than I, gave me no trouble.

I was glad when silent time came in the dormitory—but no, three of the girls must break the rule of no talking and must have the punishment then and there. So I stationed them in various places. It was about ten when I could lock up and send the sleepy girls to bed and go myself, so tired and heart sick over the day as only you can appreciate. I trust it is the worst I shall have for some time.

Now perhaps I ought to tell you some bright things or I shall have you coming to take me home. The girls in my room have got clean heads. There are no bugs in my dormitory. All my first division girls treat me well. Two who could not get along with Miss Hoppin at all are my good friends. I have the "quickest to learn" girls in the school, I think. We have just walked right along in Arithmetic and the girls are pleased with that. I can now manage my sewing class. I like the girls and am much interested in everything. Tonight I have my third $40 and the next steamer I am going to send home $103 for Mr. Williams and $6 for Aeolian. Don't you congratulate me, dearie?

I think I shall have to buy a horse while I am here. I could do without one, but it would get me out and away more and I shall never have such a chance to use one again. Miss Pope and I will probably buy together. They say we ought to get a good horse for $50 and Miss Malone out at Kamehameha has Miss Hoppin's saddle for sale. It is a nice one and cost $25. We can have it now for $16 and not pay till June. Then when we go, we can sell out again. What do you say?

By the way I have some news. Did I tell you that Miss Brewer goes home this Christmas? It is on account of illness in her family. Well at the end of this year all the rest leave with the possible exception of Miss Patch and the trustees have offered the principalship to Miss Pope. I am very glad of it for I like her very much and she has taught some years and is doing well here. It gives me quite an inside track to everything except the salary for we will be the oldest teachers. I can have the highest room if I want it to teach. I should like to have the assistant principalship offered me but I suppose that will depend on what comes at Christmas time. I seem quite young and do not look very strong so I doubt if they offer it to me. Anyway I mean to be content with whatever comes—and am glad Miss Pepoon is to have a worthy successor.

Well, this coming week I have got to get my Christmas things together. I can tell you all about them and reveal no secret because you will get them as soon as this letter. I am going to send you some photographs and I shouldn't wonder if in time you got a collection. Keep them nice, dear and sometime we will make an album of them.

December 8—I had almost given up that China steamer which was advertised to be here last week. You can imagine my joy and hopes when it was telephoned yesterday. I had 4 letters, two from you and two from Mamma. Wasn't it fine, lover, to have so much and to have almost a week to answer in? I devoured them as I always do. I wonder, dear if you couldn't find some thinner, cheaper envelopes like mine. Even four sheets with those envelopes seem to be too much. I wonder if you can know what a blessing it is to have these long letters come to me. Sometimes the present moment seems so real to me and even now I am becoming so accustomed to the scenes of my every day duty that I wonder if there is anything beside this reality and then your letters come, proofs of a beautiful past promise of a more beautiful future and words of cheer and love and sympathy from the present.

You want more particulars in regard to my health. I think I weigh about the same as when I came here. I have not wheezed once since I have been here. The mosquito sores were healed long ago. I am still some awed by those birds but they no longer affect my health. The climate makes one lazy. You simply cannot do as much here as at home and you soon learn to accept the fact. A good deal of the time the first months I have had bad feelings which I know were wholly due to changes in the climate but believe me darling, I have every reason to suppose that all will be well from now on. Don't be anxious any more dear.

No, I don't have any music to teach. Miss Patch has all that. I sometimes quite often in fact play for the girls when she is away and it is one of my treats to get a half hour to myself in the back parlor and quiet my nerves by playing. I find it hard to keep my morning prayer here. I pray with my girls at 6:20 but it is not like praying alone and I must have it to have His life in mine.

I must stop for tonight, dearie and will try to answer the other tomorrow. It has been a peaceful day for me. I have enjoyed this hour of reading your letter and writing to you. It gives me the spirit of being with you. Now I say good-night and kiss you many times very softly and daintily—Carrie.

December 11, Friday a.m.—The steamer comes in today and I hope at noon to have another letter from you. We have been having a Kona or hard wind storm. Some of our trees were blown down. A little jacket over my calico dress felt very comfortable and as for the girls, they were half frozen.

I got my paper knives the other day and they were so pretty I wanted to send them all to you. I had four made of wood. Yours in Koa and I have sent one of Koa to your father. I think you will like it. I have spent a good deal of time over the sea moss and hope you will like the result. I think one or two of them must be fruiting specimens. One or two kinds the girls like to eat and when I had a supply on hand, I would give them some to see them devour it.

> With truest love,
> Carrie

December 14, 1890, Kawaiahao Seminary

Dearest,

Here are some of the things I saw—a Chinaman yesterday on the horse-car had a five cent piece in each of his ears. I studied over it for some time and then thought  "poor heathen, he has the ear-ache and has gone to some ignorant doctor who has probably filled his ear up with something and put those in on top." While I thus thought, the conclusion came along, and the Chinaman slipped one of the pieces out of his ear and paid his fare. It was his purse.

I saw a woman over this morning at Kawaiahao Church, old and white headed dressed in a black holoku[6] with a black lace shawl over that above that a large red bandana handkerchief—then a lei of yellow flowers, and a hat tied under her chin.

We want our laundry-house renovated. It is just a plain board affair, white washed but parts of it are rotted and we want some new bath tubs put in—all of the very plainest kind and the estimate we have received is $22.00 Our little sick cottage cost $1,500 with not a bit of plaster or a chimney in it and no hard wood. I think carpenters must have good wages here don't you?

December 17—I think I am rather tired tonight but I think it will rest me to write to you. I know it would if only I could be with you and talk with you. Only two more days now till this term is over. I am not anticipating much pleasure in my vacation but think I shall be content if I get well rested. I don't know at all what I shall do and shall have to write you about it as it comes along.

Well, dear, at this point last evening my weariness overcame me. I could not write any more and I lay down and slept soundly till the girls came home from prayer meeting. I got up long enough to put them to bed and then went to sleep again myself.

We have examinations this forenoon and I have been preparing the work for that. This afternoon in addition to the sewing class I shall have a long list of girls to give extra work to. They have been talking native and that is against the rules. I shall have a lot of windows and blinds washed. Then this evening, Mrs. Dominis is coming to hear the girls sing and some people have been invited to come and meet her.

The children at the Central Union Church have a service tomorrow night and instead of receiving Christmas gifts as usual they are going to give money by classes for the little leper children on Molokai. So Miss Pepoon told our girls in chapel the other morning that she thought it would be a good idea for them to give some present to little Lizzie Nathaniel who is at the receiving station outside the city and to Ella Bridges who is on Molokai. Both these girls used to be pupils here till they became lepers and Ella's sister Mary is in my room.

Miss Pepoon thought some of them would like to give five or ten cents or more if they wanted to. Somehow it touched the girls very much and almost every one gave a quarter and one girl a dollar. Besides that, 17 girls promised to make a garment for the girls. Little Annie Wong promised twenty cents and afterward came to Miss Pepoon with some writing paper

Mary Ellen Hanau-umi-a-Kanoena Bridges. Portrait by Gonsalves & Silva.

and slate pencils and then said "and now I think that is all I can give." It made the tears come to my eyes more than once to see how eager the girls were to give and how very sober they were at the allusions to the leper children.

Well, dear it is evening at last and the close of one of the busiest days I have known here. I am thankful they do not come often. Once I got fretted and went off myself and said, "Now, Carrie, it isn't so very hard and if you will just think you are not tired you won't be and you know just what Charlie would want to have you do if he were here and knew just how it was." As soon as I got in the schoolroom this morning, I looked into the matter of "native" and found I had 22 on hand "for punish."

I had examination in Arithmetic and Geography, written. I shall save some of the papers. I feel the need of having three divisions of Arithmetic in my room but don't know how I can arrange it quite. When 12 came I looked after punish till the dinner bell rang and after dinner till sewing-class. When I came out from that Miss Patch wanted me to help her in singing class and I was with her there till supper time. The girls were very trying and she lost all patience with them. She was so tired that I sent her up to bed and sent her supper up to her.

After supper it was easy. The company came at seven—a number of the friends of the school and Mrs. Dominis in all the glory of white silk. The girls did beautifully, singing very harmoniously and Mrs. Dominis sung quite sweetly but in a frightening tone. It was quite a short affair because she had another engagement. The girls were delighted and applauded. Mrs. Dominis is regent in the king's absence so you may judge how puffed up we feel. The girls all rose when she entered and remained standing till she was seated.

I do not think, dearie that I will write any more tonight. I have loved you very much today dear and have caught myself dreaming several times of the past and the future. I wonder if you ever do that. I think so. This is what the girls say at the end of their love letters.

"My best Aloha nui to you."
Carrie

December 21, 1890

My Darling,

There shines the sea bright and blue and beautiful and there at one side rises old Diamond Head. You will wonder where I am that I can see the ocean for at Kawaiahao we are in the city and the buildings and  trees shut it out. I came out to Kamehameha Preparatory yesterday afternoon with Miss Pope. She is going to stay here most of the vacation but I go back tomorrow morning. I was glad to come at this time. We took a nap yesterday afternoon and a long sleep last night and another nap this afternoon.

This school lies next to Kamehameha proper but they are in separate enclosures and are quite distinct in management. There are four teachers, Miss Malone, Miss Turner, Miss Lyman and Ruth Hoppin and 60 little boys. Mr. Bishop, the husband of the princess who founded the other school founded this. It is on a rounded piece of high ground about a mile and a half west of the city and right in the line of one of the valleys down which sweeps a strong cold wind and frequent spattering of rain. It is not right on the sea, but all that lies below is like a beautiful picture. Last night was a wonderful night—the

"Dormitory Row" on the Kalihi campus of Kamehameha School for Boys.

moon was very full and clear and the sky was so full of light that everything was either in strong light or shadow. Most beautiful indeed! A night to think of and long for you to enjoy its beauty with me.

Monday and Tuesday I sewed for myself. I had Victoria Ahoy work with me at the wages of 50 cents a day. She is a fine sewer, expert at the machine and did all the machine work which is especially hard for me to do. We made up a pretty light blue dress I had in my trunk and fixed up a new white basque. I wish you could see me in the blue dress, Charlie. It is very becoming. I believe you would take pleasure in seeing me in it.

There were about 60 girls left in the school and Mr. Oleson invited us to bring them up to Kamehameha and have our celebration together. It was a fine idea and I think it paid for the extra work it made. On Wednesday Miss Pepoon superintended the making of 12 loaves of cake to be taken out there. Miss Davis and Miss Pope got up the Christmas tree for the 14 little children who were not big enough to take out to Kamehameha. In the morning Miss Brewer and I went down-town and did a lot of shopping for the school. It was very warm and tiresome work for the stores were crowded and it was hard to find what we wanted. We went down to the wharf and got 100 oranges for 75 cents from a ship just in from Kauai. In the afternoon I showed half a dozen girls how to make neckties and upstairs there was another company of girls with Miss Patch fixing up bottles of cologne with pretty ribbons. The little ones had a good time in the evening with their tree and sat up as late as they wished and danced about the parlor to their hearts delight.

Christmas day, I sewed our fancy things for the girls till after one o'clock and then went off to the cottage and rested for a little while. We had a good dinner of roast duck which had been given to us. Retta came in during dessert and we made the final arrangements for the evening. One little device was an Oberlin one of leaving cards with numbers on them so that all the girls might have company to tea. All the afternoon I did up presents with Miss Pepoon and we finished just in time. There was a cup of tea and 30 girls left at once with Miss Pope while Miss Pepoon and I took the rest in the next car. The other teachers went in the carriage with the presents. We were met at the cars by a large company of the boys who escorted the girls to their large dining hall. There was music by their Glee Club and by our girls.

Miss Pope gave a recitation and I told the story of Cinderella, ice-cream and cake were served we had some games and the presents were distributed. Our girls had above 40 presents for the boys and they had about the same number for us. Some presents had been sent in for the girls and we saw that everyone received a good one. Mr. Castle sent in 150 boxes of candy and $60 was given to the girls. We saved about half of that however for the new library we are trying to get for the girls. Mother Castle sent in $25 toward our library fund. I have never been with the girls anywhere when they seemed to have so fine a time.

It is a time-honored institution for the girls to make a rumpus Christmas morning and they began it Thursday at 8:30 with songs. It was wonderful the way in which I was remembered. I expected nothing of the sort. You shall have the list:—from Mother Rice, Christmas card. Mrs. Cooke, Christmas card, Miss Flaxman, Christmas card, Mrs. Gilman Christmas card. Agnes Judd, pink & blue ribbon bag. Retta Hight pretty dust bag. Mrs. Atherton, black satin bag hand-painted with yellow daisies and containing fine linen handkerchief. Miss Pope, pretty ribbon. Miss Hoppin, fancy plate, Miss Pepoon, fancy plate, Charlotte Ioba, one of the girls, a pretty white native basket. Mrs. Charles Cooke gave Miss Pepoon $10 to buy presents for the teachers and she got us each a $1.50 China cup & saucer, perfect beauties. That left $1.50 over and with that she got oysters for breakfast, just a few brought in a can on ice clear from the Atlantic. What do you think of all that, dearie? Were not the people kind to your girl?

I was invited to Mrs. John Waterhouses for Christmas night but could not go as I was needed at our own affair. I was very sorry not to go for they are English and perhaps I should have seen some new customs. All the day there was an undertone of sadness in my heart. I think I must have always been selfish on Christmas for I missed very much the loving care that has always been mine on that day.

The China steamer came in, in the night, and dear Miss Pepoon got up before breakfast to go down and get our mail for us. I think more highly of Miss Pepoon the longer I know her. While we were at breakfast she came in and there was your letter and the two books and the picture and the Reviews and Professor King's lecture and the catalogue. How rich I was and how much I thank you for it all! I have been enjoying them all down here at Waikiki. Miss Pope and I came down here to the Castle's cottage and I am having such a beautiful restful time here. Not doing a thing but sleeping and eating and bathing and loafing. I have got through the Reviews and the catalogue and two Congregationalists and all the poems you marked.

January 9, 1891—Dearest, all last week I did not write any to you, or any this week till tonight. It used to be the law here for some reason unknown to me, that steamers could not come in till twelve o'clock, but that has been changed and they come in at any time now.

I think a good deal of my discouragement last letter over the order in my room was blueness. I fancy I am through the worst and that I am really getting so I can manage them to some extent. I find if I take down the names of the first offenders on any occasion the rest soon calm down and give little or no trouble. Tonight in study hour, Emma Ai started a tumult. I had her up at once to the front, but because she answered back and was very sneaky and impudent, I had a little talk with her and made her see that I could not allow such talk. I brought her up here to my room. Poor girls, they are coming to know and fear steamer night for then I always sit up late and am quite willing to have company. If I only always could be impartial, just and certain. I think my chief failure comes when I am all tired out and my spirit and flesh rebel. But those things do go easier with practice I find. The teachers who are here, even those who had taught years in America, speak of it with horror.

When you write about the Assistant Principal you touch upon one of the sore points here. Of course it would be a wonderful place if there were one. There always was such a person but she helped the principal in place of doing some extra work like sewing class and received $400. For some unknown reason, they give Miss Davis equal salary with Miss Pepoon. It is a trial for it makes two heads, only that Miss Davis generally runs Miss Pepoon. I soon saw how things were and so got along all right. I know there will not be such an arrangement again. Miss Davis has given out all along that she was going home at the end of this year but very recently she seems inclined to stay. I fear all will not be pleasant. Miss Appleton has been written to. We were expecting a new teacher today to take Miss Brewer's place who goes next week, but she did not come and sent back the check. I think I shall give you kisses and send you fresh love from my heart.

NOTES

1. This is Lydia Liliʻu Loloku Walania Weweki Hamakeʻeha Pākī-Dominis, who later reigned as Queen Liliʻuokalani.
2. In 1843 Lord George Paulet of the Royal Navy captured Honolulu and demanded the abdication of King Kamehameha III, but Admiral Richard Thomas repudiated his action and restored the Hawaiian government.

3. This is Ke Aliʻi Bernice Pauahi Paki (1831–1884), wife of Charles Reed Bishop (1822–1915).
4. Lilla Estelle Appleton identifies this child as Louisa, sent to Kawaiahaʻo Female Seminary by the circuit court, in her transcribed diaries in the Oberlin College Archives.
5. The Hawaiian Ostrich Farm was established near Diamond Head by Dr. Georges Trousseau and his nephew in 1890.
6. The holokū is a comfortable and elegant Hawaiian dress with a loose back, a form that originated about 1820, according to the Bishop Museum. Miss Winter often misspells this word in her text.

4

The King Is Dead
January 12–April 15, 1891

The King's funeral, 'Iolani Palace, 1891. Photo by J. A. Gonsalves.

January 12, 1891[1]

Dearest:-

The term has opened well and I think I can honestly say I have a little more hold on my girls. My room is full, every seat taken and on account of the numbers and the shortness of the time, it makes rapid work necessary in order to accomplish anything.

Your last letter was so full of such good advice I suppose because you know me so well you know just what I will do in a given situation, dearest boy to think I have such a treasure as you! My heart goes out to you especially tonight. What a rapture of happiness I would be in if I could but see your loved face.

At the Athertons they have such a pretty family custom and I should like to adopt it into our home. After morning prayers, they kiss each other all around. I understand it is a custom of many of the old missionary families. It was very beautiful to see and in a nervous high-strung family like theirs I should think it would be one of the little things to keep things smooth. They are very wealthy people but about the busiest people you can imagine. We[2] occupied May Atherton's room and a very beautiful one it is too filled with so many pretty things she brought with her from Europe. Saturday evening they showed us the photographs they gathered while they were away. They all took part in telling the story of their travels and it was interesting. They had some large photographs of some of the greatest paintings. It was such a collection as only wealth could gather.

We had a call this afternoon from such an interesting lady, a Mrs. Walker who lives the second place above us.[3] She had two pretty dogs with her and we were asking her about them and she explained that she was attached to one of them because he was with her when she was wrecked. Naturally we asked about that and she told us quite a story. Her husband is a captain and three years ago they went from Hong Kong to the South Sea Islands on a fishing expedition. They anchored in the lagoon of a barren little island and soon strong winds came up. They wanted to leave but could not and were finally wrecked and lost everything. It was not a Robinson Crusoe experience either, for as she said, this island was a fertile island and many things were washed up from his ship. Their bedding and considerable clothing was cast up but not one bit of food.

There was one man on the island in a half-savage condition. Some time before, he had been wrecked there with his ships company and had murdered his captain and mate and when the others left some time after in a small boat, they left him behind. As for the island it was low and barren just dazzling white sand with a few low shrubs and not a tree. Twenty-three years before it had been surveyed and some two or three sheds and huts put up. They took possession of these although they were almost in ruin and dug a well whose water seemed good to them though their rescuers said it was very brackish. Their food was the sea-birds eggs, the birds themselves and rarely a fish. For weeks they would have only eggs and water and often days would pass without food. The murderer kept them in constant fear but he in his turn feared them on account of a gun which would not fire. Nine of their crew deserted them in a small boat and were never heard of again. They reached the Gilbert Islands but did not tell anyone of the others. Three died and all were in a most pitiable condition at the end of the 14 months they passed there. A fishing-ship saw bonfires and brought the survivors to Honolulu. She was the only woman. When they first ate just plain bread and butter it made them very ill. It is quite a story Carl and I am sitting up much too late to write it to you so I will stop now with one of the most loving of kisses.

13th—I am having quite a time with my dormitory girls just now. They cut up a mean trick last Saturday and it seemed necessary to find out just who it was. No one would own up and the method in such cases is to take all the girls into the chapel during all their play time and let them sit there with folded hands till the girl who did it is tired enough to own up. Of course it is rather hard on the teacher or teachers. Miss Pepoon and I shared this time. It is not over yet because the girl has not confessed but there are some hints that seem to indicate a certain person. That has taken much of my time that I would gladly have spent with you.

Well, dear I must tell you of the accident and narrow escape I had this afternoon. I am glad you were not there to see it or you would have been sadly frightened. Miss Brewer and I went out to make some calls and as we were going back to an afternoon tea, I dressed in my very best, black silk, light gloves, etc. We had made our last call and were on our way home on Nuuanu Ave, a plain, smooth, straight road, when suddenly Evilani who was going at a good gait, stumbled and sank right down in the traces. Of course that tipped the brake down in front and as though I had been shot from a bow, I spread out head long, over the dash-board right on to the thills. My whole weight went onto my extended hands, my mouth kissed the dust, my hat flew off to a distance. Instinctively I made an effort and rolled to one side. When I could pick myself up the carriage was some little distance. The dashboard was broken in two but I was entirely uninjured except for the dust on my dress, and a little cut in one of my gloves. One or two men saw the performance and said it was wonderful that I escaped as I did. I don't know how it was unless it was the power of one above that I did not sprain hand or foot or get some dreadful cut if nothing worse. It shook my nerves up some but now I feel quite cool and calm.

I haven't told you anything yet about my visit out to Kamehameha during vacation and as that is the only place where I meet young men at all like those I have known in Oberlin I want to tell you all about my intercourse with them according to my agreement with you and have you understand perfectly all I am doing. I enjoyed very much the meals where I meet Mr. McVoy and Mr.

Richards. Perhaps you can realize how that would be if you imagine yourself teaching in a boy's school and day after day meeting only them and your fellow young men teachers. When you did go out you met only old people you would appreciate it when you came into the society of some nice young women. So out there I have found it great fun to have them friendly and pleasant with me. They were quite complimentary and appreciative in their remarks.

The first night I was there Mr. McVoy who seemed to quite like my society went over to Retta's cottage with me. To entertain him I showed him class pictures. When we came to your picture he caught a glance between Retta and I and at once laid it aside. I soon saw what he was aiming at. He scanned every picture and compared every one with you and then asked a number of questions which I answered directly "What your name was, where you lived, where you were now, etc." When I got Retta alone I said "Now young lady explain." Then she made confession. It seems he had dropped a number of remarks which indicated to her that he was getting up an interest in me. Mr. McVoy is a very jolly nice sort of a boy and I like him first-rate and I asked

Carrie P. Winter (leaning on the right porch banister) with Kamehameha School Faculty, c1892.

him to call and he said he would. Perhaps he never will though. I hope dearie that this very slight commotion which I have raised will flatter rather than annoy you and prove to you that I am just as charming as of old and all this bundle of perfection still belongs to you.

Retta and I have started to read Macaulay together and I go out there Monday evenings to do so. It does me a world of good for it is so quiet and cool at her cottage. I see only her when I go at such times. While I was out there I spent two mornings in Mr. Thompson's school-room. He is a married man of middle age and so I could go there with propriety. He is the finest teacher they have, a graduate of the Oswego Normal School and a teacher in Brooklyn for many years. I got a great many new ideas from him which have helped me wonderfully this term. He was very kind to show me the various devices he uses to make study interesting. I learned how to give an object lesson from him.

Dearest boy, you are my all and don't because I told you about Mr. McVoy let a trace of worry creep into your loving heart. If you worry at all I shall be tempted to keep it from you when any one gives me a pretty compliment.

> With many a loving thought, kiss and caress—
> Your own girl

January 15, 1891

Dearest,

It is a beautiful January Sabbath morning. Doors and windows are open and white dresses are the order of the day. It is hard to realize that it was way last August when I saw you last. There has been no change in the  season to make me notice the passage of the year and it is only by the calendar and pay-day that I realize when a month has gone.

Going to church this morning, we had another experience with our new horse. You know none of us like him because he is so lazy and tricky. We always take Evilani if possible and although he is a gift and cost $175.00, Miss Pepoon has complained of him to the trustees. Nothing has been done as yet and we are gradually getting out of patience. This morning Miss Pope and I started off to church, I on the front seat driving. We always have to touch him up with the whip when we start but today as soon as I began to whip him, he began to back, and the harder I whipped, the farther he backed. Miss Pepoon came out and got in and laid on the whip well. That got him out of the gate but when she tried to start him up, there he backed again and with such a vicious turning of the head that I refused to undertake to drive him and the others thought it was not best either. I am willing to encounter reasonable danger but I refuse to trust my life to that great, strong, lazy and sometimes ugly beast. My being thrown from the carriage the other day was no fault of Evilani except that he is old and weak-kneed but as for this Prince, I highly disapprove of him. Don't you, Carl? Do you want me to be backed all around Honolulu by a balky horse?

Oh, I haven't told you that we are all invited to a ball the night the king returns from San Francisco. It is a royal invitation and full dress is required. I don't know whether I am going for a little while, or not. There is considerable question about the propriety of our going and the impropriety of none of us going. I don't know what will be done.

Yesterday I was thoroughly disgusted with my girls and talked with them very pointedly and plainly and refused to give them some interesting work I had prepared for them because they didn't deserve it. Somehow it struck home and there was an epidemic of studying for today. I actually saw girls around with books in their hands and that is wonderful outside of their evening study hour. Perhaps you would like to know what we did and I will try to tell you about the method and what way I am tending. I don't mean to have any thing fixed but to take up new ways to impress old truths as fast as I learn them. We recited very carefully the 1st & 9th Psalm, by verses and then all together. Then we read a chapter in Samuel, trying to understand the story as we go. While the second Division is busy with some examples in multiplication of fractions (they were in long Division when I took them), I give my undivided attention to my first class.

It is Geography to which they have a natural antipathy. I can teach them now that I have a good large map of the U.S. on the wall. I send a girl to find Arkansas—to show if it has mountains—to trace its rivers—to put her finger on the cities I name, and tomorrow without the map, she must tell me these things.

Then yesterday I told the class something about Robert Burns and now they go to the board with ten sentences founded on what I told them. These are now put on the board and I take time to correct them carefully. Here is one "Robert Burns is a very strong passion man" "Robert Burns begin to be a drinker man."

Then this class goes to work on Arithmetic, and I turn to my stupid Division to hear what they have for me in geography and English. I try to interest them in the former today by a kind of game. I tell them a story of my journey in New York and leave gaps for them to fill with the proper city, lake or mountain. Their sentences are about a little boy "name Tommy who went to fishing" as they insist on saying. Then I look through the work they have done on their slates and send them to the board to do some more like them. They are in the first part of fractions. We have no recess but I let them have a 5-minute whispering recess.

The next half hour I take for an object lesson. I have drawn a magnified mosquito on the board with the instruments in its proboscis still more magnified. I explain it to them and have them make sentences on what I tell them. These are put on the board and tomorrow will be recited.

I try to vary my work with every new device I can. It seems to be necessary to make study pictorial to them. I don't think myself that it is the way to make the best students—they are the ones who have to buckle down to work for themselves and rely upon themselves chiefly but it is the method adopted here and it is surely very fine for me for it calls out all my power of mind.

Saturday January 24—Well, darling, I was tempted to sit down last night and write you a long string but I was so stirred up in my own mind that I knew it would do no good to write it out then but would only make me feel worse. It is all over the matter of discipline about which you asked. I have got along well with my class this term and one reason for it is that I have not put up with misdeeds but have tried to punish every time and effectively. Day before yesterday three of my girls showed ugliness and impudence in the school room and I sent them all out—one to a little hallway, one to a closet and one to my room.

The first two I kept by themselves all day long except when they had singing class and at night before they went to bed, talked with each a long time and they promised me to be good. The third was Emma Ai, a girl I like very much but one who has got into the way of being sulky and impudent to me. I have punished her in various ways but she was saucy again that day, so I decided it was best to give her a whipping. She is stronger than I, so I asked Miss Pope to come to my room with me after dinner. I used a whip that both Miss Pope and Miss Hopper have used for the same purpose. Emma took off her shoes and stockings—held up her dress and I gave it to her good about her bare legs. She did not show fright at all but took it well, wept bitterly and promised me to be a good girl.

The very next day Eunice Puni was saucy. I sent her to the closet and she started off shuffling her feet and I told her to lift them. She said "keep still" and banged the door so I had her go to my room after dinner. Miss Pope was with me again but Eunice is a wiry, spunky piece, and began to show lots of fight so that Miss Pope thought best to speak to another teacher. She called in Miss Davis. Now Eunice is a great favorite of hers and she came in with the air of one who was to settle a difficulty between two girls and asked Eunice first what the matter was. I spoke up decidedly as to what the matter was and said I preferred to give the whipping myself and straight away began it. I gave a very severe one. Eunice was really hurt and was glad to give in.

Of course it used me up, and it didn't make me feel any better to have Miss Davis tell me as soon as I got outside the door that I ought not to have used that whip but to have used a strap. Miss Pope was thoroughly disgusted and told me she thought the remarks entirely uncalled for. Then after supper Miss Pepoon took me aside and told me she did not want to have me whip without having her present. She was very kind in what she said but it was not the right time to say it and it made me feel very badly. Her request was all right too, but in so important a matter, she should have told me what she expected long before that. But the real point after all was that Miss Davis had told her to speak to me.

Well it's all over now and I am not going to feel badly any more and I don't mean to let it make any difference either about my punishing. Miss Pepoon would rather like to have me turn all such cases over to her but I shall not do that as long as she does not require it. I am quite convinced that the only way for me to stop impudence to myself is for me personally to attend to the matter. I do not think you can realize what a strain of impudence they have in them. You know colored students have a kind of inborn humility with all their blustering ways, but these Hawaiians are entirely lacking in that and if you take those who have had considerable knowledge of wickedness, and who have the temptation strong upon them to be bad girls the moment they get free from school, it does not seem strange that it is only the fear of punishment that keeps them from out-breaking insult.

Well, dearest, are we ready for a Sunday morning talk? I have a number of things to tell you. We are not having just the most peaceful time here now. This last week we ran across the fact that the girls were stealing sugar. Eight or nine girls acknowledged to crawling into the pantry window after dark and carrying off pockets full of sugar and I should say 3/4 of the girls had feasted on the stolen sweet knowing how it was obtained. Some of our oldest and best girls sent the younger ones in for them. They are now going without sugar in their morning tea and with their bread Wednesday night and rice Saturday night. Miss Davis wanted it to last the rest of the year, but came down to a month but Miss Pepoon & Miss Pope think a week is quite enough. The girls are all stirred up and we are expecting outbreaks now. The next thing was Miss Pope discovering some of the girls roasting eggs at the rubbish fire in the back yard. Four or five were in that and in one girl's pocket were found three eggs. They lied like every thing over the matter but there is no telling how long they have been thieving. Eggs are 60 cts. a dozen here so it is no slight matter.

I went to Cousin's Society last night which is a kind of a missionary library society.[4] This society supports 4 or 5 of our girls. It was held at Judge Judds. It always comes on the moon-light Sunday of the month. Last night was beautiful and Miss Pope and I enjoyed our ride. During the evening while Dr. Lyons was reading an interesting paper on Russia, the ladies near us made a commotion. They had seen a big centipede on the rug. The reading was stopped and Judge Judd gathered up the rug on which it had been seen and carried it out. Speaking of centipedes, I read in the paper the other day of a man who went out to look at his hens and when he got up felt something inside his trousers leg. He grabbed it and when he got it out found it to be a centipede 10 inches long. Don't worry, dear, I will bring one home to you surely, a nice big one too. Won't that be nice?

In the evening I had a treat, for Miss Hoppin borrowed a horse and I rode on hers. We went nearly to Waikiki. It was a beautiful moonlight evening and the air was delightfully cool. We walked most of the way out once in a while galloped. I could not help but think how perfectly delightful it would be if you were only there to ride with me. You know what a lovely time we always have when we go out together and just to think of you and I riding horse-back together around this lovely country! How you would enjoy it! Mr. and Mrs. Thompson out at Kamehameha ride a great deal together. I think when I get home we shall have to ride horseback. I don't see why we shouldn't there as well as here. I am going to buy half a saddle next month. Then I can ride the saw-horse if nothing else.

It was a pleasure to me last night to sit where I could watch Mr. Oleson. I have told you how much he makes me think of you. I think he must be Danish. He is just about your build and size and has features like yours. He is quiet and pleasant looking but he has just that clear-cut, alert, interested capable way about him that you have. You can see he is full of force and yet he is quiet in his manner—nothing put on or boastful about him. It gives me pleasure to see how people respect him and I say to myself "An all-round, honest man, and I know of another in whose heart I reign—happy me!" You understand, dear, that Mr. Oleson himself is middle-aged, that the present Mrs. Oleson is his second wife and that he has five children so my admiration for him is of the most harmless type and really means "Reflections on my dearest Charlie."

January 29—The *Charleston* came in this morning bearing the dead body of the King. It seems strange to think that you must have known of his death a week ago while the first intimation we heard of it was the lowered flags of the *Charleston* as it came into port.

January 30—Now I must write you all about it while it is "hot cakes." It makes one of the most unique of my experiences. We have just come back from the palace where the body of the king is lying in state and will be perhaps for 3 or 4 weeks. The Kamehameha schools are having their vacation now so we are the only large native school on hand at this time. At half past eleven we formed our line, over a 100 girls, two by two, bare-headed with glistening black hair tied with black ribbons white dresses and no color sashes at all.

The teachers were also in white. Perfectly silently and with straight even line we marched to the palace gate. There Mr. Atherton met us and escorted us the rest of the way. The arch that had been erected and painted with gay colors was draped with black, on either side the long straight avenue were

Kawaiaha'o Female Seminary girls in marching line. Photo by Lilla Estelle Appleton.

burning torches. As we entered, the band at the left of the palace steps struck up a funeral march, the guard on the right rested on their arms. As we entered the palace hall, the gruesome sound of the hired wailers met our ears. It seems to be a kind of plaintive word that they repeat over and over again.

We passed into the throne room and such a strange sight met our eyes. The strange feeling it gave me is on me still. In the center on a raised place was the cloth-covered coffin and above this, the officers of the household formed a hollow square, each one wearing the royal yellow cape and bearing a Kahili, a kind of a long pole with feathers fastened all the way up like a huge feather-duster. These are kept in motion all the time up, down, this side, that side, day and night. At the head of the coffin, were seated the royal family, except the Queen who stood at the coffin's head and wailed.

The Wailers who passed through the room would sometime address harangues to her and she would reply by a wave of the handkerchief. We passed around the room and out. In the halls we had to pass through a larger company of wailers who set up a doleful din. I understand that this has to be kept up day and night also, but they get good pay for it.

January 31—About noon we received a note from the palace asking to have the girls come down again and sing—so at about three, we formed the same procession. It was not the hours for the public this time, but there were the same wailers and Kahili bearers. The Queen was sitting down this time however and I noticed on the steps of the throne, a silver teapot as though they had been having refreshments. The girls sang very sweetly and beautifully "Nearer my God to thee," "Abide with me," "Rock of Ages," and "Lead kindly Light." The first was in native. I had time to notice more things than when we passed through so quickly in the morning. The crown on the coffin, the beautiful floral pieces, the huge Kahili in the iron frames beside those the men carried. They are working on the decorations all the time. Three of the ladies in attendance whispered a few words to Koni our largest girl, a very fine stately girl and in some way related to royalty, and as we filed out and as she passed the royal chair, she very gracefully dropped on her knees and kissed the royal hand of Mrs. Dominis for you must know that she is the Queen now. I have not told you all the events of the day of the arrival, how the news spread like wild-fire. I think it must have been in the air for suddenly it went around my school-room "the king is dead." Of course they cried and we had them all in the chapel and read the accounts in the San Francisco papers to them not emphasizing the fact that he died of dissipation.

In the afternoon the trustees came with Dr. Beckwith and we had short exercises. I was on duty that day so could not go downtown to see the procession when the officers and marines of the *Charleston* delivered the body at the palace. They say it was a wonderful sight for thousands of the natives followed. It was a showery day and just as they reached the palace a rainbow formed right over it. Our girls made quite an effect in their visit to the palace and we have received many compliments on their appearance.

When we had our meeting at the school, Mr. Atherton was here as he had just come from a meeting of the Privy Council of which he is a member and he told us of the transactions there. Mrs. Dominis had signed the constitution and Judge Judd had administered the oath of office and at 5 o'clock she was proclaimed Queen by royal criers on all the street corners. She is to be known as Queen Liliuokalani—say it fast and leave out or slight the "u."

I have told you some about the school work and the governing. Eunice Puni, the girl I whipped said to me last night, "Miss Winter, I haven't been punished once this week and have known my lessons every time, haven't I?" And it is true. She has been very good indeed. I really think I am gaining more of a hold on my girls. Two of my best girls last night in Bible class had to be reproved but they came to me afterward weeping to beg my pardon and I had a good talk with them.

I think I am happiest here when I am deeply engaged in my school work. It takes strong hold of my heart and brain and there is plenty to keep me interested. When I go out in society I am not so happy.

Well, we have just had our laundry fixed up and a new floor put in and 10 new tubs—some old boards in the walls replaced by new ones and a new faucet was put in every one of the 40 tubs and then an extension was built with 10 little bath rooms, just of boards white washed and sliding windows like those in cellars or hen-houses—10 good bath tubs but not finished off in painted wood like ours—not a nice door or window in the whole thing and its cost is $1600!!!

February 7—Our school has just had an invitation to march in the king's funeral procession. I do not know whether we will or not for it is a long walk. It will be as the trustees say.

With love,
Carrie

January 16, 1891, Honolulu

Dear Charlie,

I am going to send a letter by Miss Brewer and have it mailed to you in San Francisco. You may get a later letter than this before this reaches you but I want to surprise you with a letter with the American stamp on it.  I am very sorry to have Miss Brewer go. She is a good Christian girl and has done good work here filling in all sorts of gaps and doing her best at all times. We cannot get anyone better.

It is almost the end of the second week now. Lucy Aukai our best girl has been sick with pleurisy. She is the first girl who has been sent into the sick cottage. We think she is better now but these natives have very little vitality and we are being very careful of her. I have not done much myself in the taking care of her, only giving her an alcohol bath last evening. Because she was my helper in the school-room, her absence has given me more work. There seems to be a great deal of work but I think I am better able to cope with it this term than last. My health is good, I have gained in flesh and I have some experience.

Saturday Morning—It is after ten and the morning's work is all done up. I wish you could see how neat and clean my dormitory is. There is an attic above with an air hole down into the dormitory for circulation. Well every bit of this has been swept and scrubbed—attic stairs, and all. Yesterday I had the windows and blinds washed. Each bed had its clean sheet and pillow-case and under each pillow is a clean nightgown and towel. The nets have all been lowered, examined and dusted. All the dirty clothes have been taken from the lavatory to the bags upstairs. The zinc sink shines from its polishing with wood-ashes. Up stairs I have looked into all the 34 trunks and found them in order and have consigned a number of old hats and shoes. The girls who were not dressed at the proper time this morning have received extra work. The girl who was cross and saucy to me yesterday morning is down in the pasture to pick up sticks till she can be good natured. Everything is very satisfactory.

Miss Pope is on duty over Sunday and I went downtown with her to market. She does not like to drive and I do. I sometimes think that if it seems hard to get a matron for next year, I will offer to take the place. I think I have had as much practical experience as any who have had the position the last three years and there are many things attractive about the work.

I was thinking this morning of how delightful I am finding this climate. The first month and a half I was here seem dreadful now that I look back upon it. I had a fever all that time but since then, I have had very little discomfort on account of the heat or cold. One never suffers from either and is rarely uncomfortable. I wish you could have such weather instead of that sour Oberlin air. You needn't be surprised if I begin to go into ecstasy over the climate here. On Monday all the work will be changed and I presume there will be some annoyance till the girls get used to the new work.

I must close but I hope that this letter from me may come at just the right time.

Your Carrie

February 8, 1891, Kawaiahao

Dearest,

You must hear now about my visit to the Pali yesterday. Miss Carrie Castle has been very kind to the Salvation Army man who has been working here for a few weeks past. He has been called home now by two deaths in  his family and for a closing kindness, she planned this day at the Pali. He and I rode in the break and she on horse-back. I didn't have to do much talking for Miss Castle talked most of the time with my companion, indeed, between you and me, I was inclined to think her a little too sweet on him considering their relative social position. He seemed to be an unlettered but common-sensible sort of a man. I thought with a smile a number of times that I would have liked to had you there to judge of the performance. I felt quite like a third person.

We went up the valley, the mountains seeming to verge toward a center. It was just a beautiful slope all the way. At first there were pretty houses with many flowers—then came a big mill farm—then the water works where the mountain streams are collected for the cities' use. It grew wilder and wilder, the air became cooler till I needed a shawl about me. At last at the foot of a steep hill we tied our horses. Before us the mountains parted with thin knife-like edges. We walked up this last hill and suddenly the most beautiful sight burst upon us—Pali means precipice and on this side the mountains are sheer down to the plain below 3,500 ft. Way below is the green plain with the most vivid red roads, then the blue, blue ocean and the long white line of the reef.

It is 4 miles from where you stand to the coast and 4 miles back to the Honolulu harbor. It makes the island seem small. It is some 40 miles long, up against the mountains we could see white birds fluttering. These are the ones that they get the red feathers from. We walked up and down and feasted on the beauty of the scene and then rode back a couple of miles to a cottage that belonged to Mr. Atherton. Here we had our lunches, picked wild guavas, enjoyed the view of the little mountain water-fall at the back of the house, and at about three started down home.

We got home about 4 and I found a note from Retta saying that the painters were in possession of her cottage and she would spend Sunday with me instead of I with her as we first planned. In the evening, she and I took a little walk and stopped at the Atherton's. Mr. Atherton offered to take us down to the palace to hear the singing they have there every night. Only certain people can go there now but he is one of the privileged ones. All the torches and electric lights were ablaze and the grounds were well filled with natives come to hear. We went up on the piazza and sat in front of the throne room windows where many foreigners were seated. Inside we could see the fresh masses of flowers and the brilliant lights and see the women of the court in their new mourning garments, long-trained, black holokus with white silk collars. There was a chorus of men inside and a chorus of women outside and first one company would sing a song and then the other. It was all in native except one song whose chorus I caught:

> *His voice is gone*
> *The vision fled*
> *Our royal father*
> *King no more*

The song was a recitive of his life and death and sung to the native tune, was very solemn and effective.

I wish you could see how very well I am looking, Carl. I think I must weigh as much if not more than I ever did in my life before. My cheeks are round and full and I have good color in them most all the time. I think my fresh bright appearance would be pleasing to you in place of the pale and rather worn face you have many times seen. My hair bothers me by coming out very freely. I think I shall be bald if it keeps on, could you stand that? I am sure it would be a serious strain on your affection if anything would.

I wanted to tell you too, that the school-room work seems to be getting along better. Of course there are ups and downs but I know the girls so much better now and can so easily locate disturbances that I seem to anticipate their schemes and sometimes head them off. This morning I tried to lay in an extra stock of good nature for I have generally found Monday such a trying day. I am trying to arrange their work on that day with reference to the fact that what studying they may do, will probably not amount to anything.

We are to have a public concert in March and that means considerable work extra. We had decided not to have a concert but just a musical in the chapel but the trustees seemed to wish to have it so we reconsidered. We can earn some $400 in that way. When we get through with that we will have to use all our energies for the closing exercises.

How much I miss you, dearie! It is a great change to be away from your constant loving interest, among strangers, those who have not a single special thought for me. Oh dearest, you have my life, the life that is the true part of me. Don't you remember how we always enjoyed all walking and talking and reading together all music and lectures? No artificiality but pure and simple enjoyment. God grant that such happiness may come to us again and even in fuller measure than ever before.

Love, Carrie.

February 14, 1891, Kawaiahao Seminary

Hearts Dearest-

I have just been down to ask "Central" if that steamer is in and "No" comes the cruel answer. It is in vain that I say to myself "there is no more reason for its obeying the new time-table than the two who have gone before."  It must be more than a month since I have heard from you. Dear heart, I think every day makes me hang higher hopes on you than ever before.

It is Saturday and tomorrow comes the king's funeral. It does away with the church services of the forenoon in the Central Union. I am not going in the procession for I am afraid I could not stand it, it is a long walk and we have to stand and wait in one place more than an hour. Miss Pepoon and Miss Pope will be the ones to go.

Miss Pope received yesterday the official notice of her promotion to princi-palship. She showed it to me the first thing. It binds her to stay for two years more, and that is the rub with her. She would like it if she could go home a year from the coming summer with the expectation of returning then for another two years. I hope she can make such an arrangement with them.

Miss Pepoon and I took the large girls down last night to the palace to hear the singing. We stood in front of the piazza where the singers were for half an hour or more. One of the native songs was to the tune of "White wings; they never go weary." The message sad flew round the deck, "King Kalakaua is no more." The song was about the *Charleston* in San Francisco bay waiting to take the last of Hawaii's sons to his island home etc. They tell us the queen dowager sleeps under the king's casket every night![5] Think of it!

(Sunday) Well, dear, a new experience this morning! The rising bell did not ring till half past seven. I gave the girls a good talking to last night—that they must be quiet this morning and sleep all they possibly could as they had a hard day before them. I have been awake for two hours, but the girls have been very good and I have not had to go in but twice to quiet them. They won't have their breakfast till toward nine. We want it as late as possible as there is no knowing when they can have their next meal. They will have poi and fish this morning instead of the bread and crackers and tea they usually have for breakfast.

I went down yesterday and saw the casket in which the king is to be buried. It is an ancient custom that the kings and chiefs must be buried in coffins of kou and koa wood. This coffin is worth $1700 not such a very beautiful affair after all only that the wood is beautifully polished and on top there is a little silver crown, a gold and silver shield and some Masonic emblems which last were sent from San Francisco. We understand that there has been considerable strife over the coffin at the palace. The new queen wished the king buried in the casket in which he was brought from the boat. The U.S. government bore the expense of that and it was the finest the city of S.F. could furnish. Queen Liliuokalani wanted a casing of kou and koa over this in order to be polite to the U.S. but the queen dowager and most of her native followers wished otherwise and she carried the day.

There are omens that one of the chief men, a Mr. Cummings is to die soon and he has asked for the King's cast-off coffin for his own burial. The omens too indicate that the present reign is to be of short duration. Mr. Atherton told me that the Privy Council had voted $15,000 for the funeral but common report has it that it is nearer $80,000 that has been spent. The last legislature voted to devote the revenue of the crown lands to pay the king's debts but his death puts an end to that for that money goes to the present queen and cannot be used for King Kalakaua's debts—that amounting to a million must be paid from the public treasury. Immediately after the action of the legislature, the king contracted still more debts. Imagine the people of America called upon to pay the private debt of one of its presidents even if you can imagine them keeping such an evil man as this king was in power! The benefits of democracy are sometimes apparent.

We watched an hour and a half while the line formed, the men with burning rushes, the king's charger the bearer of the crown and other royal emblems, the beautiful floral pieces—the officers of the *Charleston,* the surpliced choir boys, the catafalque, the numerous large Kahilis, the Queen Dowager's carriage with its blue outriders all draped in crape and most magnificent of all, the queen's carriage beautiful white horses, red livered attendants in front and behind and walking at the horses heads—besides these outriders in the same livery and bright red Kahilis. Over the king's coffin was thrown the king's yellow mantle which shone beautifully in the sunlight. The attendants near the catafalque wore the royal yellow capes. It rained in the night and the roads were muddy but in front of the palace they had scattered hay.

(Wednesday) dearest—things are no better but rather a little worse. The *Zealandia* came in last night. I was up at Miss Hight's and was wild with joy at the prospect of news but it brought me only a paper. It reports that the "*Monowai*" left S.F. three days before it left with a heavy mail. We are all filled with anxiety about it. The paper this morning published the list of its passengers and Rose Hight was one! The thought of the possible loss of the mail is bad enough with its wait of a long time for more but the loss of passengers is worst. We hope for the best however. This goes by the "*Charleston.*"

Dear boy I love you even if I can't hear from you and I try to be good and patient.

Carrie.

Kawaiahao February 22, 1891[6]

Dearest,

Such joy as I had last night, a China steamer came in the evening bringing all the mail of the "Monowai." The "Monowai" got caught in a storm, broke her shaft, went back to S.F., quartered her passengers in the Palace  Hotel and sent on her immense mail by this steamer. Two whole weeks since she left "Frisco." Imagine the joy that arose in this whole city. You heard it on the streets wherever you passed "The Monowai" is safe! And then the mail. It was worth waiting for. Crowds around the P.O.! Miss Hoppin and I were down there and the first two that came out of the box were for me. We walked around half an hour and then got a large number. It was eight when we got home, I had 4 and it took me an hour to read them. Meanwhile Miss Pepoon and Miss Davis went down again and there were 4 more for me and it was after ten when I read the last word. I could not sleep for all the news. Just think that your letters began way back Jan 18 and here it was Feb. 21.

This morning Miss Hoppin and I went down before breakfast and brought up our arms full of papers. The 91 Psalm was read here this morning. Retta Hight sat beside me and we looked over my Bible together. The tears came to my eyes as I thought of all His loving kindness to us and last but not least that all these letters had come safe at last.

I am glad you heard Mr. Pond. He saw a great deal while he was here and was taken everywhere. He was here at the seminary a number of times. We are no small institution—but really have quite an important part in the life of the city.

You speak of the Waterhouse girls and touch a tiny sore spot. I have nothing but gratitude to them for their kindness to me and at first they were more than kind, they were friendly. This is the fact of the case as I see it here—we teachers are useful members of society here and as such we are respected, as teachers everything is done for us but as young ladies we are superfluous. The town is full of them—there are only a very few nice young men. The young ladies who hold the reins don't need any more young ladies, haven't room for them, are not going to have them on any account and so simply don't include them in any social event. It smarts a little, dearie. I think I can truly say that the few young men I have met have been very polite and friendly to me and seemed perfectly willing to know me. Mr. McVoy and Mr. Richards really try to make it pleasant for me when I go out to see Retta. They think a great deal of Miss Hight also but Miss Hight and I are not invited where they are. While the Waterhouse girls are pleasant whenever we meet, still I think they have "caught on" and have quietly dropped me. I don't mean to let it make me cynical the least bit but it is a fact. The social life is very queer—people are kind and are not kind—the uncles and aunts and fathers and mothers take us to their homes and their daughters snub us.

Miss Pepoon asked me to thank you for communicating with Miss Appleton.

She had a letter from her and she comes on the next steamer. You can't speak of annexation here—the natives have a strong love for their nation and the English are strong here with a strong faction pulling that way. This is the end of your letters and I will stop now. I have written all the afternoon on the letter, from this forenoon and now it is after supper. It has been a happy day to me, reading your letters and answering as I read. Goodnight, love.

Tuesday Feb. 24. Good-morning to you dearest. I haven't told you anything here yet and I must do so now before school time. A week ago today the natives gave a "hookupu" to Admiral Brown of the "*Charleston.*"[7] I went down to Brewers Wharf and watched proceedings for a while. There were crowds of natives and the band playing American tunes and Admiral Brown was just covered with leis. The people were coming to him and kissing his hands and thanking him for all he had done for the king. Everyone brought a present of some kind. I saw the fifth boat-load that was taken out—and such presents! I saw one old man bringing up a fine cabbage—an old woman 5 cts. worth of bananas. Another with a live pidgeon its neck encircled with a yellow lei. But some of the presents were more pretentious—dozens of turkeys, hens, duck, quarters of beef, beautiful calabashes and fans besides many things in bundles which we could not see. Eggs seemed a favorite gift and I saw many pretty native baskets with these eggs in them—one tiny one with just three eggs in it. The Admiral seemed to be having a royal good time and kissed many of the women and children. It was a warm afternoon and an old native woman stood behind him and fanned him all the time. I was glad I saw it for it was extremely "native."

We have made a fine discovery—our steed Prince who has given us so much trouble in driving is a pretty good saddle horse. The other night Miss Pope and I wanted to ride and I said I would try Prince and he went splendidly. He is a very large horse and I felt safe on him. We can hardly get him into a trot in the carriage but he quite took the lead that night and galloped for long stretches. Saturday Miss Hoppin had a riding party and Miss Pope was going on Prince but at the last minute was prevented and I took her place. We went up Manoa valley, 6 girls, the Miss Hoppins and I. We went about six miles in all. There were many guavas along the way which the girls picked for us. We went as far as we could and then dismounted and ate our lunch the girls made fern leis for us! The ride home was fine. I wish you could have seen me flying down King Street. Ruth Hoppin and I had a race and Prince would not be beaten. Ruth rides astride but I do not care to ride that way.

The time-tables are all so queer that I do not know when the next letter will go. Anyway it will not be more than two weeks.

Please remember, dear Charlie, how my heart goes out to you all the time and how every day brings thoughts of you to me. I must stop writing but that does not at all mean that I stop thinking. God bless and keep you in all your ways.

Carrie

March 1, 1891, Kawaiahao Seminary

My lover,

Just see, March already. It doesn't seem as if three years were going to be so long after all, does it? I have just changed all the flowers that I have in press.[8] Now you begin to read with increased interest, my dearie?  And where did I get my flowers and what are they? Well, yesterday afternoon Miss Hoppin was going to take some of her girls out for a pleasure excursion and asked Miss Pope and I to go too. I didn't want to very much but was very glad I did. We took the cars as far as we could up Nuuanu Ave and then made our way to a narrow ravine where a little brook comes tumbling down the rocks from the mountain. There is a good path along its side and more wild flowers than I have seen any where else. I had my little basket along and brought it home full. The flowers are very puzzling and I do not know what is properly indigenous and a number of the things I found are not new to us at all but are just our hot-house plants. Up in that wild mountain place I found growing wild Lantana, Indian Shot which is a plant that wealthy people at home have in their front yards and hot-houses, morning-glories, inch-plant and pink oxalis. One whole slope was covered with the moon flower vine which has lately become fashionable at home. I got home in time to put them in press and I have changed out the driers twice and am in hopes of making a success of them for my dearie.

Do you know, Carl, I am tempted to take time between now and the next mail and write up King Kalakaua's funeral and send it to the *Courant*.

I have had one more horseback ride which was quite satisfactory. I have invested in a good straight riding whip. One can't get along on Prince without that. I don't think I told you either about my new table-spread. I hope sometime it will adorn a table in our house. I have two little linen covers also, one

KING KALAKAUA'S DEATH.

How the News Was Received at Honolulu.

In a private letter to her family in this city a missionary teacher at Honolulu gives the following concerning the late King of the Sandwich Islands. Under date of January 25 she wrote:—

"We are expecting the King home any time now and there is to be a grand ball when he comes, to which we are invited, but which I do not expect to attend."

January 30 she wrote: "The Charleston was seen off Diamond Head this morning, and in a little while word flew all over the city that it carried the dead body of King Kalakaua. It seemed to be in the air, for suddenly a whisper went around my schoolroom, where we were busy at work, 'THE KING IS DEAD!' They had caught it from some one in the yard. Soon all the school was gathered in the chapel and the account in the California papers of his death read to them. The girls wept considerably. Of course, we did not emphasize the fact that dissipation killed him, although every one knew that. We are the only large school in session now and we have to be very careful, as the eyes of a jealous people are on all the institutions managed by foreigners. In the afternoon we had a service in the chapel. The trustees were present and Dr. Beckwith made remarks. Mr. Atherton was there and told the girls of the action of the privy council, from which he had just come. Mrs. Dominis, the king's sister, had signed the constitution and Judge Judd had administered the oath of office. At 4 o'clock royal criers proclaimed her queen on the street corners. She is to be known as Queen Lilinokulani. Pronounce it quick and leave out the u. All the gay preparations for the ball had to be stopped and the red, white and blue arch was draped in black. You knew of his death long before it was known here, and it was known in England also. Only the day before I had seen Mrs. Dominis and the Queen at an afternoon tea. The next day from 10 till 2 the King's body lay in state in the palace, and it is to lie for some three weeks. At half past eleven we formed our line, over one hundred girls in white dresses, black belts, shining black hair, tied with black ribbon. They wore no hats, and we made a slow and solemn procession, not a whisper, not a head turned to right or left. At the palace gate, Mr. Atherton met us. As we turned up the long avenue between the line of lighted torches, the band at the left of the palace began to play a slow march while the guard on the right rested on their arms. We made a very impressive sight we have been told many times since. When we reached the steps, the doleful sound of the lions wailing broke upon our ears. The palace hall was filled with natives crouched upon the floor and raising their gruesome, unearthly cry. We passed into the throne-room. In its center on a raised bier covered with velvet rested the coffin, while around it, forming a hollow square, were the officers of the household, each wearing a yellow feather cape, each bearing a *kaluli*, a long pole with feathers fastened half its length—a kind of large feather duster. These were kept in constant motion, up, down, right, left. There were many other *kalulis* in iron standards about the square, and around the edges of the room were the wailers also. The royal family sat at the head of the coffin, except the King's wife, who stood at the coffin's head, wailing and weeping. They all did their best for our large school, and our girls wept appropriately. One native woman broke out into a loud harangue to the Queen, who raised her head and waved her handkerchief. It was a weird performance. This kaluli waving and the wailing has to be kept up day and night. After dinner, we received a request to have the girls come down and sing, and at three o'clock we went. It was not public hours this time, but there was the same waving and wailing. The Queen, however, was resting in a chair, and near at hand on the steps of the throne I noticed a silver teapot. Our girls sang very sweetly in their native tongue, "Nearer My God to Thee," "Abide With Me," "Rock of Ages" and "Lead Kindly Light." We were tired when it was over, if the royal family were not."

Feb. 3.—"We have received an invitation as a school to walk in the King's funeral procession."

"King Kalakaua's Death" by Carrie P. Winter (CPW), *Hartford Courant*, January 25, 1891.

the girls have hem-stitched for me and the other is underway. All these little accumulations are with direct reference to the future in my mind. I have one more treasure which you will appreciate, love.

Last week Eddie Imum, one of the big boys of the Kamehameha School whose home is on Hawaii, brought Katy Clarke a pail full of volcanoe specimens and she, Charlie, out of the goodness of her heart, brought them to me and bestowed them all upon me. I am not very well versed in such things but they are very interesting to look at and I imagine he has done much better in collecting than I could, for he is a boy, and a native, and his home is on the volcanoe island.

I have two more pieces of lace added to my collection. Charlie will you kindly drop in some day at a stove store and inquire the price of a good kitchen stove? I think its well to begin with the kitchen, don't you? I don't want an immense one but I want one with a boiler, and six holes, only one oven, I think. I have something towards it now and in a week will have $30 or $35 more. Now I have in the bank $8.18 and the 18 cents I did not earn, but it is interest that has come to me.

Lilla Estelle Appleton, 1897. Portrait by M. S. Lovell, Oswego, New York.

We expect Miss Appleton on Tuesday—the plan now is to have her take Miss Pope's room while she goes into training with Miss Pepoon for her next year's work.

Carrie

March 12, 1891, Kawaiahao Seminary

Dear Charlie,

This is Thursday morning and the *Mariposa* is already in and so I have only a little while before school for writing and the worst of it is a steamer is due from the coast and may be in any hour but this must go. I had intended to write to you yesterday but we were all invited to the Bowen's to dinner and

I had to come home from that to take the girls to prayer-meeting. Will you hear about the panic? Yes, I see you will.

It was last evening, Miss Pepoon was home in study hour, and Miss Hoppin was off in the other end of the house taking a bath. Miss Pope and I walked home from the Bowens for we were afraid we would be late for prayer-meeting if we waited for the others. But when we came in the gate we found Miss Davis, Appleton and Patch had just driven in. We noticed a man there in the yard evidently listening to the closing exercises of the girls. As we stood looking at him, he stepped a little nearer into the light that came through the open doors. The girls saw him and instantly there was the most unearthly weird scream of absolute terror from the 100 girls and they began to rush from the chapel into other parts of the house.

It was very lucky we came home just as we did. We all rushed in at once and met the girls as they were tearing out of chapel. I put myself in the way of one of the biggest girls who was perfectly wild with terror and struck at me in her efforts to get away. I caught a glimpse of my pupil teacher rushing down the back plaza with her dress half torn off her. It was some time before we could get them into the chapel where the girls who were left were all jumbled together, crying and trembling.

Very few had seen the man but all had caught the fear. Miss Pepoon stood there as pale as death trying her best to quiet them down. There have been a number of burglaries and fires lately which the girls knew about. I never saw a panic before and I never want to see another but the incident shows considerable about the girls—their want of grit and backbone—just as though they had anything to fear from one man. Two policemen came rushing in and the neighbors telephoned to know what the matter was. We took them over to prayer-meeting but had a good guard to attend us.

This morning we have the news of the death of a girl who left here last June. After being in this school for a good many years and behaving well, she went out and went wrong, one man living with herself and mother although married to neither. If she had done as she knew she ought to, she would be living today probably. It is very sad and discouraging to the teachers. As Mr. Cooke said to me the other night the chief requisite in a teacher for this school was that she be a Christian for there are so many disappointments in the work that it is too much for anyone to carry it on in their own strength.

Lovingly,
Yours

March 15, 1891, Kamehameha Preparatory

Dearest Charlie,

You see I am out spending my Sunday with Ruth Hoppin. It is a most beautiful morning and when I am here, I always have to speak of the view from the window. I am writing by the window in Ruth's room and I look  out upon a gentle slope of smooth green seaward for quite a distance, Algarroba trees and then the sea stretching way to the horizon and as smooth as glass this morning with only a tiny line of white at the reef. Not a sail to be seen to the east or west except the few ships right at the wharfs. There is a real Sabbath stillness in the air. We would enjoy such a morning together, I can imagine our sitting together down on the broad piazza, with something to read but being very lazy and very happy.

I will answer your letters first of all, dearie. My rings? Why, a day does not pass that I do not kiss my dear opal, and I often look to see if you are thinking of me, as you are just now. Your mother's ring is always on my chain about my neck. I don't know what I should do without them.

In school instruction, we do about as we please. Miss Pepoon has only been in my schoolroom once since I have been here. We have Readers, Bibles and Geographies and writing books and Spelling, English and Arithmetic. Geography is way beyond my lowest division and I have to adapt it to them. We do use board, slate, and paper a great deal, but I do not feel any lack of equipment. I think the only change I would ask for would be an easier Geography. For my lower division, I am delighted now because we have just received our new Encyclopedias. Before we had nothing to refer to and I have begun the practice of giving one girl a day a topic to report upon.

I think I can honestly say, darling, that there is real sympathy and love between my girls and me. In the few cases where I have whipped a girl, the result has been satisfactory, the girls have at once become more obedient and at the same time more loving. Emma Puni for instance, who has been out for some time now. I have been to see her twice and she seemed delighted and always when any of the girls has been there, has sent her "love to Miss Winter." There I knew it would come!

Now will you hear a few specimens of class English that has stuck in my mind? We had a reading lesson and talked over the new words and then I told them to put them in sentences on the board, taking 10 words whose meaning they had just learned. The result was more of a criticism on myself than on the girls. Here are some. "Dr. McWayne explores us twice a year" and I have to explain that we only explore countries and not people. Another girl writes, "Mr. K. is my proportion." I am puzzled for a moment and then I tell her that proportion means the relation between things not people. "This blackboard is difficult." Didn't I tell them that "difficult" means "hard?" "The girl lapsed down the hill" and I had not told them that lapse only refers to time. The English work is certainly interesting and it seems as if I could see them improve.

I was going to tell you about my sewing class. It got very hard for me. We had a machine in the room recently and have begun to make more garments and the girls don't know how to go ahead with anything like that, but you must sit down with each one and show her just how to do it. Then the work must be carefully examined before and after and for 2 1/4 hours, I was on my feet and working hard. But I asked for a helper and now have Deborah Haina and she is a great help. Before class, I am sure of 15 minutes for rest while she distributes the bags, threads and oils the machine and wets the towel. I am not hurried and can help the girls much better than before.

Miss Appleton has Miss Pope's room with the care of the front yard and school rooms. She has relieved me of the care of the sick-cottage also. I think she ought to have the care of the meals also when Miss Davis is away for she has no sewing class or dormitory. They have tacked lots on to Miss Pope now that she is one of school—a dormitory in bad shape to straighten out, and two more sewing-classes while her morning is full of outside work. She has not as yet been allowed an insight into the money matters of the school for which purpose she was taken from the school-room. She does not feel just right about it yet for Miss Appleton could have done what she is now doing as well as she. We fancy we see Miss Davis' hand in it all. I told Miss Pope the other day that I would like an offer of the matronship but I think she understands that it will be all right on my part if another offer does not come. I fear it would meet with much criticism from outside if I were given the position and I don't think Miss Pepoon or Davis would advocate it.

Yours,
Carrie

March 21, 1891, Kamehameha Preparatory

Dear lover,

The steamer goes a day earlier than usual this time, leaving tomorrow instead of Tuesday all on account of the sugar—the wharves are loaded with it and all that does not reach the coast before the first of April, means  a great loss to the owners. The steamers and sailing vessels have taken advantage of the rush to raise their freight rates and it all means lots of work and worry to the business men. They say some are sure to lose and at this rate, the profits in the future will never be as great as in the past. They have to come down from 30 and 40% to 8 and 10%. There are several new plantations recently started that will feel the strain most of all.

I see we may rejoice over the subsidy bill. By it, the Australian ship makes about $7000 a trip and it will be in their interest to put on another steamer and run twice a month. That will mean a weekly mail for us. I feel like thanking the U.S. for its thoughtfulness for us. I am glad too for another reason. In such a place as this, one feels the English spirit very much. You know they want the carrying trade of the Pacific as well as of the Atlantic. We have heard much of their all round the world line by means of their Canadian line and well subsidized S.S. lines to Australia. But now our lines can compete with them and perhaps it will not seem quite so English in the running of the ships on the through steamers. The English mail will still probably go to the U.S. to meet the Atlantic S.S. line at San Francisco. I see too that there is an appropriation by our government to improve Pearl Harbor whose use the Hawaiian government has given over entirely to the U.S. That lies some miles further along this coast and would be of great use to our government in case of any trouble on these seas. The only railroad in the kingdom runs from here down that way and I must go down sometime and see what it all looks like.

I think it was Wednesday when I sent off my last letter to you and we were just beginning our holiday. I took Victoria to the Fort St. School.[9] It is the only school for white children distinctively which this government assists. The children have to pay something but not as much as the Punahou School which is the school preparatory to Oahu College. There are 250 pupils and 7 rooms and all presided over by a Mr. Scott who is an autocrat of genius. It is certainly the finest grammar school I was ever in. All through the school there is excellent instruction and the work of the children is fine. It only takes a half glance to see that those children are far more capable than Hawaiian children. I got a few new ideas for my work but not so many as I had hoped for because much that I saw would not do here.

True to my new principle of not doing so much extra, I did not do anything for the girls that day but rested all the afternoon. They had a fine time however for Miss Pope took her old class down to Waikiki, Miss Hoppin hers to Kalia to catch crabs and Miss Pepoon took mine up on Punch Bowl to sit with the setting sun. All the little ones had a ride behind our noble Prince and everyone was happy.

The next day I had a headache but did not give up to it till noon. Then I went to bed suffering considerable but fortunately got to sleep and it gradually passed off. I did not get up however till evening. I would not have done so then, only that a quarrel over some little matter had sprung up during the afternoon between Katie Clarke and the rest of the girls. It broke out afresh when they got up into the dormitory and I went out to find Katie and Koni in a towering rage, calling each other vile names. Everyone had taken sides and I had to quell them as quick as I could. I ordered everyone to bed and would not allow a whisper. Then I gave them a pretty plain talk about the affair and heard no more that night. Miss Pepoon talked also to the girls in the chapel the next morning and I trust we shall not have such a scene again. It all comes from Katie's adopting Miss Davis's way of bossing the girls around and as the girls are high-spirited, they object and make Katie's life a burden to her. Katie is a good girl but liable to mistakes like the rest of us.

I have talked more with Miss Pope about the matronship. She says she would like to have me as her assistant. She had already written to one of her friends about the position without knowing how much it involved. As I have thought more about it, it has seemed more than ever as if I could do so much in my room if I only had them a year longer. Then too, dearie, this next year and a half is all the time I shall have probably to be school marm and if I am to be matron after that all the time, I would like to hold on to my teaching. This is the way it stands now. If this friend comes, it is to be with the understanding that she is to be either teacher or matron and we will decide then. Miss Pope said, if possible, I should have the first choice. It is really left for Providence to decide and I am sure that is the best way.

Miss Pope and I had prayer meeting with the girls tonight and it was really enjoyable instead of the pow-wow we have sometimes had of it. We made it turn on the Easter's tide and the girls recited appropriate verses.

This is short, but will you accept it, my Carl? I send it with much love,

Carrie

March 29, 1891, Kawaiahao Seminary

Dear Charlie,

I have felt very much alone and lonely of late and as though I were standing alone a long way from any to help me and in a rather difficult place. I am afraid I have been petted and loved too much all my life to make a fine success in being a stranger in a strange place.

I can look forward to a pleasant prospect next year I think for I fully trust and respect Miss Pope and she gives me her confidence to a large degree and seems to appreciate my work. I cannot and will not write out all the unpleasantness for they only amount to that and nothing more. My class is certainly doing good work. I am not mistaken—they make the best appearance on Friday mornings when we hold our classes together in the chapel. The teaching department has, I think been really neglected in past years and I am very desirous of building up my department.

I took 24 of my dormitory girls down to the rocky beach at Kalia yesterday. It was the reward for a month's good conduct in the dormitory. In the dormitory, the girls had really tried not to break any of the regulations which are necessary there and so had saved me an amount of punishing. We didn't get through however without a misfortune. We passed a Poke (Chinese) store and I went in with one of the older girls to buy bananas for them and some of the little scamps took that opportunity to steal onions and bananas from the outside. I didn't know anything about that this evening when one of the girls "told." They were rather hard to manage for there seemed a spirit of lawlessness among them but they bathed and ate and sang and continued to enjoy themselves. It was a long hot walk but a warm bath and a nap made me all right. I am very sorry that anything should have gone wrong but feel sure that the blame lies with but few of the younger girls. Still Miss Davis couldn't tell me about it without putting in an unpleasant personal dig to the effect that the girls had been taken out too much. To my mind the girls get out rarely enough and as for the girls who got into this mischief, they are always up to something and might been into just as bad a scrape if they had stayed at home.

Last night we had another incident. It was almost nine o'clock and all were in bed when suddenly the panic cry was raised from one of the dormitories. It's such a horrible sound that I could just feel my hair rise. I am glad to say none of my girls screamed but I found them all out of bed and ready to start to my room. At my word, they got into bed again and waited to learn what the matter was. Soon someone came to tell us it was nothing at all, one child frightened at a creaking and all the rest followed suit. Then this morning early, news came that both the father and mother of one of the girls of my dormitory who were on another island had died within a day of each other. She is one of the oldest girls and it brings real sorrow.[10]

I must own that now I am blue and discouraged and home sick. I hope that the church service this beautiful Easter morning will raise me from my low and morbid state. The week has been very busy and wearisome to me. I took a four mile horse-back ride last Monday evening and it lamed me all up and I did not get over it right away either but could not give up to it either. Tuesday I had a bath at Waikiki with Miss Appleton. She is a good swimmer, quite the champion of the teachers, I think.

I have been given 20 little tots to drill in a flag drill for the closing day. I didn't ask for the task but I really seemed the only one who could do it. I have two of the older girls to help me and I think they can sometimes drill the girls without me.

Kawaiahaʻo Female Seminary's primary students. Photo by Lilla Estelle Appleton.

You will be surprised at the remark I will now make on Miss Appleton. I think she is visionary although in Oberlin she struck me as very practical. By the way, dear, I have just learned that when she got here she at once sent off an application to a school on Kauai where the salaries are $800. She told Miss Pepoon about it saying that if she got the position she would refund her traveling expenses. She did not get the place and so is to stay here. It seems to be regarded as all right for her to do so but it strikes me as a little "off." At least I don't think I could do such a thing without exciting comment. I'll not write any more today, sweet, but just dream about you—Carrie.

Sunday, April 5—Tonight we had an experience with a native. He came this morning from another island and took his daughter out for the day. He was half drunk and angry and bound to take her out. Miss Pepoon did not object to that but said he could not take the things without paying. He said he would not pay and marched up to the dormitory without so much as by your leave and began to bring her things down. We telephoned for a policeman and then we stepped over for Mr. Frank Cooke. He talked native to him and even touched him up on the back with his stick and made enough impression so that the fellow handed $12 out of his daughter's pocket and paid his bill then tumbled all into a hack and was off. I hope he will not return to burn us out tonight. He threatened to sue but he can't do anything.

I had a good rest up at Kamehameha. It is so very quiet and restful there. The more I see of that school the less would I care to teach there.

Your girl Carrie

April 8, 1891, Kawaiahao Seminary

Dear Charlie,

The mail goes tomorrow I suppose and I just use all my spare minutes to write. There is hardly anything to write about for it was only yesterday morning that I sent my last letter to you. Yesterday afternoon was my free time  and I spent it in the following manner. Once a month is woman's board meeting. The most interesting thing there was a paper read by Mrs. Damon who has the entire charge of the Chinese work on her shoulders. Her husband was at the head but he worked clear beyond his strength and last summer had to leave for the states and has been in a state ever since bordering on insanity. I think I have heard no one since I have been here spoken of in higher terms than he. His wife has struggled on with the work since then. She is going to join her husband this month. She is all worn down and depressed and with difficulty, got through her paper. I could sympathize from my heart with what she said. She said that they needed as much comfort and sympathy in their work as do the missionaries of India and China and that in the 6 yrs. she had been in the work she could count on her fingers, those who had cheered them with their presence in school and church. We are not anything as bad off as that for people like to show off the Hawaiian schools. Besides we are well established and much has been already accomplished while they have the untreated heathen. More and more do I admire Nellie Waterhouse for going into the work. She did not need to at all but she has been of great assistance. There are only two others who teach Chinese in all this city where they just swarm. I wish I could help but my hands are full and with an important work also.

We had a few errands after leaving the church. I bought two pictures of the king's funeral. One a view of the throne-room with the kahilies and coffin, the other of the palace on the day of the funeral. They cost 50 cents apiece which is surely enough. I will not send them to you at least at present, but they may be the foundation of my collection here.

King Kalākaua lying in state in the throne room, Iolani Palace, with Dowager Queen Kapiʻolani and Queen Liliʻuokalani in mourning, 1891. Photo by J. A. Gonsalves.

We made one call on a Mrs. Needham and her daughter Nannie.[11] Since I came here the daughter has become engaged to a Mr. West, a teacher in some school. It was reported to me that she said, "Miss Winter need not think she was the only teacher who was engaged." I presume that that was a Honolulu lie for I have met her a number of times and she seems to me to have more sense than the ordinary Honolulu young lady. It is a city that dearly loves gossip and anything that refers to lovers or marriage is nuts to it and somehow they all manage to cast a low and vulgar tone about everything of the sort.

We dismissed school a quarter of an hour earlier than usual this morning in order to give Miss Patch a chance to have singing. The concert is to come next week and I understand the Queen has promised to come. She has given us two songs of her own composition with native words which the girls are to render.[12]

Miss Pope and I are very much surprised at the manner in which Miss Appleton is treated here. For some reason unknown to us, her work is made much lighter than the others work and if for any reason one of us cannot do our usual work, the extra task is put on some one who already has enough. For instance, Miss Davis has gone off for a week's needed rest and Miss Pope has taken her place but yesterday when she was going into my sewing class as she always does on Tuesday, Miss Pepoon offered to take it for her. Miss Pope could only refuse because Miss Pepoon does quite enough, but only one of Miss Appleton's afternoons is occupied and none of her evenings or early mornings. It does not seem just and if there is a reason, I wish we might be told so as not to be thinking wrong things.

Your Carrie

April 15, 1891, Kawaiahao Seminary

Dearest Charlie,

About putting off our marriage. You are not to think that you must wait till you have a big salary and can buy a home. I am strong and capable as well as you and though I don't now plan to help support the family when I am  married, I should hope not to double your burden. The real point of course is to wait until we see you have a clear road to something and then you can still study and we could live on little until you got there. There are no two ways about it, we have got to wait till providence opens the way more plainly.

Well, the concert in haste. We don't know yet how much we have raised but estimate it between $400 and $500 largely for our new library. It was a grand success. All the last week has been broken up with rehearsals—every afternoon one at the church with the orchestra. Yesterday there was no full rehearsal but a 1000 and one things to attend to. I took no great burden of work upon myself.

The week had been very trying with the school work so much interrupted. Miss Pope, Hoppin and Appleton saw to decorating the church with beautiful yellow vines, ferns and pretty sugar-cane. The Queen sent up a load of flowers. I tried to fill up odd places. We made all the girls lie down in the afternoon and many of them went to sleep. I drove around and gathered up the tickets left at the different stores for sale and we were frightened at the result for only 50 had been sold. We had no need to be however, for the church was full.

Our girls looked very pretty, all in white dresses. They sat on a tier of seats on the platform. Just as they got in the royal party entered. The band played "Hawaii Ponoi" and all rose. The Chamberlain had sent up the royal chairs in the afternoon—seats had been taken up and a rug spread. At one side on an easel was the picture of the "little princess" lately presented to the school by Mr. Cleghorn, her father. She is the next in succession. There were a great many nice people there and all seemed to enjoy the music. The girls take all parts and the music is regular concert music. It would be a musical treat anywhere. Mr. Berger the leader of the band has been wonderfully kind to us. He took our pieces and wrote out 84 pages of accompaniment for his orchestra—original work. One night he sat up all night. He takes no pay you understand. It is a crack band and he got $300 a month from the government for leading it. He is a jolly rough German who has been here 19 years and who has built up the native music and bosses everyone in musical affairs. I hope we can keep his favor next year also for I am afraid we could not give a concert without him.

The Queen's songs too were quite an attraction. It was her first public appearance since the king's death. Mr. Berger came home with us and we treated him to tea and grapes and allowed him to smoke his cigar in our parlor. He is a rough fellow but has been kind to us and we like to hear him talk. He wore his medals last night and explained them to us. He was in the Franco-Prussian War, was at the siege of Paris and the other evening told us some of his experiences there. He was in Paris at the exposition just before that war and took part in a contest between all the royal bands of Europe "and the Prussian Band took the prize."

The Queen bought $17 1/2 worth of tickets. One man at the door threw down $10 for 4 tickets and took no change. I wish you could have heard it. Miss Pope and I sat up in the gallery together I think we enjoy each other's society more than that of the other teachers though they are all good company.

I close with much love,
Carrie

NOTES

1. This letter is erroneously dated January 12, 1890, but the contents make it clear that it was written in 1891.
2. Ida May Pope joined Miss Winter at the Athertons.
3. This is Elizabeth L. Walker, wife of Captain F. D. Walker, master of the American bark *Wandering Minstrel,* which was wrecked on Midway Island February 3, 1888. The ship's party was rescued on March 17, 1889. An account of the events appeared in *Te Aroha News* (4 Haratua 1889, p. 6).
4. Hawaiian Mission Children's Society, commonly called Cousin's Society.
5. While Dowager Queen Kapiʻolani kept a vigil in the Throne Room of ʻIolani Palace by the coffin of the King, there is no evidence that she slept under the coffin.
6. This letter was incorrectly dated February 22, 1890, but the correct date is 1891.
7. A hoʻokupu is an ancient Hawaiian custom that paid homage to an honored person through the presentation of gifts. Admiral Brown's hoʻokupu is described by Rianna Williams, *Deaths and Funerals of Major Hawaiian Aliʻi* (p. 101).
8. Miss Winter pressed flowers, seaweeds, and other plants as a present for her fiancé, who was a biologist. These were bound in an album and can be found among her papers in the Scripps Archives.
9. The Fort Street School was a government school that offered the first normal (i.e., teacher) training in Hawaiʻi and was led by Professor M. M. Scott.
10. Maria Kahopekaʻa Puʻuohau and her sister, Koni Puʻuohau, lost their parents, Thomas Puʻuohau and Priscilla Nohoanu Puʻuohau, who died within a few days of each other.
11. Nancy Richmand Needham (1867–1924) married Rev. Harcourt Peck in 1891.
12. This refers to the second concert given by the pupils of Kawaiahaʻo Female Seminary, Kawaiahaʻo Church, Saturday, April 18, 1891. The program lists "Maikai Waipio," a composition by Queen Liliʻuokalani that was performed by the students.

5

Leprosy and Other Ailments
April 26—July 17, 1891

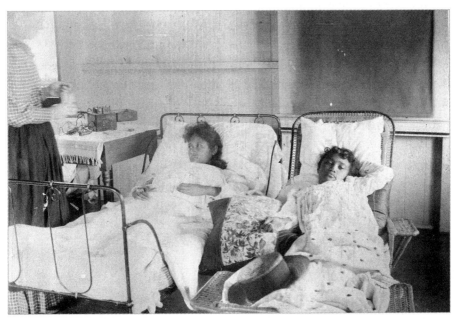

Kawaiaha'o Female Seminary sick cottage.

April 26, 1891, Kawaiahao Seminary

Dear Charlie,

Miss Pope and Miss Hoppin have a novel experience in store for them. They are going to start tonight with the Queen for Molokai and return tomorrow night. I quite envy them the chance. I don't suppose I could have  gone anyway and I knew nothing about it till after they had obtained her consent. They had quite a time with the Board of Health from whom they had to obtain their "permits." They objected and went to see the Queen and only brought them around at the last thing, last night.

    The Queen is visiting different parts of her domain which is quite praiseworthy but her Molokai expedition is exciting considerable comment. She is allowing a lot of natives who have friends there to go with her which is a bad thing, and not allowed under a careful administration. It stirs up the people there and unsettles the whole system. She is being loose in this matter anyway and has already released a number of lepers who were in various receiving stations.[1] I don't think Kalakaua ever went there. Anyway it is a rare chance these two teachers have and I should be glad to take it were I them.

I must tell you of Miss Pope's experiences on her trip to Molokai. I was intensely interested in all she had to tell. There were 400 natives about that little ship and for white people besides themselves only a Professor Bingham and Mr. Berger of the band. He made himself their protector and secured for them the last two berths or shelves opening into the dining-room. Miss Pope was sick all night long. Every where the people lay around and the Queen stretched herself up on deck where her countrymen and the tobacco smoke was the thickest and in the morning they paid their respects to her there as she sat on her mattress and ate poi from her bowl with her fingers.

At Molokai, the scenery is beautiful the dwellings of the people comfortable and there is every evidence that they are well cared for but the marks of the leprosy are everywhere to be seen. It is not the scaly Asiatic kind, but shows itself in swollen, distorted features, missing finger tips, purple bunches, etc. It was a sad sight to see the lepers greet their friends. They tried to be festive

Leper settlement, Moloka'i, Hawai'i.

for the occasion and had a decorated arch and the leper band to greet their Queen. Miss Pope and Miss Hoppin kept clear of the Queen's party and investigated on their own. They went to the girl's school—75 of them and saw little Ella Bridges whose sister is in my room.[2] They were particularly pleased with the 3 sisters who have the school in their charge.[3] They are quite refined cultivated, capable—the world does not know of them but they do everything for their girls, doctoring and teaching them and having to do everything for themselves besides. They treated our teachers so well, bringing them coffee and bread and butter and telling them so frankly about the work.

They looked up Margaret Power's mother and sister. They live in a little cottage.[4] Emma is married and she and her husband are among the worst lepers—still there was a baby a week old. They noticed there a woman and a little boy whom they thought they had seen on the steamer. She was holding and fondling the baby and Emma explained to Miss Pope that it was her husband's first wife! No comments are necessary on this story. This Emma used to be a very beautiful bright girl.

They walked over to the boy's school, three miles away and found them much worse in appearance than the girls. They sang songs of their own composition to the Queen which made everyone weep. The parting too was very sad but they brought none away as it was feared they might do.

Professor Berger and his band came and played to our girls and were treated to coffee and biscuits. The little girls were out on the grass and big ones sat on the piazzas. One of our girls has gone home with quick consumption and another has just developed a lover. We would like well to marry her off decently for she is one of the hardest cases in school.

As ever,
Carrie

May 6, 1891, Kawaiahao Seminary

Dearest,

Such a funny little incident happened this morning. I was in my school-room preparing some work and Eunice Puni came and asked if she might go to my room and mark some handkerchiefs. I was out of ink and told  her to go to Miss Pepoon and ask for a bottle of indelible ink. I then went up to my room and in a little while, Miss Pepoon came hastening in to know if I was sick. I answered "no" with surprise and she said Eunice had just come to her and said "Miss Winter has a terrible ache." After explanations we had a hearty laugh. When I asked Eunice about it she said in a shamed way that she guessed Miss Pepoon misunderstood her.

I changed the picture in your frame a short time ago to the first one I have of you, the one taken in Oberlin. I did it just to see you in another aspect. Margaret came into my room and exclaimed in a hurt tone, "Oh Miss Winter, what made you change that picture? That other man was lots prettier than this." Tonight I have been showing my class pictures to Katie Clarke and Mary Bridges. They have compared others with you and declare there is none that comes up to you. Of course now that they say so, I am sure my choice is a good one.

It's pay day tomorrow. I think I will buy a carpet and some curtains with this money, entirely in imagination, Carl. Only one more month for me. I wish it were the same for you for I know you must be getting very tired. I cannot realize that another class is getting ready for graduation. I suppose the years will pass us along rapidly now and if God please, one of these days, life will seem all new to me again because I am with you.

God bless, my dearest Carl—from me.

Letter 28: May 9, 1891, Kawaiahao

My own Carl,[5]

I have $108.18 in the bank now. Yesterday I did a little shopping, pins and needles, my perfumery both filled with a choice perfume and a fine picture of the dress. I had to pay for a big bottle of iron but I still have enough for car-fare and collections for the month.

We were invited to an afternoon tea yesterday afternoon at a Mrs. Parmalle's and I went off feeling very nice in my pretty blue dress but came home feeling quite crushed. There is something quite wrong with society here—they didn't prepare me for this in college when they told us of the responsibilities we would have to meet and how whole communities would look up to us as the educated people and how we must expect to stand in the most conspicuous places and once in a while, some of these rich, ignorant people give me a feeling as though they regarded me as of little higher social position than a mere girl. I really think teachers are looked upon here somewhat in that light. Miss Pope and I have determined however, to go wherever we are invited and do our best.

The room yesterday was full of shy little young women to none of whom was I introduced, save one, and the few I knew would scarcely answer the remarks I addressed to them. I felt positively wicked when I got out. Just wait till I can give afternoon teas and then will see if my guests shall be so treated. I don't intend to play the meek and humble here either. I had enough of that in Hartford. There are some marked exceptions of course. Nellie Waterhouse is a very sweet girl and I think it is little worldly May who is at the bottom of this. You must scold me, dearie, if I am too worldly, but I don't really see the use of tamely submitting to everything.

Saturday May 23—I'm afraid I shall have to tell you of another disappointment, the regular steamer last Tuesday brought me no letter from you, only one out of three brought me mail. I know, dearie, you write for each steamer, so there is no real neglect to complain of but I think you must be a little careless about getting them off in time. I suppose you take your timetable and beside each sailing date put another 6 days, before and then go by those in writing. It's harder for you to get yours off at the exact time than for me, for I always know just when the steamer goes and when the mail closes. If I fail for any of the regular steamers, it is malice aforethought but not so with you love. You know if you do have a shade of a fault, it is not being always prompt to do things and, this is a case where it hurts me lots.

We have come to one of the saddest experiences in the school, perhaps, the saddest—one of our little girls, of 11 or 12, is a leper and has had to leave the school. I do not think she knows what the matter is but her older cousin and sister do and it has made them almost ill. Sarah's[6] face got very swollen and slimy and there were dark blotches on her neck and body. She is a very docile and sweet child and we feel badly over it. Still we know that if she goes to Molokai she will have a lovely home. Her life will be short, though, and she is a leper! Under the present administration many "suspects" are at large and neither the Doctor nor Miss Pepoon wished to report her to the Board of Health. Still with her face, I think she will get to Molokai before long and perhaps it's only right to let her see her family once more. We have sent out another girl, her cousin, also, as she has not been well for a long time and we half fear she will be a leper too in time.

The doctor says there is no danger of contracting leprosy from those in the first stages.

Lovingly,
Prue[7]

May 23, 1891, Kawaiahao Seminary

Sweetheart,

Here it is Saturday and not since Tuesday have I written a word to you. But I have thought of you many times every day and often long thoughts too.

I have extra work on hand today. I want my dormitory to shine for the last day and am having extra work done there as fast as I can. Today each of my four dormitory girls has two window frames to clean with soap and sand. She picks the dirt out of each corner with a pin and scours off each speck of dirt. I have had my four transoms washed and three of my five doors and some of the map boards scoured. I have to find out the best way myself by experimenting and then show the girls just how. I really am learning something valuable myself and think I could train up one little servant girl very nicely. All the girls have washed their nets and bed-spreads.

This is the way Miss Pope has arranged for the vacation. Miss Hoppin wants to take June because she wants to stay here till the *Star* comes.[8] Alice Lewis, the sewing-girl, will be with her, and Miss Pope will stay a week to see the girls off. Miss Appleton and I will have July and Miss Pope and Emma Kane, August. We will all be here the first of September to receive the new teachers and open up. I don't know what I shall do during my two months since the Maui expedition seems too expensive. I think if I can have an invitation, Miss Pope and I will visit the school on Maui where the Stiles girls are for a couple of weeks.

Sunday—There was a great deal of noise last night over away the native houses. It was full moon and that was sufficient cause. There was a drunken man too who came home late and woke the neighborhood.

This has been a long term, 20 weeks in fact. The city water supply is getting very low and for that reason I shall be glad when the girls go. Yesterday they had to carry all their water for bathing and this morning there was none in the dormitories and often of late it has been so. There has been very little rain the last winter. People are not allowed to water their yards except between certain hours.

I have lately been witness to a very sad thing. My pupil Emily Bartholomew had a brother, a nice young fellow of 16 or 17 and he came down with pneumonia and was sent to the Queen's hospital. This was some 10 days ago. Thursday night the father came to tell her that he was dying. Carl, he lived all that night and Friday and Friday night, dying Saturday morning, and not one drop of medicine all that time or any plaster on his chest. On Friday he was strong enough to sit up and held a bowl of rice in his hands while he drank it. Most of the time there was a strong draft from the window beside him blowing right on him and when he sat up he would put his bare feet on the floor. I saw him Friday morning. None of us could keep thinking that he was shamefully neglected. At the last, he died all alone between the time his father left him and Emily got there. Emily wailed and it seems this is their natural cry of grief. Dr. Trousseau[9] is in charge over there and though he has a good reputation as a skillful man, I guess he has no principle and I imagine he could be very careless. Just now he is all taken up with his ostrich farm, doctoring up his baby ostriches. Last year two of his native children were in this school.

Last evening, Miss Pepoon and I went over into the old Kawaiahao graveyard to look around a little. There was a funeral there and we had a little curiosity to look about us. In two of the little enclosures, we saw tiny huts with native families in and about them, keeping up their custom of living awhile beside their dead. They had their little fire and were cooking something over it. They didn't look very sad but seemed to be having rather a jolly time. There is much sickness and death among the kanakas now. There have been so many deaths in the girls' families!

Kamehameha, May 31—The time is really going fast and it won't be so very long. I wish I could say there would be no change when I return but I will be older and plainer. Still it's my plan to be as pretty as I can be and I know I shall be very loving and happy and just as dependent on you as ever. In one way I fear I shant be as nice. You know when we are together you can always check my little ill tempers by loving reproofs and none of the little wrongs people do me count very much after all. Here life is not all rosy as when with you— no one is happy when I do well, and proud over every little success and urging me on in every little practical matter to do my best, and sympathizing and comforting and gently correcting when I do wrong. It's infinitely better for me though to be among these young girls than out in any business life. I love them and sympathize with them and it's well known that my attitude is not that of a hard task-mistress, but of a friend.

Miss Hight told me an extremely sad thing last night. Mr. Lyman's sister who has had the highest trust I suppose of any half-white girl on the islands in being a teacher in Kamehameha Preparatory, has gone all wrong and has gone off to California. We know it here and to most it is a mystery why she left so suddenly. It's a horrible story of weakness and sin and it fills me with grief. What can we expect of our girls, when this girl who has had everything to keep her, fails so miserably. It will be a blow to Henry Lyman and of course you will not mention the matter to anyone in Oberlin.

On Friday morning, we had a review of our open day exercises in the chapel. Two ladies came to visit the school. Miss Patch was away and I had to play for the girls to sing. It was three hours strained attention drilling the girls in standing well, and speaking loud enough, and getting up and down at the right time.

I had half an hour and this is the way I filled it. Nine girls to the board who drew North America, South America and Europe in 12 minutes. To my second division, I tell one of Aesop's fables and while they are writing it on their slates, I have topical recitations on South America from my first class. At the end of 15 minutes, the 2nd Division writes their story on the board while two girls read off the English they have gathered about the yard with a corrected form after each sentence. This is considerable to make it go smoothly. Tell me what you think of it.

In the afternoon, we took all the girls over to the church to drill on the exhibition day. I have two things, the flag drill and the dumb-bells. It was a good deal of satisfaction to me to have everyone say that my girls did well and were all right. It means hours of work on my part and I sincerely hope the affair will go off well at the last. I had to learn the new march which I play but am glad to have the chance.

After supper I devoted to cleaning 32 heads with careful inspection. When study hour began, I was in the chapel putting work on the board and through the window, spied what seemed the whole back pasture on fire. Someone had set our big brush pile on fire. A very dangerous proceeding in the dry condition of everything and the lack of water and the proximity of the native houses. The Chinaman from the Castle's came over and put it out for us. Mr. Frank Cooke said it was a wonder the fire department had not come rushing up to put out such a blaze.

Later on in the evening as Miss Pope and I were going through her dormitory, we found 8 or 10 of the girls had pinned their sheets and spreads on to the outside of their curtains and we unpinned them all. Their beds had been moved and this was to keep the ghosts out!

Early that morning, I had an unpleasant scene with one of the big girls and her niece. The latter is my room-girl and objected to some work in my room. I took her to Miss Pepoon and she sent her about it at once. Then the big girl came down on me too with her orders but had to come to terms and is doing extra sewing now to pay for her insolence. Well, dearie, that was one day. It was hard.

Yesterday forenoon I desired to get my dormitory cleaned up and untangled my sewing class materials. The bags had to be washed and all the underwear we have made cleaned and neat for the sale on Wednesday. Then there are many things still unfinished and I have to coax extra girls into working spare minutes on that. The beds in the dormitory had all to be rearranged and the last hour I spent with Miss Pope in cataloguing and putting away the new books. In the afternoon, I slept considerable I was so dead tired.

I am very thankful for this lull in the rush when I can stop and think, answer your letters and even let my pen roam into some of the many loving fancies I have of you. I hope the letter will seem good and loving to you for that has been my mood so with very much fresh love, I am—Your Girl

Tuesday—Here is my postscript. Yesterday was not an over hard day. Things are coming out smooth I think. Did I tell you the music teacher we expected cannot come? I feel quite elated because a little scheme which I proposed to Miss Pope has been taken up and passed by the trustees exactly as I fixed it up. Miss Patch who is to be in town as a private teacher is to have the singing and concert in charge with nothing else for $20 a month. That is to be all her connection with the school and we are to have another teacher who can give piano lessons, take a sewing class and look after the two lowest rooms. I am pleased. It relieves us of great anxiety.

Lovingly,
Carrie

June 25, 1891, Kawaiahao Seminary

Dearest,

Saturday—We found lots of things to worry and perplex us at the seminary. One of our girls, Mary Makaimoku left school a week before it closed. She was ailing some and her mother wanted her out. We heard she was hav-ing the "grip" But it was not till a week after school was out that we really learned how badly off she was. Then we found her very sick, with no doctor for two weeks and in a little hot room with no ice or milk, impossible to help them. She was all worn down.

Miss Pope sent Dr. McWayne down at once. He reported that there was no danger but was very anxious to have her brought up to the seminary. It was Monday night before she at last got here and then her condition was worse as dropsical symptoms had set in. All the week she seemed to get worse instead of better and when I went in to see her Saturday morning, I was shocked at the change in her.

The doctor was there many times that day. She was very much bloated and he said were she his own child he should tap her at once but feared if he did so to her and then she should die, her friends would say he killed her. But by evening she was suffering so much we urged the doctor to try to get the mother's consent, so he told her Mary would die if he didn't do it and would perhaps die if he did, but that it would relieve her suffering.

The mother is an exceptional native woman.[10] She was educated here and I never shall forget how she said, "I am willing, only you stay here, I can't" and then kissed Mary and went out. It took the 3 teachers who were here to help in the operation. Miss Pope turned faint and went out but it did not affect me. I didn't know how I would act but I am glad now I was there, for I have one more accomplishment. I should think the doctor drew off 3 quarts from her. It relieved her right away. The doctor feared a collapse any moment and kept his finger on her pulse all the time and every few minutes gave her brandy. It was a time of great anxiety and you can imagine our joy to have it turn out so well. The doctor himself was all worked up over it and said he felt as if he had done as hard day's work when it was over. I think Mary has gained some every day since but she is by no means out of danger yet. She seems to be eating well.

The week has been rather trying because it is the week of the closing of the Kamehameha School and the Oahu College 50th anniversary. There have been 3 daytime exercises for them to attend—the closing exercises in the evening on Tuesday, prayer meeting on Wednesday and General Armstrong's lecture last night. Yesterday Miss Hoppin had all the girls down at the beach for her last pleasure to them. All this has made the work very much broken up. Alice Lewis is on duty with me now but she cannot take any responsibility about money matters nor of managing and directing so I have my hands pretty full.

There has been company also. Miss Smith who came up on the *Star*. She is very interesting in her accounts of her 5 yrs. experiences. She has been with Alice Little and Jessie Hoppin. She is engaged to Captain Garland of the *Star*. Her health is all broken down. She suffers greatly from neuralgia of the stomach. Mother Rice is also with us during the celebration. Do you see, dearie, that I have my hands full?

28th—I shall have $50 or $100 for you in the fall. Won't you please let it be understood that you will ask me for it when you want it. I have not told you that I went into a little enterprise all on my own account this spring. I gave $100 to a Mr. Smith for investment. He is a very good and careful man and he has done very well by some people I know and has never lost anything. I can have my money anytime I want it and he will give me an account of it anytime I ask for it. I shall not give him any more but my next venture will be to get the address of the Seattle bank where Miss Malone has her money and see if I can make a deposit there. They pay 10% and why shouldn't you and I have it as well as anybody? Am I a little rash and mercenary, Carl, or shall I go ahead? I mean to keep money on hand here in the Postal Savings Bank all the time. Miss Pepoon told Miss Pope that she took home $1500 out of the $1800 she earned. That did not include her traveling expenses. I can't do as well as that I know, I shall not have as much given me as she had but I will do my best. I have set my heart on $500. It's all for you any way or rather for our home.

July 1, 1891, Kawaiahao Seminary

Dearest,

I can imagine Nellie Waterhouse's feelings tonight as she reflects that every hour brings her lover nearer and tomorrow morn she may see his face.[11] I am not without interest in his arrival for I have thought of it many  times today because soon I shall see someone who saw you only two weeks ago and who will say something right from you to me. I am afraid I shant see him as soon as I would like to. Nellie may not think how much I am interested.

I must tell you of one pleasant result of our having so much company. The last night Miss Smith brought up a basket of the loveliest pink coral which she and the Captain had picked up for Miss Appleton and I to divide between us. I shall be very proud to show it off some time and say "from the Captain of the *'Morning Star'* and his prospective wife." It is very beautiful but so brittle as to be almost impossible to keep well. I am going to get some cotton soon and see if I can't pack it so it will be safe. It is not safe to have it around. I went down to see the *Australia* off yesterday. There were ever so many aboard that I knew. The band was there and played them off. It made me want to go, too.

Six of our girls went off yesterday and more expected. We have suddenly found it quiet and restful. We find it a little hard to get the work done by so few girls. Miss Appleton had extensive ideas of doing a big amount of house-cleaning also but I guess she will have to give it up. I hope so for I am much opposed to it myself and know Miss Pope is also.

I think I am feeling a wee bit homesick and lonesome for you dear Charlie, in this big house with 20 Hawaiian girls and Miss Appleton who for some reason, perhaps my own fault, makes me fractious all the time. Well I don't feel so very badly after all, for things might be infinitely worst and it is at least quiet and restful now.

July 2nd—Last evening I had an experience such as I have read of. When the doctor was here in the early evening, he said Mary was getting a little weaker again and he had brought a bottle of nice wine of which he wanted her to take a tablespoonful every 2 hrs. When I came home from prayer meeting, the mother came to me to say that Mary would not take any, that she said she had promised in church before God never to drink any liquor and that the minister had said if she took a little it would in time make her a bad woman. I hardly knew what to do. My sympathies were with Mary but here she has been very ill for 5 weeks and I don't know but that she needs just that thing to bring her up. I went in to see her and found her very much excited, saying over and over "I will not take rum, I will not take rum," "I don't care if I am weak, I will not take rum." The only way I could quiet her was by telling her she need not take it then and in the morning I would ask the doctor if he couldn't give her something else that would do just as well. I am a little afraid of what the doctor will say for I know he hasn't any sympathy with such views. I hope he will not excite her by trying to make her take it against her wish. I am surprised by the incident because I didn't give any of our girls credit for such an amount of backbone and conscience. She ought to get well now anyway to make the story turn out well.

I wish I could take you with me to one of the native prayer-meetings. You cannot understand a word that is said. No hours seems so long as those spent over in Kawaiahao church. I have one unfailing diversion however, my thoughts of you. The men and women take part freely and it is amusing to watch them. They seem to be natural and fluent speakers and can gesture most freely. They like to create laughter so that the meetings are not always as decorous as you might expect. One night one of the men told the story of the little girl at the lighthouse who used the Bible to reach the lamp. It was comical to see him act it all out—get the Bible, wipe it off, put it on the chair on the table and then climb up and the manner in which he said "a-a-a" when he found he could reach the light.

Your girl,
Carrie

July 4, 1891, Kawaiahao Seminary

My Boy,

I think I have half an hour for writing now and I am in much need of it for I have so much to say. I haven't told you about the fine time I had Saturday afternoon, the 4th and I will now relate that tale. Mr. Fuller, Secretary  of the Y.M.C.A. and who used to be engaged to Miss Alexander, has consumption and is going away by the next steamer. A riding party was given to him and we were invited. Miss Beckwith secured me a horse and Miss Appleton found one somewhere, we left Miss Kenwill in charge, and joined the party of 17 going up Tantalus. The party was made up of all sorts of men and women, married and single and no one went with any one in particular, but were all jolly together.

We found an unpleasant state of affairs awaiting us when we got home for our Mary's step-father had been there with a carriage to take her away. Miss Kenwill told him he could not do so anyway till we came home. Miss Appleton and she went off at once on errands and left me to face the situation. The night before the doctor had intimated to me there was something new afoot and told me to let them take their own way with her and not fix up anything for her. We suspected what it was, for you must know Carl, that all the natives are largely under the influence of their "Kahunas" who are half doctor, half priest and the most thriving representative of the ancient heathenism. Nobody knows just what they do.

We feared something of the kind in Mary's case and did not fear amiss. I rang up the doctor but he was out, and I asked to have him ring me up as soon as he came in. Mrs. Makaimoku was waiting for me and had her story to tell—that her husband was a stern man and would have his way and all the time I could see she was not much opposed herself. Moreover Mary had had a strange dream which her mother had interpreted with the result that "if she took any stimulant, she would die." Mrs. Makaimoku asked the Doctor to stay away. The doctor said to me "let them take her. If she dies there, the other girls will fear the cottage, if she dies outside, it is their own fault. But warn them of the consequence." I went into the cottage and found that man putting on our Mary's shoes and stockings. I had my say but got no reply when she was carried out and the poor little thing was too weak to hold her head up. Her sister Lydia seemed to feel very sorry to have her go. Still she claims that Mary is improving all the time. We rather doubt that, although we are not anxious to have her die in order to prove our theory.[12]

> I send you my dearest love,
> Carrie

July 12, 1891, Kawaiahao Seminary

Dearest Carl,

Last week seems now kind of a horrid jumble of rushing, hurrying hard work. I left the church with two girls to attend for a short time the annual meeting of the Woman's Board.[13] These girls had been appointed delegates and someone had to take them. We were just seated in the carriage when the fire alarm sounded and just across the street behind the Cooke's a large fire broke out. It was the ware-house of the Standard Oil Company and Carl, 35 thousand cases of oil were soon burning their best. The engines came to the nearest hydrant right in front of the school. At first we were all much alarmed, everything was dry as could be; the water supply was short and there was such a line of little, low wooden houses which seemed to be continuous though they really were some distance apart. There was a supply of gasoline and we were told to expect an explosion but they got most of that out before it caught. The volume of smoke was enormous and really clouded the city for two days but, there was no wind, few sparks and no other buildings caught.

They had quite a time getting the girls home from the church but we accomplished it by a back way. The little girls who were at home all cried and when the big ones got home they were not much better. Their fond parents began to come in and urge them to pack up. We stopped that by sending the natives off and taking the girls into the chapel where they sang until they were quiet. By one, we were all over our fear. It has been burning over there for a week now and oil went up in a few hours from 20 cts. to $1 a gallon. A ship had just come in with a lot of oil but it was just in time to be burned. Oil cannot be brought on steamers so it will be some time before a supply can get here. We are fortunate, 3 or 4 cases are on hand, and vacation here when we can easily economize.

Sunday—Wednesday was our "open day" and its early hours were filled with getting the house in the best of order and arranging the dining room where each sewing class had its table, and Miss Davis a table of bread and cakes, etc. At nine, the natives flocked in and each class gave a recitation in the chapel. I think I wrote you what mine was to be. All the girls did well. At 11, the dining room was thrown open and the crowd rushed in to inspect and buy. I took in $17 from my table. At 12:30, we were alone once more and after dinner, went over to the church for a final rehearsal for Thursday. You can't think, dear, how they have to be drilled for every movement, for if they don't know the exact time and place for everything, they are filled with confusion.

The next morning I went to the church with Mr. and Mrs. Frank Cooke who had the matter in charge to help decorate. They really did it all. At 2 p.m. came the grand finale with a crowded church. Everything went finely. My dumb-bells had the most mistakes for the girls were all tired out but you can see how the paper speaks of them. Every one expresses themselves as delighted with the exercise. I paid for the dumb-bells myself. Miss Pope and I were grateful over the result for we each had 2 exercises on the program and felt as though the success was largely ours.

We had a table over there loaded with things from the fair and Alice Lewis and I stayed to sell them. We got $40 more and since then many things have been sold bringing in, in all some $230.

When I got back to the seminary, many girls had already gone and confusion reigned supreme over their departures. I helped all I could but after dark, crawled off to Waikiki with Miss Hoppin and lay still there till Saturday morning. I scarcely got to resting for at every sound in the night I would start up thinking something was wrong in the dormitory. Saturday morning I came up to find things in as bad shape as ever for Miss Pepoon and Miss Davis were nearly wild in trying to get ready for the sailing vessel at noon. Miss Appleton was trying to get the girls into a dormitory and Miss Pope had a heavy load dropping on her all at once with all the bills coming in and all the money going out. After Miss Davis and Pepoon got off, things settled a little.

Monday came and Miss Pope was nearly wild over the accounts but by noon she fortunately got them straight. I ran around town on errands for self and school and at noon went to Waikiki again but there was not much rest

TWENTY-FOURTH ANNUAL

CLOSING · EXERCISES

OF

Kawaiahao Seminary,

AT

Kawaiahao Church, Thursday, June 4, 1891,

AT 2 O'CLOCK.

PROGRAMME—PART I.

1 OPENING CHORUS,—"Night's Shade No Longer."   *Rossini.*

2 BIBLE RECITATION,—91st Psalm.

PPAYER.

3 PIANO DUETT,—"Sans Souci Galop," - - *Ascher.*
ANNA RICE, LUCY LELEO.

4 COMPOSITION,—"Na Hana Lokomaikai a na Hoaaloha
i Hana ai no ke Kula," - - - LUCY AUKAI.

5 FLAG DRILL,—Sixteen Little Girls.

6 CHORUS,—"The Fishermen," - - - *Gabussi.*

PART II.

7 DUMB BELL EXERCISE.

8 ALPHABET IN COUNCIL, - - - - *Palmer Cox.*
PRIMARY DEPARTMENT.

9 CHORUS,—"To Thee, O Country!" National Hymn,
- - - - - - - - *Eichberg.*

10 COMPOSITION,—Changes at the Seminary.
MARGARET POWERS.

11 PIANO DUETT,—"Valse Des Fleurs," - - *Rummel.*
LOUISE ALAPAI, AH OI.

12 RECITATION,—"The Angelus."
Twelve Young Ladies.

13 CHORUS,—"Friends, Good Night," - - - *Flotow.*

☞ Ke nonoi ia aku nei ka oluolu o ke anaina, e hamau na hoo-
kamumumu ana a me na walaau ano ole ana, a hiki i ka wa e
hookuu ai o na hana hoike, a i mea hoi e lohe pono ai na poe a pau
e noho ana a puni ka hale i na leo nahenahe o na kaikamahine liilii.

Closing exercises program, June 4, 1891.

there for Miss Hoppin had 2 lively girls with her who didn't seem to believe in sleep and rest.

Dr. Gulick of Maui was down that evening and taught me to float on my back. I came up Tuesday to go over to Mrs. Cooke's as she had invited me to do. Wednesday noon, I took lunch at the Atherton's and then came to the seminary where I have been since taking over duty for Miss Hoppin who had a chance to go away for a while. She makes it up to me in July. She is back now, and tomorrow Miss Appleton and Miss Pope and myself go to Waikiki for a week for complete rest and change and then for Maui!! It really has been a very hard two weeks.

Last Wednesday was Kamehameha I's birthday and a public holiday. Mrs. Oliver came and invited 20 of their boys down here to a "luau." They furnished cream and soda and the two Miss Hights to help entertain. We furnished cake, water, melons, fresh fish and poi. From 11 till four they sang, played croquet and Old Maid at their own sweet will. They really seemed to have a charming time.

The afternoon wanes and nothing written to my dear mother so I'm going to stop now, lover, and write to her with your consent. I shall only be on Maui two weeks so make no change in your letters.

> Your loving Girl,
> Carrie

NOTES

1. Pennie Moblo rightly observed, "In the fragile political state of the Islands, leprosy became a partisan issue" (Moblo, 1999, p. 78). Doctors disagreed on the diagnosis and treatment of leprosy. Medical science could offer little insight into the transmission of the disease, and in the absence of scientific facts, those in power acted on fear and aggressively isolated anyone suspected of having the disease. The result was the painful separation of families, with resulting economic consequences and social disorder.
2. Ida May Pope's May 3, 1891, letter to Lois Pope Prosser describing her trip to Moloka'i is among the Ida May Pope Papers in the Huntington Library, San Marino, CA. In her letter, Miss Pope says she found Ella Bridges at the Bishop House. Incorrectly transcribed selections of this letter appear in Helena G. Allen, *The Betrayal of Lili'uokalani, Last Queen of Hawaii* (pp. 246–251).
3. These are the nuns at the Girls School at Kalaupapa, likely led by Mother Marianne Kopp.

4. Miss Pope's letter (May 3, 1891) says the cottage was located at Kalawao.
5. Miss Winter uses Charlie Kofoid's pet name Carl in this letter. She also calls him Carlchen, an affectionate name she gave him while in German class at Oberlin College and while they were courting.
6. Probably Sarah Kapalehua.
7. Miss Winter signs her middle name, Prudence or Prue.
8. The missionary vessel *Morning Star.*
9. Georges Philippe Trousseau (1833–1894) was a physician at Kawaiahaʻo Female Seminary in 1891.
10. This is likely Mary Ann Ua Makaimoku, the daughter of an ordained Hawaiian pastor who died soon after her birth. Her mother died when she was ten, and she was taken into the family of Asa Thurston and raised in Kailua. She was educated at Kawaiahaʻo Female Seminary, where she married on June 15, 1871, Mr. Makaimoku, a theological student and later a teacher at Lāhaināluna and Hilo Boarding School (Pratt, p. 12). The Makaimoku marriage is discussed in a letter dated May 31, 1874, from Cornelia Bishop to her husband, S. E. Bishop. This letter was found among his papers in the Huntington Library, San Marino, California. The Makaimoku family fits the description of an unnamed Hawaiian family criticized in "Kahuna Work,"an article published in *The Friend* (October 1891), for consulting a kahuna during the fatal illness of their daughter.
11. Nellie Waterhouse's Oberlin classmate Arthur Bacon Wood was invited by her family to visit Honolulu. He brought gifts and news from Charles Kofoid, and Miss Winter remarked that she wished her family was in a position to pay Charlie's fare for a visit.
12. Mary Makaimoku died in August 1891.
13. This is the Women's Board of Missions for the Pacific Islands, one of the organizations that supported students at Kawaiahaʻo Female Seminary.

Student Essay by Violet Lima

I   My life as a school girl in
My name is Violet Lima. I came to school
about five years of age. I was brought up by good white
ladies who have put me in school and are now supporting
me. And now I am about the age of fourteen years.
When I first came to school the dear old school house was
not so good as it is now. The trustees of the school have
tried their best to make every thing just as comfortable
and pleasant for the girls and also for our patient teachers.
And had had build up new buildings. We have three
big dormitories where we sleep. And in each dormitory
there is a lavatory where we wh wash our faces and
comb our hair. The names of our trustees are Mr. H. Castle
Mr. Atherton. Mrs P. S. Jones who is supporting my
school. Mrs. S. Allen. Mother Rice who gave the school
money for our new sewing house. The most of our girls
do their own washing and sewing in school. A new sewing
house was put up for the use of our girls. So that when
they have left their studies they may go in it and learn
how to sew and be fine dress makers. Since our sewing
house was put up some girls have gone out earning
for their own boarding. And some girls have already paid
their board. It has being an encouragement to our dear
teachers to hear people speak well of the Kawaiahao
Seminary girls saying that they have improved a great
deal in sewing. Our washing house is quite a big
house and in it there are   about forty washing
tubs and further in there are ten bath rooms where
we bath. On Saturdays the girls parents are allowed to

come to see them and bring them some fruits to eat but not cakes. Once in every year our work is changed. In school my lessons are Bible, Arithmatic, English, Geography and Reading lesson. I also take music lessons. We have about school rooms. For my class mates we are about 30 girls of about the same ages or little older. We do our studing in study hour so as not to take plenty of time in school. Miss Hinter who is my school teacher has being very patient with us. ✱ Right beside of our washing house is our ironing house. For breakfast we have tea, a piece of craker and bread. In the after noon we have poi, meat and salt and water. In the evening we have some times poi, meat and salt and some times bread and sugar or sweet potatoes and sugar. For school we wear uniforms the color of our dresses are blue with white tape around the cups and around the neck. When we go to church when it does not rain then we wear on our white dresses. We go to sleep half past eight and the children at half past six. We are about 132 girls in school. Since I came to school girls have being married and have gone out of school and lived in their beautiful homes and have had pretty children. The works that we do are cleaning the house, sweep the yard, prepare the ~~mils~~ meals, clean the lamps and harness the horse. Our plays are jumping rope, croquet, play base ball, and play swing. We have a teacher to teach us how to sew, how ~~the~~ to cook, how and to any thing that we do not know. Our teacher gives us pleasures such as going down Waikiki

3

Waikiki for a sea bath and other pleasures.

6

Maui Summer
July 17–August 30, 1891

July 17, 1891, Kawaiahao Seminary

My Lover,

I have been getting my outfit for my Maui expedition. I hope nothing will happen to make it fall through. I am to ride astride and have made myself a dress for the occasion. It is the kind of cloth that overalls are  made of only it is pretty for it is a fine stripe of brown and blue. There is a blouse waist and a full skirt rather short. I did not make a divided skirt because I have to wear the dress in camp and as well as on horseback and there are some men in the party. I have had heavy soles put on an old pair of shoes. I bought also a long-wristed pair of chamois-skin gloves. My hat is a broad brimmed black straw, tied under my chin by a ribbon and with a veil about the rim to keep from burning. Each one carries her wardrobe behind her on the saddle. I have a big piece of black oil cloth for the purpose. It will contain an extra dress, pair of shoes, underclothing, etc. Our provisions and blankets are carried on pack animals.

July 19—One needs more dresses here than they do at home and so many times last year I would go to my closet and have nothing fresh to put on to go out anywhere. My dresses would either be in the wash or half dirty or all shrunken up with washing and unsuitable to put on without many stitches put in them first. I have been trying to remedy that difficulty by getting the goods I had on hand made up. I have made a white, a muslin and a cambric dress which are good additions and perhaps after I come back, will have time for another dress. You don't need very nice dresses but you need plenty of them or you are in a pickle half the time. At home for most of the year if you have a good school dress and a good church dress you are all right. It must be the same with the men here for most of them wear white duck or linen much of the time—still light weight woolen is the usual dress for them. I am afraid you will hardly appreciate this dissertation on dress but it's a problem that takes time and thought and so I must let you know what I am doing and thinking.

To change the subject, since I see by your face you have had enough of this. Miss Pope brought back Miss McLennan principal of Makawao with her and Tuesday I return with her to Maui. Miss Pope's ankle was very bad indeed. She suffers much pain with it, but I was glad of one new experience it gave me. I did all the business for her that had accumulated during her absence, paid all the monthly and some of the quarterly bills—over $300 worth. It was a new experience going around to all these places of business with my bag of money. I collected three bills too. I couldn't begin to tell you all the experiences I have had in this vacation but I am very glad I had the chance to learn so much. I couldn't have had the chance in a school at home probably in many years—sickness, company, housework, marketing, cooking, children, authority over large girls, money, and business.

I don't suppose I will write again till I reach Maui but in every experience I shall wish you with me, unless it be the sea-sickness.

July 23, 1891, Makawao Seminary

My Carl,

Here I am, dearie, 2000 ft. above the level of the sea on the sides of Haleakala. Behind us rises the mountain whose long upper edge is usually hidden by clouds, below us is a long gentle slope to the sea which  is 7 miles away yet looks only two. It is very cool and quiet and restful.

The mail had come in early and I had your precious letters in my bag. In the afternoon by the time I had packed my valise, telescope and oil cloth it was about time to be off. At 5 o'clock we were aboard the *Likelike* [4 syllables]. I felt half sick all the afternoon in anticipation of the journey. The *Likelike* is a tiny affair and has no stateroom and the passengers are accommodated with mattresses on deck. Miss McLennan got ours spread in a good spot and before long everyone was camped out. After putting aside a little modesty it is really lots more comfortable than a state-room. It's cool and you have plenty of air and no bad smells and no worst sounds and sights than when one is down below. The channel is dreadful and I found at once that i could not raise my head from my pillow. We were both ill for a couple of hours and after that Miss McLennan felt all right. From one till six we both slept considerable but by that time we came into rough water again and I was sick some more. I didn't see a thing all the way up.

(It's "up" because it is against the wind) but the rise of the boat. At the landing at Kahului, there is no wharf and we go down some horrid little stairs into a row boat and thus ashore. It was nine o'clock when we reached shore and you know one person who was glad to be there.

From this place, we went on board a little train that seemed like a horse-car, except for the engine. We stopped seven miles along the coast at a little place called Paia. We went through the largest sugar plantation in the world, that of Sprecklesville. At Paia we were met by an express wagon drawn by two horses and climbed steadily up for 12 miles reaching the Seminary at about 12:30. It seemed good to walk and eat after taking a rest from such occupations for 24 hours. Still I wasn't as badly off as I might have been. We slept last night without drawing the net—there are some fleas but few mosquitoes. There are large fig trees growing all around this place and they are full of fruit too. I like the fresh figs very well.

> Yours,
> Carrie

July 29, 1891, Makawao Seminary

Dearest,

It is 4 o'clock now and I have been working fast and hard since I arose, with the others on the final preparations for our trip. I don't know as this can get up to Honolulu till after next steamer goes. Good luck to the little note anyway for it carries to you my fondest love and it is to tell you that this entire trip is for you to assure you that I shall keep a faithful account of all my proceedings and try to be a good girl.

I must stop for I must try and find someone to take this to the Post Office and then help on the innumerable things still to do. We want to start at 4 tomorrow morning and we have to ride 30 miles during the day.

> Your girl,
> Carrie

August 2, 1891, Hana, Maui

Dear Charlie,

I want to write as much about the trip while I am taking it as I can and as now I have left the rest of the company and gone off by myself for that very purpose.

I went in the afternoon for my first ride astride—it was simply awful, I couldn't gallop a step without my feet flying out of the stirrups and losing my balance and I knew I couldn't ride an hour in that way without being used up for a week. Irene and I were going to the store on errands where the gentlemen were who were going with us and the last thing said to me was "they will never go if you ride in that style" so after we got down the road a piece we decided to change horses. Irene's had a side-saddle.[1] I felt perfectly at home in that and we galloped up to the store in fine shape and had a little chat, which seemed to put us on a better footing for the trip. Then Irene and I had a talk and we decided that it was folly for me to try to learn to ride astride in two days as long as I knew the other way. She was at home both ways and said she would take my horse if she only had a suitable dress to ride in. I told her I would do anything to make one if I might only ride side so all day Tuesday I worked fixing up a dress for her.

Even on Tuesday the whole thing nearly went through because one of the young men could not find a horse. He could have hired one for $15 but he was out of work. We were in despair but we transferred that responsibility to Miss McLennan thinking that if she could look out for a whole seminary, she certainly could for such young and giddy girls as Irene Stiles and me. Well, we had the most fortunate relief from the whole difficulty.

I think I must have written you about the Mr. Thomas Gulick whom I met in Honolulu and what a lark we had with him down at Waikiki when he took supper with some of us girls there once. He is the Maui minister and he came riding up to the seminary while we were wondering what ever we should do. He was on his way up the mountain with his wife and his brother and sister, Mr. & Mrs. William Gulick, the missionaries in Spain who are here on a visit. We told him our "pickle" and he said at once, "You ladies need the trip and it must not be given up. You telephone this Mr. Aiken that I'll furnish him a horse and then you hire one from Mr. Andrews and I'll pay for it and he need never know." Wasn't that fine?

Right here I must put in a description of the members of our party so that you may understand. I can turn the ladies off on a few words. 1st is Miss McLennan, principal of Makawao, Chaperon of this party, Oberlin, over 30 yrs. old, I think, pleasant and amiable. 2nd is Irene Stiles of whom you know no evil. 3rd is Carrie Winter with whose imperfections you are well acquainted, but whose little self you love and would call an addition to any camp.

Gentlemen: Mr. Hardy—business manager. He is a Harvard graduate, from a Boston family and acquainted with all kinds of high society before he came here. He must be toward 35 yrs. old. He came out here an invalid 8 yrs. ago, not expecting to live from year to year. His health is fairly good now but he has drifted into staying here. He teaches the government school here has half the day to himself, lives an easy-go lucky life, is not working for anything ahead. He is gradually running down at the heels and unless something wonderful happens will continue to do so. I don't know whether he knows it or not for he really fills an important place in society here. Nothing goes on without him, he does his duty by his school. I don't think he will ever marry because no girl that would suit him would marry him. He smokes almost constantly but never allows it to become offensive to us. These few days with us he has been living on a higher plane than his ordinary life and he enjoys it.

2nd—Mr. Aiken a tow-headed, jolly boy, recently from his home which he still loves and talks about. He goes to sleep whenever we begin to talk seriously but keeps us all laughing by his pranks.

3rd—Mr. Mossman much the same as the above, only a little quieter and a little deeper. I think we shall know him better and like him better as we go on.

4th—Mr. Dickey who was with us only the first 2 days and nights, through the crater. He is a middle-aged, married man but is jolly and kind as he can be. He saw to everything while he was with us, from guiding and pitching tents to looking out that the ladies had dry clothing on and that my lips did not get chapped. He took special care of me.

Retinue: Portuguese boy Antoine,[2] and native boy Sam who are perfect treasures, willing to do all they can and having a good time. Each one rides a horse and leads a pack-mule, called respectively Ruin and Destruction. On the mules are our tent, provisions, dishes, blankets and a private roll for each one done up in oil cloth. The mules are good animals and do their work well.

Now for the trip and all its incidents. Irene[3] and I rode down to the store Tuesday evening to make the last arrangements. We asked them to take breakfast with us in the morning at the seminary and as they decided that we must start as early as 4 a.m. The last thing I said to them was that I did not expect to see them till 5 o'clock in the morning as I had had experience before in that line. They were so much in earnest about it however that I only meant it in fun.

Well about seven o'clock we started. About 9:30 we reached "Olinda," the summer place of the Baldwin's and the last point of civilization.At Olinda, we meet the Gulick party who had just come down the mountain. There is the most delicious black-berry patch there, the only one on the islands I presume. Irene and I ate our fill there. By 11 we had started again and rode on again till 12:30 when we stopped for lunch under a clump of trees. We had a jolly joking time there and then on and on. In the hours time we began to pass through thin clouds though there were very few above the mountain as it was a dry, hot day. The higher we went the more curious the view was. We looked down on the clouds and the clouds had for their background the sea so that it seemed like looking down into the sky and we could see a faint point of West Maui, and Molokai reaching out into the cloud land. There was just the faintest line where the sea ended and above that just a few more clouds and then the arch of the clear blue heavens. The bridle path was good all the way but very steep in places and as the air grew thinner the horses panted for breath and we had to rest them often. The rarity of the air did not affect me at all though it often does people. All the time there was this wonderful view behind up and about 3 o'clock we reached the summit.

Now, Carl, I simply cannot describe the scene from there. I can only try at it. The walls fall sheer away. The crater is immense, 9 miles wide 11 miles long—99 sq. miles. In it are clouds 800 ft. high—and as far as the eye can reach—there it is—smoother in all its outline than any painting and colored in all shades of red, purple, yellow and green with white thrown in here and there. On one side, this wonder and on the other side, cloud-land. I don't believe it can be equaled in the world. Then we had a 2 hours ride along the summit to the place of descent. I shant forget that ride—no path at all—and with rocks just hurled there, in masses—up and down and over and picking ones way here and there—just the stoniest mountain ride you ever saw and for 2 hours. That made it 5 o'clock and we knew we could not make the camping place we had desired.

The ride down into the crater was not hard, just down and down the black sand with a trail of yellow dust following us It took 2 hours just the same, although it seemed only a short distance to look down. It was getting dark and we had forgotten our lantern. No use to look for water for there is none in the crater—all we could require was grains for the horses and wood for a fire and about 7 o'clock we came upon such a place beside a steep ascent. From 7 till 7 almost constantly in the saddle, what think you of that for me! Of course I was tired but far from used up. We had to do things in a hurry that night it was so late. We started a big fire to guide the mules to us and as soon as they came up the men began to put up the tent while we got the supper bread, and warmed up canned beef and coffee. Everyone enjoyed the supper and then we sat around the camp fire and sang and joked. I even got a joke on Mr. Hardy by pinning an advertisement for wedding cards on his coat. He thinks Miss McLennan did it.

Our arrangements for the night were crude. They cut off the branch greens as best they could and reared the tent, just comfortable room for us all to lie in. They first spread a canvas over the ground, then we pinned up our oil cloths through the middle, spread some more oil cloths on the ground, then an extra blanket or two, each takes her own blanket and little pillow and makes herself as comfortable as possible. It wasn't so very comfortable that night because the ground was very uneven. I had taken medicine with me to make me sleep the first night but it didn't work very well till toward morning. It is very cold in the crater, like keen autumn weather and the cold was only increased by the misty drizzling rain that set in toward morning. That was good for the horses though for it made the grass wet, and so made it easier for them to go without water. We had canteens and demijohns of water for our own use but that was not enough to allow us to wash either ourselves or our dishes.

The men got the breakfast, ham potatoes, coffee and we ate it in the tent throwing everything to one end. We always have a jolly time at meal time. By nine o'clock we were all packed up and ready for a start and forth to see some of the curiosities of the crater. I think one of the most beautiful things I have ever seen is one of these expanses of black sand and from its surface rising a plank of the silver sword, truly silver, as pure and beautiful as anything can be. For hours we rode through the same and over the rough lava or "aa" as the natives call it, through Pele's pig-pen, an enormous lava bubble—past the cathedral rocks and then entering on the most dreary, black, rough desolate waste which reminded me of Dante's Inferno perhaps because we were on the way to the bottomless pit. Before reaching that however we had to go pass along a narrow ridge of land with a great hole in the earth on either side, the crater of two adjoining cones. It's very hard to make one's way in the crater because there are no paths only the merest trails which are easily lost. A number of times that forenoon we lost our trail and then there would be the roughest kind of riding till it was found again.

At last long after noon we climbed up the side of a mountain to make our "Annie Runie"[4] camp. We went on up the mountain to the Hunter's Cave, a wonderful, lava bubble leading out into a perfect amphitheater. A little lower down we visited the Crystal Cave where we went down, down into the earth and got some of the beautiful white crystals hanging from the rocks overhead. We walked down to the camp afterward and gathered ferns. I fear a little for them this morning lest they mould and spoil. My book is full and I have no chance for drying them. I tried to get as good many of those rare ferns knowing you could exchange them for almost anything.

I have got to close this letter now because we leave Hana today and I can mail it here and then it will catch the next steamer from Honolulu. I don't think I ever felt better in my life. When I get all cross and fretted (if I ever do) just take me out to live as a gypsy on bare-back and in camp.

Carrie

August 16, 1891, Makawao Seminary

My Love,

I found two good long letters of yours waiting for me when I reached here on the completion of my trip. How I enjoyed comparing experiences! I spent one morning since my return in making a map of my expedition, one for you, one for mother, and one for myself.

Please have the map before you as I go on. That first day's ride from the Seminary to Camp Necessity was almost 30 miles. We came back into camp decidedly wet for most of the time it had been raining. They were just getting ready to put the tent up and we had to make ourselves as comfortable as we could under the shelter of the overhanging rocks (the only dry place about) on a bed of dry ferns left there by a previous party. We busied ourselves putting our ferns into our books till the tent was up and then changed our shoes and wet clothing for dry.

It is very cold in the crater but wrapped in our shawls we were dry and warm and under the influence of our fire thawed out and each took a turn at telling a story. Before dark, the boys had cut quantities of fern for the floor of our tent and over it spread our "fly" so we had a splendid bed. That night we

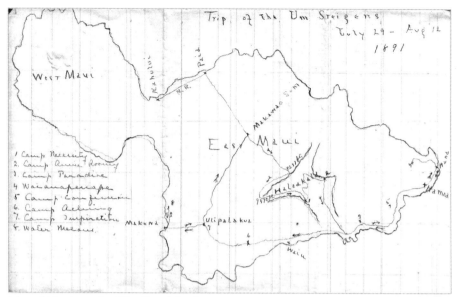

Map of Maui travels, 1891. Sketch by Carrie P. Winter.

started the custom of singing, "Savior, Breathe an Evening Blessing" after things got quiet in the tent.

There was one episode of the night that was amusing. We three women had undertaken to sleep at right angles to the men...with our curtain between of course. It was a mistake because we didn't have room to lie straight and the men were crowded. After that we always slept the other way and gave no trouble. Mr. Dickey was the gentleman nearest the curtain. I slept very soundly that night, in fact never more so and in my slumbers straightened myself out rigidly but with my feet quite outside the tent in the wet and rain. Mr. Dickey found them there and gathered them in and perhaps saved my life by so doing.

That morning dawned clear and beautiful and the sides of the crater were distinct and we could see everything at its best. We were off by nine o'clock. Here is a little outline of the view that day. We are up high here in the air riding down a sharp ridge in the air with the crater cliffs on either side and way below is the line of the crater flow against the sea. Then the blue of the sea for a distance and then a body of white cloud, still below us and rising from that the distant peaks of Mauna Loa on the island of Hawaii. Think of the great uplift to our spirits to be poised there as it were, on the narrow path with deep gulches frequently on either side and all this view before you. We had been so successful in our riding that we made a long halt at lunch and had a very merry time over it. It consisted entirely of hard tack, sardines and jam. We always took our lunch in our saddle bags and so were independent of our mules. They could follow at their own speed. Our breakfasts always consisted of coffee, rice and ham and our supper of tea, rice and canned meats. Sometimes we had bread but more often simply hard tack.

The ride in the afternoon that day was much harder. We lost our way and had to pick our way over very rough ground. We came to a dreadful hill, so steep and rough! We rode half way down but then had to get off and each one went down for himself the best way he could. Stella scrambled down beautifully. No water for our horses and they were very tired. We were getting down near the sea and it was getting late. I was getting very tired and we seemed to be riding for hours and hours and with no sign of stopping. Rain had been scarce and where last year there had been full streams not a drop of water appeared. At last—we came to a gulch with a full rapid stream. How our horses drank! We had dismounted and unsaddled and picked out our tent spot when a native man came up and offered us the use of his house. We declined that offer but when he said we might go across the road and camp in an enclosure on which we had been casting longing glances we gladly accepted. He tore down the wall for us and soon we were over in the most secluded little dell with the matted grass which here seems like moss, a foot thick beneath our feet, with a good flat place for our tent, sloping, grassy banks to lean against, a little stony place for a fire and all around great century plants that would make the fortune for a florist at home and a curious tree that branches all over and has great tropical leaves and a fruit that looks like a pine-apple. We named it Camp Paradise at once.

After supper Mr. Hardy and I found the nicest little lounging place a few steps from camp and we all went there and lay down on the grassy bank with shawls and overcoats over us and our faces turned right up to the starry sky out of which a little rain fell upon our faces but without any disturbance to us. Mr. Aiken played on his harmonica till he dropped off to sleep. The rest of us sang and told one or two stories. We got into very earnest conversation till something touched the "quick" in Mr. Hardy and he said very bitterly, "I had ideals." Then I sprang up and said we must go to bed and Mr. Aiken remarked that he thought he must have been asleep.

Saturday's ride was one never to be forgotten. It was a series of surprises and as hard riding as most people can ever expect to indulge in. The mountain comes down in ridges to the sea coast and between these ridges are deep gulches in some cases, dry but more often with a torrent of water through it.

Before I knew what I was in for I found myself zigzagging down the side of an immense ridge into a valley that must have been a 1000 ft below. The path was good in one way as there was no mistaking it and it was broad enough to give one a sense of security somewhat shaken however when you cast your eye over the edge and saw that there was no room for a horse to "act up" without sending you over and to certain death. The path was just a mass of stones mostly firmly set in the earth and not inclined to roll but full of surprising little cliffs down which our horses took little leaps and steep—o, my!! To keep my equilibrium, my body was about parallel with Stella's. I soon learned to give Stella a loose rein but hold on so as to bring her up quickly if she stumbled which she occasionally did. I should be less alarmed to go up or down a flight of stairs on horse-back than some of those "palis." Stella was afraid but her fear did not make her nervous but rather slow and careful. I wish I could get a picture of one of those "palis" to show you what I have been through. After a terribly steep climb we came up out of this gulch to the summit of the sharpest kind of a ridge with another 1000 ft. valley way below us. We had to ride up its whole length and then down again with every nerve on strain but still wild with the excitement of it.

Where we went down into the third gulch we stopped to admire the beauties—a rapid stream above us, a beautiful little waterfall, and below, another like it. It was a very tropical spot—enormous ferns in rank abundance. A half hour of its beauty and we were into quite a different scene. A large sugar plantation and then to a little settlement and a store—the first of civilization which we started. We replenished stock here and then went into a Chinese restaurant for lunch.

I must say here that on this side of the island there are really no white people living except an occasional manager of a plantation. The natives are somewhat thick and we always excited their wonder and admiration where ever we passed. This restaurant seemed to be the place for the wild, exhilarated spirits of the morning to crop out and we got into perfect gales of laughter. We had coffee and bread and pie at 12 1/2 cts. a head and provided our own spirits.

After leaving there, we had one great gulch to pass where we saw 3 or 4 waterfalls at once. We rode for an hour or two through smaller gulches and then came into good roads leading to the Hamoa plantation. Our horses were glad to stretch their legs and we rushed over the road like wild after singing at the top of our voices.

About five o'clock we reached the Von Graevemeyers who formerly lived in Makawao and have lately moved over there to take the plantation. We were invited there and received a hearty German welcome. There is only the man and his wife and innumerable dogs. They have a beautiful place but it is extremely lonely for them and our visit seemed a special providence. They did everything for us. Gave us a cottage with 2 rooms for sleeping and the whole run of the house, most bountiful meals and fed and doctored our horses up for us. I was really sorry to get into civilization again but on the whole it was best for we were very draggled and dirty from our crater experience.

August 26, 1891, Honolulu

My Love,

I am going to write up another day of our trip this morn-ing. At Hana we laid in a new stock of provisions. Hana is quite a town but there isn't a white family there. The store was the best I have seen on Maui. We went on from there to Waianapanapa a famous spring, down in a great cliff of rocks under an overhanging ledge. It is a large pool of wonderfully clear water that drips constantly from the cliffs above. The water is so clear that the darkest native looks white in it. Here in ancient times they say, a native princess took refuge from an irate husband but the reflection of herself and maid who was waving a Kahili over her, in the clear water revealed her and he descended and killed her and to this day her blood is visible in the seams of the rocks. I saw the red stain myself.

We ate our lunch here with our usual frolic and then started back. I devoted the ride to getting acquainted with our two boys who rode along with us as they had no mules to lead. I rode out with Sam and he told me the legends of the places we passed, of Peapea's hill and of the most beautiful woman on Maui. When we came back I rode with Antoine who is Mr. Hardy's best boy and bright and gentle too but over Sunday he had got into bad company, a wicked old schoolmaster over there—white too—had made him drink beer and engage in other folly. Antoine was much ashamed of it and his conscience troubled him too and he took this occasion to confide to me the whole story but said I mustn't tell Mr. Hardy or he would never forgive him. I didn't promise that and I did tell Mr. Hardy because I thought he ought to know to what temptations the boy had been exposed. The others laughed at me quite a little because Antoine chose me to make his confession to.

I must write you more particularly about Mr. Mossman now. I think in my first letter I let him pass as a quiet boy of 19. By this time, he had "come out" more and we ladies had come to like him very much. He seemed to me, more like you than anyone I have ever met, with that same gentle spirit and respectful way toward women and the constant and kind helpfulness. I soon found him out for you see I had lessons in that kind of a boy. He had just finished High School where he had an enthusiastic science teacher who was anxious to have him go to college. Perhaps it was because I took the pains to draw him out that made him and me such good friends anyway, his resemblance to my darling touched a tender place in me and I couldn't help being good to him. I often wished you had been there for I know you would have delighted in him and could have talked to him as I could not. Please tell me, my Carl, that you understand about this perfectly and are sure that I did nothing wrong. It's the first time since I have been here that I have met any boy or man where any real friendship arose and I must say I enjoyed it very much.

We were to leave the Von Graevameyers on Tuesday. We rode through one of the big gulches and about 4 went up on a side-hill and made camp under a grove of low-hanging tropical trees. It was showery that day and we had a damp time getting supper which we had to eat in the tent but in the evening it was clear and we had a big fire. That evening conversation gave the camp it's name "Confession" for Mr. Hardy started the pastime of telling around an instance of when we got "left." We all did so with some funny results but it was rather a bad thing for Mr. Hardy and Mr. Aiken for they didn't know just where to stop and they told a number of stories on themselves which became camp jokes after that. For instance Mr. Hardy told us about going out to a little country town near Boston when he was in Harvard and getting into a regular kissing party where he kissed all the 56 and then got weary long before they did and how the college boys got hold of it and made life a burden. 56 was a magic number with us after that.

Do you like my trip and my account of it? Tell me, dear, you see I can't watch your face and note every change there.

You were very comforting, love, in regard to what I wrote you. I am so glad that you are willing and anxious to be on the lookout for making the waiting time 1 instead of 3 years longer. I don't think I want to give up that Ph.D. You know what is yours is mine and I like that degree on my name but I feel now very, very hopeful that the way will open so that the time may not be 3 yrs. Please, darling, don't grow worried over it or nervous but leave it as you say in His hands for I mustn't be a burden of care to you in that way either. Your words are beautiful to me about our home and I want to fulfill your ideal and my own in it too and one thing, dearie we'll make excursions away from it sometimes so that I will always be fresh in it and not get into nervous fretful ways.

I will have to close soon for I am on duty for today and I must look after things. The Queen's husband is dead and they have all gone to see him in state.[5] Our new teachers come next Tuesday.

> I love you,
> Carrie

August 30, 1891, Kawaiahao Seminary

Dearest,

You may expect to see every letter starting out with something about my trip till I really get that written up. In my last letter I stopped at the end of our evening at Camp Confession on Tuesday evening. We got off  about the next morning and began that ride back through those dreadful gulches again. We ladies were anxious for a bath and when we got to the beautiful gulch with the falls and abundant ferns we stopped. We told the men they might go on but I guess they thought it wasn't quite safe to leave us there unprotected so near the main route. None of them had their suits so they couldn't go in with us. We all dismounted and they sat down to a friendly chat while we went up the stream to a beautiful clear pool. The water was delicious and we had such a fine time in it washing our soggy, dusty hair and our tablecloth and dish towels in the same pool.

We made a big journey that day some 15 miles over lava. We had thought the ride would not be very interesting but it was—the scenery was very unique. To our right we had the slopes of Haleakala while all the long slope between us and the sea was a mass of black, jet black lava, twisted and jagged in its wave-like crests—the hardened form of what years before was a molten flood. Strange to say we saw many fine horses and cattle over this way who somehow find enough food.

We stopped for lunch at Waiu where there is a fine spring and plenty of water for man and beast. We climbed into the cliff above the spring and acted as usual. One notices everywhere through this district the numerous deserted homes of the natives. There are the old stone foundations of their homes and the disintegrated straw huts but no people and no graves. The latter fact is explained when one learns that they hide their dead in the numerous caves.

It was almost dark when we came up with Mr. Aiken who had preceded us and had picked our camping spot. It was a high open round of land—with a thick covering of burnt grass and on the summit were the foundations of two old native houses. We named it Camp Aching at once in honor of "our guide" and the conditions we expected to be in before morning. But after we had pitched our tent inside the old house, had built a roaring fire from an old tree, had a good supper, we were in a mood to enjoy the beauties and advantages of the place. It was beautiful too for we were on a higher round of land with that long black region all above us, behind us the wonderful mountain, beneath us the sea and above us a sky luminous with starlight and a young moon.

As I write it out now I seem to be back there drinking in the beauty and the calmness of it. We took a walk that evening back to the one old grave we had seen there. When we reached the grave, the romance of the thing struck home to us and we each took a turn in expressing ourselves. Mr. Hardy made really a fine little speech and I recited a portion of Whittier's poem, "The Grave by the Lake" but when it came to Mr. Mossman's turn he quite took the poetry out of the thing by saying he doubted its being the grave of a native at all because it was contrary to their custom and that it was probably the grave of some favorite horse. How that took the wind out of our sails! We found out afterward that it was the grave of a native but a recent one.

We then went back to camp and gathered about the fire and chatted and sang till bed-time. I think our fire could have been seen for miles. The next day we were up and off once more.

Ulupalakua!! I have a subject worthy of a much finer pen than mine. This was Saturday you see and we stayed there till Wednesday and our experiences there were one of the pleasantest parts of the whole trip. Ulupalakua used to be one of the most famous places on the islands. There was a fine sugar plantation here and 7 miles below at Makena was its little port with a weekly steamer from Honolulu. There was a large mill and a large homestead all in the hands of the Makee's whose hospitality was almost past belief. Visitors were entertained in a princely manner 15 years ago then the head of the large family died and everything stopped. There were legal difficulties which prevented the settlement of the estate till six years had passed during all of which time everything remained idle. Then it was all sold for $80,000 but the man who bought it never revived the sugar works and now it is only used as a cattle ranch. There are a few native families about and the man who runs the ranch is Jim Buchanan with a native wife. They occupy one of the better houses while mansion, mill, blacksmith shop school houses and church stand deserted and empty. In character, the landscape is like New England.

NOTES

1. Irene Stiles and her sister Gertrude were teachers at Makawao School. Irene was a close friend of Miss Winter and accompanied her on the Maui trip.
2. This is Antoine F. Tavares, who wrote a letter to Miss Winter after their trip to Maui.
3. Irene Stiles.
4. "Little Annie Rooney" was a popular song by Michael Nolan performed widely in 1890. Miss Winter misspells it here, but spells it correctly on her map.
5. John Owen Dominis, husband of Queen Liliʻuokalani, died in Honolulu on August 27, 1891.

7

Back To School
September 6, 1891–January 15, 1892

Kawaiahaʻo Female Seminary students in the kitchen. Photo by Lilla Estelle Appleton.

September 6, 1891, Kawaiahao Seminary

My Own,

The last steamer brought our 3 new teachers. I have been matron and with so few girls to work, have had my hands full.[1] Miss Appleton came back yesterday and we are all ready for the start tomorrow morning and we have got our hands full too.

We are very much disappointed in our teachers and we fear what lies before us through them. Miss Harris is all right. She is the one to take Miss Davis's place and Miss Pope knew her well before. She is supporting two sisters in Oberlin. She has been teaching 4 yrs. and really has lots of grit although she is only about 22 or 23. I am a tiny bit afraid that she lacks spunk and assertiveness enough to fill her place and have also a selfish little wonder inside that Miss Pope did not think me better fitted. But the other two! Miss Hadley whom Miss Pope had met a few times, and who was highly recommended on account of her strong Christian character is a perfect little hypocrite. She is certainly toward 35 yrs. old as is also Miss Armstrong but they have made bad names for themselves on the steamer coming down. There were very fine Island people aboard but they chose their own friends among the gamblers and vulgar people.

Helen Abby Pepoon. Portrait by Davis, Painesville, Ohio.

Mr. Oleson who was aboard said of Miss Hadley that she would have been in better health if she had played cards less and drunk less wine. She has come here for her health with 4 trunks, traveling expenses of $20 where it should be $180 and a nose way up in the air. She complained all the time and has tried to order me around like a kitchen girl, without success mind you for somehow I don't hear her. She was written to quite full about the work but is surprised that we don't keep servants. If they weren't so near 40, I might try to reform them. Miss Pope is almost sick over the prospect and I suppose that if the school ever needed sympathy it is now. Six teachers and two of them such nature. Miss Appleton is not strong. Well we will see how things go. I know Miss Pope, Miss Harris and I can work together.

It's the funeral of the Queen's husband today but I don't take any interest in it and I know you don't therefore.

I think Miss Pepoon is in Oberlin. Won't you find out, Carl, and go and call on her. She is a perfect Christian lady.

All yours,
Carrie

September 13, 1891, Kawaiahao Seminary

My darling,

It is so very long since I have had a letter from you, two weeks ago Thursday. Surely the steamer Tuesday will have a rich store for me. There ought to be two long letters from you on it. We are through the first week, dear  Charlie, and we are all alive and well. We have every prospect of a fine year. At the end of the first day we had 105 and now we have almost reached 130 which is our limit.

It has been a critical week for Miss Pope and she is worked nearly to pieces but everything has gone well. When Miss Pepoon began, they had a terrible time. The girls were so wild and unruly but we have had splendid order. I have worked hard too. Miss Pope and I were really the only ones who knew the ropes and you will not be surprised when I tell you that we both found our feet blistered yesterday. I tried to help and show Miss Harris while Miss Pope attended to all the outside work. I don't see how it can be so hard this week. Our new teachers have started off splendidly.

I took Miss Harris down to a church social one evening this week and we really had a gay time, stayed clear through because we were enjoying ourselves and had quite a cluster of such young men as the city affords about us.

I must tell you how my own work has opened. I have lost 7 girls from my room but taken in as many more from the lower room and now have 30 subjects to instruct. I feel a great deal of encouragement about my room. To begin with I know the girls now and their characters. I know their capacity and can give them enough to keep them busy. They seem interested in their work and they are so much better prepared to take up the work that has to be done in my room than ever they were before. I know too how better to govern them and I have begun by being very strict. Don't be frightened, Carl. Last year they made me at times suffer untold agonies because they said I was "kind" and so they said they could do as they pleased. Experience has taught me that I may as well go if that is going to be the way and I am really gaining the power of keeping them down. I don't think Carl, you will ever know what that means till you have worked among a people so few years removed from barbarism as these are.

You will be anxious for the effect of this upon my own character and I sincerely hope that I have not lost in real gentleness, while I have gained in strength. Try, dearie, not to distrust me about this thing but to help me with your loving sympathy. I think one of the hardest things we have to bear is the attitude strangers sometimes take toward us. They see the beautiful and poetic side of the girls nature and it seems to them that we are hard and cruel and all their sympathy is for the girls which it really ought to be the other way.

Do you think Charlie that it was too extravagant in me to take that trip this summer? It cost me nearly $50. I should feel very badly if you thought it was foolish in me.

September 20—Another week has come and gone and again I turn to my lover. I have hoped to write during the week but did not. As I expected things have been much easier for me this week than last. Miss Pope has had to work too hard but not quite so much as the first week. I am delighted with my girls and every seat is taken. everyone seems interested in the studying and I am sure were you to step into my room at any time you would be pleased with my order. I really think the girls are a little worked up mentally. I got hold of a fine little book this summer on language, Powell's "How to See" and it aids me very much in teaching English.[2] In my first division I alternate Physiology with Geography with good effect. By the way, Carl, I wonder if you could get hold of any outline of gymnastic exercises. I have used up everything I have and I want something new and not too simple either in wands or dumb bells. I must pick out my class soon and train them. Every girl too in my room has a clean head and that is a great gain. I don't suppose they will stay clean but every week they have to be clean.

Saturday or yesterday afternoon I went calling with Miss Patch. We have had a large number of calls this last few weeks—50 or 60. In the evening I went to a stereopticon show over at Kawaiahao church with the girls.[3] It was a very comical performance. The girls had never seen anything of the kind before and were perfectly delighted till it came to some pictures of statuary and then they were overcome by shame at the nude-figures. The man made a great mistake in showing them because the girls were truly shocked.

I am going to run through your letters now. The first is dated Aug. 15 and evidently missed the steamer for which it was intended. I think too now that we have a perfect understanding about the "third year" and as a matter of gossip I will inform you in confidence that I expect now to be married inside 2 yrs unless something goes wrong and I shall invite you to my wedding.

You see Carl I came out of the trip not tired but tough and I congratulate myself more and more on having taken it. Oh, I expect to go camping and roughing it many times with you in the future. Aren't you proud to have a girl who can do it and who will help to get you out and into new places? I am well and happy and I love you.

Your girl,
Carrie

September 21, 1891, Honolulu

My dear Charlie,

October 4—We have a certain girl here, by name Koni Puuohau who is capable of giving any amount of trouble and who has been all stirred up this past week and not only that but has unsettled the whole school and  made disobedience the fashion. She is in my dormitory and on coming up Friday night from her punishment she kept talking till late in the night and asserted several times that she should run away the next day. I told Miss Pope what she said and yesterday Miss Pope went to see the Queen about her. She is one of the girls the Queen supports here and the Queen told Miss Pope to tell all the girls that if she or any other of her girls ran away from here she would have them arrested and put in the station house. I had Bible class last night and Miss Pope came in and gave the girls a talking to. And when she gave them the Queen's command you should have seen the change in those girl's faces. All through the school now you can feel the change and the readiness to obey. Koni has completely given in and once more we teachers can breathe freely. When she is in this fit she is like a great street rowdy, capable of committing anything. The Queen completed her good work by sending a message to Miss Pope, bidding her write a note to Anna Puuohau not to come here again and if she did come and insisted on staying, to let her know and she would have her arrested. We are delighted to have the support of the Queen.

I have had to stay at home very closely this past week and am rather tired of it, but otherwise I am all right. My school work is going well. My girls study harder than they did last year and I have much better order. I have to be very strict with them for I have a number of the worst cases in school and have lost about all of the steady, sober girls I used to rely upon last year.

I enjoy your indignation over our new teachers but you mustn't worry on my account because they haven't much to do with me or I with them. On the outside things appear to go about as usual. We are in the old ruts and that carries things along. I won't waste space on all the little annoyances. They have taken a great dislike to me and think me very cruel to my girls. Poor me, who have learned through such a bitter experience not to let the girls rule me. The girls just run right over them.

Miss Margie Brewer who is boarding here because it is more convenient to Punahou Preparatory where she is principal, while she had a sprained ankle, has done me a kindness. She has let me take her horse, Harry, in use. I rode him down from the college last evening and he was shod today at her expense. I got a bale of hay of which he is to have one meal at day. It cost between $3 and $4 and he can pick up a good many Algarroba pods as horses are very fond of them. They take the place of grain. I had a fine ride after sewing class today. It made me feel so fresh and good that I am going again tonight—to prayer meeting I mean.

I wonder if you see the "Review of the Reviews." I was going to buy a copy and send to you but there are none in town. There is an article in it on Hawaii that is acknowledged to be by far the best thing of the kind.[4] I know the Bishops pretty well. I know you would be interested could you find it. Tell me if you do.

> Very lovingly,
> Carrie

October 18, 1891, Kawaiahao

Dearest,

I have already bought Julia's Christmas present,[5] I had a pin put on a Hawaiian dime. It has King Kalakaua's face on one side and "Aloha" on the other. I think I know too what I shall send you. Oh don't you wish you did. I  had to have my ring mended also. It had come apart where you had it cut down. It cost 50 cts. I enjoy telling you that I think it your duty to keep my ring in repair since you can't very well send me the money. The man cleaned the ring all up and it looks so bright and new that I have been congratulating myself on my recent engagement.

Yesterday afternoon I had to go down to Waikiki with 10 of the girls who as a Sunday school class were invited down by their teacher, Mr. Severance. They were in the water a couple of hours I should say and I think you could have seen them diving for the sea-moss they think so delicious. I went in with them for a while. They would swim around me, letting me rest a hand on a shoulder of two girls and help me by kicking.

Bother on those natives!! They have set up a family bath-tub in their back-yard just under my windows and the men and women go there to bath without regard to my feelings of modesty. They haven't any such feelings themselves.

Monday Eve.—When we woke yesterday morning it was raining very hard, a very welcome rain I can assure you for everything is very dry. In the after-noon a strong wind came up and all day today there have been gusts of wind and little showers. It has been cloudy most of the time. The change has been a welcome one to us all. It was the hardest rain I have seen since I came.

Shall I tell you of the day? One girl thought her shirt had been stolen and I searched with her till she changed her mind, looked over the lessons for the day and got new pens for my holders. After breakfast, I cut out some work for my sewing class, made out topics for my 1st class in the new Reading Room, looked after my dormitory work, gave out two "punish work" looked up two lost pails and took my 15 minutes before school to myself. When the bell rang I made a raid on the dormitory and gathered up stray thimbles,

Kawaiahaʻo Female Seminary classroom with maps of Europe on the board. Photo by Lilla Estelle Appleton.

combs, soap, etc. for which they will have to work. Down to chapel to listen to Dr. Beckwith's kind opening words. Then to the duties of the day in my class rooms. It was a smooth day. First there were 8 or 10 "dirty-headed" girls left over from Friday to examine again only to recommend two to the use of the fine comb again with a dirty window to wash to keep along—2 classes in Arithmetic, two in English, 1 in Geography, 1 in Physiology and the morning is done. A little neat copying in their notebooks and two girls drawing the map of Europe on the board. I have got hold of a fine little book of English exercises that are just the thing for my girls. I wish you could have seen their work this morning.

It is Miss Harris' afternoon out till 2, so I must look after dinner work. I tuck in also some more preparations for sewing class and give my horse his dinner—and a little petting and salt water wash for his girth sore. Then a busy 1 1/2 hour in the sewing class for all the work seems to be done at once and I hardly sit down for the showing and explaining. Then a half hour in my own room and I go down to watch the girls get dinner. This does not prevent me from mending my week's washing while I watch till the last busy quarter of one hour. Dinner and I hang about the kitchen to see that nothing dreadful is done. Study hour quickly comes and I put my work on the board and then come up here glad that tonight I am not on "study hour" as I am every other Monday. A little sewing and then this letter.

Monday night upset the day for I had eaten some wicked salad and had to pay for it. So yesterday I was as lazy as I could be. In the afternoon Miss A. and I made a few calls—saw Mrs. Charles Cooke's twins and went to the dentist. I paid my bill. It was $19.50. I feel like begging your pardon for spending so much on my mouth. It seems dreadful but as prices go here it was all right, one gold filling, 5 silver and some treating and cleaning. I would have gone without it but the neuralgia was already after me and I would have had a hard year of it. You will laugh at my feeling so about it but I can't help looking upon my money as yours. Now I am laughing for I know you are saying to yourself, "She'll soon be thinking of mine as hers." As the girls say "Of course, Yes."

A sound sleep last night brought me back to my usual vigor, and today I have accomplished considerable even to chastising one girl but I won't tell about that because you won't understand. It was only an easy little one and I quite enjoyed it.

I hear the girls talking about "Charlie" a good deal now days and some of them tease me how to pronounce K-o-f-o-i-d but they don't get anything out of me and it is quite beyond them. They have seen it so much on letters that they think they know all about it. I have never said anything to any of them about you but they see my pictures and are on the watch every time the mail comes in.

I love you much.
Yours

October 25, 1891, Honolulu

Dear Charlie,

It is my Sunday off again and Miss Harris and I are out here at Kamehameha with the city, Punch Bowl, Diamond Head and the ocean spread out below us.

The *Monowai* was late. It was due Thursday. I tried to possess myself in patience but it didn't get in till yesterday. Our dressmaker came. I was down to the Seminary last night and saw her for a few moments and liked her appearance very much. Not a young woman but very sober and decent in her appearance.

The *Courant* is full of sensational reports about Hawaii. Don't let them trouble you at all. I suppose there are some things we don't know about but there is nothing being said or done here of an exciting nature. At least it's all nonsense about the Queen's being at the point of death.

Sunday, November 1—I cannot realize that November has come. I think I have been out of line so much the last few days. Believe me, dear, I have prayed and struggled against it and at times I think God has heard me and lifted me out. I did something wrong. I know I surprised Miss Pope and hurt her feelings very much by some decidedly sharp things said about a certain arrangement. I had thought all along that I would let it pass without begging her pardon, but I see now that I must and I will. She is the only teacher that I have real affection for here and I don't see how I could be so mean. Every other one here seems as cold to me as a block of ice while Miss Pope is truly sympathetic.

I like Miss Harris. She is really more capable than Miss Pope and she is a hard working good girl and if she could open her heart to someone as I do to you she would be lovable to everyone. We have had some good talks and she has admitted to me that so far she has always found herself the first in real capacity where ever she has been. I don't think she has ever had the experience of admitting any one on a real equality with herself and I think her ideals are all too narrow. Now you know, Carl that she and I can never be really friends till she grants me equality with herself. I have never formed a friendship of another kind.

I had intended to buy a horse this fall but I am beginning to think that Providence doesn't think it best and I am willing to rest it in his hands. I wrote to Maui about one but didn't get any satisfaction there. Then Miss Brewer let me take hers. It had been out to pasture a long time and I suppose was tender, any way in a few rides I gave him two bad girth sores, scraped his back a little which at once developed into a fistula and now it is at the doctor's for treatment and I suppose there will be a big bill. Then there is a Miss Kinney here who wanted to have me try her horse which she was desirous of selling for $50. She gave him all virtues but I have found I don't want him. He got a girth-sore in the first short ride. Beside he spent too much time in trying to look pretty and when it came down to business he was no where. I shall send him back as soon as I can. Miss Pope has got line of a fine tough little mare for $35. I think she will buy him and perhaps I can make arrangements to hire him occasionally.

November 6—The Queen visited us one morning this week. It was an entirely unexpected visit but we understand she was pleased with all she saw. She was present at devotions in the chapel and spoke to the girls and afterward spent some time in the school-rooms. I had a class in fractions and two or three examples were analyzed. The girls could not have done them a year ago.

We are finding out more and more how full of superstition the girls are. Our experiences with the Makaimokus (the girl who died) showed us much. I have been reading to my girls a history of the islands by Professor Alexander. It is not yet out but he let us have the advance sheets. The other day I was reading them about the abolishing of the ancient tabu system and commenting on it. "But," they said "tabus are not all gone yet." I drew them out a little. Generally they will not tell of such things but once in a while it will come out. They told me that a hit on the back of their heads was tabu and if they received one they would die. They also gave me the reason for Poniawa's death, the girl who died in such a short time last year. It seems her grandparents had told her never to carry pails of water and some teacher had made her carry one. What the grandparents forbid is especially tabu. Miss Appleton found today that nearly every one of her girls really believed there was such a person as the goddess Pele. She is trying to convince them now that they cannot believe in God and Pele too.

At a meeting of our trustees this last week the subject of Miss Hadley & Miss Armstrong came up and they questioned Miss Pope so closely that she had to tell just how unsatisfactory they were and they really considered the question of sending them right away but it was decided that we could not afford to do so and they are simply to be informed of the dissatisfaction with them and perhaps send away at the end of the year. I must stop—it is hot tonight and the mosquitoes are swarming.

I love you very much and this is to tell you so, dearest lover.

November 12, 1891, Honolulu

Dearest,

The last time I was up at Kamehameha something happened that you will be interested in. Since their new building has been completed the boys do not come into town to church but Mr. Oleson conducts their services  out there. I went to their evening service and heard him read two letters from John Wise. One was to the boys and one was to Mr. Oleson. He told all about his visit to Northfield and how homesick he was when he crossed the Hudson and got among the hills once more. Mr. Moody had him speak at one of his meetings. He said he asked Mr. Moody to come to Honolulu but Mr. M. said he could not. His letter to the boys was very earnest and full of love for his country. He urged more of them to become ministers. He seems to fully realize his own importance and all that is expected of him. There are two more of the boys this year at the Oswego Training School.

Sunday, November 15—Yesterday was a very festive day with us. There was an afternoon tea at Mrs. Damon's chiefly for teachers so there were both ladies and gentlemen present. Good cake and coffee were served and as I know almost everyone I had a very pleasant time chatting with them. There was a very nice young boy there—Mrs. Thrum's son who has been in Hilo as a surveyor and who goes soon to Ann Arbor, his first time away from the islands. I had a good talk with him and spent much of the remaining time avoiding Mr. Carothers, a horrid new teacher at Kamehameha. He is a perfect giant of a man to look at but dreadfully weak and melancholy in spirit and just aching to hold on to any woman's apron strings who will be a little kind to him. He has bothered me enough. I hope I shant have to mention him again.

I had Bible class in the evening and after that our girls gave an entertainment.

We had them form a club of their own and get up their own programs with some very funny results. It is all to make them a little more independent. Last night, it was a little extra because some of the Kamehameha boys were here and a few of the neighbors were invited in. They sang some very pretty native songs. Maggie Powers read a paper in which she earnestly counseled the girls to make up their minds to marry good men and bring up their children in the nurture and admonition of the Lord. The brightest thing was a take-off on an every day event. Deborah Haina was dressed up as an old woman and she called in one of the girls to re-dust the table and found fault with her work in regular teacher style. Then one of the girls dressed as a Chinaman came trotting in with her baskets on a pole over her shoulders and tried to sell them bananas, strawberries and taro. The broken English and funny ways were quite true to life and brought down the house.

All my heart

November 22, 1891, Waikiki

My Lover,

Miss Harris has been really ill for the past two weeks and she really dreaded to make the effort to come but it has been a real pleasure to see her pick up just in two nights and a day. Her appetite came back yesterday and she ate  really heartily. We rode uptown last evening and laid in a new stock of provisions without going near the seminary however. I don't suppose you can realize what a relief that was. We had a little bath just at sunset time when it is so beautiful in the water. I think you would be surprised to see how long I can keep my feet from the bottom. I can do about three times as much as I could last year only I must confess that I don't accomplish much distance in my swimming. We shall go up tomorrow morning greatly rested by our stay down here.

How curious you will be! The Hawaiian minister to the U.S. died in New York a short time ago. His body will be brought down next steamer. His sister Mrs. Lewers lives next door here and lent me this ink. His brother Mr. J. O. Carter is now in Mr. William Castle's cottage and they sent us in coffee and biscuit this morning.

I found when I came uptown that Miss Pope and I were invited to spend Thanksgiving at the Waterhouses. I am pleased at the invitation but for many reasons I would like to be at home this Thanksgiving.

November 25—Tomorrow is Thanksgiving. I wish I knew for certain whether you were going down to Middlefield today. If you go you must write me how everyone appeared.

Yours,
Carrie

November 29, 1891, Kawaiahao Seminary

Dearest,

My Thanksgiving at Mrs. Waterhouses was very good. Dr. Hyde preached in the morning at our church and I did not care to hear him so I went to the English church for the first time. It seemed odd for them to celebrate an  American holiday but the English here are largely affected by the Americans.

The other guests at the Waterhouses's were the Hights, Ruth Hoppin and Miss Helen Kinney. Our dinner cards were tied with the "crimson and gold" and the table was strewn with red and yellow roses. It was a dinner of many

Oberlin College alumnae picnic, Kapiʻolani Park, Honolulu, August 1890. (L to R) Carrie Gilman, Ida May Pope, May Atherton, May Waterhouse, Helen Hoppin, Ruth Hoppin, Iretta Hight, Carrie P. Winter, and Carrie Castle. Cyanotype by Nellie Waterhouse.

courses and very finely served. Nellie took our pictures twice after dinner and I hope I may have some copies to send to you.

I must tell you a little about a day at Waikiki. Mrs. Allen is a wealthy half white and she was made trustee this year. It was the anniversary of the king's birthday and she invited the whole school to Waikiki providing buses for the conveyance. That was great fun to the girls and they laughed and sang all the way there and back. While there most of the girls were most of the time in the water. The luau was very fine and you would have been decidedly shocked I know to see me eating so heartily and with my fingers of the Poi and pork, the "luaued" chicken and fish and the coconut and sweet potato pudding. The chicken was cooked with taro leaves and flavored with coconut. I doubt if I ever enjoy any feasting more than I did those Hawaiian dishes. It sickened Miss Hadley and Miss Armstrong and they had to leave.

I think that I am getting more real comfort out of my school work now than ever before. I am quite happy while I am really teaching. I sometimes wonder now how I ever stood last year with my almost constant weariness and the almost constant meanness of the girls.

December 2—So you think I can just as well as not write for the papers! What faith you have in me! I did send a long piece to Mahlon about my trip and asked him to publish it but I have seen no result as yet.[6] No sir, I'm not going to give you any Christmas hint. With all Boston to pick from you ought to find something pretty, appropriate and inexpensive and I want to see what you can do. Besides that is part of the courting and I'm not going to do that for you. So you think you'll let me manage "some of your affairs"! Now, if I don't have a pretty lively finger in them all I think you will be surprised.

Well this is a Christmas letter and I will tell you about what I sent you. My chief present is the "Keekui nut" watch charm mounted in gold. I have one of the nuts in its natural state to show you when I return. You will see it is a very hard nut and they are polished with difficulty. The Hawaiians hold them in great admiration, almost veneration. A string of them, without gold, costs $15. Mrs. Carter, the favorite of the Queen is never seen without a lei of them, a present I suppose from her Majesty. Very few of the ornaments made from them for women are really pretty and to my mind the watch charms are the prettiest of anything and of course I wanted one in the family, so behold your charm.

I was in talking to Miss Harris this evening when I ought to have been writing to you. My only excuse is that there are several very absorbing affairs to talk and sympathize with each other in regard to the girls. A lot of them have been taking food and money from over the fence in the pasture—some girls, we don't know who, have been over the back-yard fence and off with the boys—one of the biggest girls rebelled, refused to obey Miss Pope till a threat of the police was made—went at Miss Harris as if to knock her down. Perhaps most dreadful of all, two of the little children who were here last year, gentle little things, have been half-killed by their cruel step-mother. I am thankful to say they are no longer with the beast. The family rank among the better class. While I have nothing directly to do with any of the cases, of course I sympathize.

December 7—I have one of my free days before me and will begin it by saying, "Good-morning" to my lover. We have only two more weeks of school this term. I have just been laying out my reviews and examinations.

By the first of next month I shall have another $100 which I should like to have earning good interest. It draws only 4 1/2 now. Miss Malone had money in a bank in Seattle that was earning 10% but when I asked her about it the other day she said I had best not put in there as the bottom was falling out of things there. I don't want to put it where I cannot draw it out at any time. I am very anxious to save all I can this year as it may be my only chance. Next year, I will have to go into my traveling expenses.

Remember that I love you all the time and I send you new, fresh love now for the Christmas time.

> Yours, Carrie

December 10, 1891

Dearest Carl,

I must have a letter begun to you so that it will be handy at any time to scribble on. I haven't much ambition about writing just now after getting off that immense Christmas mail. Our vacation duties have been given  out. Miss Hadley and I have the first Sunday, Monday, Tuesday, and Wednesday of January. Beside that I expect to be here, Christmas day and the day before. I know from last year what the vacation time here means so I do not expect too much. I am not going to try to sew any this time but to rest as much of the time as I can.

We have a big wedding Christmas eve and we are invited Christmas Day to take most of the girls up to Kamehameha where they will play croquet with the boys, have a late dinner with them and enjoy a "literary" in the evening. How I wish that some kind person would invite me to her home for my vacation and I only have to stay here for the time I am on duty; but I don't expect anything of the kind to happen.

I think it will be very nice though some time to celebrate Christmas in a home of our own. You will have some vacation anyway and I will be duty bound to make it a vacation. I can just imagine all my many preparations and the lovely home festival it will be, perhaps trying to make it a bright time for some outside foreign student and then for a few days after Christmas we would run away to the big city by ourselves enjoy some of the sights and festivities. That will be our winter pleasure but in the summer we will lie us away to the haunts of fern and flower. Do you call me a silly girl for all my fancyings? Or do you approve and take a part in them?

Saturday evening—Made two calls this afternoon. One was on Mrs. Allen the sister of Mr. C.R. Bishop whose wife was the last of the Kamehamehas.[7] Mrs. Allen lives in the brother's house. To my mind it is a much finer place than the palace, the grounds are so much more highly cultivated. You would admire as I do the wood finishings in the house—all in the native woods. The great sliding doors between the parlors of "koa" were a marvel of beauty. We sipped tea with Mrs. Allen and talked with her other callers, an officer and his wife from the *Pensacola* now in port. My second call was on a government school teacher whom I do not particularly admire.

I must tell you of a funny school incident. The girls got hold of your name, from letters I suppose and a week or two ago a wave of sentimentalism passed through the school with you for its theme. I couldn't pass a group of girls but I would hear "dear Charlie" "O Charlie" murmured. One day in my presence one of the girls asked Miss Hadley how to pronounce K-o-f-o-i-d. She made her spell it over and over but couldn't make anything out of it and told them they had made a mistake, there was no such word. In the presence of all this, I was calm and composed and never showed that I knew what it all meant. In their English work the girls would bring in again and again "Charlie" and in the most unexpected places I would find "C.K." inscribed. Well after a time, as I did nothing to feed the flame, the thing began to die out only that one girl in my room in the most stolid way would go to the board day after day and solemnly inscribe above her examples on English "C.K." Time passed and I always saw the beloved letters in the same place till not long ago I wanted a girl to sweep up some chalk in my school-room and scrub the spot after school.

I hadn't a single bad girl, but I looked up and saw "C.K." so I immediately scribbled on my notes "Punish C.K." As I wrote it I thought how you would look if you could see it. When I told Maria[8] what she was to do and that I thought she had kept up her nonsense long enough, you should have seen the expression on her face! She said, "Those are my father's letter." Well that was the end of "C.K." till yesterday. Maria put at the end of her work in the very finest and faintest of letters c.k. I am going to wait a day or two and then give her a little something to do to show her that I saw it.

December 13—It's Sunday now and I have been dreaming of you this afternoon—I long for you so much. How will you seem when I see you again? I think you will not seem different at all at first and then by-and-by, I will notice little things. I think you will be very lovingly critical of me, but you will be gentle with my deficiencies when you see that all my life is in you. Won't you, darling?

December 17—Tomorrow is the last day of school and in the evening we give a musical. There are 150 invitations out. The girls are to wear their new uniforms and they are a good ways from completion.[9] I had an extra sewing class last evening and expect to have another tonight to help all I can. I have had examinations every day this week and my girls are doing so well as to give me great pleasure. Two of them were up by moonlight one night studying.

One of my accomplishments came into play last evening. I was down in the kitchen and found one of my girls struggling with a chicken. She hadn't any idea how to dress it and Miss Harris had forgotten to show her. I rolled up my sleeves and gave her a lesson in Physiology and her gratitude was pleasant to see.

Miss Harris is teaching me how to make point lace. I am going to make some for my wedding dress as soon as I know a little more about it. It is very interesting.

> With love,
> Carrie

December 20, 1891, Waikiki

Dear Charlie,

This is the first Sunday of my vacation and you will see from the heading where I am. I shall have an amount to tell you, so must possess your dear soul in patience while I ramble on. My company down here now is Miss Appleton, Van Anglen and Hadley, but we shall be a varying company, changing

probably every day. I went up to church this morning and got a few needed supplies from the seminary. Well, let me see where I was. It was Thursday morning and Miss Pope had just brought me one letter from you and I could barely open it and read a few words when the bell rang. I had to pray that morning and there was nothing to do but seal up my letter and go into chapel with a big lump in my throat. At noon time I found some more letters and your longest one among them and I was very happy with them and laughed and cried too as I read them. That was my day off so I went up to Miss Hight's to rest and reread my letters but in the evening I held another sewing class to hasten on the uniforms.

Friday was an extremely busy day. I held my last examinations that morning in Arithmetic and Reading and in between times gave out dresses to finish and the blackboards to adorn with maps for the evening. Something like a 100 people came in the evening to hear the girls sing and see them in their new uniforms (dark blue calico trimmed with white braid). They sang as nicely as ever and everyone seemed pleased.

The Queen was there with quite a large party of followers. More interesting to me was the Honorable C.R. Bishop of whom I have heard so much but had never seen before.

Kawaiaha'o Female Seminary students in their handmade uniforms, December 1891.

Did I ever tell you about Gracie Cole? She was born down in Micronesia. Her father was a white man and her mother a half-cast. They were missionaries and Gracie was always brought up with the Missionaries. She was sent up here two years ago and taken into the Cooke Family where she lived as one of the family. This year they did not think they could keep her any longer so they sent her over to us paying enough so that she could have a little room by herself and eat at our table. She is a pretty nice girl I think and has no appearance of any dark blood in her.

> With very much love,
> Carrie

December 27, 1891, Kawaiahao Seminary

Dearest,

The girls tried a few tricks this morning about their work, but I soon discovered them and they good-naturedly dropped them. A Chinaman has just been here at the door, calling for "Mamma" to look at his eggs, strawberries, etc. We never patronize them on Sunday.

I must tell you something at once that I think very interesting. I was down at Waikiki just for the day yesterday for we had to come up in the evening. The Olesons were down too and we took lunch with them. I think I have told you how much I respect and admire Mr. Oleson, and how much he makes me think of you in his clear-cut features and quick Danish ways. Yesterday I made bold to ask him where he got his name. His father was a Dane, who was born on an island in the Baltic, came to the States when he was 18 and married a Massachusetts woman, a direct descendant of the Brewster family.

This last week the large mat which I had ordered last summer to be made on Molokai, through Emma Kane came. It is a beauty. Over 2 yards square and will last a long, long time. I shall have to send down $10 for it but I am glad indeed to have it. That is cheaper than I could get it here. I think it will look very well on the floor of that study that I want so much to furnish for you.

I must tell you all about our festivities now. Tuesday evening I came up town to attend the Christmas tree at the Central Union Church. It was a mildly interesting service. I went out to the Hights and spent the night with them taking Rose back down to Waikiki with me the next morning. What a long lovely restful day we had of it and a long night's quiet sleep too. We all came home Thursday morning to find the whole house upside down with preparations for the wedding. Some of the boys were down and were helping the girls decorate the chapel and they made it look very pretty with an abundance of palm leaves and "maile" wreaths. I took the parlors in charge and with many willing hands to help soon had it transformed into a bower of greenery. All day long the wedding gifts came in and such a fine lot as there was. If I got half as much I shall be surprised. So many things came from the patrons of the two schools and from both Williams and Katie's many friends.[10] I will mention just a few. A fine tea set from C.R. Bishop—two chairs from the Olesons, an etching from Mr. Richards, an easel and picture from the Dillinghams in whose employ William is—much silver from various sources etc. etc. At the ceremony we had a good many guests with many Kamehameha boys and their teachers, New Home girls and others. Katie made a very pretty bride. Mr. Oleson performed the ceremony. Cake and cream were served and by then it was all over. Everything was done for them that could be done and we all wish them well but I am sorry to say there was very little regret over Katie's departure. By her violent fits of temper, she has destroyed most all of the friends she ever had. William seems to be a very fine young man and they think so much of him out at Kamehameha, so it would be a great blow if the marriage were a failure.

Some gifts to the school that we all shared in were oranges from the Castles, fine raisins from Lewers and Cooke, and a handsome royal palm for our front yard from the Athertons. Christmas morning, one of the girls acted as Santa Claus and distributed to the girls their presents, ribbons to the older girls and balls to the children with a box of candy to each. At ten the girls went over to the church for their exercises there. I stayed through cogitating the story I was to tell in the evening. As a grand climax to the proceedings the people all received a little bag of candy and a fancy cake.

At 3:30 P.M. all but the littlest ones were aboard the tram car for Kamehameha and the event of the week to my mind, for I had one of the most enjoyable times since I have been in Honolulu. I did not get out in time to see the ball-game for I went out a little later in the carriage. Toward five the banquet was served. I wish you could have seen the sight. By that time the boys and girls were well mingled and sat alternately at the tables. Katie held the place of honor with posies about her plate. The dining-room was nicely decorated with ferns and they had a fine feast, luaued pig and poi, plum pudding, oranges and bananas, nuts and raisins, cake and ice-cream.

After the dinner we all went over to their new and elegant Bishop Hall for the exercises of the evening. The boys and girls sat just as they pleased and two or three times there were pauses in the program when they had a chance to visit. Our girls sang three times and Miss Appleton read a poem and I told a story but the most of the programme was in their hands. How they made the echoes ring with their singing! Mr. Oleson, Mr. Thompson and Miss Hight told some very good stories and we had many hearty laughs. At the end we all stood up and sang, "Hawaii Ponoi" with all our lungs. My story was one that "took" and they gave me some nice compliments. I found a little story in an old St. Nicholas that could easily be adapted to a personal story and I added to it a good lot of lies. Mrs. Thompson said I matched her husband for story-telling and I know that is her highest praise. Someone said I was the best story-teller in Honolulu and Mrs. Oleson was extremely appreciative. The children all wanted to know if it was true. Another thing that pleased me was to have one of their oldest and best boys come and take a seat by me.

You ridiculous boy, you had better be good and drop your evil habits. Learn to eschew cider. You know you can never have any in your house after I come. We ought to have very nice Sundays when we are together. Don't you think it would be nice for us to do something for others on that day? It would be nice if we could teach in some Sunday school in the forenoon. Then we would enjoy our home in the afternoon and the early evening, all the more.

January 6, 1892, Kawaiahao

My Carl,

I think we are fairly under way. My school room work is very interesting. The girls are very good. They work like little beavers. I have been able to put the two classes together in Geography and English and that gives me  more time for the Reading, Writing and Spelling. I have felt justified in silencing them while I gave them some idea of Arithmetic, Geography and some practice in English. There is nobody to say whether my girls have done well or not or to say whether I have accomplished anything or not but I am just as proud as a peacock over them and you may always expect to hear me boasting of them. I shall be glad enough to drop all the other work but I do hate to have those girls have another teacher. Please may I bring them home with me? There are only 32.

January 8—I am going to sleep down in the hospital tonight and take care of our sick girl. I don't expect to sleep any for she takes medicines every hour besides occasional nourishment and a change of poultices. She is a little girl of about 12 and we suppose she is dying of consumption. Miss Pope and Miss Harris have taken care of her all through the week and I offered to take tonight because I have no school tomorrow. Miss Pope wrote to their friends some time ago but the inter island service has been very poor of late owing to bad storms. We hope the father will come Tuesday when the *Kinau* comes in.

I have just been up in my attic looking through all the trunks of the girls for $1.75 Maggie Powers has lost. It makes me vexed to have the girls lose their money. Miss Pope will always take care of it for them; but they want it where they can spend it. Maggie had $25 from her leper brother on Molokai for a Christmas gift. It's nearly gone now. I wonder how he earns money.

I am very tired for you this evening. I was fancying this evening as I sat on the back verandah watching the girls how it would seem to have you there too and how strange the scene, now so natural to me, would seem to you.

Yesterday Miss Pope and I called on Mrs. Judge McCully and Miss Whittier, the principal of the Hawaii girl's school. She is staying at the Hyde's and we stayed to dinner. We had a good time, a good dinner, but Dr. Hyde is certainly a most peculiar man.

We were much disappointed this morning because the sick girl's father did not come nor any word from him. The doctor thinks the child is no better, even a little weaker. There is no knowing how long she will have to be nursed. It is very hard on Miss Harris and Miss Pope.

Tuesday—A China steamer stopped here but she made no landing nor any stay because there was small pox on board and I presume she will be quarantined at the Coast. It was only Saturday that a Japanese vessel came in with over a 1000 laborers for the plantations and two cases of small-pox were discovered on board. The whole company is quarantined on an island in the harbor. Yesterday there was considerable excitement about it down town and Dr. McWayne did what he had been intending to do for some time—vaccinate the girls. It was quite a task for one afternoon but he accomplished it.

Meetings have been continued this week especially for the young. Miss Harris and I go down with my girls tonight. They are all delighted because Mr. Oleson leads the meeting and they think the boys will be there. By the way our matrimonial interests are booming. Last evening two men came here—knowing nothing of each other—to ask for girls. The first had no choice. He simply wanted a good wife. It's all very funny but I assure you quite serious.

I am writing these last few words by moonlight after coming home. It is a wonderful night. I would like to stay up and write to you but I must not for tomorrow, I will be out of sorts. So good-night, my lover. That same beautiful moon has looked or will look on you tonight. Bear him my love, sweet moon!

Jan. 13—I am tired and fractious this noon. I don't want to lie down or read or work. I have not been so fretted all this term. This Saturday I am off duty and I do wish I had a good place to go to. Perhaps the mail will come in promptly tomorrow and so aid and refresh me.

Do you remember, dearie, how you used to keep me in order. You couldn't bear to have me make faces, or do and say rude things to anybody because it always seemed just as if I did them to you. I am having a lesson on the benefits of that daily before my eyes. Miss Harris is all the time doing such horrid little things, getting heated over trifles and being rude, without sufficient excuse and there is no one who loves her enough to have the right to stop her. She sometimes is very miserable over it herself. I told her once when she half appealed to me that she needed a good lover. I am afraid lots of little new faults have sprung up like weeds in me since I have been away from my kind one. I wonder if you will put me into shape again and watch me carefully when I come again.

I was in some stupid meeting last week and I spent the hour very happily in planning out a very pretty wedding for myself. I am not going to tell you about it because it will be such fun to place all its details together. It's just an amusement I have. Do you think it would be very foolish for me to wear a veil? I think I would like too. I know I would be old but I don't look so now. One of my girls said yesterday, "Miss Winter, I'm always wanting to touch your cheek."

Evening—I am in sitting with Maria White. We wanted some of the girls to go down to Central Union to attend the last of the meetings to be held. Last night's meeting was such a good one. Mr. Oleson seemed to talk especially to our girls and he put the acceptance of Christ in such a simple and plain fashion to them. I talked to my girls some this morning, as best I could.

Miss Pope heard the other day that the Queen wished to put 20 new girls in here. We are glad of her interest and we would like the money but we couldn't possibly find room for them. Miss Pope has sent word that 6 more can come in but I don't know what we can do with them.

I send you this time one of the pictures Miss Appleton has taken of my

Carrie P. Winter in the back of her classroom, Kawaiahaʻo Female Seminary, January 1891. Annie Wong (bottom right), Violet Lima to her left, and behind her Maile Kapali. Photo by Lilla Estelle Appleton.

room. Perhaps you can soak it in water and get the lines out and mount it. I have another in my collection. Do you see little Annie Wong, a little saint, deformed but bright and quick? Beside her is pretty Violet Lima and right behind her Malie Kapali who can't keep still two minutes, has something to say on every subject and is quite likeable and amusing. I'll tell you about them all some time. You must tell me what you think of my girls.

> Carrie

January 15, 1892, Kawaiahao Seminary

Dear Charlie,

I am in the cottage again this evening with Maria and expect to stay here all night. Her father came this morning and seemed quite grief stricken but I cannot reconcile with that the fact that he soon went away and has  not been here all day since. One would have naturally thought that he would have wished to stay and take care of her today. The only solution in my mind is that he went off to see "Kahunas" and they loving drink, as they do, got him to drinking. Perhaps they are curing her from a distance. Isn't it strange, dear?

This afternoon two men with tame bears came and had them perform in our back-yard, greatly to the delight of our girls. I was on duty and improved all my spare minutes in giving extra work to my long list of "punish girls," girls whose clothing I had picked up, scattered about in the Dormitory and consigned to my box.

Yesterday was my afternoon off and I will tell you how I spent it. I went to the feed store and paid $3 for a bale of hay. I feed Miss Brewer's horse. I went to the bank and deposited some money there. My interest for the year was $.99. I have $96 there now. I had to draw out some to pay for my Hawaiian mat so I haven't quite the $100 I expected. I wanted to see Mr. Smith about the $100 I have with him as he was to report after January 1, but he is on another island now.

I went to the library and drew, what do you think, "Darwin's Descent of Man" and I am finding it extremely interesting. Much more so than Morley's "Voltaire" that I have just finished. Morley himself says such slighting, bitter things about the Bible. I really believe most of what Darwin says, but when he comes to consider the higher nature of man he seems to me to make mistakes in not defining terms and he seems to slide over that which is of the most importance to man—the power of abstract idea—and to recognize no difference in kind but only in degree to confound intellect and sensibility and not to recognize will at all. He says distinctly in one place that we give no more credit to the man who performs a right action against his natural impulses than we do to the man who does the same good deed simply following impulse. We were certainly not so taught in Oberlin. The first is morally meritorious and the second is not. He scores down the finale and makes your pleasure in receiving this either an evolution of the monkey who struts about in high feather to attract the attention of the female monkey whose fur he admires. However I enjoy it and after I got home read 80 pages. I know you will make fun of me for reading Darwin but you know I have a taste that can easily be developed for the philosophical.

1 o'clock a.m. Poor little thing. I feel so sorry for her. She has not been asleep yet and now she is sitting up for a change. She likes to have the light in the room. She seems to have some trouble in breathing and sitting up seems to relieve her. Her cough is very hard and dry. I have dozed a little but have not really been asleep for I know she was uncomfortable and heard her heavy breathing. I went off in my fancy to you once or twice but had to come back to Maria. She has to have medicine only once in three hours but her suffering makes it as hard as if I had to be up every hour. Perhaps she will go to sleep soon.

KAUMAKAPILI CHURCH.

ORGAN CONCERT

BY

MR. WRAY TAYLOR, F. C. C. G.

In Honor of the Accession of Her Majesty Queen Liliuokalani.

Thursday Evening, January 28, 1892.

PROGRAMME.

March . . . . Athalie . . . . *Mendelssohn*

Andante in F . . . . *Wely*
MR. WRAY TAYLOR.

Trio . . . . The Swallows . . . . *Leslie*

Trio . . . . Sailor's Song . . . . *Hatton*
KAWAIAHAO SEMINARY CHORUS.

Selections on the Hand Bells by Pupils of Mr. C. H. White.

Song . . . . Good Night . . . . *Abt*
MISS KULAMANU WARD.

Concert Fantasia . . . . *Hesse*
MR. WRAY TAYLOR.

Song . . . . Once Again . . . . *Sullivan*
HON. C. P. IAUKEA.

Selections on the Hand Bells by Pupils of Mr. C. H. White.

Quartette . . . . Thank the Creator . . . . *Flemming*

Quartette . . . . Chorus of Angels . . . . *Costa*
KAWAIAHAO SEMINARY CHORUS.

Air . . . . Aloha Oe . . . . *Her Majesty*

Larghetto . . . . *Batiste*
MR. WRAY TAYLOR.

Chorus . . . . The Heavens are Telling . . . . *Haydn*
KAWAIAHAO CHURCH CHOIR

HAWAII PONOI.

Kaumakapili Church organ concert program, January 28, 1892.

Sunday last evening I spent in reading aloud to Retta and Rose from "Descent of Man" and they were as much interested as I was. It is a very fascinating book. I learned one very interesting fact and one of great importance to me. It was in the Chapter where the arguments are collected both pro and con for placing the different races of men as different species and one argument is that the parasites that infect different races are plainly different species and as an example he tells of a sea captain in the Pacific who vouched for the fact that some Sandwich Island sailors who were swarming with lice gave some to the white sailors but that they did not live in their heads longer than two or three days. I am convinced of the truth of the fact because we teachers do not take them from the girls. Would you like to have me preserve a few in alcohol for you?

Jan. 20—Mahlon sent my letter to the news-paper but has not yet seen it in print. He says if I will take notes and write a book when I come home he will publish it, or rather find a publisher for it. I see it in your eye. I shall have to write a book. I think I would like to if I could do it when I was not tired.

NOTES

1. The matron was responsible for overseeing all housekeeping work at the seminary and for teaching the students to cook, according to Lilla Estelle Appleton's essay "Kawaiahao Seminary," presented to HMCS in 1888. Appleton Papers, Oberlin College Archives.

2. William Bramwell Powell, *How to See, or, First Steps in the Expression of Thought* (Couperthwait and Company, 1886).

3. The *Hawaiian Gazette* (September 22, 1891, p. 7) reported that the stereopticon exhibition by Ben Hogan at Kawaiaha'o Church was well attended and about two hundred views were shown. Mr. Hogan's remarks were translated by W. R. Castle: "As each picture" of a Hawaiian scene "was flashed on the screen, voices from all parts of the house called out the name of the familiar locality."

4. Sereno E. Bishop, "The Hawaiian Queen and her Kingdom," *Review of Reviews* (1891, pp. 146–163).

5. The present is for her younger sister, Julia Flora Winter.

6. Carrie sent several articles to her brother, Mahlon Alpheus Winter, but he was successful in getting only one published, "An American Girl in the Hawaiian Islands," which appeared in *Southern Magazine* (November 1892).

7. Mrs. Cordelia Bishop Allen was a first cousin of C. R. Bishop, not his sister.

8. Maria Kaaumoa.

9. The *Hawaiian Gazette* (September 17, 1891, p. 5) reported, "The trustees of

Kawaiahao Seminary have decided to put the girls in uniform. The object is to check extravagance in dress which was becoming a serious nuisance. One girl last term had seven hats."

10. Katherine (Katy, Kate) Clarke of Kawaiaha'o Female Seminary married William Rathburn of Kamehameha School on December 24, 1891.

8

Politics and Punishment
February 2–April 10, 1892

February 2, 1892, Kawaiahao Seminary

Dearest Carl,

I have a number of interesting things to write you about and if you please my dear, I'll begin on politics. They are great fun here. Once in two years there is an election here and the last one took place last Wednesday. Each  island is divided into sections which send one representative to the legislature. There are 8 sections on this island and I don't know about the others. Certain 6 year, 4 year, and 2 year nobles were also to be elected. Well for months the "Liberals" have had their candidates out and have been stumping all the islands. Their leaders are R. W. Wilcox, the leader of the "Revolution of 1889." Bush, a 7th Day Adventist and Ashford, in the employ of the Canadians and a regular fraud of a man who harangues the natives, abusing the "pious missionaries." I must try and find one of his speeches to send you. They are all angry at the Queen because she will not treat with them and their avowed purpose is to call a convention to change the constitution—depose the Queen, found a republic—all with this precious trio at the head.

The other issue is the new treaty with the U.S. Now it's absolutely essential to the business interest of the island to have the treaty. Since the McKinley bill[1] most of the plantations are running at a loss and every where there is great embarrassment. It really is distressing and its going to be worse unless they get the treaty. But—to get that treaty they have to let the U.S. have Pearl Harbor for a naval station. That's pat and its right too. But these fellows work on the feelings of the natives and that means the beginning of their loss of independence and that only the "rich missionaries" have anything to gain thereby. Well, the country has just been deluged with this kind of talk. Various opposition tickets were put up and a certain extent of speech making on the National Reform side. Thursday morning we had the results for this island—the national Reform Nobles elected but of the Representatives all Liberal except one—Bush, Wilcox, Ashford all in!!

This is the worst island and they were hoping for help from the other islands. Some of the steamers came in yesterday and at the last reports, the Liberals had a majority of one in the House of R's with several districts yet to hear from. I think tomorrow we will know the full result. Anyway we may expect some lively times in the Legislature and perhaps outside. You are not to feel any alarm for the *Pensacola* will stay here and of course more will come if necessary.

I held an election in my room Tuesday and like the rest my girls, elected a majority of Liberals. The next day I gave the girls a stump speech and I really believe I opened their eyes to some things. They had elected Ashford. They were sure they didn't want the U.S. to have Pearl Harbor. I asked how many girls Mr. Ashford supported in our school. I told them how a number of people had given us word that they could not support the girls next year and how Cousin's Society had cut us down 1/2 and all on account of the low price of sugar. I drew some strong conclusions, carried my audience with me and made them at last quite enthusiastic for National Reform Party. Don't you see how very interesting all this is? It's so much plainer and simpler than the Tariff. You're quite sure here which is the right and which is the wrong side, so I prefer Hawaiian politics.

Friday afternoon the school visited the *Pensacola.* Most of the girls went and all the teachers but Miss Appleton and myself. It was my day on duty and I did not care to go anyway because I was still tired from my ride of the day before and couldn't bear to think of a long walk in the sun with a procession of girls. They all seemed to enjoy it immensely and had long stories to tell me when they got home. Miss Hadley made a goose of herself with one of the officers and that interested the girls.

While they were gone, something happened to me, very funny and very horrid. That atrocious Mr. Carothers came with his carriage and asked me to go riding. Of course I had a good excuse for not going but as he went down the steps he turned to say, "Perhaps some other time," and I who lacked the moral courage to step out and say, "No, Mr. Carothers, I won't under any circumstances ride with you," murmured an ambiguous, "Thank you" and went back into the house to gnash my teeth with rage. The fact is, my dear, you ought to be here to squelch that young man for me, to protect me, though if you were here I presume you would make me do it and stand back and enjoy it. I remember what perfect delight you took in watching that poor Mr. Griffiths that I once had to refuse to attend a lecture with. The others think it is great fun and I think it's funny but horrid too. You can't conceive what a great big namby-pamby he is. I can imagine your glee over all this. I'll stop for the present now with "aloha nui."

Tuesday evening—I am so tired tonight that I must come to you and make my little plaint. It began this morning with company that did not find me time for my quiet 15 minutes before class when I pray and read my Bible and collect myself for the day. Then every single girl in my room failed in one or more lessons and I made them make these up which kept me in the class room from 9 till 3:30 except 1/2 hour for dinner. I had a little ride with Miss Van Anglen which helped me out—after supper came gymnastics and more recitations and I even had a class in my room after study-hour. It has rained all day and I fear we cannot go to Palolo. Such a day as this makes long very much for that dear home and "my rest."

We have just received our invitations to Mr. and Mrs. Hosmer's reception which takes place Friday night from 8 to 11. I think I can wear my white silk to that.

Your examinations must be over. I hope they went well. I hope too that you are not all tired out. I fear you are and that you are sadly in need of me to come and rest you, but be patient, dear. I'll come soon and I love you now, and think of you, and when I pray for myself in the morning, I pray for you too. I am not too busy to plan and fancy for the future. I am very contented. I trust you are too, dearest, and you must not worry at all.

Carrie

February 16, 1892

Dear Carl,

Now I will tell you something that I think will please you. I wrote you of the young lady, Miss Needham, who visited my school last week—well, she came another day and spent the whole forenoon in my room. She had  Miss Kinney with her and this morning they came again and spent all the time they had in my room and when they went away, Miss Needham told Miss Pope that it was simply wonderful, the work I got out of those girls and she didn't see how I did it. Now she is an older teacher than I and I think has had Normal training so I am way, way up. It is the first time any such thing has happened and I think Miss Pope was as much pleased as I. I think you ought to kiss me for that. Those girls are pretty nice anyway. Emma Ai asked me the other day when I was going home and I told her sometime next year and she said, "I don't want you to go. You are the best teacher of all. I like you."

Feb. 17—Just a few words. I have my report from Mr. Smith about my money. It has gained $3.50 since June. He said he could have done much better with it if it had been a little larger. I think that is pretty good. It is much better than the bank. I am told that Mr. W.R. Castle invests money. I am going to ask him if he invests small sums for teachers.

Feb.18—Miss Hadley had to whip 6 or 8 girls after her study hour last night. She has very little control over the girls. They say very saucy things to her and she doesn't seem to mind.

Sunday—I am just up from a good, sound nap. My domain is as quiet as sleep can make it, but I think you would smile if you could see my room. Deborah Haina, Lucy Leleo and Maggie Powers are stretched out across half of it, in their blue and white uniforms and beneath their heads they have stretched the papers I gave them to read. Yet they have been calmly sleeping all the afternoon. You will want to know their offense. On Sunday morning, the rising-bell does not ring till 6:30 but my girls were making a hubbub long before that. I went in and gave them a settling—everyone to her own bed and forbad whispering till the bell rang and told them I should not come in to devotions this morning but they were to have them, themselves. I often do this Sunday morning for my own selfish ease. But when the bell rang at 7, I was up and dressed and saw the crowd go down stairs. I went down too, to speak to Miss Harris in the kitchen and then came back to my dormitory and found these three ladies just rising from their couches, still clad in the robes of night. I immediately invited them to pass the day with me and they accepted the invitation.

This forenoon we had a funny time. We have a horrid lump of a girl here named Hannah Opeka, a thief, a liar, and a sneak. Miss Pope is off on her monthly rest but before she left she put Hannah in a closet for some mischief. This morning the closet was wanted for something else and Miss Harris told her to go to the office intending to put her somewhere else after the girls were gone to Sunday school. Well, the whole school was out in the front yard ready for their start. Hannah thought she saw her chance, and down she dashed through the back yard and pasture. I saw her and called after her then rushed down stairs and squeezed Miss Harris's hand and down we sped after her but we took a wrong turn and lost her in the net-work of native houses and lanes. Meanwhile some one was there and telephoned and off Miss Appleton started in the carriage. She found her couched and whining in a corner at her home. She wouldn't come back and the whole forenoon was a maze of telephoning and cross-telephoning till noon time brought the relatives back with the girl in tow—her pocket full of pea-nuts. She tried to make terms to avoid punishment but did not succeed and is now reposing in the closet under lock and key where she will stay till she is tame enough for a whipping and I hope after that that, she will be sent home. Life certainly has spice in it here.

I wish you could see the little glimpse I have out of my window. Off in a slanting direction the trees open so as to form a regular vista. That gives me a peep across a few back-yards with their young banana trees and papayas. One porch thrusts itself into view, a perfect bower because of its luxuriant orange-flowered vines—next in my range comes the full view of a native home—the men and women lounging on its verandah and then further on and higher up, a great tree covered and aflame with a most magnificent view—just one mass of purple and red up to the sky stands the outline of the distant mountains.

Feb. 25—Retta sent down a note inviting Miss Pope and me to dinner so we mounted our horses and sped up to Kamehameha. We had such a good time. After dinner we sat up on the balcony of their new stone recitation hall and watched a most glorious sun-set to the music of the glee songs of the chorus who were practicing within.

Sunday, Feb. 25—That girl who was sick and with whom we had to be up at nights for died at her house.[2]

It came on me as a beautiful surprise that you were thinking of and planning for our honeymoon. I love to have you take the whole charge of that. Then I am sure it will be fine. Dear, dear Charlie, I do love you so much.

    Carrie

March 6, 1892, Kawaiahao

Dearest,

Sometimes I get a little sad and think something dreadful will surely happen in another long year and I look in the glass and think how old and homely I am growing. But then my vanity comes to the front and I  say I shant look much worn surely in June than I would be in February.

My girls all did much good work in the school-room except Eunice Puni who took a notion not to learn her lesson but to get through by cheating and use her fine time to write letters, so I excused her from school for a couple of days and kept her at work. What a lot she did do! She washed all the hospital blankets, cleaned out the drains, pulled weeds in the pasture, washed down all the walls of my dormitory worked the 3/4 toilet bags and then said she would like to go to school again and she studied like a little trooper when she got back, too. Miss Harris spent one morning in my school-room and seemed to like it very much. My girls were a little inclined to show off and Maria Kaaumoa took her usual way, for when I came around to her English work on the board to correct, there was "C.K." as big as life. It was a surprise to both Miss Harris and myself and we nearly laughed aloud. You will be pleased to know that for that, Maria mounted a step-ladder and scrubbed down the four walls of my schoolroom.

I must tell you a story of the Kamehameha boys which I think is very good. Retta told it to me from the account of one of the boys who took part in it. Some of the older boys went around the island during their last vacation to give concerts—but one of the last events before they left was a talk some man gave out there about superstition referring specifically to the other side of the island. It so stirred the boys that they decided to undertake some missionary work along with their concert-giving. They camped out the first night and early in the morning gathered in a little valley to have a little meeting by themselves. All around were mountains and a brook run through the valley. They sang, "Jesus lover of my Soul" and other songs and it seemed to them their voices had never sounded so sweetly. Then as they looked at one another they found tears in their eyes and soon they all turned toward the mountains and were all still. After a while they prayed and it seemed to them that they were filled with love not for their parents or friends, but a different kind. They went on till they came to a valley where they were told was a fish-god. They found it, a large carved stone, surrounded by gifts of awa and poi and leis. Someone had told them it was death to touch this or jump over it. They all jumped over it and then pulled it down, carried it to the sea and broke it in pieces and threw it in. The next day which was Sunday they spent in the little village. The people flocked to the church to see them and to tell them they would die, but they talked to and told them it was not true and they ought not to believe such things, that it made God angry, etc. In the evening they held another service which more people attended than the pastor had ever seen in the church before.

Yesterday the pleasantest event of the week happened for I was invited to lunch at Mrs. Jordan's. She lives a long way off up Nuuanu Valley. As the lunch hour drew near it brought with it Mr. & Mrs. Babb, Miss Malone, Ruth Hoppin and Miss Pinder. I must tell you of the nice thing Mrs. Babb said. She met me with much cordiality and said if she had been wishing for some other teacher to be there, she would have said "Miss Winter" that both she and her husband had a warm place in their hearts for me. Wasn't that nice of her? I like them very much. They are plain quiet people from Maine but haven't seen a great deal of the world—a little provincial but more the warm for that.

Monday—I was thinking last night that I did need you so much to have a good talk with. I think if I could meet you somewhere on the sly for half an hour—and have you tell me to cheer up and keep interested in my work and still try to gain out of it for myself and best of all take me in your arms for a little while and show me that we were still one spirit of time and distance—it seems as if it would be much easier to go on for the 1 year, 3 months still before me here.

> Very much love my dearest,
> Carrie

March 13, 1892, Oahu College, Punahou

Dear Carl,

Can you make out from the heading just where I am? I wonder if I have ever really made clear to you about this place. This is the first time I ever came here to visit and I am the guest of Miss Margaret Brewer whom I have  mentioned to you many times but I will outline the principal facts in regard to her right here. She is principal of the preparatory school located down in the city. For 4 1/2 years she was a teacher in Kawaiahao. She boarded with us last fall when her ankle was sprained. It was her horse I liked and gave a sore back to and tended (thankful to say it didn't ruin it). She is a person of very taking appearance, shrewd, ambitious, and biased toward common-sense. I have a very curious feeling toward her. I have a strong inclination to like her unreservedly, without suspicion or reserve as you know I like to feel towards people. Something about the situation checks me. Something tells me it is simply the nonsense and the feeling that will grow up among all the people interested in a school like ours—wire-pulling, circumlocution, etc. That's one of the bothers of this place and I suppose every place. If we are all good and straight forward—why don't we believe it of each other? I have no answer for this "dilemma."

And now I must give you a good full account of yesterday's doings. It was our riding-party up "Manoa." There were 14 of us—5 from Kamehameha—5 from here—Carrie Gilman, Mr. Walsh, Miss Kinney and myself. I had come up here the night before. We got off somewhere between nine and ten and my horse the first thing started for home. I pulled her around with the only result of having her turn in a circle and prance and rear if I whipped her. The others stood looking on with little screams from the ladies. I never could have got her started, having no spur, in the right direction, had not our red headed friend Mr. Anderson, taken her by the bit and dragged her on for a piece. Then she was all right. She is a fine horse and likes to fly over the ground and is not easy unless she is at the head of such a cavalcade. To get her over her tricks I took a long gallop down the road ahead of the others.

I suppose that was really a challenge to Mr. Walsh on his fine horse and in a few minutes he came pounding after me and we had a long conversation. I must tell you a little of him. He is a self-made man, a lawyer, worth a million, a widower and looking for a wife. There are some good points about him but still I think he would be very distasteful to me but for one thing. I think Miss Pope has quite a little leaning toward him. It seems she met him last summer at Mr. Castle's and I believe if he would pay attention to her she would be glad of it. I know she would like to marry. It seems a little horrible to me that she should fancy such a man, but when a woman is towards 30 she isn't so particular as when she is 20. But anyway I am willing to do all I can to throw them together and next Saturday they both go on a riding-party together.

He paid me a very blunt compliment. You see I had been bouncing around at a great rate and was as red as a wash-woman and Mr. Walsh said, "I hope you won't think me rude, but that color is very becoming, you have a beautiful complexion" and my first thought was "if that is so, I wish my Charlie were here now to see me and take delight in me." But I wish so afterward he had not said it for it made me uncomfortable and vain for the rest of the day.

Saturday, Mch 20—I must record a few of the events of the past week. It has been a hard one for me for I did not get much rest over Sunday. I will have to own up that I was very cross and irritable in the school room though it seemed to me at the time that the girls had taken an especially mean spell. Wednesday afternoon we took a half holiday one that had long been due the girls. Miss Armstrong's girls had been acting up so she would not allow one of them to go. Miss Pope marshaled the company on horse back and we took the long walk down to Kalia, through the old coconut plantation. There was a fine breeze that day so the walk was not hard. I think I have told you of this place before. It is a long, flat, rocky stretch almost out to the reef and a great place for the girls to catch crabs, shrimps, and tiny fish which are all devoured as soon as caught. On the shore there is nothing as far as one can see but a single native hut and a tangle of Algarroba trees.

Such a funny thing happened! A white man had gone down there to bath, leaving his clothes out from shore on a rock. He chose just the spot we came to. We had been there a long time and all the other teachers had gone ashore. I was out paddling with the girls—when the absurdity of the thing came over us all at once. The poor fellow hadn't a thing on and was trying to crawl up to his clothes in the center of 40 or 50 girls. Such a tangle as the girls set up! Meanwhile the tide was coming in and wetting all his things and his shoes were floating out to sea. I had the girls gather them up and I had one of them take a garment out to the poor fellow. I suppose he thought he was in a se-cluded spot when he went in, and didn't expect a whole female seminary down upon him.

Thursday night a state ball was given. I wanted to go very much out of cu-riosity and at first some of us thought we would go as everybody in town seemed to be going but when Miss Pope found that one of the girls, Alice Lewis, wanted to go she decided to stay home and I stayed because Miss Appleton expressed her opinion very strongly about it and I didn't care to give any one a chance to say mean things about me. If I had had you here for an escort I think I should have teased you hard to take me unless it had been on Alice Lewis' account for the foolish girl went in spite of Miss Pope's request that she should not do so and paraded around with one of the worst men in town till after one o'clock. She is in deep disgrace now and it may end in her leaving.

Wednesday, Mch. 23—Yesterday the Mail came in bringing me a business letter from Mahlon. He has recently become interested in a new *Southern Magazine* and has already given the publisher permission to announce that during the year there will be a series of articles by "An American Girl in the Sandwich Islands," and he would like the first article from me at once—drop-ping him a line as to how soon he may expect it. He doesn't know if I can get any pay for the article. I am not to expect any. It is to equal in length some 8 to 10 magazine pages! What do you think of that?

Sunday, Mch. 27—this is the Sunday after the concert. It was very much like the one of last year, only in my opinion not so good and there have been so many things of late and last night was so showery that we didn't have a crowded house but it was a good one. I am afraid we did not clear over $250. We made nearly $400 last year but our expenses were larger this year. Miss Patch had to have $25. We are not in a very good condition financially although we have such a full school. Miss Pope tells me there are projects afoot for putting the school under the Kamehameha trustees so that we may have the use of some of that money intended as much for a girl's school as a boy's school. It would be a good thing and I wish that our salaries might be raised.

Mr. Berger came over home with us last evening and partook of light refreshments with us. He stayed and talked till 11 o'clock. He has been bandmaster here 20 yrs and we got him to telling of his experiences with the natives—with the Queen and with King Kalakaua. He knows the natives thoroughly and his experiences with those grown men are of the same kind as those we have with the girls. We asked him how he managed them and he said he "licked" them.

Afternoon—We had a very long service this morning. Mr. Bingham gave the sermon. He and his wife were for many years missionaries in Micronesia but for the last 10 yrs they have lived here and having been making a translation of the Bible into the language was completed 2 years ago and the time since then has been spent in making corrections and carefully looking it all over. He showed us the manuscript and the box in which it is to be carried. He and his wife go Tuesday to take it to New York. It is 25 years since they have been back East and it seems to them a great undertaking. I shouldn't wonder if I should chance to see them there, for it is not likely they will return here before '94. It is a privilege to have known them.

I am in hopes of receiving from Mr. Gulick on Maui an invitation to join the camping party he is getting up in honor of the Stiles girls to visit the volcanoe on Hawaii. Irene has already written me of how much she would like to have me go but did not feel free to ask. Last week he wrote down asking Miss Brewer and some others from Punahou to go. None of them can go but without telling me, she has written and suggested that I go. It would be a wonderful opportunity for Mr. Gulick knows all about Hawaii and has friends. No I shall go if I get a chance. What do you say to it, dear?

There was such a sad thing in church this morning. The Bowens baby was baptized. Right in front of us sat Mrs. Charles Cooke who only a few weeks ago lost the little girl of her twins. She has only just begun to go out and the

Third Annual Concert

OF

KAWAIAHAO SEMINARY

→Assisted by the "Royal Hawaiian Orchestra."←

AT

Kawaiahao Church, Saturday, March 26, '92

7:30 O'CLOCK P. M.

PROGRAMME—PART I.

1. Overture........"Enchantment"............._Herman_
2. Chorus.. ...."A Welcome, We Sing "........._Wiener_
   KAWAIAHAO SEMINARY.
3. Gavotte....... "Queen's Jubilee"..............
   Her Majesty Queen Liliuokalani
4. Solo............." My Queen"..........._Blumenthal_
   HON. PAUL ISENBERG.
5. "The Dearest Spot on Earth to me" .. .._Benedict_
   PUPILS OF THE FIRST CHORAL CLASS.
6. Solo and Quartette ...." Kanani o ka Pakipika"
   KAWAIAHAO SEMINARY.
(Words composed by Mrs. A. A. Haalelea ; music by Naone.)

PART II.

7. Chorus.................... " Full and Harmonious "
   (Arranged from Gibby La Cornemuse.)
   KAWAIAHAO SEMINARY.
8. Duet........"Onward, Bonny Boat " ...._Kucken_
   PUPILS OF FIRST CHORAL CLASS.
9. " Egyptian Midnight Parade"............... _Isenenman_
   ROYAL HAWAIIAN ORCHESTRA.
10. Chorus............. ...." Song of the Hop-pickers"
    KAWAIAHAO SEMINARY.
11. Duet and Chorus.." Puahi a ka Lani".._Queen Liliuokalani_
    KAWAIAHAO SEMINARY.
12. Solo. ....." Burst, ye Apple Blossoms".._Stephen Emory_
    MISS MAY C. ATHERTON.
13. Waltz Trio..."O'er Blooming Meadows"........_Wekerlin_
    KAWAIAHAO SEMINARY.
    HAWAII PONOI.

The Audience is respectfully requested to remain until the conclusion of the Concert.

E oluolu ke anaina e noho a hiki i ka pau pono ana o na hana.

The Fine Kimball Piano is kindly loaned for the occasion by H. H. Williams & Co.

Third annual concert program, March 26, 1892.

sight so unexpected, quite overcame her and it was only after a long struggle that she retained her composure. Mr. Cooke's position touched me so much. He was at the other end of the seat with the two boys between but I could see it was very hard for him not to be able to go to his wife to comfort her. He wanted to very much.

Write me of everything that befalls you, my Carl.
Carrie

March 30, 1892, Kawaiahao Seminary

Dear Charlie,

I am very glad now that I did not wind up my last letter by telling you about the Revolution for you would have been in a panic for two weeks and now you can linger with me over the whole absurd thing. You must know  that the whole country is in a very mixed condition. The only reason I don't write you an intelligent account of affairs is because the rumors are very vague.

The Bush and Wilcox party in secret meetings and the public try to stir up the natives against the government. Since the U.S. has refused a treaty with us the planters are vigorously talking "annexation" and indeed that seems the only solution to the financial difficulties because then they could claim a bounty on their sugar. But the rumors of war became so threatening that Sunday night a barricade of sand-bags—three deep was placed all around the palace, only to be removed Monday night.

Tuesday the *Australia* was to leave with many of the most important business men aboard evidently going up in the interests of the sugar business. The Revolutionists thought it was a good time to make a demonstration so that the disturbance could be reported in the U.S.—for what purpose I don't exactly see—except to perhaps put a stop to annexation.

Many people really believed that the palace would be fired upon Monday night. The country is really in a very curious position and with so much ignorance among the natives and with such demagogues as Bush, Wilcox, and Ashford who really are popular among the people no one can exactly say what will happen. All the rifles in town have been sold. The *San Francisco* is prepared to send its troops into town at any time.

Apr. 1—I must tell you our latest political event. Yesterday morning someone had the folly to mount the American flag on Punch Bowl where the national salutes are fired. There was much indignation over it and the soldiers went up and took it down.

We have been "fooled" in various ways today. Mr. Frank Cooke sent in over a bill for the use of their saddle $62.25. I had a box of candy in my room—white pebbles and some of the teachers chairs were tied at the table. Miss Harris's was attached to a rat-trap which went off like a cap when she sat down. All this delighted the girls.

I was calling on the Hyde's yesterday and had a fine long talk with Mrs. Chase. She remembers just where we used to live. I heard more Hartford gossip than I have heard in some time. This morning they both visited our school. It has really been a pleasant episode.

Now Charlie I just 'fess. I don't know what you will think of me. I have bought that Fairchild horse for $60.[3] But she is such a fine horse I couldn't bear to let her go. She is really a fine animal and I hope to get back every dollar I put in her. I am in hopes of letting her to the other teachers to pay for her feed. Please be kind to me about it, Carl.

I am a little anxious for all the changes and chances that may come next year. There is one, perhaps, foolish fear in my heart about you, but I think I will tell you. It seems to me that next year will be your time of trial in being true to me. Pardon me, dear. This is why I say so. You are mortal and besides you know how happy and comforting it is to be loved and it's not natural for you to be kept from ladies' society as you are now. I think next year you will meet more and every year you are becoming more important and more attractive in the eyes of most young girls and I fear you will find yourself tempted as you didn't know you could be. Dearest I can't bear to have you anything but strong and that is why I write you so.

Sunday—Now I will write you what made me feel so badly yesterday. It was Mary Alicia, a tangled specimen of a girl. I have got along in the school-room with her very nicely. Friday she had a dirty head and I gave her some windows to wash. In the afternoon I discovered she had not done them and spoke to her again but yesterday morning they were still untouched. I told her that after her regular work was done she must do it. She growled some and along in the forenoon I went to see if it was done. Still untouched! She is one of the Queen's girls and was to go out for the day. I went to her dormitory and found her dressing and told her she could not go out till she had finished her work. She started down stairs but when some 20 minutes after I went down, the work was still undone. I was wrathy. I went to the dormitory and found her all dressed to go out and as soon as she saw me she hid behind one of the beds. I told her to go to my room and I got the strap and went to her. She seemed to be all right, stood out in the room, held up her skirts and I laid on two good strokes. Then she seemed to go wild and just flew at me with both of her hands into my hair. I couldn't do anything alone. She is a great deal stronger than I, so I stepped out, turned the key on her & sent for Miss Pope. Miss Harris came instead and we went in to get her. She did her best to hold her arms while I lay on with the strap.

Charlie, I used every bit of strength I had in that whipping. Mary was just crazy. When I stopped she just raged up and down the room screaming at the top of her voice and tearing at her clothes. It was really awful. When she was some calmed down I took her to the closet and she was locked in all day. When I went upstairs to repair damages I combed a good bunch of hair out of my head and found my watch chain broken.

Last night after the whole house had gone to bed, I went down to Mary and had a talk with her and she acknowledged how naughty she had been and promised all things for the future. Then I told her I was going to whip her again because she fought in the morning. She cried at that but promised to take it "properly" so with a lantern we went off into one of the empty school-rooms. She took her whipping all right. I hadn't the heart to lay it on very heavy for her poor legs were sore from the morning. But I gave her enough to see if she were truly submissive. Then she broke down and wept in my arms while I told her how sorry I was. She acknowledged that she had always fought her mother and I know she struck Miss Armstrong one day though Miss Armstrong would never own up to it.

There were two things about the affair that worried me. Her mother came while I was whipping her and made some commotion & we didn't know but she would make more when she came back. But she was sweet as honey. The other thing was that in the fray, Mary got one lick in the face that stung her eyelid and made it swell. I was sorry to mark her at all. But I kept brown paper on it all day yesterday and it is about well today. You can imagine my feeling yesterday and how sick it made me. Don't think for a moment I liked it. I do beg your pardon, Carl, for telling you about such a vulgar thing but it's been a little relief to me. Do tell me you love me in spite of it.

We have all been having a hard time this week. Lots of disciplining after the concert. Miss Pope is out now looking for a girl who ran away last night.

We found out that some boys had been coming over the fence while the teachers were at dessert and the girls out in the yard.

Afternoon—Well, dearest, here comes something pleasant right on the lines of something unpleasant. Today I had a letter from Irene Stiles. Mr. Gulick has asked them if they have any objections to having me of the party and dear Irene is delighted. Imagine my joy. I am the luckiest teacher that I know of. Charlie this chance is worth everything. There are 4 ladies—the Stiles, myself and Miss Hammond. I suppose Mr. Gulick will have to hire someone to take care of mules for us. He is in Hilo now and will make arrangements for horses. We are to take a tent and camp. They plan for 5 days at the volcanoe and the rest of the time in Hilo and as much of Hawaii as possible. We are to start the 28 of June. We have to dress a little finer than last year for we will be among Mr. Gulick's friends in Hilo. Still they propose to wear sun-bonnets to ride in.

Apr. 7 Thursday—The "Tea" came off yesterday. It was quite an affair. It was given in honor of Miss Knight and Mrs. Chase. Mr. and Mrs. Admiral Brown were also conspicuous figures. Sandwiches, salad, cake, coffee, and "tutti frutti" were served. The flowers were pretty. At one side of the room a mass of Gardenias, at another, an aisle of pink, blue and white water lilies that would have delighted your heart. I knew most of the ladies and so had plenty to chat with but there were many handsomely-dressed half-whites and women of fashion whom I did not know. Mrs. Brown[4] herself is a half-white and a great "snob." The Hydes brought her up. She was at one time a pupil in this school. Retta was down last evening and I was saying how embarrassing it would be to the Chases if she should visit Hartford. They would have to entertain her and yet people would think she was a Negro.

I went to prayer-meeting in the evening with the Cookes and we drove to the hotel after it was over and listened for a while to the concert by the *San Francisco* and Hawaiian band.

We have received several loads of wood lately as a gift. Wood is anywhere from $10 to $18 a Cord here and we have cut down all the trees we can spare from our place. By a mistake the bill for this wood came here—$46 for 4 cords. It took our breath away at first.

Are we going to have war with England and over a frozen sea? I do hope not. Seems to me they have been fussing over that for a long time. Do you want Harrison again as President? I don't think you have written me much about politics and see how much I have written you.

I send you a portion of fresh love and beg you to warm your fingers at my heart.

Yours, Carrie

April 10, 1892, Kamehameha

Dear Carl,

Out in the harbor lies the *Morning Star* which came in this morning. I hear that Gracie's mother and brother are aboard. Gracie has promised to let me see the curios her mother will bring up and buy what I want. I do so  wish I could get money for writing. There are so many things I want to get.

Poor Mrs. Babb had a fall out of the break day before yesterday, scraping her face and hurting her back. When we came in from dinner last night their room door was open and he sat beside her rubbing her head. I had to turn my face the other way and run up the stairs.

It is very pleasant to be with Retta now she is so full of the home going plans. She came this week to the seminary to have Miss Van Anglen fit her new black silk and wedding dress. She has done much herself in fixing over old gowns. I have begun a little piece of lace for her best gown's neck. I got one pretty idea from her. I am going to make a white linen tea cloth and have one of the girls draw the map of the islands on it and have the other girls write their names on it and I will work them in, in outline stitch. That will make a pretty and useful souvenir.

Last evening Retta entertained three of the old pupils of the school. Sam Kauhane is an especially noble fellow. He has been teaching in the Kauai Industrial School but that school is about to be given up and he is on his way home. Did I tell you that Miss Katherine Pope, our Miss Pope's sister is to have Retta's place next year.

I shall see to your clothing when I become your housekeeper and trust not to let you go slovenly. I happen to know that you look as fine in handsome ties, hats, shoes and gloves as any gentleman I know and I shall keep a sharp eye on you. I mean to make such a pleasant, pretty home for you that you will be surprised. It will be happy and we will do good with it and our whole time will be happily filled with congenial work and joys. I am learning much here in ways of making a pretty home and entertaining and dressing nicely.

Apr. 17—"Christ is arisen." How tender the associations of this day are! At about five this morning I was awakened, and my whole dormitory for that matter also, by one of the horses down in the pasture. At first I could not make out what it was. I thought they must be killing a pig in another yard but as soon as I realized what it was, I sent Jessie and Maria down. I went down myself barefooted. Jenny, Miss Pope's horse had been left tied and she had pulled the rope and was choking, and our big carriage horse, Ioba, was standing beside her biting her. She is a very gentle little thing and allowed Jessie to loosen the rope. We gave her water and this morning I bathed out all the bites and applied glycerin. I should say she had 15 bruises and there is a little piece taken right out of her nostril. I am glad it was not my horse. Mr. Anderson has Mattie up at Kamehameha breaking her of a little willful trick of turning around. I think the girls will be more careful of the horses after this.

I must tell you about last Monday night. The Y.W.C.T.U's sent me an invitation to their auction sale of lunch baskets.[5] It was held at May Athertons. Well, the sale was very amusing. The limit was 75 cents and a Mr. Mossman bought mine. He got someone to introduce him and we sat at a little table and ate and chatted. He is only a boy with an incipient mustache but he had good manners and seemed delighted to talk with so old a young lady as myself. Moreover he is a cousin of the Maui Mr. Mossman I liked so much last summer. I could see a shade of native blood in him. After the lunch was over we were still chatting and Mr. Cooke came rushing up in his usual manner. "Well, Miss Winter, have you made any arrangements? Have you any one to go home with?" "No, Mr. Cooke," I blandly replied. Something took his attention and Mr. Mossman improved the time to ask if he might go with me. Then I had to inform Mr. Cooke that I was going with Mr. Mossman.

Thursday we had vacation and a big time. The whole school went on the cars to Remond Grove.[6] Arrangements were made so that we had the round trip for 15 cents. Miss Malone took her little boys also, greatly to the delight of our girls who romped with them to their heart's content. We had breakfast at 6:30 and left here at 8. The Cookes joined us at the last moment to our joy. Somehow through Miss Pope we had gotten it into our heads that we were going to go on to Eva and visit the big sugar plantation there. I had taken notebook and pencil with me to take notes and was much disappointed when we had to leave at Remond Grove. That is a regular picnic ground and made a nice place for the girls to play. I went with a party of the girls over through the rice fields to a wonderful spring to bathe. This spring runs the rice mill near at hand but was so deep that we turned back and had them bathe in the lower stream. I waited for them at the native pastor's house and had a long talk with a native woman, an unusually intelligent one. She told me how the natives cure broken arms and legs by putting on a paste of coconut leaves. We have a little girl here with a broken arm and her grandmother wanted very much to take off the splints and put on "native medicine." This Mrs. Smith told me that she herself took off the splints from her daughter's leg after they had been on only a day and cured her with this paste. It was five o'clock before we got home and everyone went to bed early. I for one felt much better for the change and the long night's sleep.

Friday night a funny thing happened. We are occasionally bored by old Mr. Tenney who from time to time makes his home at the Castles. He isn't a saint even if he has gray hairs but he is quite devoted to us. Friday is my day on duty and when it was all over and I had seen the last girl into study-hour, I carefully avoided the front of the house where I knew Mr. Tenney was conversing with Miss Appleton and went to my room. It was bright moonlight and I was very happy moving about in it, putting on my holoqu and old slippers and putting away the articles that had got tossed about during the day. Finally I lighted my lamp and took out this letter to write to you and then Miss Appleton came in and asked if I wouldn't go down and entertain him awhile. They were just going out for a walk. I didn't want to, but with a sigh I dressed and went down. He stayed till after study-hour was over and you didn't get any word from me that night. The worst was that he asked me to go down street and get ice-cream with him. I declined (old sinner) because I was "too tired." I think he was quite hurt for he said "I don't often ask ladies to go with me." By the way Mr. Carothers told Mr. Anderson that I gave him the "grand bounce." I do think some things are too funny!

Mrs. Cole gave me a South Sea Islander dress made of banana fiber, about 6 in. by 1 1/2 yd, quite a curiosity. I have bought Professor Alexander's history of the Islands just out though he let us have the advance sheets before. It is now the standard history.

Apr. 24—How this month is hastening by. Last Tuesday brought the mail and a good, long letter from you. I haven't written to you during the week because I was very anxious to get that paper ready for Mahlon and I am happy to say that by this mail 18 1/2 pages on "My trip" will go to him. It is not as good as I would hope to write under different circumstances. I do hope it will be published and that I shall get some pay for it.

I am so glad you are having a chance to know something of Boston and its

Kawaiaha'o Female Seminary students (Annie Wong in Chinese dress).

surroundings. Charlie, can you look me in the eye and say you did not intend that time to go down to Boston city and buy yourself a pair of shoes and that you strayed into an auction sale and spent your money on books and very likely got tonsillitis through the holes in your shoes? I see you cannot. You try to cover it over by calling me names—"Miss Winter"—forsooth my girls can do better than that!

Miss Hadley and Miss Armstrong are just full of horrid little tricks and schemes but I will not waste paper writing about them. The past week has flown like its predecessors. Miss Harris and I visited Kamehameha pretty thoroughly. I think Miss Hight and Mr. Thompson are the best teachers there. Mr. Babb will be better after he has had more experience. I got some very helpful hints and was encouraged by finding that their pupils do some of the same annoying things that mine do.

Last night we had a funny experience. We have lately heard that there have been men hanging around our grounds at night. Robert Pahau an ex-Kamehameha boy who lives behind here, told us about it and yesterday I learned that he had again seen a man come in here and go into our wash house. We are assured that some girl must be going down there and last evening Miss Pope, Harris and myself, after the girls were abed, went down into one of the school-rooms and sat there in the dark in front of an open window to see if we could catch any girl going down. We sat there till toward 11 but saw nothing. We acknowledged that if we did see a man we should probably yell and run. This morning however there are indications that there were prowlers around. There was a chicken with its wings tied in our pasture.

Monday—My troubles as horse owner have begun. Mattie was left down in the pasture and so climbed over the fence and made her escape. I have sent two girls out for her but don't know whether they will find her. Last night 1/2 our bag of oats was stolen. I suppose by the prowlers. I have put a padlock on that door now.

I want you to know that I love you very, very much and now too and that I would like nothing better than a glimpse of your dear face.

> As ever—Carrie.

NOTES

1. The McKinley Tariff Bill, enacted in the United States in 1890, imposed duties on imported sugar, which greatly aggrieved the sugar interests in Hawai'i and convinced some that a closer political relationship with the United States would be advantageous.
2. Maria White, age twelve, a student at Kawaiaha'o Female Seminary, died at her home around February 25, 1892. Miss Winter attributed her death to consumption.
3. Mattie is the name of the mare Miss Winter purchased.
4. Miss Winter speaks not of Mrs. Brown, the admiral's wife, but of her hostess, the Kawaiaha'o Female Seminary trustee Irene 'Ī'ī Brown.
5. Young Women's Christian Temperance Union (YWCTU).
6. Remond Grove was a picnic area in the vicinity of what is now Sunset Memorial Cemetery. Excursion trains of the Oahu Railroad stopped there.

Student Essay by Annie Wong

I

My life as a school girl in Honolulu

I would like to tell you how I became to be in the Se
Seminary. I asked my mother day after day & week after week that I want
to come to this school to learn something, she like to put me in school,
but she have not enough money ~~money~~ to pay my board, so she asked
Mr. F. W. Damon who was the trustee of the Chinese Church. and he said
to her "I will put your daughter in the school." So afterward I know that
I am going to be put in school, I pack up all the ~~my~~ things that I neade
& came to the school of K. S. I am a chinese girl my name is
Annie Wong. my age ~~was~~ was forthteen when I came, now is abut 17.

This is a large school have about hundered & twenty girls.
We have Three dormetories, Three school-rooms, Office, reception,
sewing-room, Parlar, Libery, reading-room, Dining-room
& Kitchen. beside all these we have sewing-cottage which wa
build from Mother Rice & little Hospital for the sick girls.
Now I think I must tell you about our work in different ~~es~~ classes
Miss Appleton was the teacher of the first class in the chapel. Mes
Winter ~~was the~~ teaches the second class, ~~have~~ ~~I~~ My self was in she's
class ~~so I must tell what is~~ ~~our~~ ~~our work during the school. we have~~
~~English, Arith. in D~~ Miss Armstong have the third class, Miss
Kane have the fourth class & Miss Hadly have the fif class that is
the little baby. We have sewing class in the afternoon at
2 o'clock. There are five different classes I'm the first class.
~~I~~ And singing class right after sewing class. We all
have work, some work in the morning some work ~~the the~~
~~before~~ at noon get the diner ready. some work in evening
~~my work but~~ I work in the parlar only dusty that is my wort
~~because~~ I cannot do the other parts of the house not storng engugh
to do it ~~so~~ every one of ~~us have~~ the girl have ~~work~~.

not one have none.

I do not like to play always sat on the stair or in the sewing to do my own sewing I sleep in the dormitory. all we make up in the morning at 6 o'clock only have 20 min for us to dress 10 min for prayer & Bible recitition. Half past six we all go down stai to do what we ought to do. at) o'clock we have our b we have tea, crack & bread. dinner the girls have I have rice & meat. the girls wear english drea own chinese dress. We have pleasure if we a the teachers.

9

Riding Mattie
May 1–June 26, 1892

Carrie P. Winter on her horse, Mattie, Kamehameha School for Boys, December 1892.
Photo by George Babb.

May 1, 1892, Kawaiahao Seminary

Dearest Carl,

My horse is back. You can't think how badly I felt over it. I said to myself "I don't quite think Carl approves of your getting that horse and now if you have lost her out right he won't love you anymore and he will say 'I'll not  give her a chance to lose $60 for me.'" But she is back, Carl. She had wandered 6 or 7 miles to Manoloa into a native man's place. He saw the advertisement in the paper and brought her back. I paid him $5.

Perhaps, dearie, you don't like these details but they are a part of my life—my horse life. I haven't had such a good time in a long time as on that ride yesterday. We were off about four and went up Nuuanu Valley. The road is good all the way. You know that is the road to the Pali. We stopped at Luikalia, 5 miles up, where the Athertons have a cottage and ate our lunch and enjoyed the waterfalls music and the mountains about us and came down in the dark of the evening reaching home about 7. I am afraid Mr. Anderson rather likes Miss Knapp which doesn't agree with my plans, for I want him to like Miss Harris.

I've got a hard month before me and I guess everyone else has. I must begin my fan drill of the little ones, increase my rehearsals of "wands" and labor to bring all my work in sewing class to completion at the proper time. I am going to work up an English exercise with an ear of corn as the object for closing day and get my second division if possible to do some rapid work in fractions.

May 4—We had a big thunder-storm last night which flooded our pasture and the open portions of the house. Our poor little horses had a wretched time out in it. My horse is especially miserable. The girdle sore that I told you about seems to have spread and she was so cold and stiff this morning. I had one of the girls give her a good rubbing down. Mr. Anderson told me to put kerosene on the sore and it seems to do it good.

I am very tired now and so irritable. The girls make me nearly frantic at times. I am longing for the vacation. I need the change very much. I am in good health except as regards to my temper and I love you very much—

Carrie

May 5, 1892, Kawaiahao

Dear Charlie,

I can watch my girls at work and write to you at the same time. They need watching for this last month brings out all the latent meanness they possess though it don't have much chance to lie latent. The girls are getting up a big  dinner today, luaued fish, water-melon and coconut pudding for tonight is Charlotte Ioba's wedding, as sweet and obedient a girl as was ever in this seminary. I wish we were a little surer that the young man she is marrying were worthy of her. I gave her some coarse linen kitchen towels and she thanked me as prettily as though they had been something showy.

I have changed my position to dormitory where my poor little rogue Eunice

Puni is struggling with step-ladder, beds, and rag in an effort to wash the ceiling all to expiate the conversation she indulged in this morning. If you don't believe it is hard work just try washing a ceiling and see.

We sometimes feel like criticizing Miss Pope and feel that she sometimes does not say and do the right thing at the right time but if the President[1] of one of the very largest institutions can so offend the feelings and common sense of good people at large and still hold his position, I think we can well cherish a forgiving spirit toward dear Miss Pope.

I'd like to see how a nice face-to-face compliment from you would affect me. I might not feel uncomfortable but I am sure I would feel very happy over it. I suppose I really am a good horse back rider for a woman. I am not fearless by any means but I keep a good seat, an easy balance and it does not tire me to ride for hours. The other teachers here can only ride a little. I must ride with you sometime.

May 8—Miss Harris and I are again at Dr. Whitney's enjoying a rest and their good milk and cream. The *Alameda* came in yesterday and we went down-town in the afternoon and called at the doctor's office where our mail had been left and there was the letter from you. Three letters from my dear boy in one week! Mrs. Whitney asked me quite particularly about you this time and I was very happy to tell her something of you.

You know our school has no endowment, so in these hard times everything helps—concerts, fair and all. It is going to be harder next year. We really have not suffered at all this year but I don't see how we can avoid losing some of our pupils next year. Undoubtedly our school will sometime become "Kamehameha." I think about year after next when Mr. Richards assumes the principalship. I know he favors the idea. It will be too late to benefit me. I don't think anything could induce me to stay here longer.

It would be great fun to go to Germany together but would it be possible on $750? Of course we would live in the simplest manner possible there and we wouldn't have to buy furniture there. One has to have some ready money to set up housekeeping with. Does your $25 range include pots and kettles, gridirons and coal-hocks, the pans and boilers? My $50 range does. About chairs—you know that all Hawaiians sit on the floor and I am learning to do so also.

I am so glad you approve of my horse. I have not ridden her much since I have had her. I told you about her girth sore. Well by Mr. Anderson's advice I dosed her with kerosene and it took the skin right off from a large place and now I have got to wait for that to heal. I expect to find her much better when I get back this Monday morning. I hope to get around this island on her this summer.

May 10—When we got down from Dr. Whitney's yesterday we found in the morning paper that *The City of Pekin* was so long overdue that it was probable that she had smallpox on board and so had gone on.

Friday, May 13—I think you give me good cheer in your words as to your faithfulness next year. It will all be passing before we know it but I do pray that we may be spared any severe trial in it and that we may each be kept in safety till we see each other again. I do trust you, my Charlie, but I am jealous of every evil chance that may befall you.

Like other weeks I don't know where this week has gone. The week has gone much smoother than the last one. Probably my Sunday rest helped me out. I got down-town Tuesday and bought some pins etc. and a dark-blue cotton dress that you may sometime see. Thursday I went down again, paid for some oats, got some stamps and put $30 in the bank. I made some calls—Mrs. W.R. Castle—Mrs. Atwater who came down when I did as Miss Brenner, and has just become the third wife of Mr. Atwater. His wife died last August and it was only public sentiment that kept off this marriage the few months that it did. I should think she would not like herself. I called also on Miss Mary Green, city missionary and in the evening Miss Harris and I took a pleasure ride down to Waikiki. It was rainy and dismal but there was the sounding sea which told of you and home.

Sunday, May 22—It's a week since I have written and I have a number of things to tell you of. There is first of all the mail. Three of the dearest letters from Julia, mother, and you. Julia's begins "My dear and best of sisters" and is a very delightful letter all the way through. Mother is firm in the belief that I must write a book.

I will send you by this mail a paper with an account of our political excitement in the city. It is very quiet in view of the arrest of 17 for treason in one day. The legislature meets in about two weeks and several of these men are members of it. I was told that their trial would not take place till July but I am not sure about that. There is difference of opinion about the wisdom of the arrests. It depends upon the evidence the government has. They claim that they were already for a revolution just before the opening of the legislature. W.R. Wilcox has publicly declared himself the candidate for the Presidency of his own republic. Only the other day Bipikane advised his hearers to sell their pigs and buy rifles.[2]

Good people would rally to the Queen more if she would dismiss from office Marshall Wilson, concerning whom and herself, there are vile stories afloat. He is plainly in league with the opium men and quantities of it are shipped into the country under his very eyes. It's all very strange. Miss Armstrong was asking Mr. Cooke last night who the Prime Minister was here and he said, "Sam Parker when he isn't drunk or gambling."

We are having a fine musical treat here now. The violinist Ovide Musin is here with his wife and Mr. Scharf the pianist. Did he play in Oberlin? Did you ever hear him?

Miss Harris and I went to hear him Thursday night and we were quite carried away with his playing. It has been so long since I have heard anything but amateur playing that it may be I exaggerated the wonderfulness of it but it seemed to me quite the best violin playing I had ever heard. The people went wild over it. I didn't care much for his wife's singing. Her skill was wonderful but it was not a quality of voice that I admire. They are going to do a kind thing for us. He is going to play for the boys and girls together up at Bishop Hall at Kamehameha. The public are not admitted to this. I hope I will not have to stay at home with the children as I want very much to witness the effect of his playing upon the boys and girls. They are to sing their best for him. We had a remarkably fine service this morning. Mrs. Musin sang and a Baptist minister from Chicago named Wolfenden preached the best sermon I have heard here. It showed it had not been written in this climate. There was too much energy in it for that.

Yesterday afternoon Miss Hadley and I took 30 of the girls to the ball-game between the Honolulus and the Kamehamehas. It was my project and I got them in for 10 cents apiece. The Kamehamehas lost their first game this season. It was too bad for the girls cheered them heartily.

Friday I was watching two of my girls at work. I went out of the room for a few moments and when I came back I noticed the fingers of a hand bent over the edge of the door. The queer appearance of the finger arrested my attention. The end seemed to be gone and it was not treated. I went in and found that it was Mary Ahia. When I asked her about it she was very much confused and said something about Nancy cutting it with an ax. I made inquiries of Miss Pope and she knew nothing of it. In fact none of the teachers had ever seen

ROYAL HAWAIIAN OPERA HOUSE,

LEWIS J. LEVEY.............................Lessee and Manager

OVIDE MUSIN CONCERTS

OVIDE MUSIN, The Violinist.

ANNIE LOUISE MUSIN,
The American Nightingale.

EDUARD SCHARF,
Solo Pianist.

HENRY BERGER,
Conductor.

THURSDAY EVENING, MAY 19th, 1892.

PROGRAMME.

—o—

1—OVERTURE—Semiramide,.............................*Rossini*
ROYAL HAWAIIAN BAND.

2—VALSE—From Gounod's Faust,.............................*Liszt*
EDUARD SCHARF.

3—BRILLIANT BIRD.............................*F. David*
ANNIE LOUISE MUSIN.

4—SOUVENIR DE HAYDN,.............................*Leonard*
OVIDE MUSIN.

INTERMISSION.

5—REVERIE SENTIMENTAL,.............................*Alberti*
ROYAL HAWAIIAN BAND.

6—VARIATIONS FOR SOPRANO AND VIOLIN,...........*Ariot*
ANNIE LOUISE MUSIN AND OVIDE MUSIN.

7—SOLI FOR PIANO—
a. Norwegian Bridal Procession,.............................*Grieg*
(passing by.)
b. Mazurka,.............................*Godard*
c. Rigaudon,.............................*Raff*
EDUARD SCHARF.

8—SONGS FOR SOPRANO,
a. "Open thy blue eyes,"................
.........*Massenet*
b. "List to the voice of youth,"..........
ANNIE LOUISE MUSIN.

9—BRAVURA VARIATIONS,
On a theme of Rossini—On one single string. ....*Paganini*
OVIDE MUSIN.

10—MARCH—For Orchestra—Princess Royal,.................*Meyer*
ROYAL HAWAIIAN BAND.
HAWAII PONOI.

Ovide Musin concert program, May 19, 1892.

that finger and when Mary was spoken to about it she burst out crying and refused to show it. The doctor looked at it today and said it was all right but I don't quite believe him. She says it was hurt four years ago and I don't see why it should look so now. A while ago they were much alarmed about the mother and feared she had leprosy but she seems all right now.

Carl, my vanity has received a severe shock. Miss Van Anglen was downtown and in a store looking at dress goods. The clerk showed her some cloth and said one of the teachers had bought a dress off that a few days before that. Miss Van Anglen said "It must have been Miss Winter." Then he said "which is Miss Winter, the one with the smooth, fair skin?" Miss Van Anglen said "yes and that she was rather inclined to be stout." Miss Van Anglen was telling all this at the supper table and I exclaimed at this and asked if she really considered me stout. That gave our "ladies" a chance and Miss Armstrong said, "Why, Miss Winter, you surely do not consider yourself slender." I wanted to reply that I did not consider myself scrawny or a walking skeleton but I refrained. Miss Hadley then remarked that they had recently been in that store, and that she thought Miss Armstrong would be considered fair. Miss Armstrong's face is about the hue of this paper and both those ladies are small bundles of bones. I didn't mind Miss Van Anglen for she is a dress-maker and my waist is large but I was wrathy at those fair and slender old things! Don't you think they are horrid, Carl?

I want you dear more and more every week. I plan all sorts of things for the future. You have my heart, my Carl.

> As ever,
> Carrie

May 27, 1892, Kawaiahao Seminary

My Dearest,

Carl I feel bad inside myself. I don't think I am good or brave or anything. I ought not to write out my blueness to you, but I do so many things I ought not to. I am certain you would never have fallen in love with me if you
had met me here. I don't see how one can be among mean things and not be mean too. Of course they can if they are really good Christians but I fear I am not.

The girls are fuller of meanness than I can tell you. It is a constant struggle everywhere to keep them decent and there are so many of them. You can't help liking them and that makes it all the worse when they disappoint you. Then no word but "mean" will describe those "ladies," Mrs. H & A.

I do wish now that I had seen a little clearer six months ago and I should have made an effort to get into the Chinese school next year. You see I have nothing new to learn here. My work cannot be changed at all while in that year a new interest and work would have made the year go quickly. Then from those we have here I can see how teachable and docile they all are, the half-Chinese girls so much easier to manage. But it's too late now. I ought to have thought of that at Christmas time. Of course, I shall begin next year not feeling as I do now for I shall have been freshened up by the vacation but I think I need more encouraging from you than ever.

Evening—Even now much of the bitterness and bad feeling of the morning has gone away. I think I have fewer things to vex me this evening than I had this morning. We have just been having a call from Mrs. Mead, Mother Castle's daughter whose husband is now a Professor in Ann Arbor. She has spent many years in Germany. She is said to be very crooked in her religion but she is very charming to meet, perfectly unconventional, in dress and manner. She is what I would like to be.

Such a sad thing happened here Tuesday. It was the death of a young native man Sam Mahelona. He was 31 years old, almost white and married to a girl who used to be matron here. They had three children. He was book-keeper in a large firm here and had earned a pretty home out on King Street. They were a model family. He was a tall, handsome man, with not a bad habit, treasurer of Kawaiahao church. He was at church last Sunday. He died of asthma. There is a rumor that the doctor gave him an overdose of morphine. The whole city mourned his loss. He seemed to have been almost alone in his virtues. I went to the funeral yesterday. The poor wife was almost prostrate. Darling, don't you think it must have been dreadful for her? God grant that I may not be called on to go through such a sad experience.

Yesterday, I attended to my usual duties about the house till toward ten then went down-town with Miss Pope on a few errands. I walked back and arranged myself in my best to see the Queen open the legislature.

Later—I have donned my "holoku" and the house is quiet for all have gone to church so now I may have a good time with you. I was telling you of the opening of the legislature. We were there at 11 so as to be sure of good seats although the ceremony was not to take place till 12. We with the rest of common folk, sat behind the rail within which all of importance was to take place. The band outside gave warning at the arrival of each dignitary. Some of the official uniforms were quite fine. Most of the ladies were in full dress. The ladies of the court wore a partial mourning, black lace with lavender plumes.

Presently we knew by the strains of "Hawaii Ponoi" that the Queen had arrived. Five lackies entered adorned with feather capes, silk hats surrounded by yellow leis and cotton stockings up to their knees. Two stationed themselves at either side of the throne with fine Kahili while the fifth most carefully undid his big green bundle, shook out one of the fine feather mantles and draped it over the throne. When the Queen entered all rose and I caught only a glimpse of the diamond ornament in her hair and saw that she wore black lace. We heard a murmur of prayer in Hawaiian and the murmur of the Queen's voice as she read her short address then all made a break for a place to see them go. The last representative to enter was C. Ashford. I recognized among the nobles Mr. Anderson of Maui who helped us much in our trip last year. They have some big questions to meet and I mistrust no great quantity of brains with which to meet them.

After lunch and a nap, I went up to Kamehameha on horse-back for a ride with Mr. and Mrs. Thompson. We rode from 4 till 6 going five miles out of the city beyond Kamehameha, the same ride I once took with Miss Harris. My horse went beautifully. Mr. Thompson admires her very much, says she is a very clean limbed horse. He also accuses me of liking a little daring. At any rate, he and I, a few times let a loose rein to our horses and flew. Oh Carl, such fun. Mrs. Thompson, with you in mind, I fancy, cautioned me not to break my neck this summer.

Will you hear something about yourself now? I think you are the best man in the world. You are the most to my taste of any one I have ever seen. I mean that aside from my love for you. Here is a line I read in a poem of George Eliot's today. It is just a phrase, but there is a beautiful thought in it, "The man so rare that he could make your life as woman sweet to you." See dear, that one so rare that even a woman with rare gifts and the possibility of independent success could lay aside all that, perhaps never be known beyond the walls of her own home and her life as woman be sweet and noble to her because of him. I don't mean to say that I am any genius but I do think you are already the rare one to me, and I value myself because of you.

Thursday—One week more! I had my last examination in school today. I am anxious for this to be over. I want to begin the new, the last year. I want the time to hasten. I love you. I send you my love. Where will you be when this reaches you?

Yours truly,
Carrie

June 12, 1892, Waikiki

My Carl,

I have entered on my last year here in Honolulu and I am so thankful! Now, darling all through this coming year I shall complain to you as much as I want to and tell you all manner of horrid things and how much I  want you and how eager and impatient I am for the home going. I don't think anything could keep me here longer than this year and by a year from this date, I hope to be on the waters homeward bound. I am so glad, so glad!! Are you Carl? Will you like to see me?

Week before last was my examination week and it was not as fretting work to me as my regular school work. I was proud of the results. It is quite the best I have had. Eleven girls go into Miss Appleton's room. The one whose paper I sent you stayed the longest. This last week has been a hodge-podge. Monday I made up exercises for my school-room with five minute whispering recesses between, marks, reading, spelling, math, etc. In the afternoon I went to the church and drilled in fan-drill and wands. I had a short study-hour in the evening. Tuesday we had a rehearsal in the chapel of open-day exercises. It took an hour to arrange the children in the proper places and have them march in and out. It was all very tiresome and vexing but Miss Pope was in charge so she bore the brunt of it. In the afternoon the whole school went over to the church and it was another big mess to arrange the girls.

It was after five before we got home and I was more tired with those days' experiences than with any before or after. It was 9:30 that night when I went down to the wash-house with two girls to wash out the last garments for the fair. Earlier in the evening I had superintended the removing of the tables from the dining room. We had each arranged our fair tables.

Wednesday—the girls ate breakfast out of doors. I cleared up all my sewing room and school-room affairs and at ten o'clock all was ready. We had a crowd there. My part was an object lesson on an ear of corn and some work in Arithmetic. I will send you papers with an account of the affair.

The Queen stayed through the whole and bought over $20 worth at the fair. When 11 o'clock came and the crowd was admitted to the dining room it was a grand struggle. There was a perfect raid on Miss Harris's cake and candy tables. She sold over $40 worth. Miss Appleton had a sale of pictures of the seminary and sold over $20 worth. On my table I sold $20 worth and at the other tables enough was sold to make $200 in all. The hand work on my table was much admired. The Queen bought from all the tables and Miss Pope found her on a verandah devouring a large hunk of cake breaking out the mouthfuls with her fingers. Miss Pope found a napkin and plate for her and she ate in more civilized fashion.

At 2:30 we all went to the church again for a fine rehearsal. The band was there for Mr. Berger kindly offered to furnish our music for us again. It was late when we got home but I was not so tired as the night before because so large a part was over and over for good. I hardly know how Thursday passed. I know we all went to bed in the afternoon and that a short time before we went over to the church one girl was in a towering passion of rage and we thought someone would have to stay at home and watch her. She calmed down in time and promised to behave were she only allowed to go. One girl also appeared in a white silk dress at the last moment and there were many tears and some anger when she found she would not be allowed to wear it but had to change to a simple white dress like the others. One girl did get through with a train to her gown without our noticing her.

We took a new turn this year and had our closing-exercises in the evening and charged 25 cents admission and we had a big audience. The Queen bought tickets for all the members of the legislature. There must have been 900 there. Some of my friends were so kind as to say that my part was the most successful. At any rate, my fan drill just brought down the house and the girls in the wand drill did good work and were very gay in their red-stripped dresses. There were some compositions on house topics by Miss Appleton's girls and some other fancy pieces. We obtained about $200 by this effort also.

Our yard presented a queer sight Friday morning. It was filled with hacks, carriages, push carts, and in short, everything that would carry a trunk. The natives were everywhere over the house taking down beds and curtains. In my attic I found one of our oldest and best girls amiably conversing with her friends, 5 men at work over trunks and she clad in a simple scant garment. I had my hands full of that sort of thing. There was fun and sadness too. The Queen insisted on Maria Puuohau going out. How the child cried

EDUCATIONAL.

Annual Examination of Kawaia-hao Seminary.

Shortly after 9 o'clock yesterday morning Her Majesty the Queen arrived at the Seminary, and within a few minutes the large school was filing into the main school, or Rice hall, in her presence, and to the evident admiration of the large concourse of spectators. Among the visitors, besides Her Majesty and her attendants, were Mother Cooke Mother Rice, Mesdames Judge Judd, Dole, Severence, Hartwell, Haalelea, S. C. Allen, Lyons, W. H. Rice, W. R. Castle, Andrews, and others, besides a few gentlemen and a large number of the parents, guardians and other friends of pupils.

After opening with prayer, by Rev. Dr. Beckwith, and the announcement, by W. R. Castle for the Board of Trustees, of the date of opening in the fall, with a few words of encouragement and cheer for both teachers and scholars, the examination opened with an excellent instrumental duet by Misses Lima and Aholo. Besides this there was other music, both piano and vocal. In the latter the girls of the school excel, and always give great pleasure to the hearers, and this occasion was no disappointment.

In reading, the girls showed excellent training, and by their clear enunciation and intelligent rendering indicated that they have been appreciative pupils. The exercises in arithmetic also showed fine training with like appreciation. In short, all of the work showed thorough drilling and conscientious training. The work in English speaking and like exercises was most praiseworthy. The kindergarten class of little ones made an interesting exhibit, as did the class of Liliuokalani Educational Society girls, who were decorated with pretty shields bearing a crown and suspended with blue ribbons.

Far from being a dull and prosy affair, there was much to interest every one who is watching the advancement of the Hawaiian race.

One exercise especially, would add a desirable feature to any school. It was an illustrated lesson in anatomy. A large class of girls stood erect and graceful while they indicated the different bones of the body by gesture.

Another notable example was in language, the subject being given by an object presented. One girl described the object, another told a story about it.

Everyone must have observed the ease and skill shown by the pupils in writing letters and figures. It does seem that a people so gifted in mathematics and in drawing, must have the foundation upon which to build a well-balanced education.

Later in the morning, we saw elevated maps of Oahu most pleasingly and accurately arranged showing the native conception of proportion, which also appeared later again in the music to which we listened.

Shortly after eleven, the company adjourned to the dining room where specimens of the handiwork of the pupils were on sale. The progress in the sewing department has been very great and the plain and fancy work would have been a credit to the finest millinery establishment. The guests thought so for in less time than it takes to write this all was sold. In cookery a variety of cakes, candy and the whitest and lightest of bread spoke for themselves of attainments in the pantry. In short the whole exhibit must encourage the friends of Hawaii to hope for the future when her future mothers have done so well. All praise is due to the patient, untiring and able corps of teachers headed by Miss Pope.

"Educational, Annual Examination of Kawaiaha'o Seminary," newspaper clipping, May 1892.

for us as she said, "She had no good home to go to." I felt very badly about it but there was nothing to do.

Sunday, June 19—I realize that you are seeing all kinds of life. I am glad you told me how much you wanted me. It is really dreadful for us to be separated so far and so long. I wonder if the gain compensates for the loss. I know I don't amount to very much without you. I suppose it is good for me to find that out by experience. I hope in the future that my missionary ventures may be more truly successful and I think they will for I have undertaken them with you and be happy in them and not be half-hearted because I haven't you to sympathize with me in every success and every failure.

Now for some account of my week. Last Wednesday it was quarter of nine when I awoke. I went up town then and went shopping to prepare for my trip. It seems to me I ran all around town. I do not think you would be interested in my purchases except my bag of "pulu" which is the downy growth on the young ferns, the big kinds and is much used for stuffing mattresses and pillows. While it is new it is as good as feathers but where it gets old it is too powdery. I got it to make a couple of little pillows for our trip. The next day I hired Mary Bridges to sew for me. We went right to the cottage and sewed all day.

In the afternoon I asked Emma Ai to come and sew with us and told her I would give her a quarter. She worked very nicely for it but would not take any money. She marked my stockings, finished my sun-bonnet, made my pillows and stuffed them and made their cloths also. Mary saw me through the hard part of my new dress while I sewed here and there and got nervous and tired as I frequently do when I try to sew.

Friday afternoon—I came down here on horse-back and took a bath and then went up to see Maria Puuohau. She came rushing out and grasped my hand and seemed fairly to cling to me.

Yesterday afternoon, I went to the farewell service on the *Star* at 1:30. Three Hawaiians and their wives have gone on this trip to the Gilbert Islands. The little boat was crowded and the services conducted by Dr. Hyde and Mr. Emerson were very impressive. There were a great many tears and much wailing among the natives but the others were calm and collected. Mrs. Garland looked very happy to be going.

There are five of us down here now. Miss Appleton and I occupy the downstairs "Lanai." I brought down an extra mattress and net for the purpose. Miss Van Anglen, Miss Hadley and Miss Armstrong are upstairs. Miss Hadley has been ill ever since she has been down here. Her brother is with her now. I

Castle cottage, Waikīkī.

am sorry for its no fun to be ill here I can assure you, as I know from experience.

Tuesday—I came up from Waikiki last evening and expect to remain up today and go back again tonight. Yesterday a Mr. More rang up Miss Harris and invited her and Miss Winter to go to tea the Y.M.C.A. lecture in the evening, a stereopticon lecture on Columbus. He is a clerk in the Lewers and Cooke and is a very good young man with some common sense but rather unattractive and quite ignorant. The attraction is Miss Harris without doubt. There was no reason for refusing him so we went. He did the matter up brown for he treated us to ice cream afterward and we stopped at the hotel on our way back to listen to the band play. I think Miss Harris will soon have the privilege of squelching him.

After I get my mail ready I have my room to put to rights. My things are strewn from one end of the home to the other. The girls are using my bureau for their own convenience. I found a collection of combs and brushes on it. I don't know what else they are using. I want to get the things back in and lock it up.

You will want to know the result of the preliminary trial in the treason case.[3] Five are held for treason among them Mr. Wilcox, five more were released to be rearrested for conspiracy. Among these was V.V. Ashford who immediately fled the country. It is reported that he is on Hawaii. Perhaps I shall meet him. The rest here simply released. I want to see the *Australia* off today. Miss Adams of Kamehameha Preparatory goes and I have not seen her to say "good-by." Her health completely broke down and she had to give up and go home, a great disappointment to her.

I wonder very much where and how this letter will find you. I do so hope you will have some fun this summer and some society as well as rest.

> Yours,
> Carrie

June 26, 1892, Kamehameha

Dearest,

I am here on my first visit to Retta. I leave Thursday and she sometime during the following week so I shall not see her again. How kind she has been to me!

Where shall I begin, what shall I say!! My state of mind is distracted between Waikiki experiences, hurried preparations and sad anticipations of that dreadful sea voyage. It takes from 2 P.M. Tuesday till early Thursday to reach Hilo. I can only write today and will have to leave this short letter here to go on Thursday's steamer. I will have that mail sent to Hilo.

I came up yesterday morning from Waikiki for good having spent the greater part of two weeks there. I had had a very good time there. The house-keeping was very easy for we took turns getting the meals and that left most of the day free. I had to sew almost all day long and that is why I did not write.

The Parmalus at the big Castle cottage and the Lewers on the other side were extremely "chummy" with us. They both had young ladies from town who were full of fun and jokes and our particular stretch of beach and our "lanai" was the gathering place. All day long they would be around with their "taro-patches" and guitars and fancy work and fresh crops of practical jokes. I couldn't begin to tell you all they did. Millie Beckwith was prime mover over in it all. The last night she pinned my sheets together in 15 places.

There have been very high tides all the past week and the beach has been caving in greatly to the distress of the Castles who have been at great expense to build the break-head and get the Algarroba trees growing. The evenings were especially delightful down there. A large group of us under the trees, with beautiful star light—the Southern Cross low in the sky before us and the soft noises. There were a few stray gentlemen about, nothing much however in the way of men. I must not forget the high-tide bathing on the big swells. Friday's experience was almost too much of a good thing for it was impossible to keep our

SWEET SEMINARIANS.

Closing Exhibition of Kawaiahao Girls' Seminary.

The annual exhibition of the Kawaiahao Seminary took place Thursday evening in Kawaiahao Church. The sacred stone edifice was filled to overflowing, many having to take standing room. Her Majesty the Queen graced the occasion with her presence in the royal pew. The program opened shortly before 8 o'clock with a march by the Royal Hawaiian orchestra. A chorus, "Welcome, We Sing," by the Seminary was a pleasant rendition. A Bible recitation from the Psalms was next, followed by prayer by the Rev. S. L. Desha, of Kona, Hawaii. Lucy Leleo and Lucy Aukai manipulated deftly the piano in a duet, the "Victoria Nocturne," in a pleasing manner. Two compositions, "How to Make Home Happy" and "House Keeping," by Emma Akana and Lydia Makaimoku were interesting reading and would prove profitable if followed by the rising generation of the Seminary at maturity. A historical sketch on "Alexander the Great," was also given by Louise Kahili.

The fan drill by twenty-four wee tots of the primary department, was gone through without a hitch. A chorus by the whole school, "Pauahi o Ka Lani," composed by her Majesty the Queen, was nicely sung, ending the first part of the program.

The primary department caused much laughter in their rendition of "Can Birds Talk?" A trio was pleasantly rendered, the school joining in the chorus. "Reveil du Lion," a piano duet by M. Powers and Louise Alapai, was applauded. The grammar department then rendered a recitation simultaneously. A song by the school closed the evening,s performance.

The exhibition throughout was a grand success, and credit in due the trainers of Hawaii's blooming young damsels. The musical department under Miss Armstrong has reached a high standard in that branch, and that lady deserves all commendation.

"Sweet Seminarians," The Daily Bulletin, June 13, 1892.

head above the water. I think by the time I came away, I had quite worn out the good it did me, the cooking, hard bed, mosquitoes and rather tiresome company with their constant pranks that became a little tiresome to me.

Monday eve—I asked Retta yesterday if her last year had seemed long to her and she said "no, very short." That encourages me. My last visit at Kamehameha was very pleasant. I went down to church in the forenoon. Mr. Anderson of Kamehameha joined me on the car and we had quite a chat. I had on my new Hilo dress and he said, "Where did you get that dress, its mighty pretty. I don't often notice dresses but that took my eye." Of course I immediately wished you had been there to appreciate my dress too and see if it fitted me well about the waiste a duty which needless to say, did not enter our red-headed friend's head.

The latest excitement in town is the engagement of Mr. Henry Castle to Miss Wing. The lady is a teacher out at Punahou who came this last year. She is an earnest Christian and he is very heterodox and there are many comments on the affair. I guess on the whole it is a suitable match.

Darling I felt a little lonely to be starting off on this trip. How I wish that with me, you could gaze upon the marvel of nature that I shall see before the week is done. God bless and keep us both.

As ever,
Carrie

NOTES

1. This is a reference to Charles William Eliot (1834–1926), president of Harvard University (1869–1909), who was often criticized in newspapers at the time. In 1892 he led an effort to standardize high school curriculum and college admissions requirements.
2. J. W. Bipikane, a Hawaiian politician and member of the Liberal Party, and fourteen others were charged with treason by the government of Queen Lili'uokalani. Bipikane never went to trial.
3. Marshal Charles B. Wilson had spies infiltrate the formation of the Hawaiian Patriotic League, and on May 19, 1892, warrants were sworn out for the arrest of R. W. Wilcox, V. V. Ashford, Lot Lane, J. W. Bipikane, and others on charges of treason. The preliminary hearing was held May 26.

10

Big Island Summer
July 3–August 26, 1892

Lilla Estelle Appleton, Kīlauea Volcano, Hawai'i, 1893.

July 3, 1892, Island of Hawaii near Volcanoe Kilauea

Dear Carl,

I left you last Tuesday morning, finishing my packing with the aid of dear little Zelie.[1] Word came to me indirectly at lunch time that Mr. Oliver Emerson was going on the trip also. At the last moment he rushed aboard with his arms full of papers.

I must tell you a little about him. I have known him slightly ever since I have been here. He is one you are likely to meet. He is a minister, about 45 yrs. old and holds under the A.B.C.F.M. a kind of general superintendence over the native churches. I think the families have always lived here though receiving fine educations abroad. There are 4 brothers and all have peculiarities and it's rather the fashion in Honolulu to make fun of Mr. Oliver. I long ago took rather a fancy to him. When you get him a little off his guard and he is talking to you, he seems to me to have a beautiful light in his clear honest eyes and a quick appreciation of fine points. That reminds me of you so I like him. He is a little apt however to fly back on his guard again and leave you in some ridiculous situation. He is generally supposed, truly I think, to be devoted to Miss Margaret Brewer. In fact Miss Brewer confided to me some about him. It seems doubtful if she will ever marry him though I can't see why she shouldn't accept his love and be most happy in it. He is the most interesting man to me in the party.

He saw that my things were taken to my state-room and in a few moments, I followed for the *Kinau* began to rock up and down in a most disgusting fashion. The men outside said it was a "strong trade." All across the channel till in the lee of Molokai, I was ill. That was from 2 to 6. Then I plucked up courage to ring for some water and crackers. When the steward came I found Mr. Emerson still had me in mind for he came and stuck his head in the door to ask how I was, tell me where we were, suggest poi, fished a lime out of his pocket and sliced it up for me. I supposed he would let a woman die before he would enter her state-room. His little mothering did me a world of good.

About 9:00, we came to anchor at Lahaina and I went out on deck to enjoy the fresh air. I was quite well then. I went to bed and to sleep to wake at one when we stopped at Wailea Bay where the rest of the party was to join us. We kept awake till the ship anchored at Makena and then slept till day-light. We didn't know that the ship had lain there in harbor all night long till we were out and dressed and the ship was just starting across the channel to this island. I was talking with Dr. Lyons. He said "the channel is very rough this morning." We soon found it so.

I stood it as long as I could and then crawled into my berth again. Two more hours of sea-sickness and we were anchored at the northern part of Hawaii. I was feeling all right again. Drank a bowl of beef-tea, dressed, went down to see Mrs. Gulick, Irene and Gertrude and we were soon all on deck. Everyone had been ill. Mr. Emerson goes to all the islands twice a year and he said he had never made so rough a passage.

By evening I was the only one of the ladies who was not feeling miserable again. I never felt better. I promenaded with Mr. Gulick and when the beautiful stars and new moon came out and the ship had weighed anchor and we started for a little town on the leeward side of the island, I enjoyed a long pleasant tete-a-tete with Mr. Emerson on deck. About 9, the ship turned back and we were in rough water again. All said, it would be a bad night, rough as possible.

We had caught glimpses of a beautiful green shore through our window but had been far too ill to enjoy it. At last we were called forth—our baggage gathered—before us a stretch of water and then the green bowered, coconut beset little town of Hilo. The little boat was surging up and down and it was a struggle to get safely down into it. You had to wait till it bobbed up near the stairs and then make a flying leap. At the landing was the worst of all for we had to climb up a kind of iron rope-ladder and be hauled to the top by native men. Miss Hammond and I were transported to the home of Mr. and Mrs. Terry. How thankful we were to be in a stationary house. I think you must know something of Mrs. Terry for she was the famed Miss Reamer of Oberlin.

Monday July 11. Now to go back to the Terry's. I think you know she made a marriage that did not please her friends. She was principal of Kamehameha Preparatory and he was teacher of carpentry at Kamehameha an ignorant but good man. She is now principal of the Hilo boy's boarding school and he is her assistant. I was interested to meet them for I had heard so much about them. I found her a strikingly handsome woman with a fine capable manner about her but rather bitter and on the defensive. It didn't take me long to get quite weary of his conversation. They treated us very nicely.

In the afternoon they took us all over the school farm. They have fine sugar and taro patches growing dry and not in water as on the other islands for you must know that in Hilo it rains all the time. There were bananas and coffee and sweet potatoes also doing well. This school does more in the line of farming than any other on the islands and is a most worthy school. It got very much run down under the administration of Mr. Burt but has picked up under the Terrys.

Mr. Emerson came up in the afternoon to get all the things that were to go up to the volcanoe and we had quite a scramble to get them all ready. A long, calm night's sleep seemed good after the turbulence of the nights at sea. Well, Friday came and at half past seven, we all meet at the Austin's (where I am now boarding) and packed into the wagonette drawn by 4 horses. Let me name them: Mrs. Gulick, Mrs. Severance—we four girls, Irene, Gertrude, Miss Hammond and I. Mr. Gulick, Emerson, Nickol. The first two are perfect hosts in themselves—the last is a good strong hearty young Scotchman, good voice for singing, willing to do anything to help but not particularly versed in polite ways.

We had a ride of 18 miles in the wagonette and a fine experience it was too. I will say "Hilo Woods" and when I say that, you must let your fancy picture fresh tender green, huge lines that coiled around the stately stems, the tall "ohia" or mountain apple with its beautiful red shining fruit, huge tree ferns with many a leaf fully 18 ft. long, wild bananas, wild alligator pear trees and a world of vegetation quite unknown to me.

Mr. Emerson is a "Kamaaina" and so knows everything and he was constantly darting out of the end of the wagonette to bring a piece of "ava" root to let us try its narcotic powers. It did make the tongue tingle and then grow numb but none of us got to its dreaming effects. We all had the leaves of the fragrant sweet ginger to crush in our fingers and enjoy its odor.

Once we met a party of Japs. Their open umbrellas frightened one of the front horses and off he plunged into the ditch. Fortunately no serious harm was done though it might easily have been. The breaks in the harness were repaired and we were on our way again.

It was 2 when we reached the end of the road and we were glad of the hot coffee and the substantial lunch furnished by Mr. Staples who has charge of all the prisoners who are at work on the volcanoe road. After a short rest we mounted our steeds. Mrs. Gulick left us here returning to Hilo as she had decided she could not endure the hardships of the trip. She is a very lovely lady and we were very sorry to lose her company.

You will laugh when I tell you that I rode a mule. Mr. Gulick rode one also and on the whole, they stood the trip best of any of our animals. It is an especially good animal for such a trip, as it is very sure-footed and has a long easy walk. Its gallop isn't so good. It is not free and springy like a horse but short and hard. We rode for 1 1/2 miles over that portion of the new road which is as yet unfit for wagons but all right for horse-back. We passed the prisoners at work and then turned off over a Corduroy horse-trail[2] into the thickest of the forest.

The ride beyond the forest is not so interesting. It is like very rough brambly, New England pasture land only that you must say to yourself these rocks are portions of old lava flows—those brambles are not huckleberries but "ohelos." It grows long and wearisome when mile stretches after miles and you must hurry or night will be upon you and you are on a mule! Toward evening you come out into an open road and then the most absurd thing happens. It is very cold and the ground all around is moist and green but here and there rise from it little wreaths of steam. It seems utterly out of place in such damp, cool, surroundings.

At last we reached the Volcano House, a comfortable new building, steam rising from the bank in the rear and in front, a sudden descent into the crater itself. We rode on about 1 1/2 miles beyond to a ranch house belonging to a Mr. Shipman with whom Mr. Gulick had made arrangements. There was no one at the house but a Chinaman—Luna of the place and his workman. Our tent was already up and Manuel unpacked. We had the use of the pasture for our horses—poor feeding—an old shed under which to shelter our saddles and the little porch of the house for our provisions. It wasn't very pleasant because we were in full sweep of the winds and it was very damp. We got a lunch with some hot tea as soon as possible, kept on our rubbers and waterproofs and kept up our spirits. We were even a little social though we were depressed over the desertion of both chaperones and did not feel quite at ease with one another. We had prayers, sang some, gave quotations around and I told a story which seemed to give pleasure and at once gave me a position in the party which I have not since lost. While we sat there in front of the hut we saw the sky at a little distance turn red several times and we knew Madam Pele was at work.

Shortly after nine we pinned up our oil-cloth curtain, spread our blankets and lay down to sleep. After breakfast, the question of a permanent camp came up. We felt we must have a more sheltered spot. It soon came to a question of the romantic vs. the practical. There was that beautiful koa grove in which I began this letter where a camp would be so beautiful and so much koa about for fine camp fires. Its disadvantages were the dampness of the ground, the numerous pigs which would be sure to invade our tent when we went away and the distance from water.

In the middle of the forenoon Mrs. Severance, Miss McLeod and Dr. Wiggins joined us. We feared beforehand that they might not enter into the spirit of the party but they did and we enjoyed their stay. Mrs. Severance is a very beautiful kind woman and makes me think of Mrs. Atherton. Miss McLeod is an ordinary oldish school-ma'am. Dr. Wiggins is like some funny dried-up old man you have seen, only he is young. Everyone here seems to like him. He has a fund of funny stories, comic songs and a whistling accomplishment that makes him good company in camp.

July 14—It is only about an hour now before we leave Hilo. I am writing my "good bye" of it to you. It has all been a full, rich experience and has added to the pleasant store of my life's journey. Perhaps it has added to my chances of doing good. It has added many acquaintances who I hope will remember me as kindly as I do them. I think too that it has added one or two permanent friends of the kind whose friendship is truly valuable. It is much to have had in a familiar way the society of Mr. Gulick—an able man, of well known family who has met famous people. It is more to have the confidence and friendship of Mr. Emerson. Miss Hammond has idealized me. We four girls have been like sisters. We have met with the greatest of courtesy from everyone. A great deal has been done for us and given to us.

July 16—Honolulu. I reached here at about five this morning. I have been airing and sunning my musty, dirty things, napping and chatting with Miss Harris all the day. I take the thread of my story right where I dropped it. Well, the day wore on till four o'clock when we started for the crater. We all rode to the Volcano House where the guide whom we had agreed to take with us joined us. He was a very stupid Chinaman but we paid him $15 at the rate of $1.50 apiece for following us in and out of the crater and carrying the lanterns. It is some 600 ft to the lava—a long winding descent of a mile or more. It is nothing to the lava we rode over last year on Haleakala. Along the way are little piles of stone to mark the trail.

At last we seemed to be coming to a big hole in the earth. We could see a blue, darkish smoke rising from the center. We stopped on a bench and before the crater, the active lake of Kilauea. The name of this portion is Halemaumau. Before us was a great circular hole, toward 300 ft deep and about 3 miles around it. A large part of the bottom was just black lava but in the center was the burning lake, perhaps a half mile in diameter.

It was very cold and began to rain so about 9 we lighted our lanterns and started back. At last we reached the bank, found our skirts wet, mounted and rode up. I remained at the Volcano House that night. I did not dare risk the danger of going back to camp in the condition in which I then was. I am glad I went to the hotel for Mrs. Lee was very kind, brought me toilet articles and a hot foot bath. I donned the long woolen robe she brought me, crept in between the woolen blankets and though the wind blew a gale outside was as warm and cozy as possible and had such a good sleep.

I found in the morning that Dr. Wiggins, Mrs. Severance had stayed at the hotel also. We rode back to camp before breakfast, hastening a little to be on time which was quite unnecessary as they had been very lazy and did not have breakfast till ten. It was a grand affair when it did come and we did it full justice. Mr. Nichol and myself, Mr. Emerson and Irene took a walk over the hill for flowers and ferns for our church service in the tent. Our services at 11 were somewhat unique we had reading, praying and singing.

As usual, I was called on for a story and told about the Chinese Mission in Hartford as suitable for Sunday. We sang a great deal. We tried telling the thoughts that the songs brought to us in turn about the fire. We tried having each one tell a talk of the occasion on which they felt the most gratitude toward another person. This was so successful that we took the opposite and told of the times of greatest chagrin. The most striking story was Mr. Gulick's gratitude when as a boy of 12 he with his father was wrecked between Maui and Molokai. He had been tied to the mast and when the boat keeled quite over of course he couldn't come up. A native by the name of Ioba released him by diving under. They floated for hours before they were picked up.

I do not remember any particulars of the 4th of July. We were not disturbed by any ringing of bells, or firing of crackers. We devoted ourselves quite steadily to breakfast and its duties and the getting ready for that days expedition. We got off sometime in the forenoon. When we were all up and off on horse-back, we made quite a noble cavalcade and in passing the hotel, all the guests would rush to the windows to see us pass by.

Whenever we were gathered in the tent, resting or repairing damages, Mr. Emerson's volume of Tennyson would come out and there would be reading and discussion of the problems he so delicately puts. Mr. Emerson and I put up the lunch that day. After the lunch was ready the horses were ready and we were ready for our excursion. We rode off down through the pastures through the dead and dying koa groves where our way was intercepted by the trunks of fallen trees. 7 miles from camp we came to the forest. There is not another like it in all the islands—miles and miles of great koa trees—like a live oak forest—their great boles reaching high in the air and 10 to 15 ft in circumference. There is no tangle of undergrowth here only that we sometimes rode through ferns that came to the top of our saddles. When we came to a big patch of briers and found that they were full of great yellow and red wild raspberries we thought we had best stop. We made a perfect nest for ourselves in the fernery. When we were tired of sitting up we would throw ourselves back upon its greenery and find ourselves on a springy fragrant couch. The berries added a fine flavor to the bread and beans we had with us.

July 21, 1892, Kawaiahao Seminary

Dear Carl,

To begin with I must say that none of us were satisfied with what we had seen of the volcano. We wanted to get down to that fire and we soon saw that Mr. Gulick was encouraging us in it. In fact we would not have  thought of it but for him. He shared with us that Saturday night the difficulties. The sides of the crater for the first 75 ft were a precipitous wall and below that, a mass of stones small and large that made up the slope to the bottom and that in a descent it would be easy and dangerous to dislodge one. He scoffed at the idea of danger at the bottom itself if we would let him lead the way with his experience of lava. He warned us to be quiet about the whole matter if we really wished to go there. First he consulted the hotel people and the guide and they declared that it was altogether too dangerous. They did not allow their guides to take anyone down. We said mentally that the next time we went, there would be no guide.

Sunday when Dr. Lyons was with us we talked over the advisability of going down with him. He was up there you know collecting specimens for the world's fair. He said "Oh no, it would be impossible to go in. He had been assured of the dangers." We were not daunted and fixed our second expedition for Wednesday.

We had an early dinner and then Mr. Gulick delivered a little lecture. We were on no account to get separated. What one did all were to do. We girls were to be especially meek. We promised everything most faithfully. By one, we were on our way. We took a little lower trail into the crater so as not to go by the Volcano House and left our horses half way down on a grassy slope to feed. Gertrude and I trotted all the way down the rest of the slope with joined hands, stopping once to repair the monument to the man who died of heart disease in the ascent some years ago.

At the bottom we put ourselves in marching trim. Mr. Emerson made himself a walking dry-goods store with all our wraps and rubbers. Mr. Gulick took the big demi-john of water. Mr. Nickol carried the lunch which we girls furnished at our own sweet will. It was dry so we were happy. We passed Dr. Lyons hard at work who said he would join us in the evening. Arrived at the crater we deposited our loads at the bench and at once started off. Sure enough about half a mile from the bench we came upon a great crack in the lava made by an earthquake.

Here was our opportunity and down we started. Such a climb, I shall never forget. Our short skirts were of incalculable aid—in fact we could not have gone had we not been so dressed. We were very careful of the stones and if one was loose the others were warned most of the way we could help ourselves but a few times it became necessary for one of the men to take hold of our hands, another to guide our feet and so lower us down a longer descent than usual.

When we were about half way down a wonderful thing happened. That portion of the lake to which we were nearly opposite was much higher above the lava floor than the rest of it—15 ft we judged while in other places it was not more than 7 or 3 ft. Right there before our eyes the lava began to flow over a red rushing fire fall, 15 ft wide, surging and pouring as water would do. We were wild to get to the bottom to get nearer that marvel. I had been receiving less special aid than the others and the last third of the way I got some what fagged. My heart was beating like an engine and my limbs were all trembly. Mr. Emerson saw and came to my rescue steadying me all the way to the bottom.

Then, O Carl, what delicious fun, what delicious fear. While we were down there, My Carl, it overflowed in 7 places. Once I went off a little to one side by myself but stopped suddenly when I saw in the crack beneath my feet the red glow of lava. We could not get so very near our fire-fall but we went around to another flow, running more gingerly and ran up with our sticks and thrust it into the molten stuff and pulled it out while it was still red, put coins into it, stamped it in with our heels and then carried it on pieces of cold lava till we could touch it. I have such a specimen, Carl which I helped make myself—are you not glad? All too soon they said we must return or darkness would be upon us. When we got to the wall we rested. I lay right down upon the lava to try and get my breath. We would have given any thing then for water. Our throats, lips, and tongues were so dry that they fairly crackled. Mr. Emerson took charge of me. I couldn't have gotten out without his help. I was exhausted.

We stopped occasionally to rest and sooner than one would think were at the top. When we were half way out we heard a shout from the direction of the bench and looking up and discovered Professor Keep and John Waterhouse Jr. We hastened out and reached the bench as dark was coming on. I do not think it entered their heads that we had been to the bottom. They thought we were just climbing around on the rocks. I was so tired that I threw myself right down on the rocks.

Mr. Emerson brought me some wraps and I very much mistrust that he gave me a little larger portion of the water we had left than he did the others. You see before we went down in the kindness of our hearts, we kept drinking the water so that poor Mr. Gulick should not have so much to carry! We repented that! Mr. Gulick had made us promise secrecy but as I lay there, I heard him telling Professor Keep what we had done. Wasn't Johnny mad because he hadn't been there to go with us! But the best joke was when Dr. Lyons came up and he had a full canteen of water, bless him!!

Mr. Gulick motioned to me to show him my specimen. I pulled it out. Dr. Lyons smiled kindly. "Did you bring that way here from the hotel?" "No." "Oh, you got it before at some other lava flow?" "No." "Well, you haven't been down there?" "Yes." "What, all of you?" "Yes."

I never saw a more tired-looking man. He is a very quiet, silent man but his face is expressive. After a while he walked off with Mr. Emerson to look at the crack and said to him, "I guess if those young ladies can go down there I can." He wasn't 24 hours older before he tried it too but he missed his best opportunity. I forgot to say that while we were down in there, it overflowed in 7 places and before we left that evening quite a 1/3 of the floor was covered with new lava and when he went down the next day it was too hot to go out on the lava at all.

We had a wonderful evening there—the moon was full. Our exhilaration made us quite blissful. I was so full of the thoughts of you and what you would say to what I had done and so proud to think I had done something that you would be pleased with that I could not keep still. Mr. Emerson knew before that I was engaged though I had not spoken of it out. I spoke of you then and he was so very kind, dear. He asked me all about you and seemed real interested. He was confidential too and told me much of his life and all about his love for Miss Brewer. I could sympathize with him and encourage him from my heart for I believe him to be one of the few true, refined men it has been my lot to meet. I did not discover a low or mean sentiment in him. Carl you must understand. He cannot help being drawn to me for he knows Miss Brewer thinks a good deal of me, has confided in me and I am the nearest approach to her that he has. Besides that, he honors me as a woman of intelligence with pure and noble ideals. (Pardon my vain-glory, dear.) I don't think he has ever met anyone before who came so near what he wants Miss Brewer to be like. He has known few women and yet like you he reverences and idealizes womanhood. In our companionship he did a great deal for me. To have someone respect me and look up to me like that, someone who was really of much more account in the world than I made my heart young again. I think it will make all my work this year lighter to know there is someone in Honolulu who is firmly convinced that I am a good and noble woman with the prospect of a beautiful home before me and not simply a Kawaiahao drudge.

Well, the ground seemed soft to us that night but how lame we were the next day! It was painful to me to step on or off the verandah and I noticed that all were happiest when they were lying quietly in the tent. Our expedition that day was a quiet one—it was simply to the hotel for a sulpher bath. It was a very funny experience to be shut up in a little closet with only your head sticking out and be steamed. I didn't know but I should quite dissolve. There was a good shower bath there to wash off in and all we girls took the opportunity to give our heads and hair a good washing. We looked around the hotel and sat before the fire in the old billiard room. I found the old record book and the story "Mark Twain" wrote in it when he was there years ago. The woman who has charge there gave us a bag of mangos and bananas to take back to camp with us.

That was our last night in camp and we had quite a time. We wanted a camp-fire but it began a misty rain so we had to light candles and stay in the tent. We girls had to ask permission of the gentlemen to let our hair loose so that it might dry before we slept. However, after we had retired, my suppressed excitement would out so after trying one girl after another I got Gertrude stirred up and we had a "tear." We giggled and laughed. We tried the native wrestling Mr. Emerson had taught us. We danced the skirt dance— we made saucy remarks to the gentlemen and when they told us to keep still we said we would go outside. We pulled up the end of the tent and laid our heads out on a log there while it rained softly in our faces. The gentlemen thought we were all outside and I heard Mr. Gulick say, "Emerson, have we got to go out and lasso those girls?" That brought us in and we subsided. Mr. Gulick said he thought I must have been drinking wine.

The next morning I had to be up at five to help Mr. Nichol get breakfast. By seven, that was eaten, the mules were packed and by nine we were on our way to Hilo. At the Volcano House they all came out to see us off. When we got out on the road again it began to rain and by the time we had reached Mr. Staples at the half-way house at 2 o'clock, we were pretty damp. They had telephoned ahead to have coffee for us there but instead of that he had quite a hearty lunch and to our surprise would not let us pay anything. I suppose we ate at the expense of the government as he has charge of the prisoners there. We went over their barracks and by about 3 were mounted again. With good roads the miles sped past us. Every mile is marked. Once we did a mile in 6 minutes. We stopped once for "ohelas" or mountain apples. It was really a delightful day and the 31 miles that we rode did not over tire us.

The Austins were at their six o'clock dinner when we arrived. Before we had our dinners we were trying to assume again the dress of civilization. Mr. Baker, the minister of the foreign church came in to say that he had told his people the previous Sunday that brothers Emerson and Gulick were up the mountain and although he had not consulted them he would postpone the Wednesday evening prayer-meeting to Friday evening when he was sure Mr. Gulick would preach the Preparatory sermon. Wasn't that ministerial cheek? Mr. Gulick refused to preach but said he would assist.

The bell was ringing while we ate. Stiff and tired as we all were we went to prayer meeting where Mr. Baker made a long prosy talk during which Mr. Gulick went sound asleep, waking up however at the proper time. Mrs. Gulick was much shocked for you see the story of our going down into Halemaumau had been brought down by Johnny Waterhouse. Judge Austin thought it a very reckless thing to do and Mrs. Gulick was a little disturbed over it.

Saturday brought new events. That evening Mrs. Severance had the "literary" at her house.[3] It seems to be a very erratic sort of a society that they have whenever they want to entertain company. They gave an exhibition of camera pictures. It was all on our account as the rest had seen it before. Mrs. Gulick sang a most charming Spanish song. Then Mrs. Severance came to me and asked if I would tell a story. It made me a little cross for I knew she had asked the others before hand and I thought she might have done as much for me. I really think though that it had not entered her head that I would do such a thing in public and I think someone told her that I had. I rushed into the dressing-room to bang my head against the wall to find an idea for a setting for the story. Gertrude sang while I was out. I started in. My compliment to the scientific spirit of Hilo took and I had the best of attention. I could tell from the kindly look of the eyes of my party that I was doing all right and that they were pleased so I sailed ahead and had a storm of applause when I was done. When I came back in Mr. Gulick was right there with "You've made a great hit." I heard much about it thereafter, somehow it just seemed to please their fancy and you shall see what the paper said about it.

Mr. Gulick preached in the foreign and Mr. Emerson in the native church and got over to the foreign in time to assist in the communion service. Mr. Emerson lunched with us and then all went to the Japanese chapel where both our ministers took part again in the service of welcome to the Japanese minister Okabe who had just returned to them. In the evening there was a grand union service at the big native church where we preached some more.

I must tell you of a little scheme I worked that day. In the middle of the night the *Kinau* had come in again from Honolulu with lots of Honolulu people aboard, a regular teacher's expedition with Punahou, Kamehameha, and Kawaiahao all aboard to say nothing of the Punahou Glee Club. Miss Brewer was among the number, to be the guest of Mrs. Scott for the summer. Mr. Emerson had been planning with me for some days to take me to see her. He wanted me, because he thought he might have a better time. I said I would arrange it.

She was at church that morning and you would have laughed if you had seen me manipulate things. Poor Mr. Emerson could only get the barest word with her but she was quite effusive over me. I told her I must see her to talk over the trip as I considered it was really hers since she had gained me the invitation. Mrs. Scott who was right near and had shown a soft spot for me all along then asked me to come out Monday to dinner and in an aside said she would send for me. I said, "Oh don't trouble, Mr. Emerson has offered to take me out." She said, "All right" then a minute or two later I was beside Mr. Emerson and said, "We are invited to Mrs. Scott's tomorrow for dinner." Of course he was delighted.

Monday was a very different kind of a day. All the rest of the party except Mr. Emerson and I went on an expedition to Akaka falls which was to last into the next day. I felt rather badly not to go because I knew I was putting myself into rather a false light with people in regard to Mr. Emerson, but I knew how much that dinner meant to him and that he wanted my help and so long as my own party understood I could endure a little for his sake. I know it was a real grief to the others that we did not go as it took life from the company.

After I had seen them off, Mr. Emerson realized that I was giving up something for him so in a short time he was around to tell me he had secured Mr. Anderson our red friend to go to Coconut Island if I would get some ladies. I could only get Carrie Gilman and he got Miss Elisa Hitchcock. They called for us with a double carriage and we took a ride of about 1 1/2 mile along the beach then entered a little boat and rowed out over the breakers to the beautiful little island.

We got back to lunch about one and I had a chance for a nap till three when

Mr. Emerson came for me with a nice carriage to go to Mrs. Scott's. It was a very beautiful home to go to, beautifully terraced grounds—a home full of pretty comfortable things pretty children, pretty wife and a blue-eyed, clear-eyed Scotchman at its head. Things were off very nicely.

Our party left right after lunch for our last expedition. About 29 miles from Hilo we stopped to visit Pepe Falls. I think I counted 9 of them and below each fall is a big rock hole into which the water pours and froths giving them the name of the "boiling pots."

As it grew towards dark Mrs. Gulick and Miss Hammond left us to return to Hilo while we four went on to spend the night in the woods and the forest cottage of the Hitchcock's or "Bougainville."[4] We found Miss Eliza Hitchcock and May Waterhouse there with the Jap and his wife who does the work. The house is a long shed like all open on one side with a huge fire place in the center and a row of bedsteads in the rear separated from each other by calico curtains. Right at one side a beautiful spring bubbles up and all around is the stillness of the forest.

We were to be in Hilo by breakfast time but Miss Eliza was up to serve us hot coffee. Mr. Gulick went to see about saddling and sent back word that the mule had escaped and he had gone after it. Our seven mile ride down to Hilo was delightful. Mauna Kea was clear and cloud-free. We reached Hilo by 8 had breakfast and then fell to work on last things packing and settling bills and saying "good-bys." At 12 we were at the wharf with half of Hilo there to see us off, Miss Brewer among the rest. Somehow that seemed to me a good omen for Mr. Emerson.

> With love,
> Carrie

August 1, 1892, Kawaiahao Seminary

Dear Carl,

August 11—I think you will like me, dearie, when I come home. This summer has given me a little more assurance for I know I have given pleasure to some with whom I have been thrown and that they trust and like  me. I have had more social attention since I came home than in all the time I have been here before through the influence of Mr. Gulick and Mr. Emerson.

The time does indeed fly—only 3 weeks more before school begins. Carl, I really had to get a new hat for church. Millie Beckwith trimmed it for me and our big naughty yet bright Koni[5] cried "Miss Winter you are pretty." I said, "Oh Koni, that's flattery." "No," she cried, "from my heart, you are pretty." O just to hear my Carl say that once with his eyes full of genuine admiration! I'm just going to win him over again when I go home and make him think the second time is better than the first.

I start on a trip around this island tomorrow at 4 a.m. I am to have an alarm clock in my room to waken me. Then I go over and waken Miss Katherine Pope and we go down and ring up (by telephone) Mr. Emerson. At 5 we will be at Kamehameha where the Babbs and Mr. Thompson will join us. We are to be at Waialua—Mr. Emerson's old home and Mr. Gulick expects to join us there. We may be gone all the week. We ought to have a fine time. I wanted our Miss Pope on this trip very much but she could not go on account of Miss Harris, who seems to get weaker all the time. I want so much to get away for it is hot. I am all broken out with the heat. I have been on duty 24 1/2 days. Am sorry to be in a hurry now. We ride 28 miles tomorrow.

I love you—Carrie

August 14, 1892, Waialua Oahu

Dear Carl,

Six of the clock on a beautiful Sunday morning. We are at the old Emerson homestead. The family still keeps the property but it is all rented to a ranch man by the name of Lawrence and they turn some of their large old house to profit by keeping travelers. It seems much like an old New England inn. I have just pursued the apparition of a colored man with two foaming milk-pails around the house till I cornered him in the dairy and persuaded him to let me drink my fill of his new warm milk.

All this country was once thronged with natives and in the 40's the Father Emerson came here and had this region for miles around as his parish. He got the coral rock, made the plaster and with the help of natives, built this house after the approved pattern of Connecticut River houses—from time to time additions had to be made to accommodate the seven sons and one daughter. The only other white neighbors were the Gulicks on the other side of the little Waialua River. There were 7 boys and one girl also. It is nice to have Mr. Emerson along. Mr. Gulick joins us tomorrow and he will have another set of stories to tell us.

I must tell you of the ride yesterday. I was awakened by Mr. Emerson down in the yard getting the horses up. He took care of them for us and by the time we had had our breakfasts and were ready to start it was nearly six. We stopped once to eat some bananas but did not overtake the Babbs till we were about 10 miles from town. They are traveling in their little break and are able to take most of our bundles in it. We ate some sandwiches there and then started on again reaching here sometime after two. Most of the way was over a high grassy plain with mountains in the distance on either side and the road was very good. It was somewhat hard because there was no green about us, only dry brown grass and we became quite sun-burned. A bath and lunch and a nap refreshed us and we were ready for a walk about the old place last evening and even down to the "far-sounding" sea. Mr. Emerson preached in the native church today and he asked me to talk to them a little in the evening meeting and he would interpret.

We all went out under the great tamarind tree in the morning and had a chapter in the Bible read and some poetry and a little conversation. At 11 we went over to the native church where the pastor Mr. Timoteo greeted us with effusion and gave us the front seat.[6] We couldn't understand anything and could only assist in the collection and the singing.

Sunday, August 21—I will go on with my story. I thought it was to be a kind of prayer meeting in the evening but prepared what I had to say on "true Christian womanhood" with points on cleanliness, thrift, cheerfulness, purity and sane life—the result of what I want for native women after seeing and knowing them for two years. Truly, dear, I didn't do it to show off but because I thought it might do a little good. I was a little taken aback however. There were a good many natives there and only our party for white people, and after singing, reading and praying Mr. Timoteo indicated that I was to speak. Of course it made it twice as long with the translation and when I was done, the benediction was pronounced, and we went home. I had to laugh inside myself at the idea of my being the speaker of the evening. What do you think of that, Carl?

I think that Monday was the gem of the whole expedition. Carl, if you could have been there! We did not use our own horses but Mr. Emerson secured four good ones from a native friend of his—fine large spirited horses used for chasing cattle. Miss Pope[7] and I discarded riding skirts altogether and just wore our short tramping skirts and were every bit as good as boys. I doubt if you would have known me.

I was with Mr. Emerson most of the time because he is lots nicer and more fun. Somehow we get along splendidly together. For miles and miles we rode. I think the wind and the fine horses made us a little wild.

It was quite dark but we had to go to the sea for a bath. We put our suits on at the house and carried down dresses to put on at the beach. Of course there are no bath houses but they rigged up a shawl on some sticks. It was so dark you couldn't see anything anyhow. The water was alive with phosphorescent life; little spots would fasten on your arms and legs. When we came out, Miss Pope lost her head. Some fishermen were coming down the beach with lanterns. Mr. Babb came to drive them back and that only made matters worse. There was no real trouble only a good laugh at Miss Pope for her fears. We had a good sleep. Wasn't that a fine day, Charlie?

Aug. 24—I am 26 years old today and I have no birthday kiss from my lover. What shall I do? I'll go to him before the next one comes. Tuesday we left Waialua, fording the wide stream, accompanied by Mr. Timoteo who was to be with us for a day or two. All the way on that side of the mountains it is a narrow lane averaging ½ mile between the mountains and the sea. The mountains are precipitous on that side, gently sloping on the other and the road is always excellent. Sometimes it verges toward the sea, sometimes toward the mountains.

It was when we were down near the sea that Mr. Timoteo urged us to go and see the idol that the natives in that region worship. We left our horses and climbed down to a rocky point where we found a rough large rock balanced on end. They call it "Kane-aukai," the God who swims the sea. All around were the bones of animals, birds that had been offered there. We tried to overturn it but with our united efforts could not do so till we had dug away the foundation stones and then over it toppled. We road on feeling like iconoclasts.

At Kahuku, is the ranch on which Katie and William live.[8] We rode in to greet them. The Dillingham's and Whitney's who are spending the summer there were off on a picnic. We saw Katie and met William on the road. We rode on to the mill and took our lunch in a restaurant kept by Chinamen. There was a special table for white people and the lunch was very good.

I don't remember any incident of the afternoon ride except that we all got quite tired before we reached our stopping place. This was a home owned by a Mr. Lane, an Irish Catholic who has a native wife and family.[9] Mr. Lane himself was away. In fact there was no one there but a party of boys, some his sons, some over from Honolulu who were having a fishing vacation. We had quite an experience here.

There are three or more cottages on the place and they assigned us our rooms at once and proceeded to bring forth the clean bed linen before our eyes and make our beds. Our rooms were very satisfactory. There was no curtain in the one given to Miss Pope and me but we pinned up a shawl and were all right. The water was just a little way down from the house and we all went in for a bath. I swam out to a boat a little distance from the shore and with the aid of Mr. Gulick climbed into it. He tried to teach me to swim on my back and we were all stung by the blue Portuguese men-of-war which were very abundant. It didn't smart very long though.

We made ourselves look as fine as we could for dinner which consisted of stewed chicken, rice, fried taro, warm biscuit and tea. We made a hearty meal. Meanwhile we heard the boys playing on their guitars, outside and when we assembled on the verandah after dinner they all came and gave us a concert. The best singer was dubbed "Romeo" on account of his flashing eyes and teeth which he would turn on us in the most thrilled manner while he sang sentimental Hawaiian love songs. He is a student at the St. Louis College (Catholic) in this city and his manners were quite charming. For some reason the gentlemen didn't enthuse over him as we did.

It rained torrents that night and we feared for our expedition up the valley of Kaliuwaa. At breakfast somehow we lost our appetites for day light revealed such an array of filthy dishes as almost made you sick to look at. Till the rain stopped, we whiled away the time in reading—they had a number of good books.

About 10 we started leaving. A short ride brought us to the entrance of the valley which is simply a crack in the earth. I never saw so narrow a valley. The men had told us before we started that we must not pick any of the fruit on the way up or the stones would fall on us and kill us. But the first fine guavas we came to, Mr. Timoteo picked for us, and then with a fine flourish called on the rocks to fall on him.

We went for a long way on horseback, fording the foaming little brook again and again. All the way up someone had made little votive offerings, carefully placing fresh leaves under stones. We upset as many as possible of them. At last we left the horses and climbed up the river channel. Mr. Emerson wanted or rather preferred to help me but Mr. Gulick cut him out. In the short time, our feet were quite wet for we had to cross the river so many times but they managed to keep us girls out of the water for the most part by placing stones, etc. Mr. Timoteo carried Miss Pope on his back once or twice.

Now I am going to tell you the unpleasant thing of the trip. Mr. Gulick is very fond of ladies socially and I have felt from the beginning that he hadn't as fine a fiber as Mr. Emerson. Well, when he was helping me, I thought once or twice he was not quite nice in touching me and thought I would try to manage to not have him help me. At one side is a round scooped out place with a little water trickling down where the natives say the pig-god once slid down but which Prof. Dana thought must once have been a steam hole with one side broken out. After admiring the beauty of the place—I got by myself and in the splash of the water-fall, forgot all but you. But I soon found there was no mistaking Mr. Gulick's actions. He was not treating me with respect and I seemed powerless to defend myself. I just made an opportunity to say to Mr. Emerson "Please help me. Mr. Gulick is not helping me in the right way." He murmured something in native under his breath. I said "Is it evil to him whom evil thinks?" "No," he told me later, "tis a fault of his."

We rode on home, lunched on the rice and chicken, took a long nap and then went bathing. I found that my persecution was renewed in the water. Mr. Gulick just would not let me alone. He must teach me to swim on my back and he wouldn't hold me by the back or shoulders. Mr. Emerson carried him off once and I ought to have gone in, but I foolishly stayed in. I didn't know what to do and began to think seriously of speaking to him for he was a constant terror to me in that way.

The boys gave us a fine supper that night and we ate heartily again. They had made yellow-flower leis for all the ladies that evening. After dinner we had a repetition of the concert increased by one musical instrument. A new man, Mr. Coney, had come over from the city that day and the bass viola which he played was a broom stick drawn across his thumb which rested on a large table as a sounding board. He made it chord well too. His mother is a rich woman, a friend of the Queen's. He has an American wife and is quite superior to most natives.

Mr. Timoteo told us a long native story which Mr. Gulick translated. It was full of life and action and kept us laughing. Thursday morning I proposed that we go fishing and so we did. Miss Pope was afraid of the water but the rest of us were provided with hooks and lines and rowed in two boats nearly to the reef. I fear you won't believe me but I caught the first fish and the most fish of any body. Mr. Gulick said he would give me 10 cents if I would catch the first fish and I can show you the money to prove it by.

For the last meal, those boys prepared a duck stew but they forgot and left the feet in the stew! We were glad to go on. They had done their best for us and would only take $10 for all their trouble.

I got Mr. Gulick behind when we were on horseback and told him just what the trouble was. It took lots of courage Carl, but I am sure it was the best thing to do. It was like a thunder-clap to him but he is truly a good man and then and later when he spoke of it, he begged my pardon and said he had no excuse and thanked me heartily. He has been all right ever since but somehow I shall be glad when he goes home.

Aug. 25. I must tell you of the only recognition my birthday received. The day before Mr. Emerson was talking of the "bloom being lost from the peach" and I said "Oh dear, what will my lover say. I am 26 tomorrow." He promptly replied, "He will say the tropics have given you color and health." Then last night after prayer-meeting he came up here with a nice box of candy for me and 26 of the prettiest kind of land shells.

Well here is the end. It is not a very good letter but I love you very truly and I long to see you.

Carrie

August 26, 1892, Kamehameha School

Dear Charlie,

I was very glad to get your letter this morning. I am glad you take such an interest in our friend Mr. Emerson. I hope I have not given you a wrong impression about Mr. Gulick. Though I can't profess to fancy him now particularly, I feel perfectly safe in his company.

When you are in New York I think you had better drop in at the Potter building and call on Mr. Theodore Richards. He is located there now. He is the next principal of Kamehameha and you know has just married May Atherton.[10] You must give him my "aloha nui."

After calling at the Judds we had a very pretty ride to the edge of the sea. Once we charged up a hill to inspect a big cave and then turned in at a little cottage to give me an opportunity to speak to two of our girls who lived there.

Toward 6 o'clock, we arrived at the Collin's where we were to remain over night. It was a family like the Lane's, white father and native family. They did everything for us turning out the three best rooms in which were comfortable beds for us. His wife was a superior native woman and one of the daughters teaches a little school. She got her education at the Catholic school in the city. The dishes were clean here and the food good—very nice bread, sweet potatoes, luaued fish and pork. We had the house to ourselves and the family went off somewhere and slept on mats.

The next morning was raining and we sat around till 10 and after reading one of Mark Twain's books and then mounted our horses to visit Waiahole valley. Only Miss Pope, Mr. Emerson a native boy and myself, survived to the fall. The mud drove the others back. The native boy had to carry us on his back repeatedly. Around the fall were bananas and the boy took a bunch down. When we reached the house at one, the Babb's had started on. We packed up, ate our dinner and were off by 2:30. I left my old shoes and dress to be burned. I stopped once to call on one of our girls, Ellen Ku who lives over there.

I don't know what next week will hold for me. I think I will make a thin dress. I have finished my long piece of wedding lace. It is beautiful. I must make sleeve pieces next. I dreamed about you last night and I send you today's love by this letter.

> Yours,
> Carrie

NOTES

1. Zelie Lima.
2. The road was made out of trunks of ferns and is often mentioned in guidebooks of the time.
3. The Hilo literary and musical event took place on July 9, 1892, and was briefly described in the *Daily Bulletin* (July 16, 1892, p. 4).
4. The family of attorney David Howard Hitchcock (1832–1899) had a house called Booganville located above Hilo near the Kaumana caves.
5. Koni Puʻuohau.
6. Rev. Enoch S. Timoteo was pastor of the church at Waialua and was later associated with Kaumakapili Church. Queen Liliʻuokalani mentions him in her memoirs, and he remained her loyal subject after the revolution.
7. Miss Winter refers here to Katherine Pope.
8. William Rathburn and his wife, Katherine Clarke Rathburn, former pupil at Kawaiahaʻo Female Seminary.
9. This is the family of William Carey Lane. Several of his sons were imprisoned for their efforts to restore Queen Liliʻuokalani to the throne in 1895.

10. Theodore Richards and Mary C. Atherton married June 29, 1892, in Honolulu. Caroline Babb remarked in her letter of May 18, 1892, that it was difficult to select a present for a bride whose father and uncles were millionaires. Babb Papers, The Bancroft Library, University of California–Berkeley.

11

The Queen in Crisis
September 4–October 23, 1892

September 4, 1892, Kawaiahao Seminary

Dearest,

What a country this is! Of course you know the country is on the verge of bankruptcy and that there is little prospect of relief and now comes Satan in the form of a branch of the Louisiana Lottery and last week this  proposal was made in the legislature: "If you will let us come here and establish our lottery, exempt us from taxation and give us free use of the mails for 25 yrs. we will give to your government $500,000 a year $75,000 for the new cable, a lot for Pearl Harbor and a number of other appropriations which I have forgotten." It is a great temptation and it has spread like fire among the people. I suppose it is safe to say that the majority are in favor of it. The Queen is supposed to wink it. There are many private bribes. One member of the legislature is to receive $10,000 a year and a bonus of $30,000 if he gets it through. I will try and get hold of their tract the "Golden Era" and send it to you.[1] They have their petition with many influential names upon it.

What of the missionary party! I wish you could have been in prayer meeting last Wednesday night! The chamber of commerce has its counter petition in circulation. The women have held a man's meeting and started their petition. I am on a committee to get up a petition for the school children. Who ever thought I would be engaged in a lottery fight. Our party is the smaller numerically but it's that portion of the community which expects to be heard when it speaks. The men say they do not think it will pass and yet they dare not speak too confidently. Many of the legislators can be bribed. The only thing that gives us any confidence in this legislature comes from the fact that last Tuesday night they turned out the ministry which they ought to have done two months ago.

Now comes the test to the Queen. Her favorite, Marshall Wilson, is believed by many people to be the Queen's paramour.[2] Since the beginning of her reign, it has been the annoyance of all good people that she did not send this man, openly in league with the opium ring away. She has stuck to him through thick and thin.

Well we don't know what is before us. This last thing has quite distracted public attention from the famous Horner Bill for the printing of unlimited paper money to relieve the situation. Already the raid on the bank has begun. People say it's probably safe but not certainly. I gave notice for my small amount August 12 and I hope to get it some time this month. I can't afford to let it stay on probabilities for too much depends on it in my case. When I get it, I don't know what to do with it—send it home or deposit it in the Bishop Bank where it will draw no interest. Last night was "Cousin's society" and after a long discussion it was at last decided to give up the "Girls Industrial Home" a prospect over which there has been much partisanship. Tomorrow school opens and the Queen still refuses to appoint a cabinet.

Lovingly,
Carrie

September 11, 1892, Kawaiahao Seminary

Dear Carl,

I am glad to say that we have reached a degree of calmness, which is very desirable after our tempestuous week. Dr. Beckwith, who is home again, preached on the lottery this morning. A very good sermon.

Evening—The Queen still continues to be obstinate in regard to the new ministry. It is almost two weeks now since the vote of "want of confidence." She doesn't follow well in the lead of her model, Victoria. Mr. Oleson tersely put it "Wilson or annexation," and it does look as if she were heeding very bad counsel for her own best interests. She evidently wishes to return to the old constitution. I'd like to see annexation come while I was here. I believe I'd almost be willing to stay an extra week to see the stars and stripes over this country.

Today is Monday and since I have the matron's work, it makes a very full day for me. I have been simply buried in marking sheets and pillow-cases, expounding decimals and prime factors, urging comparative silence while dish washing was going on, snatching Mary Moe from the charms of baseball, to station her firmly before the spoon pan, serving dinner with one eye to the wants of the teachers, one to entertain Miss Hoppin as company and one on

120 girls. The last was to take a girl to the doctors to see if he could extract a needle which she had got in while washing. That doesn't begin to tell!

I hope you are having some fine evenings now in September. What a beautiful month it is at home. Perhaps God will let me spend the next one with you. I don't quite expect it though for I fancy we must wait a little longer. Anyway I do want to see you Charlie. You must court me all over again. I'll be new you know and I'll know how to act this time. What do you say? Ice-cream, rides—moonlight walks, rowing, horse-back riding. Perhaps you don't think I am pretty enough for so much trouble. You wait and see!!

Tuesday Evening—I got dizzy in sewing class this afternoon and gave it over to Maggie Powers while I went to bed. By dinner I was clear headed again but the house had been so noisy that I longed to get away from it and ordered my horse. Soon I was at the rear of Punch Bowl where the breezes came fresh and cool from the mountains and I could see a beautiful valley and the luminous sea.

Maggie Powers received today the appointment to a school on Hawaii. She is to be assistant to Miss Helen Hoppin and live with her, salary $400. It is a fine chance for Maggie to do well by herself.

The Queen has appointed a ministry which we all expect to see turned out tomorrow, as two were in the former ministry and the others are not satisfactory.

View of Honolulu from Punchbowl with Diamond Head on left. Photo by Lilla Estelle Appleton.

Mr. P.C. Jones and family are back and many would like to see him made minister of finance.

>God bless you,
>Your Carrie

September 17, 1892, Kawaiahao Seminary

Dearest,

One of the girls in my room has not come back this year and we hear that she has gone quite wrong. It was the horrid girl who was always getting off "C.K."
   What can I tell you of politics? The legislatures with a majority of one, sustained the Queen's evil cabinet. Now the question is up "Majority of those present or of all members." Several of those voting to retain them will vote "want of confidence" in a short time if they do not turn out Marshall Wilson. The Queen won't do that if she can help herself.
   I caught quite a cold this last week and it quite used me up one day but now I am feeling more like myself than I have since school opened. I was very tired and homesick. It seemed as if I simply could not stand it to stay here through this year but I think I can now. Carl does a year ever pass? Do you think this one ever will?
   Dearest, do you know I am quite a little worried about the cholera. All my dear ones are right on the coast, so near to infection. I am so glad it is late in the year. It is a terrible thing. What if they should quarantine vessels on the Pacific side! I don't believe they will unless the cholera goes to Australia. God grant it may not come here. It would be awful among the natives. These are unnecessary forebodings.

>I am sorry this is so short,
>Carrie

September 25, 1892, Waikiki

Dearest,

Ruth Hoppin and I are here this time. The cottage has been moved way down the beach on a perfectly barren plot of ground without a bit of shade or grass. The cottage is as cozy as ever but it will be a good many years

before the surroundings are as good again. There is a pretty view of the Waimea huts and Diamond Head. The steamer came in 1 A.M. Friday, but was not allowed to enter the harbor till day light and then the 70 bags of mail were fumigated and it was 5 P.M. before we got our letters. All the letters had the corners cut.

It seems as if, if ever any people had reason to have the most beautiful of homes, you and I have. My life here has taught me much about that. I think I have made it something of a business ever since I was engaged to you. If ever I get a chance I mean to attend a cooking school to get just the best ideas on that. We can't look forward to wealth but there is a certain kind of elegance I do look forward to—a well stocked linen closet—a clean and neat and orderly house. I think I know too much to become a slave to my work. I appreciate outdoor life and intellectual pleasures and social pleasures and I propose to be my husband's companion in those things. My, what a busy woman I shall be!

Was glad of the Oberlin news you wrote. My objection to dancing in Oberlin is this. As it is now with so many young men and women, there is a great deal of the excitement of social life—more than in most places where one may live, and that is enough without adding dancing, whose chief evil is the excitement it produces.

Mr. Gulick did all in his power to make that thing right. I fear he has been guilty of such carelessness before but has never had his attention called to it before. He is truly a good man and it was real sorrow and shame that he experienced when he realized what a slip he had made. I trust him perfectly now and count him a good friend. He did me many a good turn. One of the last things he said to me was, "You have a real gift in speech which you ought to cultivate. When you go home you will doubtless have opportunity to tell of your experiences here and you must improve them." It is much for a man of 50 to recognize a woman of 26 as his intellectual equal.

About Mr. Emerson—I am glad you wrote and your slightest wish in regard to him is my law. I mean to tell you everything in regard to him and you must never hesitate to sound the alarm. The man is the soul of honor and so appreciates the friendliness I give him and so holds your honor as his own that I believe he would cut his right hand off before he would allow himself to offend. I am kept safe by my position. I defy any man to pay much special attention to a teacher at Kawaiahao.

I had a busy day yesterday marking clothes for Keluia Kiwaha. How is that for a name?

With much love,
Carrie

October 1, 1892, Kawaiahao Seminary

Dearest Carl,

In eight months time now I will be making active prepa-  rations for going home. This evening there was a concert at the Opera House for the benefit of the Central Union organ fund. Miss Pope and I went with Mr. Emerson. The house was full and it was really quite an elegant affair, the ladies dressed in evening dress and without hats. Miss Pope wore her dainty blue and I my white silk.

I went that afternoon to Kamehameha where I rested an hour in a quiet room, enjoyed the dinner where all the teachers were assembled. I sat beside

Kamehameha School Faculty. Standing (L to R back row) Levi C. Lyman, George Babb, Miss Katherine Pope, William B. Oleson, Uldrick Thompson, Miss Nancy J. Malone, R. Anderson, and Miss Alice Knapp. (Seated L to R in second row). Mrs. Uldrick Thompson, Mrs. Andrews, Miss Ruth Hoppin, unidentified. (L to R in front row) Mrs. Babb, Jeanne Bates.

Mr. Oleson and we had quite a spirited conversation. In the evening there was music in the Preparatory. Miss Halstead their extremely pretty new teacher sings charmingly. I also met the new teacher Mr. Ruevsky who takes Mr. Richard's place. He is from Boston Divinity School but I found he had spent a year at Hartford Seminary, so we had material for conversation. He seems a modest and gentlemanly man. Mrs. Babb thinks the Olesons and Thompson's do not fancy him. I stayed till quarter of nine and then Mr. Babb rode down with me in the moonlight. Mr. Thompson said he was to be envied. You see, dear, I have a few very kind and appreciative friends.

Oct 11—[27 yrs.] A whole week has flown and it contains much that I must tell you. I have just been rereading your two letters. The *China* and the *Australia* sailed the same day and the *Australia*'s mail was put on the *China* as the fastest sailor. It took a whole day to fumigate it. The *China* was not allowed to come into the harbor. The *Australia* came in the next day and was quarantined till yesterday. Our new music teacher was aboard but we did not get her till after 5 last evening.

After church—I am aware of the fact that today is your 27th birthday. I know you are wishing today that I were with you to make it a festive day. May every coming year add to your worth.

We all think the alarm here is disproportionate to the cause in regard to cholera. Dr. Trousseau is largely responsible. They are not often over careful about anything. By the way, he was here yesterday visiting two of his children.

I don't think much of the naval men I have seen. Let me correct you, dear, "They look like some of them belonged to a hard set." I was teaching my girls the other day "use like for word comparisons and as for sentences."

You say you are often down hearted. Wait till I come. I hope never to give you cause for it. I wish I had the power even way off here to banish it from you. Just now if there is any in your heart, "Dear sweet-and-twenty" banish it for my sake.

Evening—Tuesday is Miss Armstrong's birthday also. I shall have to remember it in some way since she gave me a little apron the other day for my birthday. It seemed to me like quite a desperate effort on her part to be sure of remembrance for herself. Poor, cranky old thing!

That brings me to the new teacher. I have only known her for a day but she didn't make a very good impression to begin with. Isn't it a pity we can't get just plain ordinary common-sense people! Her name is Burgess and she is quite young and would by many be considered good-looking. To me she is coarse looking without a line of refinement in her face. She has fine teeth and an agreeable mouth. She is good-natured, strong, and ready to work but her ideas are way off. The people on the ship filled her with tales of Miss Patch. She announced at once that she expected to give a concert in 3 weeks, half of whose proceeds should go to the church as everybody would be anxious to hear her. Also that she enjoyed society very much and expected to go out a great deal that she was not "pious" as she didn't think it necessary for a music teacher to be, and that she expected to take outside work.

Miss Pope had a talk with her last night and "sat" on her to some extent. She said she should appeal to Mr. Atherton[3] on the dancing question and if she didn't like things she should pack her trunk and leave. She has given herself away here right and left, in this short time. Poor little idiot! I shouldn't wonder if the girls would knock the nonsense out of her right speedily and then she would prove a very satisfactory teacher. It's decidedly sickening as it is. I review my intention of keeping out of the way of the fuss and mess as much as possible. It sounds rather distant as a policy but I really think it's the way to get along in a school of this kind—not be particularly friendly—do your work as well as you can—but take your recreation in another set of people if possible.

We had our first pay this last week and had to take it in "paper and silver." We made so much fun over it that Mr. Atherton has promised to secure gold for the coming months. I doubt if I can save more than $5 this month. I am very sorry about it. I owed the Seminary, $4 for shoeing, $4 for feed—about $10 for dressmaking. I paid Miss Pope $7 for her share in the saddle—pictures $3 and dentistry. There were some little things I had to have.

I will stop now with my dearest love. The girls are home from church and I must go down and have a serious midnight talk with the two Chinese girls I have had in the closet all day. The proof is very strong that they have been stealing but they deny it up and down.

Oct. 11—I spent an hour at the dentist's this afternoon, and after supper went to the hospital to call on Miss Harris. She is facing an operation and everything is very sad to me about it.

Our new teacher can sing even if she is faulty in many of her speeches. She absolutely refuses to pray at morning devotions. Well, darling, I wish that my prayers for you this day might be answered. One thing I pray is that I may grow more worthy of you.

> I love you very much,
> Carrie

October 16, 1892, Kawaiahao Seminary

Dearest,

The lottery bill came up last week and the motion to in-
definitely postpone was lost by a small majority. It was
referred to a committee.

Last Thursday Miss Burgess went with me to Waikiki
and we had a bath and supped with Miss Kinney. It was quite a tame diversion
but she was very happy over it. I have been making something of a study of
her and am going to try and help her as I mistrust she needs helping just at
this time. She came down with extremely inflated and false ideas of the part
she should take in Honolulu life. They have all been overthrown. Naturally
she is a frank, good-natured girl and it seems to me that it depends now very
much on what she does and whom she goes with as to how she develops
whether into a deceitful, artificial society girl or into a whole-hearted girl who
is going to get the blessing out of the outdoor life that is the real merit and
blessing of this place. I want to introduce her to the latter.

I have just had my first little fracas with Miss Hadley. She is taking Miss
Kenwill's place in the kitchen and she sailed into me for taking half a dozen
biscuits without asking her. As I have never asked Miss Kenwill or Miss Harris
or Miss Davis when I wanted a lunch but helped myself and as every other
teacher does, I "sassed" her up a bit. She tried to make me think she always
asked. I was too polite to contradict her to her face, but I will here.

October 19—Well the cabinet has been voted out again. The grounds given
were their failure to advance any policy for relieving the financial depression,
for not doing anything toward new treaty relations with the U.S. and for making
no effort to clean out the police department. I suppose the Queen will do just
as she did before—refuse to call a member of the opposition. I would if the people will stand it. I suppose she thinks she is abused in having so many changes.

October 20—I went down to prayer-meeting with Mr. Frank Cooke. It was
the annual meeting of the W.C.T.U.[4] of which Mrs. Whitney is president. There
was the usual talk about Miss Frances Willard ad nauseum. A funny thing happened to me at the close. I stood a little while alone in the door as I was going
out meditating as to whether I should speak to Mrs. Atherton about dining at
her house today or not and I suppose I must have looked forlorn and forsaken
for Mr. Brenner, one of the Y.M.C.A. young men stepped up and asked if he
might walk home with me. I said, "Oh thank you but I am with Mr. Cooke." It

was too bad for he exclaimed in the funniest tone, "And here is Mr. Cooke right here." He was right at his elbow but he didn't hear the conversation fortunately.

I go to the dentist this afternoon and Miss Burgess and I dine at the Athertons. Miss Harris gave Mrs. Atherton a talking to in regard to her neglect of Kawaiahao teachers and she has had us all to dinner in turn.

I am afraid you will think I am not saying anything about Mr. Emerson in this letter to allay any feelings of uneasiness you may have, but the fact is I haven't anything to say. I haven't seen him for the past three weeks. I do hope he has been making his way with Miss Brewer.

There is not a great deal to write this time. My days with the exceptions I have given you passed very quietly and somewhat monotonously. I live much to myself, avoiding the society of even the other teachers to some degree as it seems to lead to more unpleasantness than profit. I wish I had more to read than I have. I must try to get something. I have finished the neck piece and one arm piece of my wedding lace. I am teaching lace-making to a number of girls in sewing class now. They seem to take to it very well. I am proud of the work done there. It is all fine. I have learned much here in methods of doing nice work in various things, housework as well as sewing. You shall see what a nice house I will keep and what a pretty table I shall set and how particular in personal habits all my household will have to be. Does that send a chill to your soul, dear lover?

I understand Nellie Waterhouse is making active preparations for her marriage. She looks very happy.

> Carrie

October 23, 1892, Punahou College

Dearest,

How pleasantly circumstanced I am! Here in Miss Brewer's comfortable little parlor with a quiet forenoon before me and two new letters from you. She told me today that she did not expect to teach next year but to take a year at home.

Yesterday I went down and took a ride with Miss Pope. We went out to Kamehameha to find Mr. Anderson and Mr. Ruevsky mounted. They took a ride with us and we took dinner at the Hall. It gave us the freshening up we intended. It was half-past six when we reached the Seminary but I missed two horse-cars and then got stranded in the dark and rain a quarter of a mile below here because that car didn't happen to come up so far. I walked as fast as I could and was a good deal frightened when I met a man and was thankful to get inside the grounds though I did lose the road in the dark and got way off into the wet grass. However, I had one consolation! The "persnickety" Miss Snow is Miss Brewer's faithful friend and I always have been so unfortunate as to say the wrong thing in her presence. Lately however she has been very kind to me. Miss Brewer acknowledged that she had spoken a good word for me, but that Miss Snow couldn't but believe it was very heinous of me to go anywhere with Mr. Emerson because I was engaged. Now Mr. Emerson has asked me to call on him for any help I would ask of a brother but last night I refrained as I feared it would be too much of a strain on good little Miss Snow. I thought too as I was stumbling around in the rain and dark how proud and happy you would be that I was quite alone and not receiving the attentions of any other man.

In the early afternoon I played a couple of games of tennis with the teachers. I have not played so much in over 2 yrs. I didn't play so very poorly either. I think with a little practice I would play better than when I was in college. I seem to have more strength in my arms and wrists and more endurance. I was pleased to find it out.

May Waterhouse (with tennis racket), Ruth Hoppin, Helen Hoppin, Iretta Hight, Nellie Waterhouse, Myra Davis, and Carrie P. Winter. Cyanotype from Nellie Waterhouse.

I think Charlie I have done wisely in depositing $150 with Bishop & Co. I must have some at hand to get home on in case of emergency. My $100 with Mr. Smith is drawing 6% all safely and now the Postal bank has offered 6%. Those who know say there is no danger and I think I will put my year's savings there. Couldn't save a cent of my first month's salary! The rate on drafts is so high that it would cost me more to get it home, and back in an emergency than to let it be safe here though without interest. I am almost sure to lose on my horse as everything is going down here. Mattie is a jewel and I wish I could keep her for the next 10 yrs.

No new cabinet as yet though there may be one at any time. I don't see how the people stand it. I'm glad there are two U.S. men-of-war in harbor—the *Boston* and *Alliance.*

Nov. 2—I will endeavor to talk high art, literature and science with you to prove my intelligence and education. Its funny dear what a test this life is on the love of such things. My colleagues say they haven't time to read and don't, except for novels, or magazines from one month's end to another. They don't even follow up on a good paper. I have to read—be it ever so little—and must always have something good about, in poetry or prose.

The scrub ministry put in yesterday was voted out again by high noon.[5] We are in suppressed revolution surely.

> I am sorry not to finish better, but I love you—
> Carrie

NOTES

1. Gavan Daws mentions "The Golden Era" by T. E. E. in *Shoal of Time.*
2. There is no documentation to suggest that the Queen and her marshal were lovers, and historians reject this assertion.
3. Likely Joseph Ballard Atherton, who Caroline Babb says in a letter dated May 17 [1892], is president of the trustees of Kawaiahaʻo Female Seminary. Babb Papers, The Bancroft Library, University of California–Berkeley.
4. Women's Christian Temperance Union (WCTU); Mary Sophronia Rice Whitney was superintendent.
5. On October 17, 1892, the Legislature issued a vote of no confidence in the cabinet, which was dissolved and replaced on November 1 with a new cabinet appointed by the Queen. A few hours after the appointment, the new one was also denounced.

Student Essay by Helen Kalola

I.   My life as a school-girl in Hono[lulu]
      My name is Helen Kalola a a Hawa[iian]
was brought in school by the white people they
brought me to shool when I was about 9 years old,
and I am now about 15 years old.
I haven't time to tell you about my native nation
but I must tell you about my school life.
When I was first brought to school I was in Miss
Kane's class a Hawaiian girl and then I was put
in the third class Miss Helen Hoppin was my school
teacher but now I am in the second class we have
in the morning prayers in chapel and even our
prayers in chapel is done then our music teacher
plays us a marching tune and then we march
around the chapel and each class goes into her
own school rooms and then we have our lessons
that we being studying in the night at haff past 9
in the morning we have our bible recelation and
after that first division takes their arithmetic
lesson while the second division recites their english
lesson after they had recited then the first division
recites their english while the second division writes
down on their slates their arithmetic after that
then feirst division recites there arithmetic while
the second division learns their reading and after
that the second division recites their arithmetic
while we study our physiology or reading and at
half past eleven the norman classes goes into
diff school-rooms to read their lessons with the norm[an]

teachers, while we have our physiology or reading in our own school rooms from half past eleven to half past twelve o'clock then we have our sewing from half past 2 to half past 3 and after that then the second singing class will go in the chapel from half past 3 to 4 o'clock and then the first singing class goes in the chapel from 4 to half past 4 our school hours is ended and now I will you what time we eat and kind of food we eat at 7 o'clock in the morning we have our breakfast we have tea crackers and bread prepared on our table, at 12 o'clock in the afternoon we have for our dinner poi and meat and in the evening we eat from 5 we have poi and meat sometimes we have poi and salmon and sometimes we have potatoes, sometimes we have bread and sugar sometimes rice and sugar but we like it ever so much. On our school mornings we have uniforms on to wears for school and we we ar white dresses for church we have three dormitories we sleep in some girls sleeps in the new Rice Hall some in the old Rice Hall and some girls in the Pauahi dormitory our bed is every girls has an iorn bed Miss Winter has the charge of the Old Rice Hall, Miss Hoddly has the charge of the New Rice Hall, and Miss Appleton has the Pauahi dormitory. now I will tell you about our work all the girls in school has a part of work about the house sweep scrub and wipe some girls has the meal work prepare the food on the table and wash dishes and wipe.

I will tell you what kind of games we play in school some girls play catch, play rope, and many other games that I cannot tell them all to you.

We have about 9 teachers our principal is Miss Pope first class Miss Appleton the second class Miss C. Winter the third class Miss Armstrong the fourth class Miss Lane and the babies teacher is Miss Haddly and our matron is Kenwill sewing cottage teacher is Miss Vanangallen and our music teacher is Miss Burgess On Saturday we have for our pleasure a croquet game every Saturdays and every holidays we b some trustiss invites us to go down h have a sea bath and also have a party also invites us down Eva to have a tra We rather stay in school than staying homes not knowing anything the school pleasant to us then our own homes.

12

Down with Malaria

November 9–December 25, 1892

November 9, 1892, Kawaiahao Seminary

Dearest,

I knew you would worry if I didn't write and I suppose  when I tell you I have a light attack of fever, you will any-way.[1] Well dear, don't any more than you can help, and hold on for just a week and you are sure to hear that I am well. It began Saturday. The doctor says it may last a week. Miss Pope is kind and I have perfect confidence in Doctor Andrews. Last night I slept the best. In the morning is my best time. During the day I am unhappy. I have no pain. These fevers are somewhat common. The girls have them often for a few days.

> I long for you very much, dear Carl.
> Carrie

Dictated Letter: November 16, 1892, Honolulu

Dear Mr. Kofoid,

Miss Winter was laid by with an intermittent fever on  the 5th, and though somewhat better, is directed not to write; even to you. At the present moment she sits in a reclining chair pulling her handkerchief and declaring herself as well as necessary, and of the opinion that she would refuse to take care of any person no sicker than herself. No one else shares her views how-ever, and you, as well as she, must submit to a third party in correspondence—

> Yours very truly,
> Margaret Brewer

Dictated:

I said last time that there was no cabinet, but there was, as I presume you saw in the Boston papers, Wilcox (G.W.) Brown, Mark Robinson & P.C. Jones. The

Queen did call a leader of the opposition. The only drawback is that no member of the Liberals is chosen, and they threaten to vote the cabinet out if Wilson is not ousted. This is a fine set of men, except Cecil Brown, who is smart but not very good. You called at Mr. P.C. Jones' house in Newton Center to see Nellie Waterhouse. I was told that he lost $50000 in Boston. They are working well in the Legislature now, much business done every day; and they have openly declared themselves against the Lottery, and are going to borrow a lot of money around the country, so I think my money is safe here.

Week before last Miss Burgess and I were invited out to Kamehameha to dinner, and were late because I missed a car. They were very nice about it, tho' it broke up Mrs. Andrew's fine dinner, Mr. Babb's military drill, Mr. Ruevsky's glee club. I think that was one reason I got sick. You know I detest being late to dinner. They all came to the Babb's after supper, & we had quite a good time.

Mr. Ruevsky & Mr. Anderson were down to the car with us and walked along in the moonlight till it overtook us. I thought they would leave us there, but Mr. R. was so charmed with Miss Burgess that we all came on together with not very much reluctance on Mr. Anderson's part. He was even reconciled to ice cream when Mr. Ruevsky paid for it. They even went so far as to weigh us. I recorded 129 lbs. That will speak for itself, I guess. You need draw no morale from young men, ice cream, & fevers.

The kindness and goodness of the people—Mrs. Frank Cooke sends me fresh milk every morning, sent me squab, comes to see me, etc. But you ought to be sick among seven women! Miss Pope & Miss Kenwill walk their legs off for me; some come and tell me the awful sufferings through which they have gone in the past, or are enjoying at that present moment, which may I die before I experience; some come in and talk loud and hard for hours. Dr. Andrews refuses to make any charges; and I shall have to take pleasure in proving my gratitude to him. Mrs. Babb came right down, took care of me on one of my worst days, & offered me her heart & her home. Mrs. Thompson nursed me all one morning because her husband loved me, she said. She is a trained nurse, & I learned some good things from her. Mr. Emerson has inquired one or twice but they forget to tell me till two or three days afterward.

November 17, 1892

Dearest,

Dear boy, I know you have worried, but you must stop now. My fever is all gone and the doctor said that tomorrow I might go up to the Babbs. Mrs. Atherton is going to take me up in her easy carriage. I shall rest just as long  there as I need to, for there is a good substitute, Maria Forbes, in my place. The doctor rather congratulates me on my illness for he thinks the complete rest will take me through the year in good shape. It's a mystery to me where I ever got a fever but don't you worry one bit about it. I have some brains and if this comes on once more showing a tendency to fevers, I shall pack my baggage and take the first steamer home. I want to stay here and earn my fare home and a little more, but I am not going to stay here to be sick, risk my health for good, become an object of public charity, a martyr to Kawaiahao Seminary or a burden on the already over worked teachers. I hope you approve my determination. Now that my wretched fever has passed, I am quite happy. Yesterday I sat up for the first time and today I have been up most of the day.

I could have written yesterday but I was weak and it was nice to have Miss Brewer put down some of the things I wanted you to know. She has been as kind as she could be but I think it came home to her as never before that you can't do much without a home to do it from. When we build our home we must have a sick-room on the 1st floor.

In the long, restless hours alone how I have longed for you, Carl. It seemed as if just you would make me well. I fear I have allowed myself to get a little too anxious for home and you. I am waiting for your letter of tomorrow. I love you all the time, darling.

Carrie

November 23, 1892, Kamehameha

Dear Carl,

If tomorrow were not Thanksgiving Day I should go back to the Seminary today but as it is I indulge myself in one more day away, eat Thanksgiving dinner with the Olesons and then return home. I came up here Friday  morning. Mrs. Atherton brought me up in their easy carriage. It made a hard day for me. I had to hurry to get off. Miss Kenwill and Miss Pope did every-thing for me but I was very tired. The ride did not hurt me but the change of air was so great that I thought I should freeze that day. But a change was com-ing over me by Saturday evening and I began to liven up. My head was up and I was ready to walk and talk or anything. I still look somewhat thin and pale but my appetite is almost natural now.

November 24—Thanksgiving Day. All have gone down to church. I am quite alone in the house. It is a bright warm sunny day. My woolen dress and flannels are not too much for me now that I am not so very robust. I wouldn't mind having a home to play the pretty invalid in for a couple of weeks longer but I think now it will be better for me at the Seminary than here. I need a little richer diet than the Babb's can quite afford. How good they have been. I fear Mrs. Babb has tired herself out over me this week. She is not very strong. They have no servant and not an oversupply of money, but I was welcome to all they had. I am sure a word of thanks from you would please them. I don't wish to burden you at all, only it makes me all more real and it's of the poetry of life.

November 26—Kawaiahao—Well, I am back again. I think I have improved much since being here. The fare is much better for me. The girls gave me quite an ovation Thursday night coming to my room in numbers to welcome me back. The work on Friday went very well. I had time for a long rest in the af-ternoon. Yesterday, I did my usual work about the house and then rode down town with Miss Pope to do a few errands that it seemed to me could not wait longer. I was surprised to find myself quite an object of interest. A number of the business men came out to shake hands with me and there were many kind smiles and bows. I went into Castle & Cookes to be weighed and found I had lost 9 1/2 lbs, now weighing 119 1/2. I'll be weighed again in a couple of weeks and tell you the result. I think I will have gained 5 lbs. at least. The morning tired me very much but in the afternoon I had a nap and a good "bath" and was ready for my Bible lesson in the evening. In a little while I have to go over to morning service at the church.

November 29—Tuesday evening—I feel much better every day. I am so glad the *Australia* comes in tomorrow. I wish some kind spirit would give you a glimpse of me now as I sit writing and munching my big apple between times. It is a very good apple. Have a bite?

Friday evening—December 2—The mail brought me a good letter. There were letters from father and mother and was it not odd father devoted half a sheet to telling me to be careful of my health while mother bewailed the fact that I was so far away if anything should happen to me. What a dear mother she is! I would like a little more of loving if you don't mind, Charlie dear. I think it will come in the next letter.

Sunday, December 4—This must be the Christmas mail. I have various packages and letters ready to go. Yesterday morning was the dedication of the new Central Union Church. I had not been to church for what seemed a long time. I thought the exercises were beautiful. The church was crowded 1,037 being present. It is a beautiful audience room, amphitheater in shape with beautiful windows and handsome finishings. Speeches were made by Mr. Oleson, Mr. Emerson, Doctor Hyde and Mr. S.E. Bishop. The music was very good for Honolulu.

I can tell you in a few words our worry about Miss Burgess. She has a charming temper and voice but we think must have got in with a fast operatic set in San Francisco. She doesn't seem very ambitious for she won't have a thing to do with the people who could really benefit her. Her boon companion is a painted milliner down town and whenever the *Australia* comes in she is off every night till the small hours. Nobody knows where or with whom, for the men or man never comes here. Once she went to a dance at Remond's Grove, quite out of the way and she has stayed at the Eagle House over night. She point blank refused to go to the Atherton's on Sunday so that she might go off with her friends last night. To say the least she is very indiscreet and is likely to get into no end of trouble.

Did I tell you I saw the *Hiram Bingham* at the wharf—the tiniest steamer that ever cruised the ocean? It is on its way now to the Gilbert Islands.

Yesterday was the last Trustee meeting of the term and four of us handed in our resignations—Miss Pope, Miss Kenwill, Miss Van Anglen and myself. I confess there were no regrets in mine.

The time draws near but not too fast for me. Some of my dearest love goes with this letter to you. God bless and keep you.

Carrie

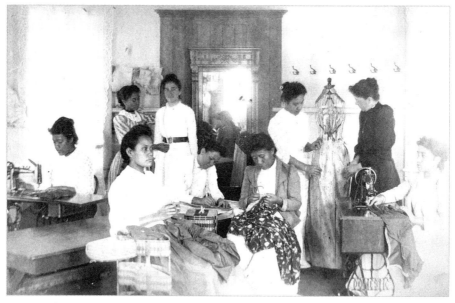
Dressmaking with sewing teacher Annie Van Anglen, c1892.

December 18, 1892, Kamehameha

Dearest,

Once more I have reason to be happy. I am at Mrs. Thompson's for Sunday and they are so kind and friendly and the four children are so pretty and fresh and interesting. It gives me pleasure to be near children that I can take hold of and squeeze.

Mr. Ruevsky came in this morning and asked me to tell the boys a story tonight. I promised to do it but I am afraid without the best inward grace for I don't fancy that gentleman at all. I know it's not because he appreciates the fine points of my story-telling, but because he is glad of the chance to get out of some work himself.

Well, darling, what are you doing today? Think of me a little bit in it—but I know you'll do that. How blessed am I. To have the surety of your love—the prospect of a happy home life in the future and the privilege of lavishing on you all that love in my heart for you.

December 18, 1892, Kawaiahao Seminary

Dearest,

Miss Harris is with us now occupying our hospital guest room.[2] She had no place to go, was bound to leave the hospital. People were saying unpleasant things and it seemed the best thing to take her in here till she either  found some work or decided to go home. It isn't a very pleasant thing but it is the best thing. She seems better but she acts "off" and none of us know what to think of the case. My own determination is to be more discreet than ever for she tells everything to everybody. There is a chance of her being matron at the hospital with light work at first. I often wonder if her sudden improvement is due to any operation they perhaps performed upon her when she was out of her head as she says she was for two weeks.

Sunday—I have just come from getting after two of my dormitory girls both bigger than I. I went in to see how the work was done. They were dressing for church but a glance under the beds showed they had not touched their sweeping. I mounted guard, sent all others from the room and there was some fine sweeping done there.

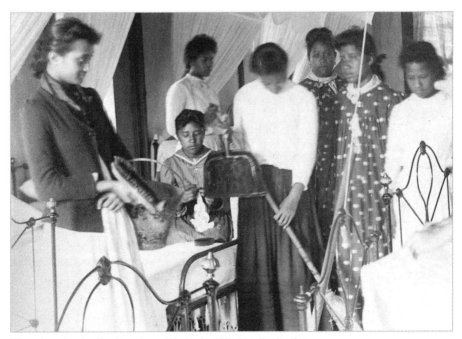

Housekeeping in the dormitory. Photo by Lilla Estelle Appleton.

Eliza was inclined to be ugly but when I told her the next bed she slammed would send her to the closet for all day, she calmed down. I'll invite them into my room for the afternoon and they'll lose that Sunday nap they so highly prize. The girls all need lots of squelching just now. I think I am able to look ahead and keep my temper a little better than I used to.

Thursday I took dinner with the Miss Forbes who was my substitute. Her mother is in charge of the Lunalilo Home for indigent Hawaiians.[3] This institution was formed by King Lunalilo and to it, he left all his wealth. They have a beautiful brown stone building and ample provision for every need. We went over the building. There are about 33 inmates—for the most part, old people. They have native nurses and a night watchman and as they do not work and do not have to be entertained in any way, it cannot be a very hard institution to run.

Tuesday, December 13—The *China* brought a mail yesterday. I have a variety of emotions over the new picture.

Charles A. Kofoid, Harvard, 1891. Portrait by Holland Studios, Boston.

Of course I went for it first and you may be sure I knew there was a kiss for me there without your telling me of it. Then while it seemed like you in feature there was a different look somehow. Lots more grown up—weighty—no frivolity—solid and wise. I had to turn back to my dear old smiling picture and kiss to put myself in countenance again and every time I came near the new picture yesterday, I would begin to blush most furiously—then would laugh at myself and then at the man in the picture. I'm crazier than ever to see you now and find out if that picture is true and if I really shall be in awe of you and have to learn you again.

Your thanksgiving note was very dear. It was truly loving. Of course I forgive you that the letters were not more loving. It was a fine point in you to remember about it all yourself.

Evening—Now darling, I like to have you buy books and especially such bargains if you do not need the money for shoes or something like that, but even a presentation set of Agassiz would fail to console me if you should die of pneumonia because you were not properly clothed this winter.

Good bye, darling.
Carrie

December 25, 1892, Honolulu, H.I.

Dear Charlie,

A "Merry Christmas" to you my darling. I wish I could put my arms about your neck and give you a Christmas kiss. We have already had two days of Christmas celebrating and today is the real day and tomorrow is the  legal holiday. Many very pleasant things have happened to me and I want to give you a good account of it all as this is my last experience here of Christmas. I am across the street with Mrs. Frank Cooke now. I was very glad to have her invite me. It seemed to mean real "aloha." I mean to be agreeable company.

I must give you a list of the things I have received. You will be pleased too, I hope and I plan that many of them shall go into our home. Miss Pope gave me a polished coconut calabash. That's a very fine thing and a nice memento. Miss Kenwill a Chinese fan of white silk embroidered, very dainty and pretty and a little compass that I "might find the way to her again." Miss Appleton combined Christmas and wedding gift in a fine large album for island photographs. Miss Armstrong gave me a dainty, square china dish and Miss Hadley ½ doz. little blue dishes which I had much admired. Mother Cooke gave me a card. Mrs. Frank Cooke an arrangement of sachet bags. Miss Katherine Pope, a yellow silk tie "to wear with my brown dress," Miss Parmalee, a fancy watch-pocket. Miss Brewer and Miss Snow, the most beautiful white cracked vase. One of my girls gave me a handsome hat braid which I will have made up when I go home. Miss Hadley gave me a little silver salt spoon made from a Hawaiian 10-cent piece. Mrs. Gilman gave me a little Christmas book. That makes 14 and I think there will be one or two more. We had a Christmas dinner at the school last night. The turkey was from Mr. Charles Cooke, the butter from Mrs. Atherton, the plum pudding from Mr. W.R. Castle, the cake from Mrs. Lowry and Miss Wickenan, and the flowers from Mrs. Atherton.

Now I must go back to Friday and tell you of the events of that day. The little ones went home in the morning but the higher rooms had school till 11 o'clock. After dinner we arranged ourselves in our best, and at 2:20 three cars stopped in front of the school to take 90 of us up to Kamehameha. It began to rain just when we wanted to get off but stopped when we were in the cars. When we had reached the other end however, down it came, good and hard and before we could reach Bishop Hall the white dresses were all bedraggled, the color turning out of the ribbons and the shoes heavy with mud. There were only two or three umbrellas for the whole company.

It broke the ice at once for there was a big scurrying around to get the grumpy girls out of their wet waistes and into boy's coats. The rest scampered around till they were dry. It spoiled the boy's ball-game but Bishop Hall doesn't often hear such shrieks of laughter. Dinner came early and such a dinner! Well on toward 300 in the dining hall for the Preparatory was there also. The boys and girls had luaued fish and pig, pork, poi, oranges, cake, ice-cream and candy. Our table was set for 30. Our names were written on bits of tapa cloth and at each plate was a carnation.

Mrs. Andrews delights in dinners and this was one of her grandest efforts. There was a whole squad of boys to wait on us so it went off without hitches. 1st—soup. 2nd—fish, limes, potato. 3rd—Turkey and all that goes with it. 4th—chicken pie. 5th—salad. 6th—pie and cake. 7th—plum pudding. 8th—coffee. 9th—nuts, raisins. 10th—fruit. 11th—ice cream and cake. There were lots of things that no one even touched. The palm and fern decorations should be mentioned. The boys and girls had a fine time strolling about the grounds to the music of the Hawaiian band stationed on the Oleson's porch.

As soon as it grew dark the big bell rang and we all gathered in Bishop Hall for the literary exercises. All three schools took part and it took most 3 hours but nobody minded for we were all so interested. There were recitations, music and farces—thoroughly enjoyable, every bit. By half past nine it was raining, pitch-forks again. The Thompsons asked me to stay overnight and after consulting with Miss Pope I concluded to do so. They got thoroughly wet going home. We drank milk and chatted over the affair for an hour.

On Saturday I came down and established myself at Mrs. Cooke's, received and gave presents, ate Christmas dinner at the seminary. Took a long nap and in the evening, went with Mr. and Mrs. Cooke to the Portuguese Sunday School where as the paper said, I presided with credit at the organ. I had practiced with them twice before. The singing was very dreadful but I suppose very creditable to them. Mrs. Cooke asked me some time before if I would play and I was glad to do so. They had a small tree with presents for those who had been to Sunday School 20 Sundays. The little church was full to the doors.

The Emersons are much interested here. The Doctor is the superintendent and Mr. Joseph Emerson talked with us about his trip to Kohala where he had been with Doctor Whitney examining the mummies in the caves there.[4] Someone said Doctor Whitney wanted to get a lot of good teeth cheap. Anyway they brought away four bags of skulls and some fine tapa.

The service was cheerful and good at the church Christmas Sunday. In the afternoon I went again to the Portuguese church to teach Mrs. Cooke's class as she was all tired out and to play the organ in her place. They seemed quite grateful. In the evening I stayed at home with Mother Cooke while Mr. and Mrs. Cooke went to church. Mr. Henry Castle was married that afternoon very quietly to Miss Wing. We caught glimpses of the bride after the ceremony.

Monday the Cooke's went off on a family picnic and according to previous invitation, I went out to Kamehameha to a tennis party which the young men gave there. They entertained some 25 there. It seemed rather difficult for the teachers and the town girls to assimilate. I didn't mind much for I was playing most of the time. I played 7 sets, some with a Brown boy and the rest with Charles Atherton. It was great fun and I entered into it heartily.

(L to R) Nellie Waterhouse, Iretta Hight, May Waterhouse, Ruth Hoppin, Helen Hoppin, Myra Davis, and Carrie P. Winter.

Last night we had a little experience. I told you of Miss Harris' being a little flighty at the hospital. Last night the doctor brought her back from his office where she had been in the same condition. I saw him and he gave me some directions in regard to her. Miss Kenwill and I went to his office today and had a very satisfactory talk with him in regard to the whole matter. He says it is hysteria and not mania that even her pain is largely mental—that she is not accountable for much that she does and says. I believe I will write to Jo and ask her to talk with her sisters.[5] The family act very queerly and do not seem to respond to the information that has been sent them. It is a very trying case. Today she seems like herself again.

On Tuesday, Misses Pope, Hadley, Van Anglen started on a trip to Waialua intending to remain in the mountain cottage till Saturday. The Atherton boys went with them, and it rained most of the time and I fear they have had serious difficulties. Miss Van Anglen has Mattie. We expect her back tomorrow. Between you and me, I shall rest easier when I see my horse back again. She would mean to do well by her but it might be out of her power.

I have just tomorrow more of duty for which I am devotedly thankful and I hope never to have such a thing as "vacation duty" in the Kawaiahao sense in my life again.

Saturday—'Tis the last of the old year. I look for much happiness in the new. May it be full of blessings for you.

> Your girl Carrie

NOTES

1. Caroline Babb wrote on November 14, 1892, "my friend Prudence Winter, who teaches at Kawaiahao has had a strong dose of malarial fever—overwork and poor location combined." Caroline Babb, also called Carrie, refers to Miss Winter by her middle name, Prudence. Babb Papers, The Bancroft Library, University of California–Berkeley.
2. Caroline Babb wrote on November 14, 1892, "poor Miss Harris is still at the Hospital…in her sick days…she lies and wraiths and twists in agony and nothing can be done for her." Babb Papers, The Bancroft Library, University of California–Berkeley.
3. This should be Lunalilo Home for Indigenous Hawaiians.
4. Dr. Nathaniel Bright Emerson and his brother Joseph Swift Emerson wrote several papers mentioning the Kohala caves.

5. Miss Winter's Oberlin classmate Blanche Alice "Jo" Anderson was a teacher at Oberlin High School who was acquainted with Miss Harris' sisters. Miss Winter apparently wrote Jo, requesting that she discuss Eva Harris' health problems with them.

Student Essay by Keluia Kiwaha

I.

My life as a school-girl in Honolulu

I am a pure Hawaiian. My name is Kiwaha, and I am twelve years of age. I know all of you would like to hear some-thing about our school, but I will tell you what I know. It is a large building. It has three dormitories, one chapel and three school-rooms, one large dining room, kitchen, bedrooms for the teachers, hospital, parlor, library, and a ~~new~~ little cottage has been build for the Sewing Department. I enjoy the school very much. When I first came to school it was not a large building.

In the dining room ~~there~~ are seven large tables for the girls to eat, and one table for the Teachers. There are few piano's and one organ.

Some of the girls take music lessons. In the office there is a Telephone. The reception-room is for the parents who come to make a visit. In our school-room there are about thirty pupils.

We are divided among two divisions. The first division and the second division. Our teacher is Miss C. P. Winter. I hope you all know her.

Our studies are Geography, Reading, Physiology, and English. I will tell what we eat, ~~wear, sleep, work, and play~~. We have Tea, bread, and cracker in the morning. Poi and meat in the afternoon and Evening. ~~On every other days.~~ We wear Uniform dresses when we

we have school, but when school finishes each
girl goes to her own dormitory and ch[...]
uniform. We are not allowed to go the t[...]
our uniform. We sleep on iron bedsteads[...]
to buy our own bed-steads. Each gir[...]
bring a curtain, and a white spread[...]
Sewing-room work to do.

13

The Revolution

January 1–March 19, 1893

January 1, 1893, Honolulu, H.I.

Dearest Carl,

So you see at last this year has come to its opening. I suppose in many, many lives it has been the year of promise for a long time. How many have we heard say, "I will do this and so when '93 comes." Even for me, it  must contain trial, disappointment and weariness, but I must confess my hopes and anticipations are high. It seems to me no year will ever come that will contain more variety of happiness. I expect the happiness of becoming your wife, but there are many other precious joys to look forward too. I hope the rest of my time here will be full and rich.

Mrs. Soares, the Portuguese pastor's wife[1] telephoned me yesterday to know if I would play in their church service today. Their organist was disabled. I was the only English one there and of course I understood nothing of the service. Attracted by my blue dress, little Ray, the oldest child came and nestled beside me and patted and smoothed my hand.

I was glad of a nap this afternoon for I was tired from yesterday afternoon and everybody celebrated last night with crackers, bells and cannon. Mr. Emerson got back from Molokai yesterday morning and sent me a half dozen sweet snails and fern leis. I distributed them among the teachers and we all decorated our rooms.

I have long been intending to have him to dinner and so asked him last evening. I must confess I was a little tried because my dinner didn't go off very well. The girls forgot the corn and salad till we were almost through and then came bringing them in and the biscuits were yellow with saleratus. All the teachers did their best at entertaining end. Miss Burgess sang for us. He had to go early and Miss Van Anglen arrived wet, tired and hungry and I had to attend to her.

Tuesday morning—Mrs. Cooke was telling me last night some old love tales of the islands and rather heart-rending scenes. Mrs. Atherton was engaged to Judge Judd, but he went away to Yale and became so absorbed in his work there, she fancied he did not care much for her. She broke the engagement. When Frank Judd got the news, he was made sick by it and her own brother and sister who were in New Haven at the time sided with him.

Mother Cooke felt it all so deeply that she would not speak to her daughter for 3 months and many of their friends left town to avoid attending the wedding. Everything is all smooth between the two families now. There were several other similar cases. I think I told you that the same misfortune happened to Mr. Emerson. He was engaged to Mrs. Baldwin, whose husband is one of the wealthiest men on the islands, and while he was off at school, she broke it off. The moral of all which is for you and me dearest, is that we must not let the cares of this world keep us from knowing the true state of our feelings toward each other and to keep each other informed as regards to that state. Dear heart, our dangers are almost over and surely we will be saved from mistakes for the rest of the time.

Miss Kenwill and I spent most of the day yesterday with Mrs. Needham and her daughter Mrs. Peck. They were very kind but it's hard for me to spend a day like that as a prim visitor. It rained, so we sat and talked and talked and at the proper time, ate rich food. When Mr. Peck came from the Y.M.C.A. of which he is secretary, he showed me his immense collection of shells of which he really knows nothing. Mr. Needham was much more entertaining to me with his tales of sea life for he used to be steward on a whaler. We got him to talk whales to us which he did at a great rate telling us how good doughnuts were fried in whale oil and the great excitement of the whales themselves. I listened with all my ears as I am not likely to meet whalers again.

January 3, 1893, Kawaiahao Seminary

Dearest Carl,

How it rained all day yesterday. In fact it began on Wednesday and there was no going to prayer meeting for either girls or teachers. It has made a rainy, tiresome week. The pasture was afloat and the girls had to stay  in the house. During the night I woke several times to think of poor Mattie, out in the storm with no shelter. She was as wet as a rat and trembling with the cold. I gave her some oats with a condition powder in them, a pail of Algarroba pods, and set a couple of girls to work rubbing her down with old rags and soon she looked as well as ever. Her back is so well now that I shall venture to ride her as soon as I have a chance.

I have been working off a long list of "punish girls" this afternoon—garments picked up in the dormitory and my own clothing nicely mended up once more—even the end of my new horse rope I had sewed and bound in red so that I can tell it from the other's ropes.

Well, dear one, I certainly have a number of things to write about to you today and I would like to do justice to my topics. The first regarding Miss Pope. She told me yesterday. No one but Miss Kenwill and I know it as yet. Friday she was summoned to a trustee meeting at which the trustees proposed to her that she should take this week's steamer for the States, take Miss Harris with her, and either put her in charge of her friends or in Clifton Springs Sanatorium[2] then herself go on to New York and take a term training in Pratt Institute and look up various matters of interest to the school with a view to her return next fall.

It produces in me rather mingled feelings. Her salary is to continue just the same. She has not yet come to a full decision but in my opinion the only thing that will stand in the way of her going will be whether Miss Harris will consent to go or not. You see the community is nearly in despair over that girl. She's out of her head most of the time and is very trying. Her true pride seems all to have left her and she does not seem to realize in the least how much she is receiving from the community at large. She's threatening to kill anyone who shall write to her parents of the true state of the case. There is an insane asylum here but it is not at all the proper place for her to go and she is not having the right treatment. Everyone says she must go, but the difficulty has been to get anyone who would look after her and to get her willing to go.

This plan will remove the first difficulty. The plan for the school for the rest of the year is to put Miss Kenwill in charge, hire someone to look after the kitchen department, put the concert a little later than the present plan, and have no closing exercises and only a simple open day. Mrs. Charles Cooke has given $50 and Mother Rice $100 toward Miss Harris's expenses. Now for my comments on the situation. It is a good thing for Miss Pope and she deserves it. I can't keep down a little hurt feeling that they should be willing to do so much for Miss Harris and Miss Pope and recognize me in so little.

Personally, it is a relief not to have that closing exhibition expected of us which means so much extra work for me and I would just as like to have Miss Kenwill at the head as Miss Pope. I am a confidential friend of both. Miss Kenwill is a much more intellectual woman and able in many ways and is capable of being a much trusted friend. She has a quick temper well under control, but it will be a constant trial to her to have dealings with certain members of the faculty. In fact none of them like her as much as I do. Then of course there are many matters which she does not know about that will give her some trouble. Miss Pope is in a whirl now with many things to think of.

Afternoon—Now, dear for my second subject. You know that imaginary, ideal maid servant about whom I have occasionally written. What do you say to my bringing her home with me? Now I can fancy just what is flitting through your brain, but dear, just give me a favorable hearing. Helen Wilcox or Keoike has been in my room two years and I know her thoroughly. She is a quiet, shy girl—not particularly bright in her studies but I think she easily stands first in the school now for goodness and willingness. She might easily pass for a white girl, is always neat and clean and smiling, does not seem to have a bit of that insolent upstart bearing which is so trying in many of the girls. She is so good that on the few occasions when she has been naughty, the sorrow over it has made her nearly sick. Girl after girl failed to do Mrs. Cooke's ironing work till we sent Helen and she thinks her a treasure.

Lately she has been attendant for Miss Harris and we have been much surprised at the brightness she showed in managing her. She knows how to manage little children. During all my vacations, Helen has done my washing beautifully and on the way taken care of my room. She can scrub floors, wash and iron, make fires early in the morning (hear that, Carl), and she would soon learn cooking. Do you know it seems to me she might prove a perfect treasure to us when we begin housekeeping and I think I shall go so far as to ask Mr. Albert Wilcox in a letter this week if he will pay her expenses if I give her a home and assume responsibility of her as far as I reasonably can. I do not think it would be a wrong to the girl.

A decent Hawaiian girl has a very poor chance in this country. She is not pretty and there is little for her to look forward to here. She could save her wages with us and if she wished, return. I doubt not I could get a good situation for her here on account of her story in America. Of course if Mr. Wilcox objects, that is an end to the matter. He disclaims her but those who know, are very sure she is his daughter and that means good blood. I asked Helen if she would like to go to the States with me and she hid her face in her hands and said, "Yes, but Mr. Wilcox." Don't think too much about it Carl for its all in the air. It would be nice to have her in Middlefield next year. She is a good server and mother has no help. What do you think, Carl?

We're in a peck of trouble and we don't know how we are coming out at present. I have a few forebodings as to the next 4 months but I shall get through all right. The one thing that stands out all others now is Miss Harris. She appeared here yesterday morning. Miss Pope got her off as soon as possible so that the girls should not tell. She wouldn't hear of going and was all worked up.

During the day, Mrs. Coleman, Mrs. Cooke, Mr. Atherton and Dr. Wood talked to her and in the evening to everyone's surprise she began to pack her trunk. She wouldn't stay here all night and she wouldn't let any teacher go back to the hospital with her. Mr. Emerson was here calling and we called on him. He has been away a long time and had just heard of her state from Miss Brewer and wanted me to go too as he did not know how to manage her. She was all right and I rather demurred but finally yielded and it was well I did, for she was quite "off" by the time we got started and said for one thing, that she was not going home. We were all more or less stirred up over this all day yesterday.

School matters have rather taken a place in the back ground. Monday night I had a little talk with Miss Appleton. Time and again change has come here and she had never been preferred and so I ventured on a word of sympathy. To my surprise, she burst into tears. I went to Miss Kenwill and said we must manage to give Miss Appleton the matron's place. It was a difficult thing to manage but the chance came that evening for Miss Kenwill to put a word into the right place and it was offered her.

Thursday—Miss Appleton declined the position and was somewhat disagreeable about it. She said she would give up her sewing class and dormitory and supervise the rest of us in our teaching for the additional salary. At the present crisis, that is absurd. It would leave the new matron whoever she chanced to be, and the principal, a sewing-class and extra dormitory. They might pick up rags about the yard while Miss Appleton presided with dignity over the rest of us. Miss Kenwill talked with me yesterday. She wants me to take the place. It's all in the air and when I see myself there, I will believe it. Miss Harris wants me to take one of her Japanese pupils. I have to see about that this morning. I am a little stirred up but tell myself to be calm. I would like the place for the extra pay and the experience.

January 4, Wednesday—The steamer goes this morning. Yesterday afternoon, Miss Kenwill and I went to an afternoon tea at Mrs. Lowry's. It rained all day long and of the 25 she invited, only 7 were present. She is a very pretty woman with a wonderfully pretty house. We all worked fancy work and talked. For my part, I listened to the others and it was as good as a play. So many events in the social life of the city that I know nothing about were talked over. At last they got on the subject of duties and two of the women revealed such depths of depravity as I did not know existed among such elegant ladies. For instance, it had never entered my mind to put any but the true value on a parcel post package but their way is to record $20 as $2 and pay duty according. Millie Beckwith says, "I don't think that right." "But," replies Mrs. Lackland, "What else can you do?" Silence!!

We had fine cake and cream served in the daintiest manner. We returned to Mrs. Cooke's in time for dinner and Mr. Sam Alexander was taking his last meal before returning to his Oakland home with his mother-in-law, Mother Cooke, an active, traveled, wealthy man. He wanted to talk and we all did our best and I must confess he directed much of his conversation toward me and I was duly appreciative. At last, Mother Cooke said something about someone's going to Oberlin and that it was a good thing for them. "Well," he said, most heartily, "I'm glad of that tho' I don't think much of Oberlin" and this right to me in the most beaming of ways. Mother Cooke said but you mustn't say that to her. "Why," he said, "I was just going to add judging from the people I had met." "Well," he said, "I would never have thought you were from Oberlin." Which he meant for a compliment. I have to laugh every time I think of it.

> I love you the same as ever,
> Carrie

January 8, 1893, Kawaiahao Seminary

Dearest Charlie,

It isn't real daylight yet but it's my best time to begin this letter. School opened yesterday. Almost all the girls were on time. A few do not return. I lose two from my room. Aden is to be married and Caroline's father can  no longer pay for her. Her departure ought to relieve me from much nervous strain. One might as well have placed a large porker on its hind legs and have tried to teach it fractions. Their places are filled by new girls. One very nice girl came from Hilo, Carrie Nakapuahi. I wrote that name on a big pile of her clothing yesterday so I ought to know it well.

I have an entirely new program of school-room work and I am interested to see how it goes. I want my last term to be my best. For one thing I am going to take a few minutes each morning for a little sermonet having them write the main proposition in their note books. The first series will be, "Why I should be a Christian," and this morning the answer will be "That I may have a happy everlasting life."

I feel very seriously the amount of responsibility I have in this matter. Many of the girls never go beyond my room, life is very uncertain with them, my time here is short and I don't know what sort of a woman my successor may be and I don't know how practical for them the instruction is at their church.

I spent the last four days of my vacation up to Kamehameha. Miss Van Anglen paid me $3 for the use of Mattie going to Waialua which was tolerably cheap as she broke a strap on the saddle and scalded her back. It won't be long before that's all well.

I must not forget to tell you. I have finished the lace for my wedding dress. It has taken about a year to make it and it is very beautiful. There are pieces for neck and sleeves.

January 10—I have a little to write of matters political. There is a flood of corruption which if it has full head way will utterly ruin the country. Some time ago, a bill for licensing liquors in all parts of the kingdom was introduced, it is only licensed now in Honolulu, but it was defeated. The next was the opium bill to license its sale to Chinese. There has been a strong opium ring here which of course was opposed to the bill, but their efforts and the rather futile efforts of those opposed to it on moral grounds, were not sufficient to prevent its passage. A committee of ladies waited on the Queen to supplicate her to sign it. They were much encouraged by her manner, but nevertheless she signed the bill yesterday. It is characterized as "one more death blow to the Hawaiians."

Most alarming of all at the present moment is the fact that they sprang the Lottery Bill in the House yesterday and it passed its second reading. They will try to complete the work this morning. Only one white man voted for it. They took their opportunity when several members known to be opposed to it were absent. All are hoping for the arrival of the *Oceanic* this morning to bring two members. She isn't here yet however. I went to prayer-meeting last night and it was a pretty serious affair. Such a disgrace as it is to the country! Mr. Oleson thinks the low ebb of Christian activity is to blame for the state of affairs but I never saw more united and fervent effort than was put forth in every way when the Bill first came up.

January 12, morning—Well, all the Lottery Bill needs now is the Queen's signature. There is great sorrow throughout the city. They tried to keep it out of the prayer meeting last night, but it would creep in. It was characterized as a dark day in Hawaiian History. Judge Judd nearly broke down when he thought of the land of his birth to which his parents had come, consecrating it as a new land to Christ, where they were buried and thus disgraced! Mr. W.O. Smith who has worked nobly in this long 8 months session was there and perfectly fagged. He said "The bill is an absolute franchise for 25 yrs. I add that to my years and I will be 70 before this is over." He has a large family of boys and girls. If the whole thing seems so dreadful to us who are strangers here, what must it not seem to those whose all is here? There is talk of proving it unconstitutional but the blot exists.

> Yours,
> Carrie

January 15, 1893, Kawaiahao Seminary

Dear Charlie:

Yesterday was a day of political excitement. I wrote you in my last of the passage of the Opium and Lottery Bills. Thursday the white members stayed away from the legislature with the exception of Peterson who alone of  them all had voted for the Bill. Thursday afternoon, I was out calling at the Hyde's, Hobron's, Bishops, Judd's and took dinner at the Waterhouses and it was during that afternoon that the good cabinet was ousted. Everywhere I went, the people were furious. They were mad at the Queen and the legislature, the absent members who might have saved things and the captain of the *Boston* and U.S. minister Stevens who were down to Hilo on a pleasure excursion. Mr. Henry Waterhouse was so wrought up that he couldn't join into light dinner conversation but left the table early to go and pacify his father who he said would be fighting mad.

Friday added to the indignation when the Queen announced her new cabinet, Sam Parker, Cornwell, Peterson, and Colburn. I'll try and send you the *Advertisers* statement of them. A good many of the natives were angry at this. Yesterday crowned it all. The Queen in the morning signed both those wicked bills and at high noon in a most gorgeous new robe of lavender satin attended by her new cabinet, she prorogued the legislature.[3] Not a white member was present and all are ladies, wives of Judges and members of legations in fine attire.

Only a few tourists were present as spectators. I tell you this town was hot but worse was to follow, for on return to the palace, a petition was handed to the Queen by a native society asking for a new constitution and she immediately submitted it to her ministers for them to sign. Sam Parker signed, but she met an unexpected obstacle in the other ministers, for the other three said "Your Majesty, we cannot sign this." "You must," she replied, bringing her fist down on the table or "I will myself proclaim it." She told them to resign then but they refused to do that.

By this time, rumors of the matter were all abroad and there had been so much running to and fro and the foreign ministers came to tell her what was what. The *Boston* had come in the forenoon and they say Stevens gave her a good talking too. At any rate, late in the afternoon, she had to come out on the balcony and tell the crowd of soldiers and natives that she cannot give them a new constitution now and that was an end to that plan.[4]

What do you think of it all? We are all so stirred up we hardly know what to think. Certain it is that people will no longer put any confidence in her and that she has failed in this attempt to get absolute power for herself. They are all full of schemes and no one knows what to expect yet. Of course many things were said whose truth we are not sure of. It was said that at any movement of the Queen, the *Boston* was ready at a moment's notice to land its men, declare the Queen a rebel and take the islands in the name of the U.S.

A more authentic report was that a community of 13 men were around watching affairs and getting names to found a provisional government. They were to have reported to a man's meeting last night but the condition of affairs did not warrant it. Mr. Emerson and his brother were here last night and we questioned them to our heart's content. I am anxious to see the faces of people in church this morning, after the strain they have been through. I went around the palace myself and saw the soldiers and stacked guns. For some reason the girls don't seem to have gotten hold of these matters at all. They are generally so excitable but I haven't heard one speak of the matter.

It is late, but I cannot let the day end without a word on the latest rumors. The 13 have been hard at work all day and the papers are out for a man's meeting tomorrow. I came up for our church tonight with Mr. Cooke. He says the business men are determined now and that the outlook is that she will be deposed, a provisional government established, looking toward annexation. All the business houses are to be closed. No one knows what tomorrow will hold. I am glad you are not in it. I should worry to death. We may have our hands full with the girls.

January 17—I will send you a full report of the man's meeting yesterday. It was noon when the Queen's "By Authority" came around, backing down and throwing the blame on her "native subjects." My dear, it's exciting times and we are almost in the midst of whatever excitement there is. Opinions and theories as to what the Committee would do were filling the air all the afternoon. At evening the *Boston* landed its troops. They stayed in town all night. Some were around the U.S. legation. Early in the evening, a company was at the Atherton's where it is supposed a committee meeting was held. The girls have been remarkably quiet through it all. The fire alarm rang twice during the night for slight fires and it was rather noisy.

At noon today, there were more rumors. Miss Pope found only men down town, heard one man ordered to find two more rifle-guns, saw the marines around the legation and heard that much more was to happen. The school children were sent home early. Early in the afternoon a police man was shot but not killed down on Fort St. He was trying to stop a team containing arms.[5] That is all the shooting so far but the committee and their adherents took the government building, proclaimed a provisional government, made Judge Dole, Governor, W.O. Smith = Attorney General, P.C. Jones = minister of finance and Mr. King minister of the Interior. They had quite a time finding the old ministers but we hear this evening that the Queen under protest and after long hesitation has signed the abdication paper and the police station is now in the hands of the committee.

A number of the parents have been here to take away girls. They say they are going to fire on the missionary houses tonight. There are a good many men under arms for the night and we feel safe. We at least are safe with all these Hawaiian girls in our charge. I know now what it means to sit around and wait for news. I'd have given a good deal to have been a man today. Miss Appleton and I did go over to the church and climb up into its tower but we couldn't see much and after a little time, some natives below saw us and began to point at us and we thought we had best get down before they came up.

Morning—There is a rumor that the *Claudine* goes to the States today. All was quiet last night.

Carrie

January 20, 1893, Honolulu

Dearest Carl,

If one could only have revolutions, time would go on quickest wings. There is little political news. We have the palace, barrack, the guards, paid and dismissed, and the Queen drives about in a one horse gig. Everything is well guarded.

The *Claudine* got off all right with Thurston, W.R. Castle, and Marsden Wilder as delegates, and the only purpose annexation. For once I was very energetic and by using every spare minute and I got an article for the *Courant* written. I didn't even have time to look it through once. I suggested to them that they pay me for it but very likely they will prefer to take their news from the Press and my effort will come to naught. You must say, "good girl" just the same.

Friday evening—It is glorious moonlight evening and I wish you were here to take me out into it. I was out at Rainbow yesterday afternoon with Miss Brewer and went riding with a party from there in the evening. Mr. Crocker was quite willing to ride and talk with me since I asked him about Maui and was willing to mention Irene's name to him. It is quite understood that he is in love with her. We went to the top of Punch Bowl. How beautiful it was there in the calm of the flood of the moon light with the lighted city below the ocean and the strains of the band coming plainly to our ears, mainly American airs— we had to return early on account of martial law. Today it was extended to 11 o'clock.

I wonder if you are reading today the telegraphic news of our Revolution. The *Claudine* ought to have reached there today. Everything goes quietly and well here. The Queen thinks she will be back in power in 3 months but no one else thinks so. Every time we look back upon those few days the wonder grows greater. The Queen's party had an immense quantity of ammunition. Had they just turned their guns upon us, killed two or three of the leading men and roused the natives to deeds of violence, all of which it is now known they had carefully planned, one doesn't dare to think what would have been the consequences.

Sunday morning—I was surprised to see Mr. Gulick on the plantation with Dr. Beckwith. He couldn't stand the pressure but had to come up and find out for himself. Dr. Beckwith gave us a fine sermon on "half-way reforms." I never

HAWAII'S CRISIS.

Story of a Young Woman Student.

LETTER TO "THE COURANT"

In the Mail of the Steamer That Brought the News.

HONOLULU UNDER MILITARY RULE.

Scenes Attending the Proclamation of the Provisional Government—All White Residents Under Arms—Waiting in Suspense the Decision of the United States.

[The following interesting letter written from Honolulu, capital of the Hawaiian Islands, was a part of the mail of the steamer Claudine that brought the news of the crisis in the islands to San Francisco. It bears date of January 18. THE COURANT'S correspondent is Miss Carrie P. Winter, a student in Kawailiao Seminary, Honolulu. It is, we believe, the first letter of the sort published in the East from an American who actually witnessed the Honolulu revolution.]

An Interesting Narrative.

HONOLULU, H. I., Jan. 18, 1893.

To the Editor of THE COURANT:—

This is the first day that ever dawned in these islands without a king or queen as ruler. To-day we are under a provisional government and martial law.

Since 1871, in the days of King Kalakaua, there has been almost constant struggle on the part of King or Queen to regain the royal power held under the old constitution and lost at that time in the new. At the accession of Queen Liluokalani, almost two years ago now, it was hoped that these contests would end, but from the opening of the Legislature it was apparent that she was pursuing the policy of the last King, her brother. One cabinet after another was voted out till at last the Queen seemed to give way a little and we had a ministry in whom all had confidence and who it seemed would be able, if anybody would, to restore financial prosperity to the country so largely crippled in its leading industry, the production of sugar, by the McKinley bill.

Cause of the Outbreak.

Popular indignation was aroused by three bills which were brought into the Legislature. These were for the manufacture of liquors in the islands, the licensing of opium and the granting of a franchise to the Louisiana Lottery Company for twenty-five years. It was in August that this last bill was sprung upon the people. Every sort of public demonstration against it was made that could be. Numerous petitions were presented to the Legislature against it, mass meetings were held and the papers filled with articles against it. The excitement died down, the bill was referred to a committee and many thought that an end

tion on "her native subjects" and promised to keep within the laws next time.

Queen Dethroned.

Over 1,200 citizens were present at the mass meeting and unanimously ratified the action of the committee of safety and gave them power to go on with such action as they deemed for the public good. Yesterday was a serious day. All houses of business were closed. Armed men from the United States steamship Boston were ashore guarding the American legation and American property. About 2 o'clock in the afternoon an attempt was made to arrest a load of ammunition by a native policeman. He was wounded in the fray. This incident seemed to furnish the signal and the armed citizens advanced to the government building, taking possession of it and stationing their guards without resistance. The proclamation of provisional government was then read and copies of it scattered among the people. An advisory council of fourteen was named, with Judge Dole as its president; W. O. Smith, attorney-general; P. C. Jones, minister of finance; Mr. King, minister of the interior.

After considerable delay, the members of the cabinet were found and a deputation went to the Queen. She held out a long time, but at last, under protest, signed the document giving up her power. She surrendered the station house to the new government and night saw them in full possession.

The city is at present under martial law and the available white population of the city is under arms. The better class of the natives are with the whites in their action, but, naturally, the larger portion of the natives are uneasy. There was no disturbance last night.

Waiting in Suspense.

No regular communication could be held with the United States for three weeks, when the next steamer reaches there, but one of the inter-island steamers has been called into service and starts this afternoon for the States with the official news. It carries a mail and will take this letter. It will be a hard strain on the people here to keep up this vigilance till word can come of the action of the United States in the matter. The only hope of the country is in annexation and for that we most earnestly wish.

C. P. W.

"Hawaii's Crisis," by Carrie P. Winter (CPW), *Hartford Courant.* Written January 18, 1893, and published February 3, 1893.

heard him do so well. I wish you could have heard his description of the crisis of how "mothers went begging that the future of their sons might not be endangered by foul acts and with one stroke of the royal pen, their prayer was disregarded." And how the change at last came "through our last insane act." The feeling of relief everywhere is wonderful. Why Carl, just think, beside her salary of $58,000, she had all the revenue of the crown lands amounting to $80,000 and now all that goes into the treasury of the government.

Sunday—I am not going to church this morning. It is too far to go twice and I shall go back to the Seminary this evening. I went up Tantalus again yesterday afternoon with Miss Brewer, Carrie Gilman and Miss Hadley. I am rather anxious to visit places not quite so familiar to me now. We have been having beautiful days, cool at morning and evening so that a wrap was comfortable and warm at midday and the more glorious of moonlight nights.

School work is going well.[6] My girls have taken hold really well. I like my arrangements best of all this term.

This is my little dream of what will be our ideal life. It's only fancying, dear, so you must take it to heart should some of it not be possible. I would like to have a little waif of some kind to train as a servant and have her stay with us all the time then there will be much of the day when you cannot be with me and I would like to fill my time like this—some practical house-work every day with my own hands, some plain helpful sewing—some fine art sewing— a little reading of the English kind—some hard conscientious work on music. I should like to take lessons—a little venture into literary work—some outdoor exercise, a pretty gown for the time my Carl is with me. What do you say, love? Will you enjoy me thus? We must besides, do all the good with our home, our time and opportunities.

I have thought of you and the home people much this last two days. I feel the news of the revolution may make you very anxious but I hope not. You must tell me all about how it was taken.

January 30—A busy day ended with rumors in the air that all our guards are being extra careful that threatened tumult does not take place before the steamer goes to weaken the office of the Revolution abroad. Another story not so very well vouched for, but believed by many, is to the effect that the Queen offered sacrifices in the palace Sunday since she found herself in such difficulties.

It gets worse and worst about Miss Harris. She won't hear about going home. Things are rapidly coming to a crisis. Miss Pope sends to her family a full statement of the case by the steamer.

January 31—The last night of this month—good!! If only this rapid passage of time didn't mean that one must grow old. I must tell you of my recent reading. I have just finished a second volume of Ruskin containing his letters, poems and Love's Meinie, lectures on birds. I don't care for the book and in it he makes considerable fun of Darwin's theory. Evidently he is a Revolutionist. I have now begun on Carlyle's "Sartor Resartus" and enjoyed it as I do everything of Carlyle's.[7]

I have been talking with two of the girls. The conversation ran on "Kahunas." They plainly show that they believe in them. It is disgusting.

Well, dearest, what of our love? I'd like a fresh breath of strength and happiness from you. I find myself more and more given to fancying our meeting. Will it be you, the Carl I knew? If you don't like me very well, will you give me a chance to be myself? I am sure if I know that you honor me and love me, I shall do well and do better. Dear heart what a joy and crown it is to these years of absence to look forward to so much happiness. Often I feel as if I were in a dream here and my real home, my real life were elsewhere.

> Goodnight, dearest—
> Carrie

February 12, 1893, Kawaiahao Seminary

Dearest Carl,

I got up this morning fully intending to write you some of the love thoughts that kept thronging through my half-waking fancies before I was quite awake. I think now I could show them to you better than tell them.

I just went to the glass to see if I had the faded look that Miss Morris has, whom we are entertaining just now. She is the new teacher for Makawao in Irene's place. I think she used to be good-looking once, but now has that wretched faded look. I don't think I look so now but don't know how it will be by June.

It has been a hard busy exciting week. I am glad it is over. I think there was no ending to my last letter because Thursday night after I had gone to bed, Miss Pope came over to say that the *Monowai* was in and was going and she gave me a kiss and was gone. I did not want to go over and mix in the affair. It was raining hard outside.

Mrs. Coleman went to the hospital for Miss Harris. Mr. Atherton and Mr.

George Castle were here to help off with their carriages and men. Mr. Frank Cooke also came to see what he could do, and after all, the steamer did not go till 11 the next day. I went down in the morning to bid them both "good-by" and to give Miss Pope another letter to mail for me. Miss Harris, who had been in such high spirits the night before was "off" again. You know we sometime have a suspicion that she puts much of it on. She did not know us and wanted Dr. Wood, with whom she fancies she is in love. Miss Pope did ask me to telephone him when I got back but I didn't. I couldn't bring myself to do it. They say that to the last minute she watched for him and felt sure he would come.

The *Mariposa* came in that same forenoon and brought me Jo's report.[8] The mail came in too late for Miss Harris to get her home letters. Jo said the father had sent on money for her to come home on, but we don't know whether he did or not. Her bill at the hospital was unpaid when she went. I very much fear that her family will take no responsibility for her, that she will make a big bill in San Francisco for people here to pay and that as soon as she can get money, she will be back down here.[9]

The China steamer *Belgic* went out the night before but she had small-pox on board and would have to be quarantined so I thought it best not to send my letter by that as it would probably be delayed.

The U.S. Man-of-War *Mohican* also arrived on Friday and the town was very active. It was our first news from San Francisco since our Revolution. The *Claudine* came the same day too but the *Mariposa* brought the news as she came down quicker. Well, I think we have made all the excitement in the American world that we could hope for and everybody here is delighted at the reception given to the news. There doesn't seem to be much report from the Eastern papers and that is what I most want to see. The delegation had just reached Washington when the steamer left. It will be 10 days before we can hope for more news. I must get one of Saturday's papers that you may read of the feeling here.

We were so stirred up over Seminary affairs that we could not think of much else. No one has been found to help us and I think the trustees are inclined to rest on their oars. They are a little vexed at Miss Kenwill because she will not take a certain worthy native woman for the place. But I feel with Miss Kenwill that it is best to make every other effort first.

Friday Evening—I have to sit up half an hour with a couple of girls whom I caught dancing the "hula" so I gladly embrace the time to add to this letter.

Every day since then has been hurried and filled with the preparations for the wedding of last night. I had charge of the chapel and its decorations and 5 Kamehameha boys and picked girls to help me. We had a large supply of ferns and coconut palm leaves. These latter adorned every door-way. The girls braided long leis of fern rapidly and we festooned the walls with these all radiating from a common center beneath which the bride was to stand. There was a mass of ferns at the back of the platform and choice potted plants and roses for the foreground. I also saw to the hanging and lighting of the Chinese lanterns, window-washing and removing of seats, etc.

Charlie Blake is a Kamehameha graduate who now teaches at Lahaina Luna on Maui. Mr. Oleson married them[10] and there was much grandeur in it all. The building, refreshments, girls, presents, bride were all that one could wish. I was constantly pleased by the glimpses of the handsome young fellow, and even if he is a Hawaiian, reminded me of you and couldn't keep from thinking were that my dear bridegroom I should find some difficulty in being a proper, dignified bride. You will have to train me about those little things I think.

Sunday morning February 19—We will know today whether a certain Miss Smith who is Mrs. Dillingham's guest will come to take a place here. She half offered herself to the school on Kauai, but would prefer to come here. If she comes, she will take my work and I will be matron and assistant principal. I am full of foreboding over the matter. Miss Hadley has been pulling ropes to get the place and when she finds her plans have failed, I fear will make it unpleasant for me. Miss Appleton, who has all along advocated my taking the work indicated in a remark the other day that she thought she should be assistant principal though I think she will have sense not to press that point since she definitely refused the position. This Miss Smith is a gentle, sweet faced white-haired woman whose wildest fancies of trouble from the girls lies in the fact that they may not sometimes know their lessons.

There are so many difficulties that I am resolved to be content with whatever turn the matter takes. We must at least have help. I know that for one, I worked too hard last week and yesterday forenoon was quite played out. I went up to see Dr. Andrews and he prescribed hypophosphites and after a nap and a good beefsteak dinner, I was much better. Miss Kenwill and I are going to take the tonic together and see what it will do for us.

I have not told you about my Japanese pupil, Mr. Mori whom Miss Harris passed over to me[11] Mr. Mori works in Bishop Bank as interpreter, has been here a year and had so much experience of the English language. In Japan he attended a school taught by Germans and he knows German well. He is only a boy and as bright and merry as can be. He tries very hard indeed. He comes three evenings in a week from 6:30 to 8. He is reading from *"Swintons Third Reader"* and I use *"How to Talk"* with him.[12] It is delightful teaching him. It is positively refreshing to me. The first time he came he said he was too tired to study and I thought he had only called to make the business arrangements and so chatted away with him, small talk, but he stayed the full time and I at last recalled the fact that Miss Harris said they liked to talk for practice. He has been here five times but last night told me he was going to Maui for two weeks on business. I was sorry to have the lessons interrupted and lose the money but if I have to begin being matron tomorrow and helping Miss Smith out with her work, it may be just as well for me not to have him for a little while.

I have been greatly grieved over a letter I have had from Maui. I forgot whether I told you of it or not. It is from Miss Hammond and contains an account of the moral downfall of that Will Mossman whom I liked so much on our Maui trip. He betrayed the trust of his employer to the extent of $3,000 all for the sake of marrying a stupid native girl. To prevent that folly, his father had him arrested and he is now awaiting trial. How easy it seems to be to lose the moral balance.

I have a letter from Mr. Albert Wilcox in regard to Helen. I rather doubt whether we shall be able to come to terms. He seems to take fright at the thought of her as a "common house-hold drudge." The tone of the letter goes far to convince me that he is her father.

Wednesday evening—The *China* came in on Monday and brought me a very gratifying mail—two letters from you and one from the *Courant*. Your letter gave me the first news about my article and I was quite overjoyed. You can imagine with what eagerness I seized the *Courant* letter when it came and how I almost turned dizzy at the sight of the $10 Postal note. It was a fine letter from Mr. Clark the editor himself.[13] I don't know what higher praise they could have given me. I think I will have it framed, sometime. Here are the best parts of it.

"My dear Miss Winter. Your very enjoyable letter came to us on the evening mail Thursday and was in Friday's Courant. So far as any of us know it was the first original letter in any eastern journal. It was a good piece of newspaper enterprise on your part and we were glad to get it....The Courant would like to hear more from you and the Islands and if you will send us a letter of 1500 words by each steamer for a while now we will be glad to give you $5 each.

Also if you pick up some photographs of immediate interest send those along. There is going to be a great deal of interest over there for a while and we should like our own source of information..."

For once I really did a bright thing, didn't I, Charlie? Of course I am going to write all I can for them and let the money accumulate that and I have solemnly devoted it to my wedding gown.

The next morning Mr. Mori the Japanese pupil came in to bid me good-by and to pay me $5 for the five lessons I had given him. The good pay made me regret all the more his going. At first he said he was going to Maui for two weeks but this time he told me he was not sure.

Now there is no hope of my being matron. It has been quite impossible to find anyone who could or would take a school-room. Our last hope failed. A quite common sort of woman has been engaged for the kitchen work. I reconcile myself for the loss of the $10 by the thought that it would have been very unpleasant on account of certain people anyway. I could not have gone riding so much and I should had to staying at home more on Saturday and should have had to help the new teacher.

Mr. Emerson rang me up yesterday and asked if I didn't want to take a ride with him. I was very glad to go for I was very tired of the Seminary. He took me up a new valley, Paoa. We left about quarter to 4 and got back at six. The valley is very beautiful, a narrow one, full of taro patches.

Miss Kenwill and I are going to hear Mrs. Leavitt lecture tonight on Madagascar.[14] Come and go with us two.

Sunday February 26—I am spending this Sunday at the Bowens. They are good Oberlin people. Mrs. Bowen has been in poor health for the past two years and has entertained very little but seems to have begun again now for she has had two or three of us since Christmas. He is a half-brother of Mr. Pond. He is one of the firm of Castle & Cooke. Their home is very pretty and full of the comforts of life. Every book, chair and table looks new and substantial. The house is very complete in all its appointments. One device of theirs I like very much. All their bedrooms have ample dressing-rooms and closets with drawers and shelves in abundance and that makes it possible to keep all the living rooms and bed rooms uncluttered and in pretty order. We must remember that when we build. Mr. Bowen taught me yesterday to use the type-writer. I found it quite fascinating. I wrote a letter to mother on it and a note to Irene Stiles.

There are 5 men-of-war here now, 2 American, 2 Japanese, 1 English. I am glad you were not afraid for me at all. I shall always have tales of that Revolution to tell. It was very wonderful. The clinching argument for annexation and the one that could not be gotten over was that England would take the Islands if America did not.

No, the girls don't take notes on my lectures, except to copy my main proposition, which is extremely simple. The term did open very quietly but events have made it a rather hard one so far. We hope for an easier time from now on.

February 28—There is to be a little change in my work on account of the new matron. She is not a person you care to leave in authority or give her charge of the money. When Miss Kenwill goes away over Sunday, she does not wish to leave that to Miss Appleton for fear of no end of unpleasantness, so she has arranged to have Miss Appleton off at the same time as herself. That gives me a hard Saturday and Sunday once a month but my day off is to be Monday afternoon and hereafter I do not attend to the meal during the week when the matron is away. I used to have a very hard Monday. Well, dearest, I hope the days go well with you and that you are not thronged with petty worries.

Carrie

March 5, 1893

Dearest Charlie,

Yesterday was a very long day—rising at 5:30 to let the kitchen girls down, at the beck and call of girls, teachers, telephone and presiding over the reception of native friends all the afternoon. There was a concert in the  evening which 83 of the girls attended and I had to take their money and names for that. So far there is only one incident that I have to deplore. I let Koni[15] go to see her doctor yesterday afternoon as she has been doing for some time past and she did not come back. Her grandfather has been trying for some time to get her out and we all knew she would go soon but I am sorry she did it while I was on duty. The girls have been very good, obedient and kindly. I hope today will pass without any incidents.

11A.M.—I am staying home this morning as I am to go to church this evening with the girls. It was collection Sunday and I had to work up the $5.00 collection among the girls. It is always a hard thing to do but it was particularly hard after the concerts of last night. $20.75 came in easy enough but you would have been moved to great pity if you could have witnessed my labors this morning. It at last amounted to $5.10. Then I tied up the sore legs and fingers, gave medicine to the Sunday stomach-aches, watched the line off to Sunday Service and then came to my room. My duties for the afternoon and evening are as follows. Attend to Mrs. Leavitt at lunch which she takes here today. Preside at dinner, go down to the pasture, give out the books from the library, hear my own and Miss Appleton's Bible class, take care of my Dormitory, register the books as they come back, preside at supper, don't forget to tell the girls about church, preside at our Sunday evening Service in chapel, go with girls to Central Union and put dormitory to bed. Well it's enough for Sunday. Tomorrow afternoon is my day out, fortunately. I know what loneliness means, for there is really no one here with whom I can associate in the cares.

We were delighted and surprised when the *Belgic* came in last Tuesday. No one in town expected her. The news from Washington made everyone a little blue. Delay is a very unfortunate thing. I trust Cleveland will get to work at it at once and settle the matter up. Delay means England now for we can't go back where we were before.

The *Courant* came with my article in it. I had quite forgotten what was in it. To the best of my knowledge they did not change anything. It was in the first column. I felt a little ashamed of the big headlines. I only signed my initials but they took pains to tell just who I was. There is a letter from father. He was proud of me.

Thursday I went to an afternoon tea at Mrs. Charles Cooke's given in honor of Mrs. Scott of Hilo. I went with Mrs. Frank Cooke. None of the others were invited. It was because I as a "friend of Mrs. Scotts" thanks to Miss Brewer. You will perhaps remember that I took dinner there when I was in Hilo. It was pleasant because I know enough people now to keep up a lively conversation. The coffee cake, cream and salted almonds were exquisite. I went home with Mrs. Frank Cooke to dinner and went with Miss Van Anglen to the church social in the evening.

Oh, I didn't tell you? We heard from Miss Pope. She got along very nicely on the ocean trip, reached San Francisco Friday, saw Dr. Martin Saturday morning, took Miss Harris to the sanatorium, and left for her home Saturday evening.[16] The Athertons had a long letter from Dr. Martin who expressed great interest in his patient and thought he could cure her in the time for which she

The Hartford Courant.

HAWAII HEARS THE NEWS.

Regret That Annexation Has Been Delayed.

MR. DAVIES INIMICAL TO THE UNITED STATES.

Another Letter From Miss Winter— A Sketch of Cosmopolitan Honolulu — Passion of the Natives for Flowers and Bright Colors — Picturesque Scenes in the Capital City.

Correspondence of THE COURANT.

HONOLULU, March 2, 1893.

Yesterday forenoon the China steamer "Belgic" came in quite unexpectedly. At first the news it brought gave a universal feeling of disappointment, that Hawaiian affairs were at a stand still till after March 4th. The promptness with which the matter was first taken up had raised false hopes and we really were expecting our commissioners home next week with the treaty in their pockets. One of the native papers

THE POST OFFICE.

said the "missionaries" wore long faces. We do, however, see the reasonableness of the delay from the standpoint of the United States, but it does keep rather tight tension here and delay for us is a misfortune. The disaffected among the lower class of native and their demagogic white leaders are already beginning to talk of England. The presence of Kaiulani and Mr. Davies at Washington is merely a little by-play which ought not to affect the matter at issue. Mr. Davies was down here but a short time ago. He is a very worthy gentleman but he does not work for American interests. While here he carried on a spirited newspaper warfare on the question of Pearl Harbor. He was very sure that the Hawaiians ought never to allow the American navy to hold a coaling station there.

A COSMOPOLITAN CITY.

In thinking of Honolulu one needs to bear in mind that it is very cosmopolitan. There is an interesting colony of Portuguese here.

Hawaiian. They could not do it. They would give away their whole stock in trade to their friends; besides, they would not degrade themselves to do the same work that the "Pake" or Chinaman does. The Chinese have redeemed large tracts of marsh land outside the city, turning them into banana plantations and vegetable gardens. They do the gardening for the city. Every morning all housewives are besieged by the Chinese marketmen who come to the door with their double baskets on poles across their shoulders to know if "mamma" will buy their store of corn, peas, tomatoes, bananas, strawberries, etc. They furnish strawberries the year around. They are a feature of almost every landscape with their funny half-walking, half-running gait and their big basket hats. But this is only the beginning of what they do. They do the laundry work of the city, for people do not care to have it done by the natives. They make most of the clothing that the native men and women wear, they make their shoes and they make their food. They have more of the taro patches in their hands, so they raise the taro, make the poi and sell it to the natives. The Chinese literally wash, feed and clothe the city and do its housework. A gentleman who has a cottage up Manoa valley, told me that last summer, wishing to find some one to take care of his place, he went through the valley looking for a Hawaiian, as he preferred to help the natives by giving such work as he had to them. He found a man sitting idly in his hut and offered the work to him, but the man refused it, saying that he did not used to work. He leased his taro-patch to a Chinaman who furnished him with poi and some money.

THE NATIVE HAWAIIANS.

English, Germans and Americans are numerous in the islands, but are out-numbered by the other nationalities. All are out-numbered by the Hawaiians, though they are yearly becoming less. The drift is toward Honolulu and all those who can in any way make a living here come here. They are a fine looking people, tall and large with a great deal of physical strength, but without physical endurance. They are very gentle, good natured and kindly, willing to share everything with you, willing to help you in any way. They are very fond of color, of flowers, of music. Some twenty years ago Bandmaster Berger came here from Germany and undertook the formation of a Hawaiian band. His success was beyond belief. He gave shape and form to all the native music, composing much of it himself and succeeding wonderfully in songs especially adapted to the low, mellow voice of the Hawaiian. It is expected that Mr. Berger will have

There will not be a knife, fork or spoon upon the table. It soon becomes apparent that fingers were invented before forks. Between you and your neighbor will be a calabash of native wood or a bowl of poi. If your entertainer is wealthy it is a calabash. After timidly dipping your fingers into this once or twice and trying the inimitable Hawaiian twirl to get it into your mouth you will gladly leave that sour, pasty mixture to the more skillful manipulation of your native neighbor and turn your attention to the oily package on our plate. This is always some dainty which has been wrapped in "ti" leaves and been cooked under

HAWAIIAN GRASS HOUSE.

ground. This method of cooking gives a delicious flavor to the dainty. Perhaps it is beef which will easily break off in your fingers, or, better still, tender young pig, or more delicious mullet, which rivals shad, or, best of all, chicken. If it is chicken you will find it cooked with taro leaves and flavored with coconut. These are all dishes fit for a king. Your neighbors all share the delicacies of their plates with you. For relishes all up and down the table will be little dishes of salt, little red peppers, ground "kukui" nut, tiny raw fish, while anywhere you can lay your hand on a baked sweet potato or taro, a crab or curious shell fish, and bowls of a delicious pudding compounded of coconut and sweet potato.

HAWAIIAN GRAVE.

The one thing quite revolting to the foreigner is the raw fish which the natives are so fond of. It is quite as much of a mystery to them how we can eat rare meat. Every "luau" ends with watermelon and soda water. If there are many white people present coffee and sandwiches are served afterward.

scene any Saturday [at] There are crowds of [danc]ing natives, gay with fl[owers and] colors, engaged in rapid [talk] with much gesticulation [A] native orator is up haran[guing] on politics or religion a[nd is] very ready to interrupt [from] the stalls laden with [food] more abundant the thou[ght of] the sea.

A more doleful but equ[ally busy] scene may be seen any ev[ening] into the cemetery back [of] Church. The graves ar[e built] over with stucco work

wooden frame work, a[round which] have picket fences about [it.] of the lots you will find a[t] one corner a piece of [wood] braced up to form a shel[f. The] grave of the last member [will] be the fire to do what lit[tle they] ed. It is their custom to [put be]side their dead week[ly for] months. After the first [month] it becomes quite a jol[ly affair.] children play games on [the] various mourning famili[es at this] time. Death is apt to [be an] event in a Hawaiian fa[mily. It] loosen the family ties.

For all their love of

are not careful in cultiva[tion. You] can pick out a Portugue[se from a] Hawaiian by the present [appearance] former and their absen[ce in the] Plain wooden cottages ar[e used by] natives in the city. On[ly in] the country or up in[to the hills] find grass houses and [a few]

LUNALILO HOME.

They have come largely from the Azores and Madeira Islands. They are a very thrifty people. They have settled the slopes of "Punch Bowl," the old crater, just back of the city. Every inch of land they get hold of is in perfect cultivation. Their houses are surrounded by carefully trained grape vines, flowers and fig trees. They seem to have a special gift in the cultivation of fruits.

The Japanese are scattered all through the city. The women are in great demand his band at Chicago and there you may hear the sweet strains of "Alahaoe" and "Hawaii ponoi."

A CHARACTERISTIC TRAIT.

The natives weave all the flowers or ferns they can get hold of into garlands and wear them about their necks or hats. The boatmen, the hack-drivers, all adopt this custom and it is almost a national badge. There is nothing peculiar in the dress of the men except the flowers and the gay hat bands. The dress of the women on all occasions is the "holoqu" or Mother Hubbard wrapper. It is always rather short in

KAWARAHOO CHURCH.

as nurses for children. The men seem to be especially successful in mercantile pursuits. The work on the plantations is done, for the most part, by Japanese.

THRIFTY CHINESE.

No matter what one's prejudices may be against the Chinese, he has to admire and respect what they have accomplished here. They are a happier and better looking set of people here than in San Francisco. Their stores and homes occupy one large portion of the city, so that we have a veritable "Chinatown." Their little shops fill the city, and are on every corner; a few vegetables, or dry goods, will constitute a store. This is true all over the islands. I never saw or heard of a store kept by a front but makes up for that by a train. They wear them on the street and to church. I once saw a woman pay her respects to King Kalakaua in a most elegant "holoqu" of white satin.

A NATIVE BANQUET.

One is not long in Honolulu before having an opportunity of attending a native banquet or "luau." It is the approved style of entertainment where it has to be done on a large scale and after one has attended two or three, there are parts of it that are really enjoyable. The true way is to have the banquet spread upon mats on the ground but they are often given on tables. The mats or tables must, however, be quite covered with "ti" leaves. Each guest may have a plate and a glass but that is all.

has money to stay at the sanatorium. It is $25 a week there. There was also a letter from Mr. Harris expressing grief and surprise and saying that he would come to Honolulu to meet her. We are anxiously awaiting the next letter from Miss Pope which will probably clear up the mystery about the family.

March 8—I am reading "Schönberg Cotta Family" to the girls in devotions now.[17] Last evening after study hour I finished my article for the *Courant*. I intended it to be upon the suburbs of Honolulu but it turned out to be a letter about the different races here with a description of a "luau" etc. We expect the steamer from the colonies today.

I took a short horse-back ride alone yesterday afternoon, tried to find one of our girls who is out sick and called for a little while on Victoria who is one of my married pupils. Mattie did not go very easily and I discovered when I got her home that she was minus a shoe. I had her taken down to be shod this morning. Miss Kenwill and I went to Mrs. Cooke's tea Monday afternoon. This was for teachers. It was much like the one of the week before only humble.

March 9—The steamer is in and I must get my mail off. I hunted Koni up yesterday afternoon and had a talk with her. She was very frank and pleasant with me. To her mind "It was stay in the Seminary and die" or go as she did and she chose the latter.[18] There is worse behind that. I think much about you and the meeting which is gradually drawing near.

> With my dearest love,
> Carrie

March 19, 1893, Honolulu, H.I.

Dearest Carl,

It's such a wonderfully fresh, sweet Sunday morning. You can really taste the sweetness of the air. The warm weather is on us though. It will be hot in the middle of this day.

I had the time yesterday and wanted to take a long, long ride but had no one to go with. Late in the afternoon I went out to the Babb's and took supper with them. Katherine Pope had her horse up and we rode down into town. When we got to the Seminary I telephoned Mr. Emerson to ask if he would ride out to Kamehameha with us to get her safely home—then we rode on toward Waikiki through the crowded noisy mob around the saloons on Saturday night. It was after nine when I got home.

This year of '93, darling, is a wonderful year in all its possibilities. I just get full of excitement when I think of it all don't you? I'm rather of the opinion this morning that there's lots of joy in living and I would like to have you share it with me. I hope we won't make any mistakes in founding our home and so will always keep open the possibility of joy. There are so many things I want to do and see. I fancy in one way that I shall be the versatile one of the family though I know you will never settle into one thing. You'll have avocations. Won't it be joy to live it all out together—only we must be so careful not to let "the little foxes spoil the vines" but always urge each other on in doing and gaining higher good.

March 21—I know now what it is to live in the inside of rumors. Now the air is full in regard to the Japanese Men-of-war in the harbor. There have been two here the *Naniwa* and the *Kongo*. They steamed here in a great hurry right after news of the Revolution. There are some 20,000 Japanese on the Islands. Some little things have aroused suspicion. The *Kongo* went to Hilo closely followed by the U.S. *Alliance*. They came back again and then the *Kongo* went off—no one knows where. Meanwhile a Japanese prisoner at the "reef" escaped to the

Katherine Pope (on horse) with sister Ida May Pope at Kawaiahaʻo Female Seminary, 1893.

Naniwa and they refused to give him up when the Provisional Government asked for him.

The rumor today is that President Dole contemplated going aboard the *Naniwa* today and they sent him word that he would not receive the salute if he did. Is there anything in all this? Are the English behind it? Is it "big head" on the part of the Japanese? Everything lies low till tomorrow when the *Australia* is due and I guess we are all a little uneasy that she will not bring much helpful news. Perhaps if Japan does make a little stir it will help the U.S. to make up its mind with a little more alacrity. Someone said the other day that the meanest thing the British Lion had done in this affair was to keep so still. If he had so much as uttered one growl, the U.S. would have known what to have done.

On Saturday evening, Huntsman, one of the Wilcox men, a white man with some brains, but little savory reputation, and editor of the "Liberal" was shot by a half-white. He died yesterday, was buried today. It is the first thing of the kind since I have been here. It was a cold-blooded affair and miserable throughout. He had no religion. We were once warned to look out for him on account of one of our girls.[19]

Kawaiahaʻo Female Seminary students with musical instruments, c1890.

Tonight there is an annexation meeting in back of us. It seemed necessary to stir up popular feeling a little. I can hear the meeting over at the rink. They are letting off "Americanism" in shouts.

Meanwhile, Miss Kenwill, Mr. Emerson and I went up Pauoa valley yesterday. We started at two and didn't get back till long after dark. There are more little native houses and more cultivated land in this valley than any other I have been in. There are no cattle, no lantana. One climbs steadily up till Punch Bowl is quite below and then even higher on to a plateau and then a long way beyond over a ridge and you are in a mass of cloud land and right below a vision of beautiful valley land again—the head of Manoa valley. We found a few skulls up there, the "alba" and ate our lunch and had a fine ride home.

March 28—Last Thursday I was invited to Mrs. Charles Cooke's for dinner. Mr. Wood and Miss Brewer were also guests. They were very cordial to me and I had a fine time. Mr. Cooke told me of many of his experiences on his recent trip to Washington carrying extra dispatches for the government. He talked to me most of the evening and then brought me home again in his carriage.

It was my Sunday out and I went to Mrs. Frank Cooke's Friday evening and got a good night's sleep. Saturday morning went very rapidly in hearing the children practice and doing an errand or two for Mrs. Cooke. They were to go to the Thompson's for lunch and so I went to Kamehameha with them and lunched and visited coming downtown early morning to see to getting potted plants over to the church for a little decoration for the concert of the evening. This was an extra concert of local talent which Miss Burgess got up to help the school out in its present financial stress. We had a $200 house. I had hoped for $300 but the natives were attending an anti-annexation meeting in Emma Square. Miss Burgess sang so well as to bring pleasure to all. We were glad to get to bed early. The wind made sleeping hard work and I was very tired from all my extra work. It's almost the first of April. I am so glad. I thought this month would never pass.

> Yours,
> Carrie

NOTES

1. This is Rachel Fernandez Soares, wife of Antonio V. Soares, pastor of the Central Union Church's Portuguese mission beginning in 1890. He is listed in several Honolulu directories as principal of the Portuguese mission school.

LATEST FROM HAWAII.

Decided Stand Taken by Japan.

ESCAPED PRISONER NOT RE-TURNED.

Provisional Government Not Recognized — Is England Back of the Scheme?—Annexationists Hold Meetings.

Special Correspondence of THE COURANT.

HONOLULU, H. I., March 23, 1893.

During the past week the air has been full of all kinds of rumors, most of them lacking in comfirmation. Many of them refer to the presence of the Japanese men-of-war. There are 20,000 Japanese on the islands and as soon as Japan received news of our revolution she sent over two men-of-war, the Kongo and the Naniwa. They came in a hurry, for they steamed across and they were well armed. The Kongo left this port for Hilo closely followed by the United States Alliance, and they returned together. The Kongo soon after left again, ostensibly for home. Meanwhile, a Japanese convict escaped from the prison out on the "reef" and reached the "Naniwa." The provisional government asked for his return and it was refused. It was also said that when President Dole proposed to visit the "Naniwa" he was informed that he would not receive the salute if he did come. All this raises a multitude of questions. Would England allow Japan to lay hands on this country? Is England behind Japan in any plans she may have? How will the United States government take it to have Japan hovering about her possible possessions?

Annexationists Meet.

On account of these rumors and some little discontent and agitation among the natives a meeting of the friends of annexation was called two nights ago. There was a large attendance of all the better portion of the city and every annexation sentiment was applauded to the echo. One of the speakers was Judge Hartwell, a man of known caution, and among other things he denied the insinuations that have come from abroad. He declared that the overthrow of the Queen was no preconcerted plan, that it was not the action of a company of sugar speculators, that it was not the work of the "missionary" party. It was like a thunder clap from a clear sky. It was an act necessary to the preservation of law and order.

Another speaker was Mr. Oleson, the principal of the Kamehameha schools. He said that while the government of the United States might disregard the argument for annexation furnished by the need of a naval station in these waters, furnished also by increased commercial advantages should the Nicaragua Canal be completed, the financial benefit to herself also as shown in Mr. Thurston's article in the *North American Review*, even the preservation to herself of American property, missions and business interests in the islands, she could not disregard the argument for civilization, for progress.

England's Course.

There is an opinion abroad here that the course of the British lion in this matter has been very disappointing. Had he but uttered one growl, shaken his head but once, America would have known immediately what she must do. It was only a short time ago that England took possession of Johnson's Island to the south of us and while a chief of the Gilbert Islands was in America asking for American protection for his islands, English ships went there and took possession of them. England is surely not indifferent to the situation, but t is her policy to keep quiet for the present. Yesterday the Australia came in. There was a great crowd to meet her, for all were hoping for further news. We are all well satisfied that a commission should be sent to invistigate the condition of affairs here, though it puts an end to our hope for a speedy termination of the matter. We hope they will be here next week and will make a thorough investigation.

Kaiulani's Manifesto.

For the first time also we saw the text of Kaiulani's manifesto or rather Mr. Davies's manifesto. It does not seem to occur to her that the very fact that it is the sons of the missionaries who years ago gave to their people independence and recognition among the nations, that because it is their sons who wish to annex the islands to America there is a probability of its necessity and of the common sense involved in it. The earlier kings were glad to sit at the feet of the missionaries and learn wordly as well as divine wisdom of them and used their power to protect their people from outside evils and to promote advancement in every line of growth, but the last two monarchs drew quite away from that influence, formed their "court party," advocated a return to ancient superstition and were quite willing to introduce vices to their helpless people for the sake of the money gain, till Liliuokalani wished to flood the country with liquor, opium and the lottery at once. One of those very same old missionaries who came around the Horn in the early part of the century and is now a very lovable and gentle old lady said to me last night that she feared we would be obliged eventually to banish the Queen to escape from her ntrigues.

ANTI-ANNEXATION FACTION.

There have been one or two open-air, anti - annexation meetings of late well attended by natives. One of the leaders of this faction, a Mr. Burle, has lately returned from the coast and tells the natives of a number of important communications he made to the people of the United States and services he rendered Hawaii; among other things that he kept the people from sending an army down here to quell the natives. All their speakers are very much afraid to touch the subject of annexation, they do not care to openly oppose it, for if it comes they wish to reap the benefits of it as well as others. They do cry for civil rights of the natives, knowing well that unless the natives have the vote they will never reach any office. C. P. W.

"Latest from Hawaii," by Carrie P. Winter (CPW), *Hartford Courant*. Written March 23, 1893, and published April 15, 1893.

2. The Sanitarium at Clifton Springs, New York, was founded in 1849 by Dr. Henry Morgan for the treatment of invalids.

3. Miss Winter was not present, but Miss Appleton was and wrote in her journal, "Miss Catherine Pope, Mrs. Babb and Mr. Anderson came down from Kamehameha to attend the prorogation. Miss Kenwill and myself hastily dressed and went over with them. We were fortunate enough to secure good seats. The Royal Band played in the Government Building Yard and when they struck up the National Anthem we knew Her Majesty was approaching. About a minute or two before twelve she entered. Four Kahili bearers preceeded [*sic*] her, carrying magnificent kahilis. The Queen wore the most magnificent costume. Her robe was rich lavender silk or satin. The Royal Feather Cloak was spread over her chair, a tablet was handed her from which she read her prorogation address first in Hawaiian then in English ending with the words, 'I now declare this Legislature prorogued.'" Transcript of Appleton Journal, page 34, Appleton Papers, Oberlin College Archives.

4. Again, Miss Winter was not present and is repeating gossip. Miss Appleton reported in her journal that she was downtown with Miss Pope and met President Hosmer of Punahou: "He said the Queen had told the natives in her address that she has wanted to give them a new constitution but would be obliged to wait." Transcript of Appleton Journal, page 35, Appleton Papers, Oberlin College Archives.

5. Miss Appleton and Miss Van Anglen witnessed this event, according to Miss Appleton's journal. She wrote that upon their return to the seminary, "We talked under our breath lest the girls should find what was going on and precipitate a panic. Our ears and eyes were on the alert for the first symptoms of such trouble. Miss Pope turned back the clock to keep the girls in sewing class longer or we did not know but firing might begin at any moment. Then both classes met together for singing for the same reason—to keep them from scattering in case anything should occur to frighten them." Transcript of Appleton Journal, page 38, Appleton Papers, Oberlin College Archives.

6. Miss Appleton wrote in her journal on January 19, 1893, "The Queen gave notice that she should take out her four girls on Monday next and would consider in regard to the twenty-three paid for by the Liliuokalani Education Society and give further notice on Monday. I suppose they will go and it will be a heady blow to the school." On January 23, she wrote that to Miss Pope's surprise, she received a message from the Queen through Mrs. Ahia that the girls supported by the Liliʻuokalani Education Society would remain in school. Transcript of Appleton Journal, pages 42 and 47, Appleton Papers, Oberlin College Archives.

7. John Ruskin, Love's Meinie: Lectures on Greek and English Birds. George Allen, 1873–1881. Thomas Carlyle, Sartor Resartus, 1832.

8. Blanche Alice ("Jo") Anderson to Carrie Prudence Winter, A.L.S. January 1, 1893, but internally dated January 20. Kofoid Papers, Scripps Archives, University of California–San Diego Libraries.

9. Caroline Babb wrote on April 8, 1893, that it cost $500 to get Miss Harris to San Francisco, a sum she implies was raised by Joseph Ballard Atherton, trustee of Kawaiahaʻo Female Seminary. Babb Papers, The Bancroft Library, University of California–Berkeley.

10. Charlie Blake married Harriet Lewis. Miss Appleton described the wedding in her journal: "Last night we had another interesting gathering, the occasion being the marriage of one of our girls, Harriet Lewis, to Mr. Charles Blake. He is a handsome fellow and Hattie looked very pretty in her pretty white dress, white veil, slippers etc. and artificial orange blossoms in her hair. President Dole gave the bride away and Mr. Oleson married them." Transcript of Appleton Journal, page 51, Appleton Papers, Oberlin College Archives.

11. Miss Appleton wrote in her journal on February 6, "Miss Winter and I are to take two of Miss Harris' Japanese pupils. Miss Winter's pupil is a Mr. Morey who works in Bishop's Bank. My pupil is Mr. Imanisha who was sent from Japan to establish a branch bank in Honolulu, in the interest of the Japanese laborers who come to the plantations. He is wealthy and intelligent and interesting." On page 54, she identifies him as "Mr. Imanishi." Transcript of Appleton Journal, pages 51 and 54, Appleton Papers, Oberlin College Archives.

12. William Swinton, *Swinton's Third Reader* (New York and Chicago: Ivison, Beakeman and Co.), issued in many editions. *How to Talk: A Pocket Manual to Conversation and Debating* was one of many self-help manuals by phrenologist Samuel Roberts Wells and was first published in 1857.

13. Charles H. Clark to Carrie Prudence Winter, A.L.S. February 4, 1893. Kofoid Papers, Scripps Archives, University of California–San Diego Libraries.

14. Mary Greenleaf Clement Leavitt (1830–1912) was a famous feminist, lecturer, and president of the Women's Christian Temperance Union (WCTU).

15. Koni Puʻuohau.

16. Dr. George Henry Martin held the chair for mental and nervous diseases at Hahnemann Hospital College, San Francisco.

17. Elizabeth Runcle Charles, *Chronicle of the Schönberg-Cotta Family,* 1868, a book about Martin Luther.

18. Miss Appleton also called upon Koni Puʻuohau at her family residence in Waikīkī, according to her journal, and failed in her attempt to persuade her to return to the seminary. Transcript of Appleton Journal, page 55, Appleton Papers, Oberlin College Archives.

19. Charles August Hering was indicted for the murder of D. L. Huntsman, who was shot on March 18, 1893, and died on March 20.

14

Homeward Bound
April 1–June 13, 1893

April 1, 1893, Kawaiahao

My Darling,

I am coming to the conclusion that love letters are not all they sometimes are claimed to be. What dry bones they are! I want something infinitely better. I am not at all satisfied with these paper sentiments, are you? Let's  raise a revolt, let's strike, have a Revolution or something.

I'm not so tired as I was a month ago tonight. I had Bible lesson tonight. I think my last one. I was glad it was the Easter lesson for it means so much to me. The girls were very quiet and attentive. 53 of the girls have gone to a concert tonight. I had to sell them tickets for that and make arrangements for their going.

Mr. Gulick telephoned me this evening in regard to steamers. I fear it will be difficult to secure a berth on any steamer before June 21. We have a trustee meeting Monday morning and then I suppose we may know just what day school closes and I can make more vigorous plans. I can't and won't stay here till June 21 unless absolutely compelled to do so Sunday morning—How the days glide by and how much I must put into all of them—the flannel skirt is nearly all embroidered; the lace handkerchief is well on its way. I must do some necessary sewing for my journey—those red seeds at Mrs. Cooke's which I must collect, shells, etc. etc. I wish I had a little extra money right at hand for extra things. Did I tell you of my two shares of $172 Makaweli instead of Pahala which Mr. Castle has for me? It's a better plantation, pays dividends this year. If it does well, I wish we could keep it there and see what comes of it. Perhaps we can.

The *Rush* came in Wednesday.[1] The town went into red, white and blue galore. Yesterday the American flag of the protectorate was taken from the government building and "Camp Boston" abandoned, all the men going on the ship again. Of course we are in midnight darkness as to what it all means. They say Minister Stevens looks satisfied and that is really all we have to hope for the present. Perhaps this step is necessary before annexation but if the citizens have to keep up guard duty from now till next December, there is going to be trouble.

The natives misunderstand it and are stirred up. Our girls were saying last night "our Queen Liliuokalani is coming back this month we are so glad!" The last rumor is that the Japanese will reinstate her if they may receive civil rights for it. It would be just like the natives to turn their backs completely on America and make everything of Japan. I don't know any public event which would be more typical of their character.

There is some growling about Cleveland that Harrison deserves the credit for all that has been done, and had he only been in office longer, it would have been completed by this time. I think Cleveland will do it in time but while he is making so much of himself over it, the delay is very hard for this country. The political situation has been very interesting but I shall be glad to leave even though it's going to gall me like everything if America doesn't come up to the mark in this thing. I'll do all I can to make public opinion.

I went to the Judd's to dine on Friday. It was a very unhappy affair. They had several family quarrels—no family discipline at all—those boys need to be caged. Mrs. Judd lamented that she had not seen more of me. I think it's a little late in the day to make so much of me but they were afraid of me at first. Can't quite blame them for that when there are such curious specimens here.

Oh I nearly forgot—there's a young man, Mr. More Clerk in Lewers & Cooke who paid some attention to Miss Harris while she was here. I once went with them to a lecture. Yesterday he telephoned to ask me to go to the concert with him. Of course I gave as excuse my Bible Lesson. Poor young man, a clerk!! He wants to know nice people and be somebody, and have a lady friend—but not through me.

I may get your letter today. It seems as if I were never more anxious for it than I am this time. I want you very much.

Yours,
Carrie

April 7, 1893, Honolulu, H.I.

My Darling,

Now there is a rumor of a China steamer stopping here  tomorrow or in a day or two. I know I can't get anything less than $65 on the steamers. They are iron-clad. If rates are equal on the Northern Pacific & NW and Rio Grande, I think I shall prefer the Northern Pacific. I have seen people who traveled in tourist sleepers and found them very comfortable indeed. Mr. Gulick says buy a cheap mattress and a blanket and you are all right. I fancy that will much depend on who is with me. I can't run any risk of insects, but if I have someone with me and it is at all feasible, I would be glad to save the money. They say they are cooler. I am more particular about there being a dining car where I can get good food. It does not pay to eat poor things. It's risky.

I received yesterday a *Courant* with my first $5 letter in it. I think I have sent five but I am encouraged to try to get off another one today.

Miss Kenwill and I think Miss Burgess rather wrong-headed. She has tried to get the trustees to advance her the rest of her salary—$120 and says she will return in May and give the concert and then take summer duty. She is really having a good time here and wants to come back, but her past record has not been much as to make the trustees care to have her back again and they don't wish to risk the money. They have point blank refused her proposition. I guess she is somewhat angry over it. It's just one thing right after another in this school.

> With much love,
> Carrie P. Winter

April 14, 1893

Dearest,

Annie—"Is you father living, Miss Winter?"
Miss Winter: "Yes."
Annie: "What is his business?"
Helen: "Why, don't you know? He is a minister. That's why she is good."
Miss Winter: "Helen, do you really think I am good?"
Helen: "Yes, we think you are our best teacher only we like to be naughty."

FINE HAWAIIAN SCENERY

Precipitous Cliffs and Beautiful Valleys.

A BIT OF NATIVE SUPERSTITION.

Travel on Horseback Among the Mountains—Phases of Native Life—Hard Climbing.

Correspondence of THE COURANT.

HONOLULU, H. I., April 8.

Since we are at a stand-still in matters political we may return to some scenes of Island life. There is a little story going the rounds this morning that is worth relating. The Queen's agent, Paul Newman, and Prince David arrived here on the steamer yesterday and during the day attended a "luau" given in their honor. While the guests were busy with the repast the heavy bough of a neighboring tree fell with a quent guave bushes and the silver of the "kukui" trees and the grass.

A Fearful Precipice.

We climb the last gentle ascent on foot, round a corner and are struck dumb with amazement, for the land has fallen sheer away from our feet for about 2,000 feet and way down below us stretches a beautiful level plain to the ocean, a couple of miles from us. The wind blows a hurricane here and we creep under the over-hanging cliffs to hear how long ago Kamehamaha came from Maui with all his warriors, met the chiefs at Waikihi and drove them back little by little into the mountains to this very spot and thrust the surviving desperate men over this deadful "Pali." We run to the wall and look down the fearful precipice. At one side there is a winding, stony, steep trail and as we watch some pack animals resolve that we will never venture our necks on horseback in any such dangerous place. In a year's time if you are fortunate you will be doing much worse riding than that. This is the only pass across the mountains. The only other way to get to the other side is to go to the extreme end of the island and go around. One realizes how small the island is when in a short afternoon's

MOUNTAIN CLIMBING ON HORSEBACK.

"Latest from Hawaii," by Carrie P. Winter (CPW), *Hartford Courant*. Written March 23, 1893, and published April 15, 1893.

crash without apparent cause, as there was no wind blowing. The "Kahunas" say this means the downfall of the present government. Perhaps it was from the same reliable source that the story started yesterday that the Queen would be on the throne again at 2 o'clock. She certainly did not get there and never will again.

Famous Valleys.

After one has lived in the islands a little while one finds he must know something of the valleys to appreciate them fully. From the central mountain ridge of this island extend mountain spurs, which make a series of wonderful valleys all their leeward side. On the other side the mountain descent is chiefly precipitous as if we might be a part of a huge ruin of some ancient crater and all but about forty miles of the crater's boundary walls had fallen into the sea. The first valley for the traveler to visit is "Nunanu."

ride they can go from one side to the other and wonder why all the water between here and San Francisco does not melt it all up and wash it away. "Nunanu" valley is the only one that has a good carriage road up it, the others must be explored on horseback.

Native Country Life.

"Panoa" lies next to Nunanu. One sees native country life at its best in this valley. The cattle are shut out and lantana has not got started. The little native huts are surrounded by their banana and mango trees and a taro patch close at hand. The valley itself is not very long, but rises in a plateau where it is very delightful riding. At last you come to the end, mountains quite shutting you in, and look down a sudden descent into sunny "Manoa" valley. If one's eyes are very bright and they know just how to look they may find a few of the famous achintinellidee or tree shells, for which this island is famous. They are beauties and it is a real pleasure to find one for one's self.

MOUNTAIN ROAD, SHOWING THE PRECIPITOUS CLIFFS.

You pass out Nunanu avenue past the homes of the wealthy citizens, the home of Minister Stevens, the Japanese consulate, and at the outskirts of the city the cemetery and the Royal Mausoleum where King Kalakaua is buried, past the electric light building till you are fairly in the country with mountains rising on either side and mountains before. The ride is very beautiful, a gradual ascent, a refreshing coolness in the air, the glimpses back upon the sea. We pass the chain of reservoirs that store the frequent rains among the hills for the city's use. We pass "Lui Kahaha," where is a group of cottages, summer homes of city people, and soon reach a wilder region. We see a distant waterfall on a mountain side, a few large white birds against the green, the birds that furnish the yellow tuft of feathers for the royal cloaks. At the roadside the "hou" tree has so often lowered its branches to take root in the ground again that it makes an impassable jungle of stem and trunk. There is the scarlet of the Indian shot, the yellow of the fre-

Manoa Valley is quite given over to Chinese cultivation. After passing the narrow entrance to the valley, it opens out into a large circular plain and there are great stretches of taro, rice and banana. There are numerous waterfalls in this valley, charming in their tropical surroundings. To the left of Nunanu valley is Kalii valley. By making a long climb up a narrow ridge one may look down upon the other side of the island. Beyond this again is "Maunalua," given up wholly to cattle, who kill many of the trees, and so do much to destroy the beauty of the valley. Every valley one visits is a fresh surprise, and they all repay a visit. Fording the mountain stream again and again, following up vague trails, breathing the cool air, dismounting for lunch in a shady spot, hunting for rare and beautiful ferns, scanning the trees for shells form, the pleasures of valley exploration. There are no spiders or snakes to fear and no colds to catch.

C. P. W.

You ought to have the inflections, Charlie. All I care about it is to have the girls really think me sincere.

Blount still preserves his reticence, is petitioned by the royalists—today they say the Queen goes back tomorrow. May it always be "tomorrow." The China steamer of last Monday brought me a letter from father. He wavers a little on annexation. He is very proud of my letters in the *Courant.*

Miss Burgess acknowledged to Miss Kenwill and me the wrong of her course here and the mistake she had made in not availing herself of our friendliness. She said to me "I have admired you very much and I want you to forgive my mistakes." I wrote a little to her this morning urging on her a little higher type of womanhood. I hope she will not take it amiss. I did it humbly.

Monday afternoon Miss Kenwill and I went to Waikiki for a rest at the cottage where the Punahou teachers are spending their spring vacation.

Thursday evening Mrs. Cooke had a little entertainment by the children in aid of the Portuguese organ fund and I told a dragon story as a grandmother to a lot of children. They raised $15.

Quiet day Friday, but yesterday I went out to Mrs. Frank Cooke's picnic at Remond Grove. We had a fine time. Quite a party went on to Ewa and visited the sugar mill. The party consisted of the families of Mrs. Frank Cooke, Mrs. Charles Cooke, W.R. Castle, George Castle and the Lowries beside some teachers. The event of the afternoon was the arrival of Mr. W.R. Castle.[2] We got him into a corner and had a splendid long talk from him about his experiences as Commissioner. It was really fine and worth a dollar at least. I'll make a clear $4 out of that day's events.

Sunday Evening—I had a long talk with Mrs. Charles Cooke yesterday. She wanted to draw me out on the subject of Miss Hadley and Miss Armstrong. I did not allow my personal feelings to get into my remarks about them but I held to the opinion I have always held that they are not the right women for the place. I think from what she said that it will come to a head this week and I shouldn't wonder if they got their invitation not to return this week. I do think it is rather late to do it, but though my feelings are very strong on the subject, I have nothing to do with it. If it comes, we can't expect them to be very happy over it and I presume they'll make the rest of us suffer from now on. How horrid it is!

Then there is Miss Appleton bound to pour her confidences into my ears, venting her spleen at the trustees, Miss Pope and Miss Kenwill. I do pray earnestly each day for wisdom and judgment to get through what comes to me without mistake, but I shall be very glad when it is over.

I received a kind letter from Mr. Gulick today urging me to get off on the May 24 steamer or at least engage my berth for the steamer of June 1 or 6 and he will visit in San Francisco and travel east with me but I fear our school doesn't close till the 9th and there is no knowing now how or when I can get off.

Did I tell you that Mrs. Thompson had asked me to tell a story to the children on Children's Day? I believe it will be a fitting public close to my life here. For that reason I will try very hard to do well.

Thursday evening—I am going to the Milk Maid's Convention[3] this evening with Miss Kenwill at her invitation. I hope it will be real funny. Every afternoon this week has been given up to rehearsals at the church. There are a good many "bosses" in the affair and that makes a crop of unpleasantness.

Well, we had a delightful surprise in the arrival of the *Australia* on Tuesday instead of Wednesday. It broke the record. That was because Spreckels was aboard. It was a delight to go down at noon and get the mail myself. There was a short note from the *Cosmopolitan* very courteous but stating they had an article on Hawaii, and would not need one from me. I presume you would like to have me try somewhere else but I don't know just where and even if I should get a chance, I don't feel much inclination to write a long article.

April 23, 1893—Time is passing darling, but when I remember the long vacations in college days, then I get discouraged. I got somewhat morbid too when I think as I often do that there is so much opportunity for making sad mistakes and getting wrought up over little things. My sole dependence is on the grace of God to keep me from error. I am afraid of being unjust to others, of not keeping out of things. How good I shall be when I have my own home.

The last papers told of the death of Mrs. Perkins of Hartford who was my benefactress of college days.

April 25th—The trustees had a meeting today in which it was decided to close June 7th. The steamers after that are June 19 and 21. The first a China with no teacher's reduction, the second, the *Australia*. I found out today that a number of sailing vessels go in June and if one goes shortly after the 7th, I think I will take it. I can't wait here two long weeks.

The trustees also decided to dismiss Miss Hadley and Miss Armstrong. They'll get their little notes tomorrow and I haven't any idea what will happen then. I am something of a coward and would like to be somewhere else. However they might as well make me suffer in a good cause as in a bad one. They are as serene and high and mighty as ever.

I don't think I would like to have you look at me working without my knowing you were there. You might catch me being very cross to the girls and then you wouldn't like me.

I think my sugar venture is all right. They are turning out 70 or 80 tons of sugar a day at Makaweli and sugar has just gone up in the New York markets.

I had a fine ride around Diamond Head with Miss Kenwill and Mr. Emerson on Monday. We started after four and didn't get back till after eight. We rested awhile on the sandy beach beyond Diamond Head. It was fine moonlight and made one of the most delightful of rides. I rode Mr. Emerson's own big white horse. No woman had ever ridden him before.

Well, dearest, I have an examination this morning and must prepare the paper. It is an important occasion.

> Yours
> Carrie

April 28, 1893, Kawaiahao Seminary

Dearest Carl,

A little time for you in the quiet of my room this Friday evening. I shall be glad when tomorrow and Sunday are over. Miss Kenwill goes away and there are so many chances for me to make mistakes and I feel that I am  much more criticized. No one knows how or when Miss Hadley and Miss Armstrong may light. While we were shaking in our boots, unbeknown to us, Mr. Atherton had sent the notes of dismissal up to them. We did not know till next day that they knew. Mr. Atherton showed Miss Kenwill their replies. They were very curt, saying they would leave at the end of the term and quite omitting, "Dear Sir," or "Yours truly" that made both Mr. Atherton and Mr. Castle mad though to me it really seems a small thing compared to what we are hardened to here. Miss Armstrong had all along laid her plans for a visit home this summer but intended to return and I think she has quite convinced herself that she is going of her own accord. She is really quite amiable. I think Miss Hadley feels it very much. She has had little to say but her face betrays her feelings. Neither has mentioned the subject and both have been treated with perfect consideration.

The crowning misfortune has happened to my saddle. I am going to take it to Hammer's tomorrow and see what he can do. If he can fix it up for me perhaps he will give me something for the trappings which are all new. Mattie is looking much better now. I am fattening her up on barley and as soon as her back is well, will try and find a chance to sell her.

Well, it's 12 o'clock Sunday and I took a long rest this morning while the girls were at church. The island mail has just come in and I have looked over the girl's letters. I had a note from Mr. Gulick. That man will be the death of me. Now he writes that he wouldn't mind taking a sailing vessel himself. If I can have another lady along I wouldn't mind his preference.

This is the last day of April. I think it is a shame we do not close before the 7th of June. We haven't had a holiday this year. I mean to give my class one on Tuesday if I can find a place to go to. Darling, don't you think I have been a pretty good girl to stay away all this time and not fret or worry you or tease any more than I have? But now I do want to go so much. Sometimes it seems as if the days would never go by. Will May seem as long as April did? I think after May is gone I shall be quite content for the last days and the packing will fill my mind. It will be harder for you then, than for me.

May 2—I went down to the bank today to deposit $30 and give notice that I wished to draw it all out next month. I made inquiries there some time ago and thought I had the matter all straight but they tell me today that I can draw $100 but 90 days notice is required for the rest—some $20—I gave the notice, pocketed my $30 and came home. I'll have about $200 to get home on and that is ample, especially if I go on sailing vessel. Makaweli shares are now quoted at $87. You remember I bought at $86.

The girls in their Lima Kokua Society by voting $10 to the Woman's Board made me a life member.[4]

Such good fortune. When we came down this morning there was the news of the *Mariposa* and before school I had read my nine letters. I judge from your political talk which must be a reflex of much you see in the papers that they have been doing a good deal of talking lately. That is not so about Blount's associating with the baser sort. He has conducted himself with great circumspection. Lately there has been very little about him except that he is very busy. I am quite stuck up over the reception my letters are receiving. Mother writes me all they say. They do send me the papers as fast as they can and they are in the Dailies and Weekly's too but it takes forever for them to reach me.

You know now of my decision to go on the Northern Pacific and to take a sailing vessel as soon after June 7 as possible. I suppose we must allow 3 weeks for the voyage. That is dreadful but if I am well, it will be a good rest.

Mother wrote me how bad the weather was while you were in Middlefield and that you got little benefit from the trip. She said too that you were not looking well. It fills me with anxiety for you. I long to be where I can help you take care of yourself. Your picture of affairs at home was very realistic. It has always been so more or less and it makes me desire very much to have some regular work next year that I may be quite independent in money matters. Poor father, he has done well considering the great burden of weakness he has had to bear. He has always been a most kind and indulgent father to me. I must never forget that.

I shall look eagerly for your exhibit at the world's fair. You like me just as well don't you, my Carl?

Carrie

May 5, 1893, Kawaiahao Seminary

Dearest,

I think by tomorrow that I may be able to scratch up enough for a political article if I can get the time to write it. You see I must get my story in shape for Sunday. We are pleased that all the papers are making such a fuss  over Cleveland's giving Blount power to pull down the flag. We believe though that Blount is doing wisely. I'll reserve the rest of this for the *Courant.*

I had a letter from a teacher in Meriden, Connecticut who because she has read my letters in the *Courant,* wants me to send her some stamps. Next mail I expect a request for my autograph.

Sunday, May 7—It is after church now where I spent more of the time in dreaming of you and my return home. I allowed $10 this month for expenses and it is almost gone already. Money goes a very little way here. $10 seems a big amount at home. I feel that I must take the sailing vessel now to save money. Mattie needs a little more time to let the hair grow on her back and then I shall make vigorous efforts to sell her. I expect to sell her at a loss but I must get something.

I realize the flight of time more than other days. It is really the 7th today and that makes it just one month to closing. You'll get this about the 19th and perhaps I can get an answer if there is a steamer going right off. You will have letters for me at the "Occidental" in San Francisco and the "Endeavor" in Chicago of course.

Dear one how much I want to be to you.

Goodnight, Sweetheart

May 12, 1893, Honolulu, H.I.

Dear One,

I really am so full of plans and schemes these last weeks that I hardly know which way to turn. Here are two big girls who were into each other's hair just before study-hour to be settled. I guess I'll keep them sewing for me.  I want to finish my lace handkerchief next week and I am pushing my other sewing as fast as I can, keeping offenders busy. It will be full work from now on. I'm glad of it too.

Mattie was not sold yesterday. There seems nothing now but to accept Mr. Emerson's offer. He will find a place to pasture her for the summer and in the fall I will have him bring her here for a month for the new teachers to try and if no one then wants her, she shall go to auction and sell for whatever she will bring. It's too bad that I can't sell her now but everyone is going away now.

Mrs. Cooke is going to give me a piece of tapa cloth. That makes one curio that I will not have to buy. It is three weeks and a half now to closing and I want to do it all in good shape. I do want to do that story well this morning. If you were here I should want you to say a little prayer for me.

I quite understand the feeling of restlessness you have and I am sure it is only a temporary thing. While it is farthest from my desire make you drowsy or inert, I shall be very unhappy if I do not content you and make next year much more interesting to you, add point and zest to all your experiences and give you a good healthy interest outside yourself. My, what a bother I shall be!

May 21—2 1/2 weeks more. I must tell you the after remarks on my story. I did not feel that I had done very well because I knew that those in the back part of the church could not hear me but it seemed to have made a good impression. Dr. Whitney said "She is an artist." Mrs. Charles Cooke said that her two boys came to her in the evening and asked her to tell it to them again. Mrs. Coan, who could not hear very well, said "It was such a pleasure to hear someone who did not put on airs" and there were many other kind things said.

On Monday, Miss Kenwill and I made some calls and went to Mrs. Charles

Mary Sophia Hyde Rice (Mother Rice).

Cooke's to dinner. We had dreaded that a little as it seemed a little perfunctory, while it turned out a very pleasant occasion. When we went away, Mother Rice gave me a note for Miss Appleton. It turned out to be a gift of money for her and $5 of it was to be given to me. I was glad to have some recognition that she did not disapprove of me. She has never taken much notice of me.

It is very kind of your father and mother to feel so about my coming there, but I know you will quite understand my feeling that I cannot go there till I have been to my own home.

Its Tuesday now—I came home Sunday evening. Went to church. Mr. Gulick preached and came up with me and had his talk out. He stayed till almost 11. I was never so bored in my life. It was the old folderol that he got off last summer with very little new in it about him and Irene. I was disgusted and tired and cross. I think he must be unbalanced. I wish I had never seen him after our Hawaii trip. He is a good man but he lacks judgment.

> As ever,
> Carrie

May 26, 1893, Kawaiahao Seminary

Dear Charlie,

It has been a satisfaction to take down my long list of things to do and take off the tasks I had imposed on myself. I got the Japanese carved mask for Dr. Lee that he asked Carrie to have me get. It is horrible and cost $2.
I will have him get it off me when I pass through Minneapolis. I could not resist getting one of the smaller ones for you—they are so perfect in their way. I have had to indulge myself in that way several times of late. I began to think I shall have a full trunk of curios.

The *Australia* generally leaves promptly at 12 but it was a little late this last time and Miss Appleton and I rushed down to see it off. The bridge was just down but we had a chance to pick out almost every one we know and wave them a farewell. There was a great crowd, music, leis and tears.

For a review, we had a Geography match in my room today. The girls studied very hard. I know some could have said the whole 7 pages of the big geography forward and backwards too. They invited Miss Kenwill and all went off well except that the losing side fell into a fit of Hawaiian sulks from which it took the united efforts of Miss Kenwill and me to raise them.

Tomorrow is Miss Kenwill's day off and the last time I have the responsibility of the whole school on my poor shoulders. Heaven preserve me from many conflicts. It was only yesterday that three girls went off without permission to make a visit. I have the Bible lesson on "The Excellent Woman."

I am extremely tired and a little inclined to the headacheing. I had a good nap this afternoon and presume I shall feel better in the cool of the evening. Three girls who stayed out over time yesterday and two who did not stay but forgot to report, gave me great anxiety all the last part of the afternoon. It really came out pretty well but by 6:30 I was more impressed with the failures of the faulty woman than with the virtues of the "Excellent Woman." However I made an effort as it was my last time and did my best for them and was rewarded by such attention and remarks of approbation as they have never before accorded me.

I move like a machine through my various duties which my mind is projecting itself with the departure, or travel, or you, or even our future. I was much interested in the article I was reading this morning on "Taking Root." I do hope it will be our lot to find ourselves at once in the work to which we can give our whole interest and that we may found a home with the prospect of its being permanent. I experience even now a little terror at the thought of a year of transition. Had I the misfortune to be a school teacher, all my life, I should feel forced to root myself here.

Later—The sailing vessel *Irenegard* is in with the news of General Armstrong's death. He is so well known and loved here that the whole city goes into mourning. The *Irenegard* came down in 9 days and went up in 10. That is the vessel for me if it will only go on the right time.

Monday evening—Miss Kenwill, Mr. Emerson and I went for a long ride this afternoon. We were in the saddle most of the time from two to six. We had a fine gallop to the 5-mile point beyond Kamehameha and then branched off up a ridge where we had delicious mountain air and a glimpse of things green and beautiful and restful. We saw the *Boston* go out on target practice and wondered if we were safe with only the *Adams* in port. There's a man's meeting of "Republicans" tonight. We heard that Mrs. Blount said to a lady who was about to leave in disgust at the delay in annexation "Stay a few weeks and you will see some fun."

> I love you very much.
> Carrie

June 1, 1893, Kawaiahao Seminary, Honolulu, H.I.

Dearest Carl,

The steamer from the colonies came in last night. I have been following up the sailing vessels diligently of late and they all seem to go the last part of this week or the first of next. I had my hopes pinned on the *Allen* and  she came in, but only to go on the marine railroad. Besides, there doesn't seem to be the slightest rumor of anyone else so much as thinking of going that way and I can't start off with a with a company of men on a 3-week voyage. I haven't felt so depressed over anything for a long time. I was willing to stay here 3 school years but as to 3 years and 2 weeks, that's a different thing.

On Tuesday, I had a very happy time in taking all your letters from the envelopes and arranging them in the order of their dates. There is enough manuscript there for a good signed volume and I don't believe any woman had a more beautiful nest of letters. I would not part from them for their weight in gold.

> With much love—
> Carrie

June 4, 1893, Kawaiahao Seminary

Dear Charlie,

I think this is my last letter from Honolulu to you. My good news—two sailing vessels are going out Wednesday—the *Allen* and the *Irwin* and I am going on one of them. I think it will be the *Allen*. Mr. Cooke thinks that  is the better vessel and the captain's wife and little girl are aboard so that it is all right for me to go on her whether anyone else goes or not.

I called on the Waterhouses and the Judd's. I shall make very few calls and leave no cards. Last night I finished going through my letters and papers and burned what I wished to destroy. I have many willing helpers and I sent down many loads of old papers. I am going to give my bed clothes to the Portuguese. I have a dread of the long journey between here and home.

Tuesday, A.M.—The *Allen* doesn't go till Thursday. I am delighted. It was going to be too hard to get off tomorrow. Now I can see the girls leave, have time to pack see the *Morning Star* off, attend one more prayer meeting and perhaps get in a short ride. It removes the strain entirely.

I got very tired yesterday. Miss Kenwill gave me some Polia Jam and Guava jelly for mother. I called on Mrs. Coan, at Punahou, and at the Beckwiths. Went to the Athertons in the evening and sold a point lace baby cap for $5 for our fair. Everybody says very nice things to me. Mr. Corhew's going to fix up my trunk for me and he has spoken to Captain Thompson about me. I think the girls are getting up money for a present.

I am looking forward to many happy dreams of you on my long journey over. Mr. Atherton says don't be surprised if it is 30 days. I shall have a long letter to send you as soon as I land. I have to use my wits hard now, to get everything in, but it will soon be over.

I love you truly—Carrie.

June 13, 1893, "S.C. Allen," Pacific Ocean

Dear Carl,

I fancy you of an evening strolling about somewhere in Newport in the most correct of surroundings, perhaps gazing out for a few moments over an equally correct sea-view and indulging in some loving thoughts of me,  wondering where in this great world I may be and making a half-prayer to the Ruler of wind and wave if perchance I am upon the high seas. I wish you could have a glimpse of the reality. It is a strange experience, quite endurable, though sometimes I almost fancy it is not.

We left Honolulu six days ago. Many pleasant things happened at the end of which you shall learn sometime. I suppose my weariness affected me on the ship, certainly I have never been so sea-sick or so slow in getting over it. Even when I feel pretty well, I am so utterly lazy.

June 14—The captain hopes to have good enough winds to make S.F. in a week. I would be delighted but I fear that is a little too much to expect. We are going along very lazily now, about 3 or 4 miles an hour with some 16,000 miles still to go. Doesn't that seem rather hopeless? I am learning all I can about ship life as I never expect to have such another opportunity. The captain is delighted to have a pupil in navigation.

June 15—I got ill again yesterday and remained perfectly irritable till after supper in the evening. I am going to try eating every little while today and see if I can't keep up. We are going splendidly now—due east, 7 miles an hour straight for San Francisco. At first we had the trade winds and could only go due north— they fade out gradually and then comes the time of danger before you get the westerly winds. Last trip, the ship was 14 days in getting round the corner, this time about 4 days and now we expect to go straight on. The captain has an extra sextant and yesterday I took the sun myself and worked out the latitude.

June 16—I am getting discouraged. I no more than get up and turn around a few times than I have to go back to bed sick again. I fear I was most too tired to begin with to get the good out of such a trip. Our outlook for fair winds quite failed us—instead of a west wind coming up it was a N.E. or head wind and we are veering off into the South as much as the East. If it continues, we will tack today and perhaps find westerly winds before night.

I was on deck a long time last evening, bundled up to the last degree to keep me from freezing watching the heaviest sea I ever saw. The vessel looks like nothing with the waves coming in from either side over the main deck and even venturing occasionally over the poop deck.

They treat me like a Princess. Captain Thompson is a Norwegian, a tall fair haired, blue-eyed Viking, doesn't drink, smoke or swear and is very kind hearted and gentle. He rules the ship very well but his 3-year old daughter Edna, rules him. She is a cute little youngster and amuses me. They dress her in boy's cloth- ing. The wife who is also of Norwegian origin doesn't count much either way, spending most of her time in devouring novels of the most sentimental type. She is 23 but decidedly plain. Her great accomplishment is supposed to be her music. She has her piano along and bangs off rattling waltzes and polkas. She also sings sentimental songs in a high cracked voice. With all this, she is good- natured and virtuous. I try to be agreeable which consists here in occasionally amusing Edna and listening to the Captain who loves to talk and likes a listener.

June 17—Yesterday I managed to get through the whole day without being sea-sick so I take courage and think I may come out all right after all. I cer- tainly do a lot of sleeping, only waking at the change of watches. Please, dear, I hope you are very indulgent of this letter writing. It really is pretty hard to accomplish anything.

HAWAIIAN · FERTILIZING · CO.

Organic and Chemical Fertilizers,
Bone Meal, Superphosphates,
Sulphate and Muriate of Potash,
Chile Saltpetre,
Nitrate of Potash,
Rotted Manures,
Wood Ashes,
Lime, Gypsum and Guano,
in quantities to Suit.

A. F. COOKE, Manager.

Bark "S.C. Allen"

Honolulu, H. I., June 7 1893

My dear Miss Winter
Honolulu H.I.

I can not write all, I would
like to say, but I trust that your
going away, what is Honolulu's loss may
be again to some other spot in God's world,
and that spot be made brighter for your
having lived in it.

I thank you for all your kind thoughts
and deeds to me and mine (seen & unseen)
during your abode in our midst.

My prayer is that God may follow you
in your journeys in life, and if it is His
will, and yours too, that you find a happy
home on earth, May his spirit ever abide
with you & yours.

Please accept the enclosed ($10.00) one half from
Mother Cooke & the balance from Lily & the girls) as a
slight gift for you to use as you see fit, before or
after your wedding day.

Yours affectionately
A F Cooke

Letter from Amos Frank Cooke to Carrie P. Winter, Bark *S.C. Allen*, June 7, 1893.

Mr. Frank Cooke handed me a letter to open at sea. It contained $10, $5 from Mother Cooke and $5 from "Lily and the girls" and such a kind letter from him.

The Captain did everything himself for me when I was sick which was another great comfort as the cabin-boy is a rather skinny looking Jap. I had only to speak and there he was—he made beef tea for me himself and when I was better, had chicken broth in the middle of the forenoon. There are hens on board so I have fresh eggs whenever I wish. The food is very plentiful but the canned meats are a little too rich for me and I have to be careful. Ice and fresh meat lasted till Monday.

The captain is very blue over the wind which continues to carry us up and down here in the middle of the ocean instead of onward to our haven.

July 29—In at last, after 23 days. We struck horrible weather night before last and I slept very little the last two nights and was sick every minute yesterday, so I am in a very dilapidated condition. Captain brought me to the hotel, got my trunk thorough without trouble. I devoured your letters. It is almost impossible for me to think clearly enough to write.

This is only to let you know I am again on American soil...

> As ever,
> Carrie

NOTES

1. U.S. Revenue Cutter *Richard Rush* arrived in Honolulu March 29, 1893, with U.S. Commissioner James Henderson Blount, who was charged to investigate the overthrow of Queen Liliʻuokalani.
2. W. R. Castle was one of five commissioners sent to Washington, D.C., by the Provisional Government of Hawaiʻi to foster support for annexation. There is a fuller account of the Remond Grove picnic in Miss Appleton's journal. Transcript of Appleton Journal, page 58, Appleton Papers, Oberlin College Archives.
3. This appears to be the Dairy Maid's Convention, a fund-raising program of the YMCA mentioned in the *Hawaiian Gazette* article "Many Milkmaids in a Row" (April 25, 1893, p. 11).
4. The Lima Kokua Society, also called the Helping Hand Society, was an auxiliary of the Women's Board of Missions for the Pacific and was led by Mrs. L. B. Coan in 1893.

Afterword

At long last, Carrie Prudence Winter became Mrs. Charles Atwood Kofoid on June 30, 1894. She was married by her father at the family home in Connecticut and soon dropped the name Carrie. She took her middle name and became Prudence W. Kofoid. Carrie Winter, the schoolteacher, was forever left behind in Honolulu, and it was Prudence Kofoid who stepped forward to begin an energetic life as the wife of a distinguished university professor.

After the wedding, the couple went to the University of Michigan, where Charlie served as instructor in vertebrate morphology for one year. They then moved to the University of Illinois for another teaching appointment. In 1903, they settled in Berkeley, where Charles succeeded his colleague William Ritter as chair of the department of zoology at the University of California.

While in Honolulu, Carrie had spent much time envisioning their future home: "I will try to be always loving and kind and gentle and thoughtful and have things warm and cheerful when you come home. And I am sure it will be a very beautiful house too." In 1905, Prudence had her beautiful house designed and built by Julia Morgan, an architect best known for her design of Hearst Castle. Located near the Berkeley campus, the Craftsman home of the Kofoids was run on the strictest principles of cleanliness and good order, with everything exactly in its place, true to the housekeeping standards of Kawaiaha'o Female Seminary. The grass mat that Carrie had commissioned from Moloka'i for ten dollars was placed not on the floor of the study, as originally intended, but on the ceiling, where it remains today. The Kofoids had no children of their own, but their lives were busy and their home was always open to university students, colleagues, visiting missionaries, booksellers, and teachers. On holidays, those with no family nearby had a place at the Kofoid table.

Like other missionary teachers from Kawaiaha'o, Prudence wasted no time in

Carrie Winter Kofoid, 1904. Portrait by Frederick A. Webster, Oakland.

furthering her education. She studied history at the University of Illinois under Evarts B. Green. Her master's thesis, "Puritan Influences in the Formative Years of Illinois History," was completed in 1906. She became proficient in Latin and Russian and assisted her husband in the translation of scientific articles.

Charles gained international prestige as a scientist, and a reputation as a hard-working oceanographer. He accompanied Alexander Agassiz, the pre-eminent oceanographer in America, on the Eastern Tropical Pacific Expedition of 1905 and was closely associated with Ritter, a former Harvard colleague, in founding a west coast marine laboratory, now known as the Scripps Institution of Oceanography. His early work on plankton was praised by the great oceanographers of Europe, who received him and Prudence during a year-long visit from 1908 to 1909. That trip yielded a book, *The Biological Stations of Europe*, which was used as a guide by a generation of young American scientists anxious to work in the best laboratories abroad.

During World War I, Prudence was an active member of the YWCA, serving on the California Field Committee while her husband enlisted and worked as a bacteriologist in the Sanitary Corps of the U.S. Army. Kofoid witnessed the flu epidemic of 1918 as it devastated soldiers in military camps, and cautioned his wife to avoid crowds. When he returned to Berkeley, medical students and the sons of missionaries who wanted careers in science sought his courses in biology. Throughout their lives, Prudence used her missionary connections at home and abroad to foster her husband's career in science, and he found jobs for her protégés. During the two world wars, they united their efforts to assist scientists and other scholars who were refugees. Together they acquired a personal library of over forty-thousand rare books, eventually donating them to the University of California.

The *Berkeley Gazette* followed the Kofoids' social and professional activities closely. They were pillars of the Berkeley Congregational Church, and Prudence was a founding member of the Women's Club at Berkeley. For twenty-three years she served as president of the Women's Board of the Pacific of the Congregational Church, and she was an active member of its Board of Missions. The Kofoids and their friends were among the influential Progressive Republicans who supported political reform and the arts and who champion oned the protection of California's natural environment. Prudence used the teaching skills acquired at Kawaiaha'o to assist her as a tutor, lecturer, committee member, and Sunday school teacher.

Only one of the Kawaiahaʻo teachers rivaled her social success. Margaret Brewer Fowler did good works in Pasadena with the fortune left to her by her lumber baron husband. Few of the other teachers at Kawaiahaʻo married, but they led exciting lives nevertheless. After a lifetime of service in Hawaiʻi, Ida May Pope died at the age of fifty-two. Miss Pope served as the principal of the Kamehameha School for Girls for over twenty years. Upon her death in 1914, a newspaper eulogy published in *The Friend*, described her impact:[1]

> Miss Pope was a woman of very keen intellectual power with few peers in the Islands. She had both woman's intuition and man's power of cool judgment, a very rare combination. ... She gave herself to the cause of mothering Hawaiian girls, so many of whom had no real mothers....It is hard to think of any one person in Hawaii whose going could represent more of a community loss than Ida M. Pope.

Carrie's other teaching colleagues, Helen Pepoon and Myra Davis, left Honolulu together and went on to Whitman College in Walla Walla, Washington, where Miss Pepoon excelled as a professor of Latin and Miss Davis served as matron for the ladies' dormitory. Miss Davis died at thirty-eight, and Miss Pepoon was mired in a local scandal when her nephew poisoned his wife. She took a leave of absence from Whitman College and traveled to Foochow, China, as a missionary teacher, becoming an eyewitness to the Boxer Rebellion. Lilla Appleton earned a doctorate from the University of Chicago in 1909 and developed a touring presentation, "The Geographical Features and Social Conditions of the Hawaiian Islands," illustrated with her own collection of stereopticon images. She settled in Vermont.

When the Kofoids visited Hawaiʻi in 1930, their ship was met by two former Kawaiahaʻo Female Seminary students, Eunice Puni Rose and Elizabeth Kahanu Gittel, who shared stories about their fellow students. Many Kawaiahaʻo alumnae excelled as teachers. Among them were Lydia Kaʻonohiponiponiokalani Aholo (1878–1979), *keiki hānai* daughter of Queen Liliʻuokalani. She lived to be 101 and became the first Kamehameha School teacher of the Hawaiian language. Lucy Kapahuahuula Aukai Wright (1873–1931) became the first Native Hawaiian teacher on Kauaʻi. She taught school in Waimea until her marriage, and a park was established there in her honor. Margaret "Maggie" Powers Waldron (1873–1939) was singled out by Kawaiahaʻo teacher Helen Hoppin for her first teaching assignment at Makapala, in Kohala District on the Big Island, in 1892. She became known as Mother

Dr. and Mrs. Charles A. Kofoid, 1930, Honolulu.

Waldron of Pohukaina, an educator so devoted to her students that a park in Honolulu is named in her honor.

Many of Carrie's students had brothers and cousins among the boys at Kamehameha. Marriage to a Kamehameha graduate was greatly encouraged by both schools, and half a dozen of the girls complied. Otherwise, the husbands represented diverse ethnicities, occupations, education levels, and religions. One girl married the son of a prominent Honolulu saloonkeeper, and several married into families that were Catholic, Buddhist, or Protestant but also observed traditional Hawaiian practices. Only seven students appeared to have left the islands and died elsewhere; all the rest seem to have spent their lives in Hawai'i. While the Kawaiaha'o alumnae suffered deeply from the loss of the Kingdom, they made great efforts to transmit Hawaiian culture and language to the next generation and are remembered today for their service to their communities.

Prudence witnessed enormous changes in Honolulu in 1930. The downtown seminary buildings were demolished after the move up to the Mānoa Valley, and modern buildings surrounded Kawaiaha'o Church. The little cottages of the wealthy families in her beloved Waikīkī were rapidly giving way to hotels and office buildings. The Chinatown she knew so well had burned down in 1900, an accident occasioned by the effort to eradicate the bubonic plague. Motorcars replaced horses, and streetcars replaced the mule-driven tramcars. The Kamehameha Schools, where she had spent so much time, was about to move up to its new location, Kapalama Heights.

A new Hawai'i had emerged that matched neither the missionary vision of moral progress, nor the hope of the Kawaiaha'o students for self-government. The regime established by the foreigners who overthrew Queen Lili'uokalani remained in power for fifty years. When Prudence visited Honolulu with her husband, she knew the men in power at the time. Under their leadership, hotels and commercial centers replaced churches and missions as the dominant features of the town. The depression and war were shortly to erode the men's power, making way in our time, if not hers, for a renaissance of Hawaiian culture and a renewed discussion of sovereignty.

Carrie Prudence Winter Kofoid died on November 4, 1942, and the *Berkeley Daily Gazette* acknowledged her community service and social standing in a tribute, "Death Calls Mrs. Kofoid."[2]

Found among the Kofoid collection was a handwritten letter to a bereft Charlie from Prudence's friend Irene Fisher, who included the written eulogy she presented at the September 1, 1943, Annual Women's Board of the Pacific meeting. Fisher made it a point to remember their president as a former missionary teacher to schoolgirls in Hawai'i—one of many contributions to a "long and useful life."[3]

> No one who had known her through the years could fail to sense the modest adequacy she seemed always to have. Was it a report of General Council

Dr. and Mrs. Charles A. Kofoid on their forty-eighth wedding anniversary.

meeting, or learning to read Russian, or in later years, learning to play the piano, or being the president of the Women's association of a great church, or cataloging the scientific books of her husband, or leading in public prayer, or speaking in a memorial service of a little child, or teaching a Sunday school class of boys, or leading a group of young women in Bible study, every task was undertaken with a humble sense of her fitness and adequacy. She has gone from our sight, but she will always be to us an example, a challenge and a benediction.

NOTES

1. *The Friend* 8 (August 1914, p. 1).
2. *Berkeley Daily Gazette* (November 4, 1942, p. 1).
3. Irene Fisher to Charles Atwood Kofoid, T.L.S. September 1, 1943. Kofoid Papers.

Carrie Winter Kofoid in her home, c1920, Berkeley.

Appendix
Who's Who in Miss Winter's Letters

ABRAHAM, Jessie Student of Miss Winter at Kawaiahaʻo Female Seminary, of Hawaiian ancestry. *The Biennial Report of the President of the Bureau of Public Instruction to the Legislature of the Republic of Hawaiʻi 1896* (pp. 102, 119) lists Miss J. Abraham as a teacher of Hawaiian ancestry teaching without a certificate at the Hanāʻmaulu School in Līhuʻe (September 1895).

ADAMS, E. T. Friend of Nellie Waterhouse in Honolulu. *Hawaiian Gazette* (February 24, 1891) notes her arrival on the *Zealandia* and notes she is a graduate of Oswego Normal School. Teacher at Kamehameha Preparatory School who departed Honolulu in ill health (June 1892).

AEA, Sarah (c1878–1900) Born to Joseph Aea. Listed by Miss Winter as a member of her sewing class at Kawaiahaʻo Female Seminary. Her performance at the seminary as an American Indian is mentioned in the *Hawaiian Gazette* (December 2, 1895). The *Independent* (April 17, 1900) includes a notice that Sarah Aea, age twenty-two, daughter of the well-known musician Joseph Aea, died in her home at Waikīkī. The *Evening Bulletin* (April 17, 1900) lists the cause of death as consumption, but the *Independent* (April 18, 1900) lists it as typho-malaria fever. Seminary principal Christina Pauling notes her death and writes, "She had been a member of this school since she was a little girl and was a bright, happy-natured and faithful young woman, always ready to help others. When the time came for her to leave this world, she was ready and went gladly" (*37th Annual Report HEA,* 1900, p. 39).

AHIA, Mary (1877–1947) Born March 19, 1877, in Wailuku, Maui (birthplace also listed as Makawela), one of six children of Abraham Fred Beckley Kekapala Kepoʻomahoe Ahia and Melinda Melaina Kale. Her mother was a retainer in the household of Queen Liliʻuokalani. Student of Miss Winter at Kawaiahaʻo Female Seminary beginning 1892 to 1893, of Hawaiian ancestry. Her brother William Malulani Ahia was a graduate of Kamehameha School and later served as a senator in the Territorial Senate. Worked in the Kawaiahaʻo Female Seminary laundry after leaving school. Married (1905) Charles Burnette Wilson and became foster mother to Honolulu mayor John H. Wilson. Died July 25, 1947, in Honolulu; her obituary appeared in the *Honolulu Advertiser* (July 28, 1947).

AHIA, Nancy (c1876–1918) Born in Wailuku, Maui, to Abraham Fred Beckley Kekapala Kepoʻomahoe Ahia and Melinda Melaina Kale. Her mother was a retainer in the household of Queen Liliʻuokalani. Miss Appleton says in her diary that Mrs. Ahia was close to the Queen. Student of Miss Winter at Kawaiahaʻo Female Seminary beginning 1890, of Hawaiian ancestry. Her sister Mary attended Kawaiahaʻo Female Seminary, and their brother William Malulani Ahia was a graduate of Kamehameha School and later served as a senator in the Territorial Senate. Nancy Ahia was a teacher and is mentioned in Ida May Pope's *Memory Book*. Married (May 2, 1895) Solomon Mahelona at Kamehameha School, Honolulu; witnesses included Miss Pope and Frank Beckley.

AHOI, Victoria (d1894) Student and pupil-teacher of Miss Winter at Kawaiahaʻo Female Seminary beginning 1890, from Līhuʻe, Kauaʻi, of Hawaiian and Chinese ancestry. Her name is spelled Aoy on Miss Winter's list of former students and Ahoy in Miss Winter's letters and is annotated "Married." Hawaiʻi State Archives holds a License to Marry, which lists Victoria Ahoi, daughter of Mrs. P. Ahoi, married to George Chapman Sea in 1891. A brief obituary notice appears in the *Hawaiian Gazette* (August 28, 1894) that Mrs. Victoria A. Sea died in Hanamāʻulu, Kauaʻi.

AHOLO, Lydia Kaʻonohiponiponiokalani (1878–1979) Born February 26, 1878, in Lāhainā, Maui, to Hon. Luther Aholo, lieutenant governor and minister of interior during the reign of King Kalākaua. Her mother, Keahi, died shortly after her birth. She was keiki hānai of Queen Liliʻuokalani, who sent her to Kawaiahaʻo Female Seminary at the age of five. She is the author of an English essay written at age fourteen (c1892), "My life as a school girl in Honolulu." Her name appears on an invitation list for a party at Kawaiahaʻo Female Seminary (June 4, 1892). She graduated with the first class of Kamehameha School for Girls (1897) and attended Oberlin College, majoring in music. She had one year of normal school training (1897–1898). After college, she returned to Kamehameha Schools and is listed in the 1902 school directory as a resident of Honolulu and office assistant (bookkeeper) for the Kamehameha School for Girls. She taught Hawaiian there. She later worked at the Teacher's College of Hawaiʻi and for the Hawaiian Homes Commission. She resided with the Queen until the latter's death. She never married. She discussed her life at Kawaiahaʻo Female Seminary in an oral history interview with Helena Allen (1969). She died at the age of 101 on July 7, 1979.

AI, Emma Kaleionamoku (1876–1969) Born March 27, 1876, in Wailuku, Maui, to John "Kanaka" Ai and Kahale. Student of Miss Winter at Kawaiahaʻo Female Seminary, of Hawaiian and Chinese ancestry. At Kawaiahaʻo Female Seminary (1890–1892) when her name appeared on an invitation list for a party (June 4, 1892). The *Hawaiian Gazette* (June 8, 1894) commends her composition "The Higher Education of Hawaiians." *The Report of the Minister of Public Instruction to the President of the Republic of Hawaiʻi for the Biennial Period Ending December 31, 1899* (p. 94), mentions Miss Emma Ai receiving a certificate for public instruction at the normal school. After graduation, she taught at the Old Royal School Annex. *Hawaiian Gazette* (March 8, 1900) notes marriage of Emma Ai to John J. (Jock) McGuire, Kawaiahaʻo Church; seven children. Jock was yardmaster of the railroad depot. *Department of Public Instruction, Report of the Superintendent of Public Instruction to the Governor of the Territory of Hawaiʻi for the Year Ending December 31, 1900* (p. 208) lists Mrs. Emma McGuire teaching at Pohukaina School. After the death of her first husband, she married Harry T. Haustein/Hausten; one child. In later years, her family ran the famous Willows restaurant on Hausten Street in Honolulu. *Honolulu Advertiser* (March 21, 1959, p. B1, 3) reflected upon her life in "Mrs. Hausten Oahu's Mother of the Year." Died October 1, 1969.

AIKEN, Worth Osbun (1873–1960) Born April 24, 1873, in Robinsonville, North Carolina, to Dr. Perley Johnson Aiken and Julia Orilla Smythe Aiken. Attended Oakland High School. Married (1896) Helen M. Chamberlain; three children. Came to Hawaiʻi and taught school in Wailuku, Maui (1891); station master, Wailuku (1891–1892); postmaster, Kahului (1892–1893); bookkeeper, Haleakala Ranch, Maui (1893–1895); tax collector, Makawao (1893–1904); collector of customs, Kahului (1904–1912). Various positions in banks on Maui. Owner and operator of pineapple plantation, Makawao. Listed in *Men of Hawaiʻi*, 1921 (p. 7). Buried in Makawao Cemetery.

AIKUE, Abigail (1874–c1930) Born November 1874 to Edward Peter Aikue, a district magistrate, and Esther Kalakini. Student of Miss Winter at Kawaiahaʻo Female Seminary (1893). Listed in the 1890 Honolulu city directory as resident at Kawaiahaʻo Female Seminary; occupation, teacher. Mentioned in letter from Helen Kalola Kahaleahu (July 18, 1893). Her composition "A Loaf of Bread" is listed in the program of the closing exercises of the seminary in *Hawaiian Gazette* (June 8, 1894, p. 4). *The Biennial Report* *of the President of the Bureau of Public Instruction to the Legislature of the Republic of Hawai'i 1896* (p. 84) lists Miss Aikue as a teacher at Kawaiaha'o Female Seminary. *The Annual Report of the Hawaiian Evangelical Association 1898* (p. 30) lists Abigail Aikue as teaching in the primary department of Kawaiaha'o Female Seminary in 1898. *The Report of the Minister of Public Instruction to the President of the Republic of Hawai'i for the Biennial Period Ending December 31, 1897* (p. 70) lists her as a teacher at Kawaiaha'o Female Seminary. Married (1906) Harry Harrison; eight children. Resided at Ko'olaupoko with her family; died before 1930.

AIKUE, Dorcas On Miss Winter's list of former students at Kawaiaha'o Female Seminary. Her name appears on an undated Christmas card addressed to Miss Winter. Her performance at the seminary as an American Indian is mentioned in the *Hawaiian Gazette* (December 2, 1895).

AIWOHI, Emma Kahoopaa (b1870) Born in Kohala, Hawai'i, to Samuel Aiwohi and Ellen Paku Kamaka. Friend of Victoria Ahoi on Kaua'i. Student at Kawaiaha'o Female Seminary in 1892, when her name appeared on an invitation list for a party (June 4, 1892). Hawai'i State Archives notes Emma Aiwohi married twice: (July 28, 1892) Wallace Jackson (divorced); (1912) William Charles Brewer. Lived in Līhu'e, Kaua'i, at Grove Farm Plantation during World War I, according to census records. Her first marriage was performed by Rev. Hyde at the North Pacific Missionary Institute and announced in the *Daily Bulletin* (July 29, 1892).

AKANA, Emma Kaleiwohi (1885–1969) Born August 8, 1885, to Ng ting en den Ah chin Akana and Tammer (Tamar/Kamala) Keopuolani Davis, according to her family. Her mother is identified as Kamala on her 1910 License to Marry. Student of Miss Winter at Kawaiaha'o Female Seminary beginning 1890, of Hawaiian and Chinese ancestry. Miss Winter described her as "a slender pretty girl with nice fine hair and good eyes" in a letter to her mother (November 27, 1890). According to family genealogy, Emma's mother was the great granddaughter to Kauwe a Kanoa akaka wale no Haleakalala ka uwe ke kini o Koolau, *ali'i* and cousin to King Kalākaua. Married (1910) Henry R. Wassman; seven children. Emma Akana Wassman was a midwife and devoted member of her church until her death. The transcribed diaries of Lilla Estelle Appleton in the Oberlin College Archives commend her essay "How to Make a Happy Home Happy." This composition was also praised in the article "Sweet Seminarians," published by the *Daily Bulletin* (June 13, 1892). Died October 9, 1969, in Honolulu.

ALEXANDER, Mary Elizabeth (1854–1949) Born September 13, 1854, in Wayne, Michigan, to physician James D. Alexander. Former teacher and principal of Kawaiahaʻo Female Seminary. Principal (1898–1903) of East Maui (Maunaʻolu) Girls School, Makawao, Maui. Her engagement to Mr. Fuller is broken because of his tuberculosis. In 1912 she was secretary of the YWCA in Detroit, Michigan. Member of Hawaiian Mission Children's Society. She retired to Grayling, Crawford County, Michigan, where she resided with the family of her brother George. Died in Detroit, Michigan, (October 21, 1949) and was buried in Elmwood Cemetery, Grayling. An obituary was published in the *Crawford County Avalanche* (October 1949).

ALEXANDER, Samuel Thomas (1836–1904) Born on Kauaʻi 1836, to missionaries William Patterson Alexander and Mary Ann McKinney Alexander. Educated at Punahou School and Williams College. Married (1864) Martha Eliza Cooke; four children, including geologist Annie Montague Alexander. With his partner Henry Perrine Baldwin, purchased Bush Ranch in Makawao, Maui, in 1869 and began cultivating sugarcane, eventually founding Alexander and Baldwin, Inc. He and his company constructed the Haʻikū irrigation ditch to carry water from Haleakalā to East Maui. Moved to California with his family in 1883. Died September 11, 1904, of injuries in a rockfall at Victoria Falls, Africa.

ALEXANDER, William De Witt (1833–1913) Born April 2, 1833, in Honolulu, to missionaries William Patterson Alexander and Mary Ann McKinney Alexander. Educated at Punahou School, A.B., Yale (1855). Married (1860) Abigail Charlotte Baldwin; six children. Author of *A Brief History of the Hawaiian People*, 1891. Professor, Beloit College; professor, Oahu College (1858–1864); president, Oahu College, (1864–1871); surveyor general, Bureau of Government Survey, Hawaiʻi (1871–1901); privy counselor under King Kalākaua; member, Board of Education, Kingdom of Hawaiʻi; founder, Hawaiian Historical Society. He died in Honolulu February 22, 1913. His obituary appeared in HMCS *Annual Report* 61 (1913, p. 41).

ALICIA, Mary Student of Miss Winter at Kawaiahaʻo Female Seminary in 1892.

ALLEN, Cordelia Church Bishop (1837–1912) Born January 25, 1838, in Caldwell, Warren County, New York, to Nelson Bishop and Harriet Phillips Bishop, first cousin of Charles Reed Bishop. Her home at the time of her marriage is sometimes listed as Warrensburg, New York. Married (1865) William F. Allen. Trustee of Kawaiahaʻo Female Seminary. Died Honolulu September 23, 1912. Her obituary appeared in HMCS *Annual Report* 61 (1913, p. 42).

ANAHU, Margaret Kealamoani (1881–1957) Born December 19, 1881, in Honolulu, to John Kaluakapu Anahu and Rose Kaleiokamoku Kamaile. Her father was a musician for Queen Liliʻuokalani and proprietor of the Anahu Ukulele Factory in Honolulu. Student of Miss Winter at Kawaiahaʻo Female Seminary (1893). Kamehameha School for Girls lists her as half Chinese and age thirteen when she entered (December 1894). Several programs listing her musical performances are in Miss Pope's *Memory Book* (vol. 1) in the Kamehameha School Archives. Kamehameha alumni directory for 1902 indicates she graduated in the Kamehameha School for Girls class of 1900, resided in Nāwiliwili, Kauaʻi, and was an inter-island telegraph operator. She was an assistant at Kamehameha Preparatory School for a decade before her marriage. Married (1909) Archibald Arthur Dunn. Died Honolulu September 18, 1957, and buried in Kawaiahaʻo Cemetery.

ANAHU, Rose Kukona (1876–1948) Born to John Kaluakapu Anahu and Rose Kaleiokamoku Kamaile. Student of Miss Winter at Kawaiahaʻo Female Seminary beginning 1890, of Hawaiian and Chinese ancestry. She entered Kamehameha School for Girls at the age of nineteen (December 1894); her expenses were paid by J. A. Hopper. She became blind from atrophy of the optic nerve in 1897. She is listed as a laundress, but her grandnephew recalls that she took care of the children in the Anahu extended family.

ANDERSON, Blanche Alice ("Josephine" or "Jo") (1876–1940) Born October 14, 1876, to Holmes Shepley Anderson and Maria/Marie Fleming. Miss Winter's friend and classmate. A.B., Oberlin College (1890); M.A., Stanford University (1898); Phi Beta Kappa (1905). Latin teacher, Oberlin High School/Academy (1890–1896); instructor in ancient history, Stanford (1899–1901). Married (1901) Floyd O. Rittenhouse and resided in Santa Cruz, California. Christian Scientist and also a member of Congregational Church. Died while on vacation in Newport, Oregon, July 1, 1940.

ANDERSON, James Friend and riding companion of Miss Winter on Maui. In 1892, she sees him among the nobles in the Hawaiian legislature.

ANDERSON, R. B. Teacher in Kamehameha School from 1890 to at least 1896. Listed in Hawai'i directory (1890) as teacher of mathematics and in *Thrum's Hawaiian Annual* as superintendent of manual labor (1891, p. 151). Mrs. Babb describes him as tall, red headed, and originally from New Jersey. The *Hawaiian Gazette* (March 24, 1891) notes he is a recent graduate of Oswego Normal School. He is listed in *The Friend* in 1906 as residing in Brooklyn, New York, and continuing his work teaching boys.

ANDREW, S. J. Matron at Kamehameha School for many years who returned to her home in the United States in 1892 because of cataracts. *Hawaiian Gazette* (May 29, 1894) lists the matron as Mrs. Andrew, so she returned at a later date and was listed as matron of Kamehameha School for Boys, where her birthday was celebrated on April 29, 1896, according to *Handicraft* (May 1896, p. 2) She departed Kamehameha in June 1896, according to *Handicraft* (June 1896, p. 1).

ANDREWS, George Pierce (1838–1903) Born April 9, 1838, in Kailua, Hawai'i, to missionary physician Dr. Seth L. Andrews and Parnella Pierce Andrews. Attended Philips Andover Academy; University of Michigan; M.D. from College of Physicians and Surgeons, New York, (1862). Married (1868) Sarah Garretson Dyer; one child. A founder of Detroit Medical College, where he was professor of medicine until 1881, the Detroit Academy of Medicine, and the Michigan Medical Society. Returned to Honolulu 1889, and as physician in Honolulu treated Miss Winter. His wife was a member of the Women's Board of the Pacific. Died Honolulu, May 10, 1903. His obituary appears in the *Journal of the American Medical Association* (1903, p. 1592), and in *The Friend* (July 1903, pp. 5–6).

APOLO, Mikahala Student of Miss Winter at Kawaiaha'o Female Seminary beginning 1890; of Hawaiian ancestry. Listed in the 1890 *Directory and Handbook of the Kingdom of Hawai'i* as resident at Kawaiaha'o Female Seminary.

APPLETON, Lilla Estelle (1858–1937) Born November 9, 1858, in Victory, Vermont, to George Ashley Appleton and Fanny Reed Wooster Appleton. Graduate, State Normal School, Randolph, Vermont (1880); Litt. B. (1886),

Ph.B. (1890) Oberlin College; graduate, State Normal School, Oswego (1897); Ph.M. (1903), S.M. (1904), Ph.D. (1909) University of Chicago. Teacher, Vermont Public Schools (1875–1881); teacher, Lake Henry, South Dakota (1888–1889); teacher for three months, Santee Indian Training School in Santee Agency, Nebraska (1889); Kawaiahaʻo Female Seminary, Honolulu (1886–1888). Left because of ill health but returned (1891–1893). HMCS *40th Annual Report* (1891–1892, p. 22) says that she is conducting a normal class at Kawaiahaʻo Female Seminary to train the pupils to be teachers. Teacher, Kamehameha Preparatory (1893–1894); teacher and lecturer, South Dakota, Minnesota, Washington; head, Teacher Training Program, Upper Iowa University, Marshall College and other colleges (1907–1916); head, Department of Psychology and Education at Oxford College for Women in Oxford, Ohio (1919–1928); researcher, University of Chicago (1928–1937); author of many published articles in education, ethnology, and sociology. She prepared a stereopticon lecture entitled "The Geographical Features and Social Conditions of the Hawaiian Islands" and toured with it in 1897. Died May 8, 1937, in Chicago, buried in Granby, Vermont. Her papers are in the Oberlin College Archives and with the Vermont Historical Society.

ARMSTRONG, Anna M. (d1894) Teacher at Kawaiahaʻo Female Seminary. Arrives aboard *Zealandia* September 1, 1891, according to the *Hawaiian Gazette*. In 1892, she is about thirty-five years old (her birthday is on or about October 11). In 1894 she was a teacher at St. Andrew's Priory, an Episcopalian school in Honolulu, after leaving Kawaiahaʻo Female Seminary. The *Hawaiian Gazette* (July 20, 1894) notes that Miss A. M. Armstrong, a teacher at St. Andrew's Priory, departs on the *Australia* for a vacation in New York, via Panama. Died February 1894, according to probate records filed in the First Circuit Court, Hawaiʻi. The *Hawaiian Gazette* (February 9, 1897) publishes a notice by A. Z. Hadley, administrix of the estate of the late Miss Anna M. Armstrong of Kīlauea, Island of Kauaʻi. Probate records indicate that she was originally from Morris, New Jersey, and died without heirs at law or next of kin, leaving her modest possessions to friends under a New Jersey will dated 1891.

ARMSTRONG, General Samuel Chapman (1839–1893) Born January 30, 1838, in Wailuku, Maui, to missionaries Richard Armstrong and Clarissa Chapman Armstrong. A.B., Williams College (1862). Married twice: Emma Dean Walker; Mary Alice Ford. Entered Union Army (1862) 125th N.Y.

Regiment, rose to lt. col. 9th U.S. colored infantry. Brevetted brigadier general (1865). A founder and principal of Hampton Institute. Died April 11, 1893, in Hampton City, Virginia.

ASHFORD, **Clarence Wilder** (b1857) and **Volney V.** A politician who harangues about the pious missionaries. Miss Winter does not distinguish which brother she refers to in her letters. Clarence Wilder Ashford was Attorney General of Hawaii (1887-1890) and joined the Hawaiian League. His brother Volney V. Ashford, both born in Canada, was the leader of the Honolulu Rifles. Both brothers were implicated in a plot to overthrow the monarchy in the revolution of 1887. Both men were exiled for political activity, but Clarence returned to Hawai'i and served as a judge in 1911.

ATHERTON, **Charles Henry** (1867–1928) Born July 12, 1867, in Honolulu to Joseph Ballard Atherton and Juliette Montague Cooke Atherton. Educated at Punahou School, attended Oberlin College (1887). Married (1887) Minnie Myrtle Merriam of La Grange, Ohio (1887); three children. Trustee of Central Union Church; director of the YMCA; joined Castle & Cooke Ltd. in 1887 and advanced from buyer to vice president; businessman in Honolulu with interests in many companies. Purchased *Hawaiian Star* (1908), and with other family members owned the *Star Bulletin* (1912). A dormitory near the University of Hawai'i is named in his honor. He died in Beverly Hills, California, February 25, 1928, and his obituary appeared in the *Honolulu Advertiser* (February 26, 1928).

ATHERTON, **Joseph Ballard** (1837–1903) Born November 9, 1837, in Boston, to Jonathan Atherton and Elizabeth Robinson Atherton. Worked at A. H. Amiden, Boston. Went to Hawai'i for his health and obtained a position as bookkeeper at Castle & Cooke (1858). Married (1865) Juliette Montague Cooke; six children. President, Castle & Cooke (1894) until his death; member of the Privy Council (1889–1891); treasurer, Ewa Plantation Company; president, Wai'alua Agricultural Co., Ltd.; member, Board of Immigration. Active in church work and founder of the YMCA in Hawai'i. Trustee of Kawaiaha'o Female Seminary for many years, beginning 1887; trustee, Oahu College; president for many years, Hawaiian Evangelical Association (HEA). Died April 7, 1903, in Honolulu. His obituary appeared in *The Friend* (June 1903, p. 5) and in the *40th Annual Report of the Hawaiian Evangelical Association* (July 1903, p. 14).

ATHERTON, Juliette Montague Cooke (1843–1921) Born August 21, 1843, to missionaries Amos Starr Cooke and Juliette Montague Cooke. Educated at Punahou School. Married (1865) Joseph Ballard Atherton; six children. Artist whose still-life paintings are in the collection of the Bishop Museum. Philanthropist who left part of her fortune to establish the Atherton Foundation. Died Honolulu, August 25, 1921. An obituary appeared in *The Friend* (September 1921, pp. 209–210) and in the *Honolulu Star Bulletin* (August 26, 1921). Listed in *Women of Hawaii* (1938, p. 16).

ATHERTON, Mary Cushing ("May") (1869–1951) Born April 21, 1869, in Honolulu, to Joseph Ballard Atherton and Juliette Montague Cooke Atherton. Graduated from Punahou School (1887). Married (1892) Theodore Richards; four children. Lived in New York (1892), then returned to Honolulu. President of Women's Board of Missions for twenty-six years. Author of several books, including *The Chiefs' Children's School.* Died April 18, 1951, and buried in Mission Houses Cemetery, Kawaiahaʻo Church. Biography appears in *Notable Women of Hawaiʻi.*

ATHERTON, Minnie Myrtle Merriam (1865–1947) Born August 4, 1865, in La Grange, Ohio, to physician Eurotus Driggs Merriam and Laura Ann Bartholomew Merriam. Married (1887) Charles Henry Atherton; three children. For genealogical information see *Merriam Genealogy in England and America,* (1906, p. 215). Died Honolulu February 26, 1947.

ATWATER, William Olmstead (1849–1908) Born in Fairfield, Connecticut, to William Woodruff Atwater and Elizabeth Olmstead Atwater. Married three times: Ellen Whipple Stanford (d1871); Emily Sophronia Baldwin (1844–1891), one child; and Annie Eckfeldt Benner (d1922). General secretary, Postal Bureau of Hawaiʻi; treasurer, Central Union Church. Listed in 1900 Honolulu city directory as bookkeeper, Honolulu Iron Works. Died May 17, 1908, of Bright's disease, according to *Genealogy of the Olmstead Family of America* (1912, p. 422). His obituary appeared in the *Hawaiian Gazette* (May 19, 1908, p. 10).

AUKAI, Lucy Kapahuahuula (1873–1931) Born in Anahola, Kauaʻi, to S. Aukai and Kapa Aukai. Listed on the program for the closing exercises of Kawaiahaʻo Female Seminary at Kawaiahaʻo Church (June 4, 1890), performing a piano solo of "Sternennacht" by Spindler. Miss Winter calls her "our best girl" at Kawaiahaʻo Female Seminary (1891) when she was ill with pleurisy in January, and notes that she was a helper in the classroom. Friend of Victoria Ahoi on Kaua'i; had an aunt in Anahola. Listed on the program as performing a composition, "Na Hana Lokomaikai a na Hoaaloha i Hana ai no ke Kuia," at the closing exercises of Kawaiaha'o Female Seminary (June 4, 1891). *Daily Bulletin* (October 26, 1892) reports she left the seminary to assume a position at Anahola School, Kaua'i. First Native Hawaiian schoolteacher at Waimea; listed in the *Directory and Handbook of Honolulu and the Hawaiian Islands* (1892) as a teacher at Keālia in Kaua'i. *The Biennial Report of the President of the Bureau of Public Instruction to the Legislature of the Republic of Hawai'i 1896* (p. 120) lists Miss Lucy Aukai, nationality P.H. (part Hawaiian), holding a teaching certificate, second class, as a teacher at Waimea School beginning August 1892. *The Report of the Minister of Public Instruction to the President of the Republic of Hawai'i for the Biennial Period Ending December 31, 1897* lists Mrs. Lucy Wright as a teacher at Waimea on Kaua'i and on Ni'ihau in September 1894 and says she received her teaching certificate in August 1892. *Department of Public Instruction, Report of the Superintendent of Public Instruction to the Governor of the Territory of Hawai'i for the Year Ending December 31, 1900* (pp. 61, 214) mention Mrs. Lucy Wright at Waimea. Married (1897) Walter Albert Wright; five children. Died 1931 in Waimea, Kaua'i; buried at Waimea Foreign Church. A beach park on Kaua'i is named for her.

AUSTIN, **Caroline Hannah Clark** (1836–1915) Born June 26, 1836, in Honolulu, to Ephraim Weston Clark and Mary Kitridge Clark. Married (1856) Stafford Lapham Austin; seven children. Died April 29, 1915, in Kealakekua, Kona. Her obituary appears in *The Friend* (1915, p. 107). Her letters are archived at HMCS, Mission Houses, Honolulu.

AUSTIN, **Stafford Lapham** (1825–1896) Born April 10, 1825, in Saratoga, New York, to Benjamin Hale Austin and Anna Lapham Austin. Arrived in Hawai'i on a whaler in the 1850s. Married (1856) Caroline Hannah Clark; seven children. Resident on Church Street, Hilo, when visited by Miss Winter in 1892. Lieutenant governor, island of Hawai'i (1856–1857); circuit judge, island of Hawai'i (1857–1862); founder, Onomea Sugar Plantation. Samuel Clemens stayed with the family during his visit to Hawai'i (1866). Died October 2, 1896, in Waimea, Hawai'i.

BABB, **Caroline May Holden** (1866–1924) Born April 27, 1866, in Casco,

Maine, to Jesse Francis Holden and Sarah Books Sawyer Holden. Married (August 19, 1891) George Herbert Babb in South Windham, Maine; four children. Arrived in Hawai'i aboard steamer *Australia* (September 1891). Taught at Kamehameha School. Died April 22, 1924, in Sebago, Maine.

BABB, George Herbert (1864–1950) Born January 8, 1864, in Sebago, Maine, to John Calvin Babb and Annette Douglass Babb. BME, State College, Orono, Maine (1890). Married (August 19, 1891) Caroline M. Holden in South Windham, Maine; four children. Arrived in Hawai'i aboard steamer *Australia* (September 1891). Manual arts teacher, Kamehameha School (1891–1895); teacher, then principal, Manual Training School, Portland, Maine (1895–1917); member, Maine State Senate, 2d District (1919–1922). Died December 4, 1950, in Augusta, Maine.

BAKER, Edward P. (d1896) Minister of the Foreign Church near Hilo from the 1880s until his resignation (1894). The *New York Times* noted that he observed the eruption of Mauna Loa (March 1881). Died in a bicycle accident in Santa Cruz, California, at the age of sixty-five. His obituary appeared in *The Friend* (August 1896, p. 1).

BALDWIN, Lois Gregory Morris (1837–1924) Born December 28, 1937 in Bridgeport, Connecticut. Married (1857) David Dwight Baldwin. Resident in Maui, affiliated with girls' school there. The Baldwin summer home was known as Olinda. Died November 3, 1924, in Ha'ikū, Maui. Her obituary appeared in *The Friend* (November 1924, p. 268).

BARTHOLOMEW, Emily K. (1872–1928) Born in Līhu'e, Kaua'i, to Wallace Bartholomew and Kaehakoni Kameaaloha Bartholomew. Student of Miss Winter at Kawaiaha'o Female Seminary beginning 1890, of Hawaiian ancestry. She and her classmates presented a dialogue listed on the program for the closing exercises of Kawaiaha'o Female Seminary at Kawaiaha'o Church (June 4, 1890). Miss Winter's letters note Emily's brother Fred died May 23, 1891, at Queen's Hospital of pneumonia. Polk (1892, p. 106) confirms that Fred Bartholomew of 118 Nuuanu Avenue died on May 23, 1892. The *Hawaiian Gazette* (September 5, 1893) notes that she accompanied Emma Kane on the steamer from Moloka'i, returning to Honolulu to attend Kawaiaha'o Female Seminary. Married (1896) Mormon missionary Edward Ailuene Ingham; three children. Her husband ran for office in Hawai'i as a Democrat in 1908. Moved to Alameda, California, in 1909 and later resided in Oakland.

BARTHOLOMEW, Fred (d1891) Born to Wallace Bartholomew and Kaehakoni Kameaaloha Bartholomew; brother of Emily Bartholomew. Died of pneumonia at the age of sixteen or seventeen at Queen's Hospital, tended by Dr. Trousseau. His death is cited in Polk (1892, p. 106).

BARTHOLOMEW, Hattie Student of Miss Winter at Kawaiahaʻo Female Seminary (1893). The *Independent* (June 30, 1899) announced the marriage of Miss Hattie Bartholomew to W. L. Austin (June 26) in Honolulu. William L. Austin and wife, Harriett, are listed in the 1910 federal census as resident on Fort Street in Honolulu. His occupation is listed as foreman.

BECKWITH, Edward Griffin (1826–1909) Born in Great Barrington, Massachusetts. Williams College (1849). Principal, Royal School, Honolulu (1852–1854); president, Oahu College (1855–1859); pastor, Central Union Church (1887–1894) and Makawao Union Church, Paia, Maui (1894–1905). Active with Salvation Army. Married (1853) Caroline Porter Armstrong; five children. Buried Makawao Cemetery. See W. D. Alexander, "Remarks on the Pastorate of Rev. E. G. Beckwith, D.D., in Central Union Church, 1887–1893," *The Friend* (April 1909, p. 5).

BECKWITH, Millie C. Daughter of Rev. Edward G. Beckwith. Listed in the1890 *Directory and Handbook for the Kingdom of Hawaiʻi.*

BENNER, Annie Eckfeldt (1859–1922) Born August 4, 1844, in Fairfield, Connecticut. Married William Olmstead Atwater. Had a sister named Bertha.

BERGER, Heinrich Wilhelm ("Henry") (1844–1929) Born in Potsdam, Prussia, to Wilhelm Augusta (Dehne) Berger. Studied music in Treuenbrietzen, attended Conservatory of Military Music, Berlin. Entered military service (1862), 2d Life Guards, Berlin. Participated in military engagements in Denmark (1864), Austria (1866), France (1870–1871). By request of King Kamehameha V was ordered from Berlin to Honolulu by the minister of war to introduce European music in Hawaiʻi. Arrived Honolulu June 3, 1872. Naturalized Hawaiian subject (1879). Composer and musician, organist at Kawaiahaʻo Church. In 1877 advanced to leadership of the Royal Hawaiian Band, a position he held until 1915. Became a close personal friend of Queen Liliʻuokalani and accompanied her on her royal visit to Molokaʻi (1891). Married Rose Margaret Clark (1899); one child. Associated with

Kamehameha Schools, where he enlarged the music department (1893–1903). Died October 14, 1929, in Honolulu. David W. Bandy documents his career in "Bandmaster Henry Berger and the Royal Hawaiian Band," published in Hawaiian Journal of History (1990, pp. 69–91).

BINGHAM, Hiram II (1831–1908) Born August 16, 1831, in Honolulu to Hiram Bingham and Sybil Moseley Bingham. Yale University (1853). Married (1856) Minerva Clarissa Brewster and departed immediately for Honolulu. Congregational missionary to Micronesia (1857–1875). Commander of the missionary vessel *Morning Star* (1866–?). After developing health problems, settled in Honolulu 1868. Accompanied Queen Lili'uokalani on her royal visit to Moloka'i (1891). Translated the Bible into the language of the Gilbert Islands. Died October 25, 1908, in Baltimore, Maryland. His obituary appears in *The Friend* (December 1908).

BIPIKANE, John W. Married Kuikini. Listed as a driver in the *Directory and Handbook of the Kingdom of Hawai'i*, 1890. Member, 1892 legislature; vice president, Ka Hui Hawai'i Aloha 'Aina (Hawaiian Patriotic League), in 1893. Hawaiian politician who advised others to buy rifles. Charged with treason by the government of Queen Lili'uokalani (1892) but never brought to trial.

BISHOP, Bernice Pauahi (1831–1884) Born December 19, 1831, in Honolulu, to Abner Paki and Konia, both of whom were *ali'i* with distinguished chiefly ancestors. *Hānai* daughter of high chiefess Kinau, *kuhina nui* (1832–1839). Educated at Royal School. Married (1850) Charles Reed Bishop. Member, Kawaiaha'o Church, Stranger's Friend Society. Refused offer to be Queen of Hawai'i (1872). Died October 16, 1884, of cancer, buried in Royal Mausoleum. Her will established a trust that founded Kamehameha Schools and many other institutions serving the Hawaiian people.

BISHOP, Charles Reed (1822–1915) Born January 25, 1822, in Glens Falls, New York, to Samuel Bishop and Maria Reed Bishop. Arrived in Honolulu (October 1846). Married Bernice Pauahi (1850) and was made a lifetime member of the House of Nobles. Joined the Privy Council; became collector general of customs; helped organize the Royal Hawaiian Agricultural Society; opened Bishop and Company (predecessor of First Hawaiian Bank); served several Hawaiian monarchs in a variety of positions, e.g., foreign minister (handling treaties with Austria, Germany, Denmark, France, Russia, and the United States), president of the board of education, and chairman of the legislative finance committee; sat on the boards of many charities and donated generously to Hawai'i schools, hospitals, churches, and social-welfare organizations. His wife, Bernice Pauahi, died in 1884. As one of five trustees she had selected to manage her estate and as the co-executor of her will, he set in motion the process that resulted in the establishment of the Kamehameha Schools in 1887. In 1889, he established the Bernice Pauahi Bishop Museum to honor his wife. He departed Hawai'i in 1894, repudiating the revolution that overthrew the Queen. Died June 7, 1915, in Oakland, California.

BISHOP, Sereno Edwards (1827–1909) Born February 7, 1827, in Kaawaloa, Hawai'i, to missionary Artemas Bishop and Elizabeth Edwards Bishop. Graduated Amherst College (1846), Auburn Theological Seminary (1851); ordained New York (1852). Married (1852) Cornelia Ann Sessions; five children. Returned to Hawai'i (1853). Served various churches; principal, Lāhaināluna Seminary (1856–1877); member, Board of Trustees of Kawaiaha'o Female Seminary until 1887; member, Hawaiian Government Survey Department (1877–1881); editor, *The Friend* (1887–1902); author, *Reminiscences of Old Hawai'i.* His obituary appears in *The Friend* (May 1909).

BLAINE, James G. U.S. politician and secretary of state. Unsuccessful candidate for president in 1892.

BLAKE, Charles E. (1870–1916) Born March 7, 1870, in Kōloa, Kaua'i, to Alva Scott Blake and Kanohi Kuaalu. Graduated, Kamehameha School (1891); his school expenses were paid by J. K. Smith. Married twice: (February 16, 1893) Harriet Kawaikapu Lewis(divorced), five children; (October 10, 1906) Annie Kamakawai Tell, one child. Teacher of mechanical drawing, Lāhaināluna on Maui; attorney in Kōloa, Kaua'i; magistrate on Kaua'i (1894–1900). In 1895 he wrote a circular letter as secretary of the Kamehameha class of 1891, published in *Handicraft* (May 1895, p. 3). Died December 16, 1916, in Kōloa, Kaua'i.

BLOUNT, James Henderson (1837–1903) Born September 12, 1837, in Jones County, Georgia. Graduated from University of Georgia (1858) and admitted to the bar (1859). Married (1861) Eugenia Wiley Blount; three children. Served as enlisted man, promoted to lt. colonel, Confederate Army. Represented Georgia in the U.S. House of Representatives (1873–1893). Commissioned by President Grover Cleveland in 1893 to investigate the overthrow of the Hawaiian monarchy. Arrived in Honolulu and ordered that the American flag be lowered and the Hawaiian flag raised on March 29, 1893. The Blount Report (October 1893) included testimony from a wide spectrum of Hawaiian residents and condemned the coup d'état. Died March 8, 1903, in Macon, Georgia.

BLOUNT, Eugenia Clopton Wiley (1843–1936) Born January 19, 1843, in Bibb, Georgia, to physician John Barnett Wiley. Married (1861) James H. Blount; four children. Died January 5, 1936, buried at Rose Hill Cemetery Macon, Georgia.

BOWEN, William Alfred (1853–1919) Born March 17, 1853, in York, Medina County, Ohio, to Calib Alexander Bowen and Mary Jerusha Castle Bowen; nephew of S. N. Castle, half-brother of Chauncey N. Pond. A.B., Oberlin (1878). Arrived Hawai'i (1878) and became a bookkeeper with Castle & Cooke. Married (1885) Emma Viola Kennedy; two children. Clerk, Honolulu (1878–1880); employed at Oberlin Treasurer's Office (1880–1881). In 1888 purchased a share in Castle & Cooke; partner, then treasurer until 1906, and finally director, Castle & Cooke. Superintendent, Portuguese Sunday School, Hawai'i (1894–1906); superintendent, Central Union Church Sunday School, Honolulu; president, Honolulu YMCA; commissioner of education, Territory of Hawai'i, for three years; secretary, Hawaiian Government Commission on Public School Funds; member, Hawaiian Board of Missions. Worked for the Mid-Pacific Institute. President and treasurer of Anti-Saloon League. Died March 2, 1919, in Honolulu. His biography appears in *Men in Hawai'i* (1917), and his obituary appeared in *The Friend* (March 1919).

BOWEN, Emma Viola Kennedy (1856–1927) Born June 22, 1856, in Brunswick, Medina County, Ohio, to William Kennedy and Elizabeth Hamilton Kennedy. Attended Oberlin College summer sessions (1907, 1908). Married (1885) William Alfred Bowen and accompanied him to Honolulu; two children. Baby baptized at Kawaiaha'o Church (March 1892). Member, Central Union Church. Died March 1, 1927, in Honolulu. Her obituary appeared in the *Honolulu Advertiser* (March 2, 1927).

BREWER, Margaret Abernethy (1863–1931) Born September 23, 1863, in San Francisco, one of three daughters, to lawyer John Hiram Brewer and Margaret Abernethy Brewer. After graduating from Oakland High School, she taught at a school founded by her friend Anna Head. Teacher, Kawaiaha'o Female Seminary (1883–1891); teacher, Punahou Preparatory School, where she taught for a decade; principal, first and second grades, Punahou Preparatory School (1890). The *Hawaiian Gazette* (July 10, 1896) announced her engagement to Dr. Jared Smith, a government physician at Kōloa; he was murdered the following year to prevent him from signing an order for the removal of a Hawaiian girl suspected of having leprosy. M.A., New York University (1899). Married (1903) businessman Eldridge M. Fowler, a widower, and settled in Pasadena, California. Associate, California Institute of Technology; long-time contributor, Pasadena's All Saints Church; benefactor, Pasadena Hospital. She founded Boys Republic (1907), a youth facility and school for troubled boys, and settled in Casa Colina to be near the school. There she met the early faculty of Scripps College and served as a founding member of its board of trustees. Died July 1931.

BRIDGES, **Ella Kamakea** (b1876) Born to George A. Bridges and Maraea Kapule Ka'ainahuna; sister of Mary Bridges. Listed in the 1882 *Circular of Kawaiaha'o Female Seminary* as a student. Miss Winter wrote her brother Alpheus Winter (December 19, 1890), that Ella Bridges was on Moloka'i. A letter from Miss Pope (May 3, 1891) published in Helena G. Allen's *The Betrayal of Liliuokalani* (1982, pp. 246–251) describes her visit to Ella Bridges at the Bishop House on Moloka'i in1891; the original of this letter is in Huntington Library. Married twice: (1901) James K. Pahu (died); (1907) David Kaai, six children. Resided on Moloka'i, working as a farmer for the rest of her life.

BRIDGES, **Mary Ellen Hanau-umi-a-Kanoena Kanoina** (1872–1919) Born October 4, 1872, in Honolulu to George A. Bridges and Maraea Kapule Ka'ainahuna; sister of Ella Bridges. Listed in the *1882 Circular of Kawaiaha'o Seminary* as a student; student of Miss Winter in 1890. Listed in the *Directory and Handbook of the Kingdom of Hawai'i* (Polk, 1890, p. 144) as a student at Kawaiaha'o Female Seminary, residence Queen, Honaukaha. Married (1894) Robert Kolomoku Pahau; two children. Her name is on an invitation list for a party at Kawaiaha'o Female Seminary (June 4, 1892). Died August 26, 1919, in Honolulu. Obituary published in *Ka Nupepa Kuokoa* (September 12, 1919) entitled "Ua Mae Ka Pua O Ka Ilima I Ka Ehu Kakaiaka" and was translated and published in *Hawaiian Genealogies* (vol. 2) by Edith Kawelohea McKinzie.

BROWN, George (Rear Admiral) (1835–1913) Born June 16, 1835, to William J. Brown, secretary of state for Indiana and later a U.S. congressman, and Susan Brown Tompkins. Joined U.S. Navy, midshipman (February 5, 1849); passed midshipman (June 12, 1855); master (September 16, 1855); lieutenant (June 2, 1856); lieutenant commander (July 16, 1862). Commanded an ironclad during the Civil War and participated in many engagements, including Vicksburg; wounded, captured, and exchanged. Promoted to commander (July 25, 1866); captain (April 25, 1877); commodore (September 4, 1887); commander-in-chief, Pacific Station (1889–1892); rear admiral (September 27, 1893). On retired list (1897); commander, Norfolk Naval Shipyard (1893–1897). Highest-ranking naval officer until his retirement (1897) to Indianapolis, Indiana. Married (1871) Kate Morris; three children. Died June 29, 1913, in Indianapolis.

BROWN, Irene Haalou Kahalelaukoa-Kamamalu ʻĪʻī (1869–1922) Born September 30, 1869, to John Papa ʻĪʻī, companion to Liholiho (later King Kamehameha II) and advisor to his successors, and his second wife, Maria Keawe. After her father's death, she was placed in the care of Justice Albert Francis Judd and raised in the home of Rev. C. M. Hyde in Honolulu. Educated at Kawaiahaʻo Female Seminary and Punahou School. Married twice (1886) Charles Augustus Brown (divorced), three children; Carl S. Holloway. Lady of the court of Queen Liliʻuokalani; attended the Queen on her visit to Molokaʻi (1891) and is mentioned in the Queen's memoirs. Trustee, Kawaiahaʻo Female Seminary; president, Kawaiahaʻo Alumnae Association. Member and leader of many Hawaiian societies and civic organizations and was noted for her charity and philanthropy. Died August 26, 1922, in Honolulu. Her biography is in *Notable Women of Hawaiʻi*.

BUCHANAN, C. H. Overseer, Ulupalakua Ranch, Maui. Had a Hawaiian wife. Listed in T. G. Thrum's *All About Hawaiʻi* (1892). This may be Charles Augustus Buchanan (1860–1946), husband of Namahana.

BURGESS, Etta Augusta (1868–1958) Born April 1, 1868, in California, to artist William Hubert Burgess and Henrietta J. Haskel Burgess of Oakland. Attended University of California, Berkeley, as a special student in the class of 1888. Her love affair with Lincoln Steffens is described in Kaplan (1974).Teacher of music at Kawaiahaʻo Female Seminary (1892), departed Hawaiʻi (1893) and returned to her home in San Francisco because of her mother's illness. Performances as a contralto in Honolulu are mentioned in the *Daily Bulletin* (November 24, 30, 1892). Performance of her Kawaiaha'o Female Seminary students in *"The Flower Queen"* is praised in the *Hawaiian Gazette* (April 25, 1893). Attended New England Conservatory of Music in Boston (1896). She is listed as a vocalist in Oakland, California (1900). Married (1901) Stephen Graham Nobbs, in Massachusettes. Mrs. Etta Burgess Nobbes is listed as contralto, Boston Symphony Orchestra (1910), and music instructor, in New York. The *New York Times* (February 21, 1910) says she is on the faculty of the Normal College on Park Avenue. Moved to Sarasota, Florida (1940). Died September 25, 1958.

BUSH, John Edward (1843–1906) Born February 15, 1843. Governor of Kaua'i, Minister of Finance; King Kalākaua's envoy to King Malietoa of Samoa; other offices. Owner of Hawaiian-language newspaper *Ka Leo O Ka Lahui;* politician; Seventh-day Adventist; member, National Liberal Party, which was against the monarchy; representative, district of O'ahu in the legislature (1890); vice president (1893), Ka Hui Hawai'i Aloha 'Aina (Hawaiian Patriotic League). Sometimes a royalist and sometimes not. Married twice: Maryanne Peters; Mary Julia Glennie, one child.

CAROTHERS, George R. Arrived in Hawai'i (September 1891) on steamer *Australia* in company of the Babbs. Teacher, Cincinnati Technical School; teacher of drawing, Kamehameha School; superintendent, machine shop (until 1892); principal, Tacoma Manual Training School. Kamehameha School records say he was from Milwaukee, Wisconsin, but Caroline Babb says Iowa. Joined Central Union Church (April 1892).

CARTER, Henry Augustus Pierce (1837–1891) Born August 7, 1837,in Honolulu, Hawai'i, to Joseph O. Carter and Hanna T. Lord Carter. Member, C. Brewer & Co., Honolulu. Married Sybil Augusta Judd; five children. Numerous diplomatic posts for the Hawaiian monarchs beginning in 1874, including Hawaiian minister to the United States (1883). Died in 1891 in New York.

CARTER, Joseph Oliver (1831–1909) Born in Honolulu to Captain Joseph Oliver Carter and Hanna T. Lord Carter; older brother of H. A. P. Carter. Hawaiian minister to the United States. Educated in Boston. Married Mary Elizabeth Ladd; six children. Journalist, *Pacific Commercial Advertiser,* from the late 1850s until 1872; Hawaiian correspondent, *New York Herald.*

Elected to the legislature (1872). Registrar for public accounts (1874–1880). Joined C. Brewer & Co. (1880), served as president (1891–1894). trustee, Kamehameha Schools and Central Union Church.

CASTLE, **Caroline Dickenson** (Carrie) (1858–1941) Born March 15, 1858, in Kawaiahaʻo, Hawaiʻi, to Samuel Northrup Castle and Mary Tenney Castle. Student of music and voice at New England Conservatory of Music and then Oberlin College (1877–1879). Married (1905). Rev. William Drake Westervelt; one child. President Honolulu branch, Women's International League of Peace and Freedom; director, Foreign Relations Department, WCTU; director, Near East Relief Work, Honolulu; member, DAR, Daughters of Hawaiʻi, YWCA, League of Women Voters, Congregational Church. Close friend of Miss Pope and mentions Miss Pope in her Oberlin file as a person who had an outstanding influence on her life. Died July 23, 1941.

CASTLE, **George Parmelee** (1851–1932) Born March 15, 1858, in Honolulu, to Samuel Northrup Castle and Mary Ann Tenney Castle. Educated at Punahou School and in Ann Arbor, Michigan: one year at Michigan University; one year at Detroit Medical School. Married (1879) Ida Mary Tenney; three children. Clerk, Castle & Cooke (1874). In 1883, purchased a portion of his father's interest and became a partner in Castle & Cooke, rising to president. Helped with Miss Harris. Member, Honolulu Rifles; member, Advisory Council, Republic of Hawaiʻi, 1893; trustee, Children's Hospital, Mid-Pacific Institute, Hawaiian Board of Missions, Hilo Boarding School, and many other organizations.

CASTLE, **Henry Northrup** (1862–1895) Born August 22, 1862, in Honolulu to missionaries Samuel Northrup Castle and Mary Ann Tenney Castle. A.B., Oberlin College (1883); attended Harvard Law School; studied in Berlin and Leipzig. At Oberlin established a lifelong friendship with philosopher George Herbert Mead. Married twice: (1889) Frida Steckner (died 1890), one child; (1892) Mabel Rosamund Wing, one child. Editor (1890–1893) and owner, *Pacific Commercial Advertiser* and *Hawaiian Gazette.* During the revolution of 1893, he carried a rifle as a private. Attended the Hawaiian commission in Washington that investigated the overthrow of the Hawaiian monarchy. Died 1895 in steamer accident on the North Sea.

CASTLE, **Ida Beatrice Lowrey** (1854–1926) Born November 5, 1854, in South Lee, Massachusetts, to Frederick Canfield Lowrey and Alice Lovinna

Moore Castle. Married (1879) William Richards Castle; three children. Died January 23, 1926, in Honolulu. Her tombstone at Kawaiahaʻo Church lists her date of marriage as October 12, 1875.

CASTLE, **Ida Mary Tenney** (1856–1944) Born June 30, 1856, in Plainfield, New York, to Lucien P. Tenney and Mary Eliza Davies Tenney. Married (1879) George Parmelee Castle; three children.

CASTLE, **Mary Ann Tenney** ("Mother Castle") (1819–1907) Born October 26, 1819, in Plainfield, New York, to Deacon Levi Tenney and Mary Kingbury Tenney. Attended Deerfield Academy and taught at Plainfield schools. Married (1842) Samuel Northrup Castle and joined him as a missionary to Hawaiʻi; ten children. She was Samuel Castle's second wife, and the sister of his first wife, Angeline. Advocate of female suffrage and a member of Women's Board of Missions. Worked for prison reform and was a member of the Woman's Christian Temperance Union. Established (1898) the Mary Castle Trust for charities and education, later the Samuel N. and Mary Castle Foundation. Home was on King Street, next door to Kawaiahaʻo Female Seminary. Friend to Miss Pope. Biography is in *Notable Women of Hawaiʻi.*

CASTLE, **William Richards** (1849–1935) Born March 19, 1849, in Honolulu, to Samuel Northrup Castle and Mary Ann Tenney Castle. Entered Oberlin College as a prep student (1864) but never graduated due to ill health. L.L.B., Columbia College (1873); Honorary A.M., Oberlin College (1885). Married (1875) Ida Beatrice Lowrey; three children. Practiced law in New York City (1873–1876). Attorney general, Kingdom of Hawaiʻi (1876); member, Hawaiian legislature (1878, 1886–1888); president and attorney, Honolulu Gas Co., Ltd.; trustee and treasurer, Kawaiahaʻo Female Seminary; member, commission sent to Washington, D.C., to initiate annexation (1893). Served in Washington as Hawaiian minister (1895). President of Board of Education of the Republic of Hawaiʻi for three years. He and his father financed the creation of the Ewa Plantation Co. One of the founders of the Honolulu Rapid Transit Trust and Land Co.; trustee, Oahu College; member, Hawaiian and American Bar Associations, National Municipal League, National Economic League, American Academy of Politics and Social Science, Sons of the Revolution. Congregationalist. Died June 5, 1935, in Honolulu.

CHASE, **Charles Edward** (1857–?) Born March 19, 1857, in Dubuque, Iowa, to George Lewis Chase and Callista M. Taft Chase. Married Helen Smith Bourne; two children. President of Hartford Fire Insurance Company. Affiliated with Asylum Hill Church, Hartford. His biography is listed in the *National Cyclopedia of American Biography* (1967, p. 387).

CHASE, **Helen Smith Bourne** (d1933) Married Charles Edward Chase and resided in Hartford, Connecticut. Visited Hawai'i with her husband (March 1892).

CLARK, **Charles Hopkins** (1848–1926) Born April 1, 1848, in Hartford, Connecticut. A.B., Yale University (1871). Editor, *Hartford Courant* (1890–1921).

CLARKE, **Katherine** ("Katy") (1871–1941) Born July 4, 1871, in Kapalama, Oahu. Student of Miss Winter at Kawaiaha'o Female Seminary, of Hawaiian ancestry. On November 10, 1890, Miss Winter wrote her sister Julia Flora Winter that she had encouraged Katy to write to her: "She is one of my best girls if not my best—19 or 20 yrs old and very pretty with crinckly [sic] black hair, flashing eyes, olive skin and pleasant manners. She can sew nicely and cook well but she is just beginning fractions; I think a great deal of her and would like to have you answer her letter. She dresses very nicely, and if you should meet her I do not think you would look upon her as inferior." Married (December 24, 1891) William Kolo Rathburn of Kamehameha School, who was later a judge; four children. Census of 1900 and 1930 lists William K. Rathburn and his wife, Katherine Clarke, as living in Ko'olauloa, Honolulu, Hawai'i. Her obituary in the *Honolulu Star Bulletin* (March 20, 1941) notes that she died in her home in Paumalū, windward O'ahu.

CLEGHORN, **Archibald Scott** (1835–1910) Born November 15, 1835, in Edinburgh, Scotland. Married twice: Elizabeth Pauahi Lapeka, three children; Princess Miriam Kapili Likelike (1869), one child, Princess Victoria Kaiulani (1875–1899). Served in the House of Nobles and as governor of O'ahu under Queen Lili'uokalani. Died November 1, 1910, in Honolulu.

CLEVELAND, **Grover** (1837–1908) Born in Caldwell, New Jersey, to a Presbyterian minister. Raised in New York State. Practiced as an attorney in Cleveland before returning to New York to begin his political career. President of the United States (1885–1889; 1893–1897). In favor of acquiring a naval station at Pearl Harbor for the United States. He withdrew the annexation treaty proposed by the Harrison administration from consideration by the U.S. Senate (March 1893) and sent Congressman James H. Blount to Hawai'i to investigate the overthrow of the monarchy. Cleveland supported Blount's report, which found that the people of Hawai'i were opposed to annexation. He was not in favor of using American force to restore Queen Lili'uokalani to the throne and left the matter of annexation to Congress.

COAN, Lydia Bingham (1834–1915) Born December 25, 1834, in Honolulu, to missionaries Hiram Bingham and Sybil Mosely Bingham. Educated at York Square Seminary in New Haven, Connecticut. Principal, Ohio Female College. Founder, Kawaiaha'o Female Seminary, and principal for six years before her marriage (1873) to Rev. Titus Coan. Died August 31, 1915, in Honolulu.

COLBURN, John F. (1859–1920) Born September 30, 1859; part Hawaiian. Businessman and importer in Honolulu. Married Julia Appianni Kulia E Kanu'u Naoho; many children. Appointed interior minister by Queen Lili'uokalani (January 13, 1893) and served until the overthrow on January 17. Member of the cabinet that protested to U.S. Minister John Stevens the landing of American troops from the USS *Boston*. His letter to J. F. Ganz of St. Louis was published in the *New York Times* (February 9, 1893) as "The Queen's Side of It; A Picture of the revolution by One of Lili'uokalani's Cabinet." His house was raided on December 16, 1893, and searched for arms. Served as treasurer of the Kapi'olani Estate, Ltd. Died March 16, 1920.

COLE, Grace Student of Miss Winter at Kawaiaha'o Female Seminary in 1891. Born in Micronesia to white father and native mother. Raised by missionaries. Taken in by Cooke family of Honolulu. A photograph of Grace Cole with Marshall Islands students at the school at Kusaie is in the Mission Houses Library, Honolulu. She could be a daughter of W. E. Cole (born 1848), a trader on Majuro (December 1877). He was on Pohnpei briefly in early 1880, but he apparently lived on Kosrae. Died April 10, 1880, of fever aboard *Mathilde* on his way back to Kosrae, his home in later years. He left a "white" (perhaps Samoan) wife and two small children. Wife remained on Kosrae and was an agent for Capelle & Co. during the early 1880s.

COLEMAN, Harriet Angeline Castle (1847–1924) Born January 1, 1847, in Honolulu to Samuel Northrup Castle and Mary Tenney Castle; sister of Caroline Castle. Attended Punahou School and Oberlin Preparatory School

(1865–1866). Teacher, Punahou School (1867–1869). Married (1876) Charles Carson Coleman; two children. Associate of Kawaiahaʻo Female Seminary. Visited Chicago to study Froebel Training School for Kindergarteners, led by John Dewey, and Hull House, where she met Jane Addams. Member, Children's Aid Society; financial secretary, Free Kindergarten Association, Honolulu; member, Hawaiian Historical Society, YWCA, Women's Board of the Pacific, Daughters of Hawaiʻi, DAR. Died December 11, 1924.

CONEY, John Haʻalelea (1864–1944) Born June 9, 1864, in Hilo, Hawaiʻi, to John Harvey Coney and Laura Amoy Kekukapuokekuaokalani Coney (Laura Ena Coney), a lady in the court of Queen Liliʻuokalani. Married (1889) Mary Ellen Kelly; seven children. Machinist, Lucas Brothers Mill and B. F. Dillingham & Co.; apprentice, Columbus Machine Co. (1883); mechanical engineer, Ohio (1883–1890); mechanical engineer, Board of Public Works, Hawaiʻi (1890–1893); construction engineer, G. N. Wilcox, Kauaʻi (1893); deputy sheriff and then sheriff, Kauaʻi (1892–1906); representative, Territorial Legislature of Hawaiʻi (1907–1911); senator (1913–1917); alternative delegate to the Republican National Convention from the Territory of Hawaiʻi (1912). Died December 13, 1944, in Kauaʻi. His obituary appeared in the *Honolulu Advertiser* (December 14, 1944).

COOKE, Anna Charlotte Rice (1853–1934) Born September 5, 1853, in Honolulu, to missionary William Harrison Rice and Mary Sophia Hyde Rice. Attended Punahou School and Mills' Young Ladies' Seminary in Benicia, California. Married (1874) Charles Montague Cooke, Sr.; six children. Member, Central Union Church; philanthropist and founder, Honolulu Academy of Arts; member, Board of Trustees of Kawaiahaʻo Female Seminary beginning 1887. Died August 8, 1934. Her biography appears in *Notable Women of Hawaiʻi*.

COOKE, Amos Francis ("Frank") (1851–1931) Born December 23, 1851, in Honolulu to missionaries Amos Starr Cooke and Juliette Montague Cooke. Educated Oahu College and University of Michigan. Businessman who started Castle & Cooke (1875) and had many business interests in Honolulu. Married Lilanet Lydgate; two children. Served in the Citizens and National Guard under the Provisional and Republican Governments of Hawaiʻi. President of Hawaiian Mission Children's Society (1899). Died

November 16, 1931, in Honolulu. His obituary appeared in *The Friend* (January 1932).

COOKE, **Charles Montague** (1849–1909) Born May 16, 1849, in Honolulu to missionies Amos Starr Cooke and Juliette Montague Cooke. Educated at Punahou School and Massachusetts Agricultural College, Amherst. Married Anna Charlotte Rice (1874); six children. Joined firm of Castle & Cooke and later formed Lewers & Cooke in Honolulu. President of Bank of Hawai'i; associated with C. Brewer & Co. Trustee, Kamehameha School (1884–1897) and Bishop Estate. Served as "special commissioner" of the Provisional Government of Hawai'i in January 1893 and was sent to Washington, D.C. Died August 27, 1909.

COOKE, **Juliette Montague** ("Mother Cooke") (1812–1896) Born March 10, 1812, in Sunderland, Massachusetts, to Caleb Montague and Martha Warner Montague. Educated at Miss White's School, Amherst, Massachusetts; attended lectures at Amherst College; studied at Ipswich Seminary. Teacher, Upper Hadley Mills, Massachusetts. Married (1836) Amos Star Cooke; seven children. Arrived in Hawai'i in 1837. In 1838 she and her husband took charge of the Chiefs Children's School (later Royal School) on Maui and oversaw the education of royal Hawaiian children, five of whom would grow up to be Hawaiian monarchs. They were released from missionary service in 1852 and established Castle & Cooke in Honolulu with fellow missionaries Samuel Northrup Castle and his wife. Died August 11, 1896, in Honolulu. Her biography appears in *Notable Women of Hawai'i.*

COOKE, **Lilanet Lidgate** (1856–1946) Born August 2, 1856, in Rice Lake, Canada. Married Amos Francis Cooke. Died July 18,1946, in Puna, Hawai'i; Buried in Kawaiaha'o Cemetery.

CORNWELL, **William Henry** (1842–1903) Born in Brooklyn, New York. Accompanied parents to Hawai'i about 1857, according to his obituary. Father was a sugar planter at Waikapu plantation on Maui. Married; three children. Began a political career in 1890 when he was elected a noble. Knew King Kalākaua and was appointed by Queen Lili'uokalani to her staff (1891). Minister of finance, Kingdom of Hawai'i (1892); member, Colburn Cabinet (1893); mason and member Central Union Church. Died December 18, 1903, in Waikapu, Maui; obituary appeared in *Paradise of the Pacific* (December 1903, p. 69).

DAMON, **Mary Rebecca Happer** (1858–1949) Born to missionary parents; father was Rev. A. P. Happer. Married (1884) Francis William Damon (1852–1915) in Canton, China; five children. Marriage reported in the HMCS *32nd Annual Report* (1884, p. 12). The Damons spoke fluent Chinese, established the First Chinese Church of Christ, and taught English to Chinese boys in their home beginning 1892.

DAVID, **Caroline** (b1874) Student of Miss Winter at Kawaiahaʻo Female Seminary beginning 1890; of Hawaiian ancestry. Miss Winter notes she is from Honolulu. Departs school 1893. This may be Caroline Nahulewa or Nahulciva, known as Caroline David, born March 1874. Listed in the 1900 federal census as resident of Honolulu. Her father's name is listed as David Nahulewa or Nahulciva, and her brother, Kaukina Albert, is listed as a policeman.

DAVIS, **Myra H.** (c1860–1898) Born near Sabula, Iowa, the youngest of four children of a farming couple born in Maine. Father died when she was two. Attended school in Clinton, Iowa, and graduated from Cornell College, Mt. Vernon, Iowa. Schoolteacher and later principal of a school in Clinton. Her mother died, leaving her the family farm and the care of an invalid sister, who died of consumption a year later. Went as a teacher to Kawaiahaʻo Female Seminary, arriving (August 21, 1888) in Honolulu on the *Zealandia*. Served as assistant principal (1889), becoming matron and teacher (1890). Left Hawaiʻi (June 6, 1891) with Miss Pepoon on the bark *S.G. Wilder.* Spent a year tutoring her nieces in Chicago, and then joined Miss Pepoon at Whitman College (December 1893), when she was appointed matron of Ladies' Hall, the dormitory for women. Continued in that position until her death (October 9, 1898), which occurred at the home of her friend Mrs. Tapley, of Santa Barbara. Left a bequest of $1,000 to Whitman College for the purpose of helping poor girls obtain an education. Member and officer, First Congregational Church of Walla Walla; member, Women's Missionary Society. An in memoriam article appeared in the *Whitman College Quarterly* (October 1898, p. 38 et seq).

DICKEY, **Charles Henry** (1842–1932) Born August 12, 1842, in Ottawa, Illinois, to Theophilus Lyle Dickey and Juliet Evans Dickey. Maui attorney and riding companion of Miss Winter on Maui. Educated in Illinois and served in 4th Illinois Cavalry (1863–1864). Married (1867) Anne Elizabeth Alexander; five children. Postmaster of Haʻikū on Maui, and telegrapher. Established first commercial telegraph line in Hawaiʻi (1875); introduced telephones to Hawaiʻi (1879). Member, Hawaiʻi Legislature 1886, 1890; Hawaiʻi Territorial Senate, 1902–1904. President, Mission Children's Society, 1902. Alternate delegate to Republican National Convention from Hawaiʻi Territory in 1904. Died January 21, 1932, in Oakland, California; buried in Makawao Cemetery, Maui.

DICKSON, Irene Student of Miss Winter at Kawaiahaʻo Female Seminary in 1893. Mentioned in *Handicraft* (April 1895, p. 4) as performing in a vocal quartet at closing ceremonies for Kamehameha School for Girls (March 29, 1894). This is likely to be Irene Keohookalani Dickson (1881–1964), daughter of Honolulu photographer Menzies Dickson and his wife, Mary Kameeleihiwa Miner, and later stepdaughter of Cecil Brown. Irene K. Dickson is listed in the Hawaiʻi census of 1900 and 1910 as a student at Oahu College (1896–1898). Irene Keohookalani Dickson married (1921) Eveline "Edward" Wood Nehenuikalani Low; no children. Died September 15, 1964.

DILLINGHAM, Benjamin Franklin (1844–1918) Born September 4, 1844, in West Brewster, Massachusetts, to Benjamin Clark Dillingham and Lydia Sears Howes Dillingham. Arrived Honolulu (1865). Married (1869) Emma Louise Smith; four children, including Mary Emma Dillingham Frear. Capitalist with many business interests, including railroads and sugar. Died April 7, 1918, in Honolulu.

DILLINGHAM, Emma Louise Smith (1844–1920) Born June 4, 1844, in Honolulu, to Rev. Lowell Smith and Abigail Smith. Married (1869) Benjamin Franklin Dillingham. Poet. Died August 15, 1920, in Honolulu.

DOLE, Sanford Ballard (1844–1926) Born April 23, 1844, in Honolulu, to missionary Daniel Dole and Emily Hoyt Ballard Dole. Married (1873) Anna Prentice Cate. Attended Williams College; studied law in Boston. In 1884 elected to the House of Representatives, Kingdom of Hawaiʻi. Associate justice of Hawaiian Supreme Court (1886). Joined the Hawaiian Patriotic League, which sought to limit the power of King Kalākaua and imposed the Bayonet Constitution. A leader of the coup d'état to overthrow the Queen. President of the Provisional Government of Hawaiʻi (1893–1894), formed immediately after the overthrow of Queen Liliʻuokalani. President, Republic of Hawaiʻi (1894–1900); first governor, Territory of Hawaiʻi (1900–1903);

U.S. district judge until retirement in 1916; author, *Memoirs of the Hawaiian Revolution* (1936).

DOMINIS, **John Owen** (1832–1891) Born March 10, 1832, in Schenectady, New York, to Captain John Dominis and Mary Jones Dominis. Married twice: Mary Purdy Lamiki Aimoku (died); Princess Lydia Kamakaeha Paki (subsequently Queen Liliʻuokalani). Prince Consort of Hawaiʻi; governor of Oʻahu and Maui. Died August 27, 1891, in Honolulu.

EMERSON, **Joseph Swift** (1843–1930) Born July 13, 1843, in Lāhaināluna, Maui, to missionaries John S. Emerson, and Ursula Sophia Newell Emerson. Attended Punahou School; B.S., Massachusetts Institute of Technology (1874). Hawaiian government survey (1877–1903); surveyor, Court of Land Registration, Hawaiʻi (1903). Author of books and papers on Hawaiʻi and Hawaiian anthropology. Married (1898) Dorothea Lamb; one child. Died May 16, 1930, in Honolulu.

EMERSON, **Nathaniel Bright** (1839–1915) Born July 1, 1839, in Waialoa, Oʻahu, to missionaries John S. Emerson and Ursula Sophia Newell Emerson. Educated Punahou School; A.B., Williams College; M.D., Harvard (1869); College of Physicians and Surgeons, New York City. Union Army (1863–1865), wounded three times. Married (1885) Sarah Eliza Pierce, M.D.; one child. Private practice in New York. Returned to Hawaiʻi (1878) to work at Kalaupapa, the leper colony on Molokaʻi. Vaccination officer, Oʻahu. Private medical practice, Honolulu. President, Board of Health, Hawaiʻi (1896–?), before and during the outbreak of plague (1899–1900). Author of several books on the history and ethnography of Hawaiʻi. Died July 18, 1915, at sea. His papers are in the Huntington Library, San Marino, California.

EMERSON, **Oliver Pomeroy** (1845–1938) Born July 27, 1845, in Lāhainā, Maui, to Hawaiian missionaries John S. Emerson and Ursula Sophia Newell Emerson. Educated at Punahou School, Oahu College; B.A., Williams College (1868); Theological Seminary, Andover, Massachusetts (1871). Corresponding secretary, Hawaiian Evangelical Association (1889–1903); agent, Hawaiian Evangelical Association, Maui (1903–1906). Harvard Divinity School (1906–1907). Congregational pastor in Connecticut and Rhode Island. Married (1896) Eugenie Homer; no children. Author of a memoir of his family, *Pioneer Days in Hawaiʻi* (1928). Died August 24, 1938, in Intervale, New Hampshire.

EMERSON, Sarah Eliza Pierce (1855–1938) Born in New Bedford, Massachusetts. Attended Oahu College. Physician. Married (1881) Nathaniel Bright Emerson, M.D. Died November 1938.

FLAXMAN, Margaret Listed in *Directory of the City of Honolulu* as a teacher at Kawaiahaʻo Female Seminary. Listed by the Hawaiian Evangelical Association as a teacher at Kawaiahaʻo Female Seminary (1868–1878) and in Helen S. Norton's report (May 24, 1881) as principal when Miss Bingham's health failed. Listed as a teacher in the *1882 Circular of Kawaiahaʻo Seminary*. M. A. Chamberlain notes that she taught sewing. In 1890, she was teaching sewing at the Girls' Industrial Home in Honolulu as an assistant to her sister, Mrs. Stratford, according to *The Friend* (October 1890, p. 76). Her sister Sarah was also a missionary and resided in the Atherton household. The sisters came from Lowestoft, England. She was seventy-eight in 1920.

FORBES, Maria Rebecca (1865–1950) Born January 13, 1865, to missionary Anderson Oliver Forbes and Maria Jane Patten Chamberlain Forbes. Substitute hired at Kawaiahaʻo Female Seminary when Miss Winter had a fever (1892). Died September 21, 1950.

FORBES, Maria Jane Patten Chamberlain (1832–1909) Born April 25, 1832, in Honolulu to missionary Levi Chamberlain and Maria Chamberlain. Educated at Punahou School and Mount Holyoke Seminary. Returned to Honolulu (1854). Married (1859) Anderson Oliver Holmes (died 1888); four children. When she was widowed, she took charge of the Lunalilo Home for Indigenous Hawaiians in Honolulu and remained there as matron until 1901. Died January 21, 1909, in Honolulu. Her obituary appeared in *The Friend* (February 1909, p. 17).

FULLER, Samuel D. (d1895) Listed in *Directory and Handbook for the Kingdom of Hawaiʻi* (1890). Secretary of the YMCA. Formerly associated with the YMCA of Sacramento, California. Engaged to Miss Alexander. Departed Honolulu with consumption (July 1891). Died August 14, 1895, in Newburyport, Massachusetts, according to the obituary in *The Friend* (October 1895, p. 75).

GARLAND, George Francis (1852–1947) Born March 16, 1852, in Medway, Massachusetts, to George C. Garland and Harriet Ellis Garland. Served as mate on the missionary steamer *Morning Star;* promoted to captain (1887–1904). Married (1891) Sarah L. Smith; three children. In 1908, Captain Garland and wife took charge of the Missionary Home at Oberlin. Died May 12, 1947, in Oberlin.

GILMAN, **Sarah Fletcher Atherton** (d1910) Born to Jonathan Atherton and Elizabeth Robinson Atherton in Boston; sister of Joseph Ballard Atherton. Married Henry Dearborn Gilman; two children. Honolulu resident; mother of Carrie Gilman. Died September 26, 1910, in Honolulu.

GILMAN, **Carrie Abbie** (1864–1942) Born April 21, 1864, in Readville, Massachusetts, to Henry Dearborn Gilman and Sarah Fletcher Atherton Gilman. Attended Oahu College, Oberlin College, American School of Osteopathy (1900). Teacher, Punahou Preparatory School (1889–1898). Listed as teacher of seventh and eighth grades at Punahou Preparatory in 1891. Studied osteopathy in Kirksville, Missouri, for two years; practiced in Honolulu for nine years. Started a home with Miss Yarrow in Hawai'i, then moved to Florida with her (1922), settling in Palm Beach (1923). Died April 18, 1942, in Palm Beach, Florida.

GREEN, **Mary Theodosia** (1865–1936) Born March 28, 1865, in Makawao, Maui, to Joseph Porter Green and Harriet Fowler Green. City missionary in Honolulu, assisted by Nellie Waterhouse at Chinese mission. Married (1892) Henry Harrison Wilcox.

GULICK, **Alice Elmira Walbridge** (1844–1911) Schoolteacher in Ithaca, New York. Married (1872) Thomas Lafon Gulick.

GULICK, **Alice Winfield Gordon** (1847–1903) Born August 8, 1847, in Boston. A.B., Mount Holyoke College (1867). Instructor at Mount Holyoke until 1870. Married twice: Alvah B. Kittridge, who died of tuberculosis the day after their wedding; (1871)William Hooker Gulick; five children. ABCFM missionary to Spain with her husband beginning in 1871. Returned to the United States (1890); affiliated with Harvard University. Established International Institute for Girls in Spain (1892). Died October 1, 1903, in London; buried in Madrid, Spain. A biography appears in Gerald H. Anderson, *Biographical Dictionary of the Christian Missions* (1999, p. 269).

GULICK, **Thomas Lafon** (1839–1904) Born April 10, 1838, in Kōloa, Kaua'i, to missionaries Peter Johnson Gulick and Frances Hinckley Thomas Gulick.

Educated at Punahou School; A.B., Amherst College (1865); Andover Seminary (1868). Married (1872) Alice Elmira Walbridge. Missionary to Spain with his brother (1873–1883), Cuba (1884), Nevada (1885). Minister, Maui Makawao Foreign Church (1886–1893). Instructor, Oahu College (September 1890). Supported the overthrow of Queen Liliʻuokalani. Directed a home for convalescents in Devon, Pennsylvania (1896–1904). Died June 15, 1904, in Kenya.

GULICK, William Hooker (1835–1922) Born November 18, 1835, in Kōloa, Kauaʻi, to missionaries Peter Johnson Gulick and Frances Hinckley Thomas Gulick; brother of Thomas Gulick. Educated at Punahou School and Andover Seminary. Married (1871) Alice Winfield Gordon; five children. Missionary to Spain (1872–1883) with his wife and brother. Died April 14, 1922, in Boston.

HADLEY, Anna Zillah (1854–1940) Born November 26, 1854, in Fayetteville, New York, to farmer Theodore Daniel Hadley and Elizabeth Ann Cornish Hadley. Teacher at Kawaiahaʻo Female Seminary, arrived (September 8, 1891) aboard the *Zealandia*. A. Z. Hadley, teacher, is listed (1890) as resident in Kīlauea, Kauaʻi, and in the *Directory and Handbook of Honolulu and the Hawaiian Islands* (1892) as teacher in Kīlauea. After leaving Kawaiahaʻo Female Seminary, she nursed Caroline Babb through an illness at Kamehameha School. *Hawaiian Gazette* mentioned (June 27, 1893, p. 4) that she replaced a teacher who was ill at Waiheʻe School. *The Biennial Report of the President of the Bureau of Public Instruction to the Legislature of the Republic of Hawaiʻi 1896* (pp. 105, 127) lists A. Z. Hadley as holding a teaching certificate, second class, as a teacher at Kīlauea School, Hanalei, commencing March 1894. *The Report of the Minister of Public Instruction to the President of the Republic of Hawaiʻi for the Biennial Period Ending December 31, 1899* (pp. 123, 144) lists Anne Z. Hadley, nationality American, holding a teaching certificate, second class, as a teacher in Lāhainā in March 1894. Briefly served as principal of that school, according to *Hawaiian Gazette* (April 16, 1907, p. 8). *Hawaiian Gazette* (February 9, 1897) includes a notice by A. Z. Hadley, administrix of the estate of the late Anna M. Armstrong of Kīlauea, Kauaʻi. *The Biennial Report of the Hawaiʻi Department of Public Instruction 1911* (p. 110) lists Anne Z. Hadley as a teacher at Central Grammar school in Honolulu (1894–1908). In 1930, she was living in Honolulu with her widowed sister; after her sister's death, she returned to the mainland. Died in 1940 in Philadelphia, according to genealogical sources.

HAINA, **Deborah** Born to Rev. George Haina (d1886) and Kaluahine (d1903), who were sent by Hawaiian Evangelical Association (HEA) as missionaries to Tarawa and the Gilbert Islands. Listed by Helen S. Norton (February 8, 1881) as one of five daughters of Hawaiian missionaries who were scholars at Kawaiahaʻo Female Seminary and whose fees were partly paid by HEA. Helen S. Norton's report (May 24, 1881) lists her entry date as May 1, 1878, at age nine. Listed in the *20th Annual Report of the Hawaiian Evangelical Association, June 1883* (p. 10) as one of the daughters of missionaries and clergymen enrolled at Kawaiahaʻo Female Seminary whose expenses were partially paid by the HEA. Listed in the *1882 Circular of Kawaiahaʻo Seminary* as a student. Rev. and Mrs. Haina were survived by nine of their eleven children. Her sisters Hattie, Sarah, and Leelia also attended the seminary. Student and pupil-teacher of Miss Winter at Kawaiahaʻo Female Seminary, and her helper in sewing class. The 1910 federal census lists Deborah Haina, age thirty-nine, living with four children in Honolulu next door to John and Rachael Antone, her brother-in-law and sister. Margaret Powers Waldron mentions Deborah Haina "or Mother Gunner as we loved to call her" in her speech on the history of Kawaiahaʻo Female Seminary published in *The Friend* (December 1914, p. 276).

HAINA, **Rachael Kailiao** (1877–1942) Born January 27, 1877, in the Gilbert Islands, one of eleven children of George Haina and Kaluahine Haina, missionaries serving in Tarawa and the Gilbert Islands. *Annual Report of the Hawaiian Mission Children's Society* (1885, p. 24) says that Rachel Haina arrived Christmas Day from Micronesia on the *Jennie Walker*. Student at Kawaiahaʻo Female Seminary beginning 1885; at the seminary when her name appeared on an invitation list for a party there (June 4, 1892). Married (1908) Richard Antone; two children. The 1910 federal census lists Rachel Antone, age thirty-nine, living with husband John Antone and two children next door to Deborah Haina and her four children in Honolulu. The 1930 federal census lists Rachael Antone, age fifty-five, born in Gilbert Islands and living in Honolulu with her husband, John. Died September 27, 1942, in Honolulu; her obituary appeared in the *Honolulu Advertiser* (September 28, 1942).

HALE, **Miriam Agnes** (1877–1939) Born November 20, 1877, in Honolulu.

Student at Kawaiahaʻo Female Seminary (1892) when her name appeared on an invitation list for a party (June 4, 1892). She was in Miss Winter's sewing class. Graduated from Kamehameha School for Girls (1897). Married (1900) Henry Joseph Auld; four children. Lived in Palama, Honolulu, according to Kamehameha Alumni directory. Miriam Auld, wife of H. J. Auld, both twenty-two, are listed on the 1900 federal census as resident in Honolulu. The 1910 census has Miriam Auld, wife of Harry Jos, resident in Honolulu with five children. The Honolulu city directory lists Miriam Hale Auld as resident in Honolulu. Obituary in the *Honolulu Star Bulletin* (July 3, 1939) lists her as a graduate of Kawaiahaʻo Female Seminary and Kamehameha School for Girls and a former probation officer for the Court of Domestic Relations in Hawaiʻi (1922–1935) and says she is the youngest sister of the late Rev. Stephen L. Desha, Sr. Died July 3, 1939, in Honolulu.

HALSTEAD, Emily Alice (1870–1953) Born in Hawaiʻi, to Robert Halstead, owner of Waialua Sugar Plantation. Music teacher, Kamehameha Preparatory (1892). Attended Oahu College (1883–1889). Married (1902) Col. John McClellan; two children. Lived in Honolulu (1910) and San Diego, California (1920).

HAMMOND, Nettie Eugenia (b1863) Born La Porte, Indiana. Persuaded by her cousin, Rev. William D. Westevelt, pastor of Wailuku, to move to Hawaiʻi (1889). Teacher at the Maunaʻolu School for Girls on Maui for five years. Cousin was Lt. Commander Ingersoll of the USS *Philadelphia.* She later taught at the Kamehameha School for Girls. Accompanied Miss Winter on vacation to island of Hawaiʻi (1892). Married (1897) Levi Chamberlain Lyman, a teacher at Kamehameha; one child. A newspaper clipping describing her wedding is in Miss Pope's *Memory Book,* (vol. 1) in the Kamehameha School Archives. Husband was principal of Hilo Boarding School. Listed as an author of *The Lymans of Hilo, A Fascinating Account of Life in 19th Century Hawaiʻi* (1979) along with Margaret Greer Martin, Kathryn Lyman Bond, and Ethel M. Damon.

HANAIKE, Emma K. (1875–1899) Born April 24, 1875, in Līhuʻe, Kauaʻi, to Joseph Benjamin Hanaike, Sr. Sent to Kawaiahaʻo Female Seminary at age five, after the death of her mother. Helen S. Norton's report (May 24, 1881) lists her entry date as July 5, 1880. Listed in a report (May 19, 1881), archived in the Mission Houses Museum Library, as among the students

HMCS supported at the seminary. Listed in the *21st Annual Report of the Hawaiian Evangelical Association* (1884, p. 11) as one of the daughters of missionaries and clergymen enrolled at Kawaiahaʻo Female Seminary whose expenses were partially paid by HEA. She returned to Līhuʻe after finishing school and became a teacher. Her brother Benjamin was a cowboy at the Gay & Robinson Ranch on Kauaʻi. Kikuchi and Remoaldo (1992, p. 132) locate her grave at Līhuʻe Congregational Church Cemetery. Her gravestone gives her dates as April 24, 1878–July 31, 1899.

HANUNA, **Ida** (b1877) Born May 29, 1877, in Hana, Maui, to John M. Hanuna and Elizabeth Naliʻikipa Aipo. Two Hanuna families are listed in the *City Directory and Handbook of Honolulu and the Hawaiian Islands* (1892), one headed by a pastor and the other by a surveyor, both in Hana. Student of Miss Winter at Kawaiahaʻo Female Seminary in 1893. Mentioned in letter from Helen Kalola Kahaleahu (July 18, 1893).

HARDY, **Frederick Wood** (1859–1920) Born January 23, 1859, in Boston, to George Dana Boardman Hardy and Olive Andrews Hardy. A.B., Harvard University (1881). Arrived Maui (1882). Married (1896) Lillian Hitchcock Aiken; one child. Schoolteacher and vice principal, Wailuku School (1883); instructor, Lāhaināluna Seminary (1884–1888); principal Makawao School (1888); president, Annexation Club in Makawao (1897). Died April 3, 1920, in Makawao.

HARRIS, **Eva L.** (1868–1952) Born March 22, 1868, in Huron, Erie County, Ohio, one of five children of farmer Thomas J. Harris and Susan Jaffrey Harris. Attended Oberlin High School/Academy. Friend of Miss Pope. Arrived (September 8, 1891) in Honolulu aboard *Zealandia* at age twenty-three as a replacement for Miss Davis. Joined the Central Union Church (April 1892), which listed her as Eva A. Harris. Assistant principal, Kawaiahaʻo Female Seminary (1892–1893). Supported two sisters at Oberlin High School/Academy: Edna Belle (Litt., 1894) and Elma May Harris. Taught English to private Japanese pupils in Honolulu. Succumbed to hysteria in Honolulu and treated by Dr. C. B. Wood. Miss Pope accompanied her back to San Francisco on the *Monowai* (February 10, 1893), which listed her as M. Harris. Her Oberlin file notes that she attended University of California, but other sources say the University of San Francisco. She practiced as a physician in Oakland, California, and was a member of the homeopathy society.

Resided at the Claremont Country Club in Oakland with her sisters until her death in July 1952.

HARRISON, Benjamin (1833–1901) Born in North Bend, Ohio, and raised in Indianapolis. After service in the Union Army during the Civil War, he represented Indiana in the U.S. Senate. Elected president of the United States (1888) as a Republican, but was an unsuccessful candidate for re-election (1892), when former president Grover Cleveland, a Democrat, defeated him. Charles Kofoid voted for Harrison in both elections. As president, Harrison favored the acquisition of Pearl Harbor, but did not take decisive action on annexation before the end of his term.

HIGHT, Iretta May (c1863–1925) Born in Genoa, Michigan, to Nathan Hight and Elizabeth Bennett Hight. Attended Oberlin College (1887–1889). Listed as from Romeo, Michigan, in Kamehameha School records. Teacher at Kamehameha School (1889–1892). Lived in the Kamehameha cottage with Mr. and Mrs. Babb. Married (1892) in Salt Lake City to Frederick Smith Retan, a Baptist minister in Niles, Michigan. Later resided in Detroit, Michigan, Parkersburg, West Virginia, and Massachusetts; three children. Died October 22, 1925, in West Newton, Massachusetts.

HIGHT, Rose Gillette (1873–1957) Born June 27, 1873, in Chilson, Michigan, to Nathan Hight and Elizabeth Bennett Hight. Student at Mount Carroll Seminary (1894); Oberlin College (1886–1890). Arrived in Honolulu (March 1891), and taught at Kamehameha Preparatory (1892). Lived in the Kamehameha cottage with Mr. and Mrs. Babb. Married twice: (1894) George Ernest A. Thrum (divorced 1895); (1895) Frederick Horton Anthony; two children. Resided in Philadelphia (1895), Boston (1897), Chicago (1899), Detroit (1900), Hammond, Louisiana (1906). Died March 5, 1957, in Santa Barbara, California.

HITCHCOCK, Eliza Acquaintance of Oliver Emerson (1892). Home of the Hitchcock family was Bouganville on Big Island. Miss Ellie Hitchcock is listed as a teacher in Hilo in the *Directory and Handbook of Honolulu and the Hawaiian Islands* (1892).

HOBRON, Anna Maria Kinney (b1873) Married (1889) Thomas William Bailey.

HOBRON, Frances Elizabeth Gray (1824–1904) Born December 15, 1824, in New London, Connecticut to William Jefferson Gray. Married William Henry Hobron; three children: Mrs. Thomas W. Kinney, Mrs. William O. Smith, and Thomas William Hobron.

HOBRON, Thomas William (1866–1922) Born on Maui, to Thomas H. Hobron. Married (July 1889) a Waterhouse cousin, Anna Maria Kinney; two children. Accountant for W. O. Smith, according to *Directory and Handbook for the Kingdom of Hawai'i* (1890). Lived in Berkeley (1909).

HOPPER, Susan V. Sewing teacher at Kawaiaha'o Female Seminary (1885–1890). Susan V. Hopper of Williamstown, Massachusetts, is listed as a member of the Women's Board of the Pacific. M. A. Chamberlain notes that she is a cousin of Nancy J. Malone and came from New York State.

HOPPIN, Helen Frances (1861–1946) Born November 27, 1861, in South Haven, Michigan, to Thaddeus Hoppin and Catherine Ann Stuart Hoppin. A.B., Oberlin College (1886). Married (March 29, 1894) Henry Herbert Renton in Hawai'i. Teacher at Kawaiaha'o Female Seminary. Died January 23, 1946, in Saratoga, California.

HOPPIN, Jessie Rebecca (1864–1949) Born January 13, 1864, in South Haven, Michigan, to Thaddeus Hoppin and Catherine Ann Stuart Hoppin. Litt., Oberlin College (1888). Teacher at Kawaiaha'o Female Seminary (1888–1890). Principal of the ABCFM mission school Kusaie in the Caroline Islands, Micronesia, for thirty-five years, beginning 1890. Retired 1935 and lived in Ashland, Wisconsin, until she died January 14, 1949.

HOPPIN, Ruth Estella (1870–1938) Born February 27, 1870, in South Haven, Michigan, to Thaddeus Hoppin and Catherine Ann Stuart Hoppin. Graduate, Oberlin Conservatory of Music (1896); bachelor of music conferred (1907). Teacher, Kamehameha Preparatory (1891–1892); music teacher, Northfield Seminary (1896); music teacher, Ashland, Wisconsin. Died March 12, 1938, in Ashland, Wisconsin.

HOSMER, Frank Alvah (1853–1918) Born November 14, 1853, in Woburn, Massachusetts, to Alvah Hosmer and Octavia Emerson Poole Hosmer. A.B., Amherst College (1875); A.M. (1878). Married Esther Hosmer. Principal, Woburn Central Grammar School (1875–1876); vice-principal, Hitchcock School, Brimfield (1876–1877); principal, Palmer High School (1878);

principal, high school in Great Barrington, Massachusetts (1878–1888), where his students included W. E. B. Du Bois. Editor, *Berkshire Courier* (Great Barrington); correspondent, *New York Herald* in Indian Reservations of the West. President, Oahu College (1890–1900); member, advisory council, Provisional Government of Hawai'i; judiciary committee; Hawaiian Sharp-shooters. Joined Central Union Church, Honolulu (April 1892). Representative, Massachusetts legislature for Amherst (1908–1909). Author of *History of Great Barrington, Manners Maketh a Man*, and other books.

HOSMER, Esther Mayo Kellogg (1852–?) Born February 29, 1852, in Amherst, Massachusetts, to Willard Mayo Kellogg and Elvira Minerva Marsh Kellogg. Married (1878) Frank Alvah Hosmer; no children. Joined Central Union Church (April 1892).

HUGO, Eliza Kaipoleimanu (1875–1940) Listed as a student in Miss Winter's class at Kawaiaha'o Female Seminary beginning 1891. Miss Winter annotates her name "out." Married (1891) J. F. Carl Hagens (b1870), listed in *Men of Hawai'i*. Eliza K. Hagens, wife of Jacob F. C. Hagens is listed in federal census (1910) as resident in Honolulu. Eliza Kaipoleimanu Hugo Hagens (1875–1940) died in San Mateo, California. Her obituary appeared in the *San Mateo Times and Daily News Leader* (June 27, 1940).

HYDE, Mary T. Knight (1840–1917) Born August 6, 1840, in Brimfield, Massachusetts to Dr. Knight. Married (1865) Rev. Charles McEwen Hyde (1832–1899); two children. Arrived (1877) in Hawai'i with her husband. President, Woman's Board of Missions for the Pacific Islands and Free Kindergarten and Children's Aid Association; vice president, Portuguese Charitable Association.

IOBA, Charlotte (d1900) Born on Kaua'i and raised by Mother Rice, according to her daughter's "Petition for the Registration of the Hawaiian Birth of (Mrs.) Lily Charlotte Gibson Pfluger," application no. 31978 (April 7, 1952). Student of Miss Winter at Kawaiaha'o Female Seminary. Charlotte Job is listed in the *1882 Circular of Kawaiaha'o Seminary* as a student there. Miss Winter describes her "as sweet and obedient a girl as was ever in this seminary" and described preparations for her wedding at Kawaiaha'o Female Seminary. Married (May 5, 1892) Henry Gibson, according to *Hawaiian Gazette* (July 10, 1892). Family sources list her husband as Henry Kalehuamakanoe Gibson, grandson of Walter Murray Gibson. Died June 13, 1900, in Lāhainā, Maui.

IMUM, **Eddie** Student at Kamehameha School; resident of island of Hawai'i.

JONES, **Peter Cushman** (1837–1922) Born December 10, 1837, in Boston, Massachusetts, to Peter Cushman and Joan MacIntosh Baldwin Jones. Arrived (1857) Honolulu. Married (1862) Cornelia Hall Jones; three children. Clerk, Wilcox & Richards (1860); partner, C. L. Richards & Co.; partner, then president, C. Brewer & Co. (1870–1899); founder and first president, Bank of Hawai'i (1897); minister of finance, Wilcox cabinet (1890–1892) and Provisional Government (1893). Supporter of the overthrow of Queen Lili'uokalani. Member, Fort Street Church and Central Union Church; trustee and treasurer, Punahou School (1875–1915). Wife was a member of the Board of Trustees of Kawaiaha'o Female Seminary beginning 1887.

JORDAN, **Mrs. E. W.** Woman of Honolulu with a young son (1892). Her sister-in-law was Emma Jordan, an Englishwoman who traveled to Hawai'i on the *Zealandia* with Miss Winter.

JUDD, **Agnes Elizabeth** (1873–1953) Born November 18, 1873, in Honolulu to Albert Francis Judd and Agnes Hall Boyd Judd. Attended Wellesley College. Miss Agnes Judd is listed as president of the Hawaiian Mission Children's Society (1915). Died November 23, 1953.

JUDD, **Agnes Hall Boyd** (1844–?) Born in Jefferson County, New York, to Rev. James R. Boyd and Elizabeth Moseley Camp Boyd; sister of Mrs. Pratt. Married (1872) Albert Francis Judd; nine children. Prominent member of the Free Kindergarten and Children's Aid Association.

JUDD, **Albert Francis** (1838–1900) Born January 7, 1838, in Honolulu, to missionaries Gerrit Parmele Judd and Laura Fish Judd. Attended Punahou School; studied two years under William De Witt Alexander; A.B., Yale (1862); LL.B., Harvard Law School (1864). Married (1872) Agnes Hall Boyd; nine children. Returned to practice in Hawai'i; served in the legislature (1868 and 1872); named attorney general (1873) by King Lunalilo. Appointed second associate justice of the Supreme Court in 1874 and served as chief justice from 1881, presiding not only during the reigns of Kalākaua and Lili'uokalani, but also under the Republic of Hawai'i. Member of the Privy Council (1891); member, Board of Trustees of Kawaiaha'o Female Seminary until 1887; second president of Hawai'i Board of Missions (1883–1900). Died May 20, 1900.

KAAE, Laurita Kaualokulani (1877–1913) Born May 20, 1877, in Honolulu, to Junius Kaae, a public official close to King Kalākaua, and stepdaughter of his wife, Jessie Kapaihi Lane. On Miss Winter's list of her former students. Her wedding announcement appeared in the *Daily Bulletin* (January 22, 1894, p. 3). Married (January 23, 1894) Giovanni Apianni Long; they are listed in the 1910 census as resident in Honolulu with five children. Died October 11, 1913.

KAAUMOA, Maria (b1876) Born to Elisha (?) Kaaumoa and Hattie K. Kaaumoa. Student of Miss Winter at Kawaiaha'o Female Seminary beginning 1890; of Hawaiian ancestry. Miss Winter annotates her name "out Ewa" on her list of former students. Married (c1894) Joe Nu (or Nee); one child. Listed in 1910 and 1920 census as residents of 'Ewa. Joe Nu is listed as a laborer on a sugar plantation.

KAELELE, Cornelia K. (b1876) Stepdaughter of Daniel K. Kaelele, sexton of Kaumakapili Church. On Miss Winter's list of former students at Kawaiaha'o Female Seminary (1892). Listed in Kamehameha School records as Hawaiian; education paid for by E. K. Amalu, of Ho'okena, Hawai'i. Entered (December 1894) Kamehameha School for Girls at age seventeen. Sent from school (May 1895) after attempting suicide. Listed in 1900 federal census as resident of Honolulu from South Kona, Hawai'i. Listed among teachers in Kona in *Hawaiian Gazette* (November 26, 1895, p. 3). Mother of Grace Mathews Mahikoa.

KAHAI, Lucia Student of Miss Winter at Kawaiaha'o Female Seminary; of Hawaiian ancestry.

KAHALEAHU, Helen Kalola (or Helen Kalolowahilani Kahaleahu) (1879–1920) Born to J. Kahaleaahu, member of House of Representatives, Kingdom of Hawai'i, and Ann Niulii, both descendants of chiefs. Author of the English essay "My life as a school girl in Honolulu." Arrived at Kawaiaha'o Female Seminary at age nine, and was fifteen about 1892. Was at Kawaiaha'o Female Seminary (1892) and appears on an invitation list for a party (June 4, 1892). Name appears as Helen Kalolo on an undated Christmas card signed by several students. Wrote Miss Winter (July 18, 1893). Entered Kamehameha School for Girls at age seventeen (December 1894), address Kunawai, Honolulu. Hon. C. R. Bishop paid for her education. Graduated from Kamehameha School for Girls with the first class (June 1897). She attended Normal

School and received one year of Kindergarten training (1897–1898). *Hawaiian Gazette* (July 6, 1897) lists her as a graduate of the Kamehameha School for Girls and vice-president of the alumni association. The Kamehameha Alumnae Reunion program for 1903 lists her as Hellen Kahaleahu, treasurer. Married (1904) Henry Walsworth Kinney; three children. Her husband was superintendent of public instruction during the Territory period. As an heir under Bernice Pauahi Bishop's will, Helen Kinney filed suit in the 9th District Court in 1919 (Kinney v. Oahu Sugar Co. 255 F. 732) to regain lands a Kapalama lost to the family in 1893, but did not prevail. The judgment includes a discussion of genealogy. The 1920 Honolulu city directory lists Helen K. Kinney, died May 24, 1920, age forty-three. Buried at Kawaiahaʻo Cemetery.

KAHANU, Elizabeth Holoaumoku (1878–1932) Born May 23, 1878, to David Kaaunuiohua Kahanu and Keliikuaaina Moluhi Kanaiama. From Anahola, Kauaʻi; of Hawaiian ancestry. Student of Miss Winter at Kawaiahaʻo Female Seminary. Graduated from Kamehameha School for Girls (1897) and attended normal school. February 1898 to at least 1902, worked as an assistant at Kamehameha Preparatory School, which listed her as Elizabeth N. Kahanu. Married (November 3, 1904) Hans M. Gittel in Honolulu; four children. In 1930, Lizzie Kahanu (Mrs. Hans M. Gittel) met Carrie Prudence Winter Kofoid and her husband on their visit to Honolulu. Died June 1932, according to her husband's obituary, which appeared in the *Honolulu Advertiser* (March 8, 1937, p. 1).

KAHILI, Louisa Student of Miss Winter at Kawaiahaʻo Female Seminary beginning 1890; of Hawaiian ancestry. Listed in the program for the closing exercises of Kawaiahaʻo Female Seminary at Kawaiahaʻo Church (June 4, 1890). In her transcribed diaries at Oberlin College, Lilla Estelle Appleton commends her essay on Alexander the Great as the "best arranged and most original." Also praised in the *Daily Bulletin* (June 9, 1892, p. 3).

KAHUILA, Eunice Friend of Victoria Ahoi on Maui. Appears on the program for the closing exercises of Kawaiahaʻo Female Seminary at Kawaiahaʻo Church (June 4, 1890), presenting a composition, "He Moolelo no ke Kula Hanai o Kawaiahao."

KAHUILA, Nellie Student of Miss Winter at Kawaiahaʻo Female Seminary (1893). Mentioned in letter from Helen Kalola Kahaleahu (July 18, 1893). Name is sometimes spelled Kahuuila by Miss Winter. Performance in the role of an American Indian mother at the seminary is mentioned in the *Hawaiian Gazette* (December 2, 1895). *Report of the Minister of Public Instruction, to the President of Hawai'i* (1900, p. 94) lists Miss Nellie Kahuila as receiving a diploma for public instruction at the normal school. *The Biennial Report of the President of the Bureau of Public Instruction to the Legislature of the Republic of Hawai'i 1896* (p. 86) lists N. Kahuila as a teacher in the Chinese kindergarten (February 1895).

KAILIPANIO, Myra (1879–1934) Born February 11, 1879, in Honolulu, to Wakeke Ululani; stepdaughter of Joseph Hewakawa Heleluhe,who resided at Washington Place. Genealogy is listed in the *Kekoolani Genealogy of the Descendants of the Ruling Chiefs of Hawai'i*. Mother was lady-in-waiting to Queen Lili'uokalani; stepfather was Queen's secretary; brother was the famous musician Jack Paoakalani Heleluhe. Listed by Miss Winter as her student at Kawaiaha'o Female Seminary beginning 1892. The spelling of her name varies, appearing as Maira Kailipinio or Kailipanio. A school essay is signed Myra Kailipanio. Entered Kamehameha School for Girls in 1895 at the age of sixteen; her expenses were paid by Queen Lili'uokalani. *The Friend* (1898, p. 37) notes that Miss Myra Kailipanio accompanied Queen Lili'uokalani on a trip to the United States and says that shortly before, she was a student at Kamehameha School for Girls. *Handicraft* (November 1898, p. 6) mentions the trip. The Queen bequeathed her money and land in Waikīkī in a will (1917). Married (c1899) George Lumaheihei Iona; two children. Myra Heleluhe Iona is listed in the 1910 census as the wife of George Iona and mother of Ululani Iona, residents of Honolulu. An obituary notice appeared in *The Friend* (July 1934). Obituary in the *Honolulu Advertiser* (May 26, 1934, p. 10) notes that Mrs. Myra Heleluhe Iona accompanied Prince Kuhio when he was Hawai'i's delegate to Congress, and served in the household of Prince Kuhio and later Princess Kalanianole. Lydia Ka'onohiponiponiokalani Aholo mentions her in her oral history interview with Helena Allen (1969). Died May 24, 1934, in Honolulu.

KALĀKAUA, David Lonoikamaka Keola (1836–1891) Born November 16, 1836, in Honolulu, to high chief Kahana Kapaakea and the high chiefess Analea Keohokalole; *hānai* to chiefess Haaheo Kaniu. Married *ali'i nui* Esther Kapiolani II (1834–1899). Reigned as King Kalākaua of Hawai'i (1874–1891). Died January 20, 1891, in San Francisco and was succeeded by his sister, Queen Lili'uokalani.

KALIAI, Lucia On Miss Winter's list of students at Kawaiahaʻo Female Seminary (1890).

KALUNA, Lucy Student of Miss Winter at Kawaiahaʻo Female Seminary (1891). Her name appears on an invitation list for a party (June 4, 1892).

KAMANA, Esther Nakaleha (1889–1934) Genealogical records list her as born in Waiheʻe, Maui, to William Makakoa Kamana and Haleaka Kauwao Kanauuao Pahukoa Kamana; spelling of her Hawaiian middle name varies. On Miss Winter's list of her students at Kawaiahaʻo Female Seminary (1892). Married (1910) Henry Nelson Range; one child. Died January 1, 1934, in Honolulu.

KANE, Emma M. (1874–1934) Born in Halawa Valley, Molokaʻi, to Opiopio and Mataio Kane; of Hawaiian ancestry. Gravestone lists her birth as December 12, 1874, and her death as December 13, 1934. Arrived (c1878) at Kawaiahaʻo Female Seminary as a student and then taught there until 1894. Attended Kamehameha School for Girls (1895–1896). The *Hawaiian Mission Children's Society 39th Annual Report* (1890–1891, p. 23), mentions that Emma Kane took a primary class at Kawaiahaʻo Female Seminary. Her name appears on an invitation list for a party (June 4, 1892). Associated with Kamehameha School for Girls (1896) and listed as from Halawa, Molokaʻi. *The Biennial Report of the President of the Bureau of Public Instruction to the Legislature of the Republic of Hawaiʻi 1896* (pp. 67, 129) lists Emma Kane, of Hawaiian nationality, as a teacher at Waiheʻe School in Wailuku District commencing September 1894. The *Missionary Herald* (October 1897) notes that she accompanied Miss Hoppin to Kusaie to teach in the girls' school with support of the Hawaiian Evangelical Association. Her efforts there were praised by the ABCFM, and its archives at Houghton Library, Harvard, include a letter from her dated January 28, 1900. Her letter to Miss Pope (August 12, 1900) from Kusaie is among Pope's papers at Huntington Library, San Marino, California. An interview on her work at Kusaie is reported in the *Honolulu Republican* (October 16, 1901, p. 5). Listed as a teacher at Pelekunu School in the *Evening Bulletin* (October 23, 1902) and at Wailua (September 2, 1908). Listed among teachers at Wailua in the *Report of the Superintendent of Public Instruction to the Governor of the Territory of Hawaiʻi from December 31st 1906 to December 31st 1908* (p. 69). The *Hawaiian Gazette* (September 13, 1907) and *The Friend* (March

1909) list her as a teacher at Wailua. *The Biennial Report of the Superintendent of Public Instruction 1908–1910* (1911, p. 113) lists her as a teacher at Halawa, Molokaʻi. *Biennial Report Hawaiʻi Department of Public Instruction (December 31, 1920)* lists her as a teacher at Kaupo. Married twice: (c1902) Joel Nakaleka, deputy sheriff of Molokaʻi (died); (1921) Samson Kalohelani; two children. Obituary appeared in *The Friend* (December 1934, p. 426).

KANOA, Hoomalu Lydia (1880–1945) Born November 8, 1880, in Kauaʻi to Paul Puhuila Kanoa Kalakau, former governor of Kauaʻi and member of the House of Nobles, and *hānai* daughter to his wife Kaleipua Kanoa. Listed in the program for the closing exercise of Kawaiahaʻo Female Seminary at Kawaiahaʻo Church (June 4, 1890). Later attended St. Andrew's Priory. Married (1898) Charles Conrad Kreuter, cornetist with the Royal Hawaiian Band; fifteen children. Listed in 1900 as resident of King Street, Honolulu. Moved to San Francisco in 1905, and died there (April 16, 1945). Her granddaughter remembers her as a very loving mother to a large multigenerational family, a very intuitive person, a meticulous housekeeper with a beautiful singing voice who had served as a young woman as lady in waiting for Queen Liliʻuokalani. She spoke of the Queen often as a loving woman, but never mentioned Kawaiahaʻo Female Seminary.

KAPALEHUA, Rose Student of Miss Winter at Kawaiahaʻo Female Seminary beginning 1890; of Hawaiian ancestry. Sister of Sarah Kapelehua. Miss Winter notes she is from "out Kauaʻi."

KAPALEHUA, Sarah Student of Miss Winter at Kawaiahaʻo Female Seminary beginning 1890; of Hawaiian ancestry. Miss Winter notes she is from "out Kauaʻi." Became ill, possibly due to leprosy.

KAPALI, Malia Born to Kapali and Kealakai, of Moanalula, Oʻahu. Age nineteen in October 1895; of Hawaiian ancestry. Listed in the *1882 Circular of Kawaiahaʻo Seminary* as a student; student of Miss Winter in 1890. First name is variously listed as Maile or Malia, and last appears as Kapale on a photograph. Maria Kapali is listed in the *19th Annual Report of the Hawaiian Evangelical Association, June 1882* (p. 12), and in the *20th Annual Report of the Hawaiian Evangelical Association, June 1883* (p. 10), as one of the daughters of missionaries and clergymen enrolled at Kawaiahaʻo Female Seminary whose expenses were partially paid by the HEA. *Annual Report of the*

Hawaiian Mission Children's Society (1885, p. 24), identifies Malia Kapali as the daughter of missionaries serving in Micronesia. Listed as a member of 1897 class at Kamehameha School for Girls, where her expenses were shared by Bishop Trust and C. R. Bishop. She took one year of normal school training in the sewing department (September 1898), but her health failed and she left school (January 1899). In 1902, she was Mrs. A. Trask, Jr., resident of Kakaʻako, Honolulu. The *Hawaiian Gazette* (July 6, 1897) lists her among the graduates of Kamehameha School for Girls and notes that her essay "A Plea for the Children" was presented during the graduation ceremony.

KAPIOLANI, Queen (1834–1899) Born December 31, 1834, in Hilo, to Kuhio, high chief of Hilo and Kinoiki, a daughter of Kaumualii, last king of Kauaʻi. Married twice: (1855) high chief Namakeha (d1860); (1863) David Kalākaua, last King of Hawaiʻi, no children. Traveled widely with the King and attended Queen Victoria's jubilee. Shared the interests of her husband, who supported Kapiʻolani Maternity Home (later Kapiʻolani Children's Medical Center) and Kapiʻolani Home for Girls in Kakaʻako, among other philanthropic interests. Died June 24, 1899, at her home in Honolulu; buried in the Royal Mausoleum. Her biography is in *Notable Women of Hawaiʻi*.

KAUHANE, Samuel (b1868) Born November 16, 1868, in Kaʻu, Hawaiʻi, to James Kauhane, a Hawaiian legislator, and Annie Manohealii Kauhane. Attended Hilo Boarding School; graduated Kamehameha School (1891). Married (1916) Emma Ululani Martin. Teacher, Kauaʻi Industrial School; manager, Waiohinu Agriculture and Grazing Company (1893–1908); supervisor, Kao District, County of Hawaiʻi (1909, 1911–1917); chairman, Board of Supervisors, County of Hawaiʻi, 1915.

KAULA, Leialoha (b1874) Born to W. K. Kaula and Keola. On Miss Winter's list of former students. Letter by Leialoha Kaula dated October 2, 1894, is in the Sandwich Islands Mission Collection in "Schools—Oahu—Kawaiahao Seminary, 1866–1905" folder at Mission Houses Library, Honolulu. Mentioned in the *43rd Annual Report of the Hawaiian Mission Children's Society* (1895, p. 30) as one of four girls whose seminary fees were paid by HMCS. Married twice: (1896) Rev. David L. Ai (died 1907); (1911) John Piimauna. Federal census of 1900 lists Leialoha as living with her husband, David L. Ai, evangelist, in Hilo. His obituary in the *Hawaiian Evangelical*

Association Report (1908, p. 95) lists him as native assistant to Rev. H. H. Parker, of Kawaiahaʻo Church, and editor of the newspaper *Ka Nupepa Kuokoa.*

KAWAO, Emma On Miss Winter's list of former students but annotated "dead."

KEALOHA, Hattie Name appears on an undated Christmas card addressed to Miss Winter. *Hawaiian Gazette* (October 20, 1896, p. 6) lists her as a teacher in a government school on Kauaʻi.

KEALOHA, Mary Neau (1873–1917) Born February 19, 1873, in Honolulu to John Kealoha and Hana Kailikoli. The 1892 *City Directory for Honolulu and the Island of Oahu* (p. 102) lists Koula Kealohapauole, resident of King Street near Alapai, an address confirmed by descendants. Student of Miss Winter at Kawaiahaʻo Female Seminary beginning 1890; of Hawaiian ancestry. Miss Winter annotates her name "married" on her list of students. The *Daily Bulletin* (April 11, 1892, p. 3) notes the marriage of former Kawaiahaʻo Female Seminary pupil Mary Kealoha to William Brede at Kawaiahaʻo Church, her family resident on King Street. The 1900 census lists Mary Kealoha, born February 1875, wife of William Brede and mother of four surviving children. The census lists her husband as an ironworker. Board of Health records list her birth as February 19, 1873, and death as December 10, 1917.

KEAMUOKU, Miriam Student of Miss Winter at Kawaiahaʻo Female Seminary beginning 1890; of Hawaiian ancestry. "Miriam Keeaumoku" signed an undated Christmas card to Miss Winter, and her name appears on an invitation list for a party (June 4, 1892). The *Hawaiian Gazette* (March 19, 1892) describes a school outing and lists "Miriam Keamoku" as playing centerfield baseball for Kawaiahaʻo Female Seminary in "The Scholars Outing—A Merry Time Spent at Remond Grove Thursday."

KEEP, Josiah (1849–1911) Born May 11, 1849, in Paxton, Massachusetts. A.B., Amherst College (1874); A.M. (1877). Married (1877) Amelia Caroline Holman; two children. Principal, Alameda High School (1881–1885); professor of natural science, Mills College (1885–1911); author of many books and papers on the seashells of California. Died July 27, 1911, in Pacific Grove, California.

KEKALOHE, Harriet K. (b1874) From Waiheʻe, Maui. Student of Miss Winter at Kawaiahaʻo Female Seminary beginning 1891. Her name appears on an invitation list for a party at Kawaiahaʻo Female Seminary (June 4, 1892). Harriet Kekalohe is listed as a graduate of the first class of Kamehameha (1897), and gives her occupation as seamstress (1902). The *Hawaiian Gazette* (July 6, 1897) lists Hattie Kekalohe as a graduate of the Kamehameha School for Girls presenting an essay "My Life at Kamehameha." Her name is spelled variously by Miss Winter as Kaloha, Kealoha, Kelohe. Married (1903) Harry H. Hanakahi, according to Hawaiʻi State Archives; one child.

KELIIAA, Eliza Poomaikalani (c1876–1930) Born in Honolulu, to Moses Keliiaa and Laika Keliiwaiwaiole. In the Kawaiahaʻo Female Seminary group photograph (c1888) in the Mission Houses Museum Library. Student of Miss Winter at Kawaiahaʻo Female Seminary beginning 1891; on Miss Winter's list of her former students. Eliza Kaluaa is listed as a student in the *1882 Circular of Kawaiahaʻo Seminary*. Her performance at the seminary as an American Indian is mentioned in the *Hawaiian Gazette* (December 2, 1895). Married (1904) George Kealoha Gilman; one child. Member of the Kawaiahaʻo Alumnae Quartette, mentioned in *The Friend* (December 1914, p. 275). Died January 1930, in Honolulu.

KENWILL, Margaret A. (1853–1904) Library Science, Pratt Institute (1893). Teacher at Hampton Institute (1880–1890). Arrived (August 30, 1890) in Honolulu on the *Zealandia*. Teacher at Kauaʻi school. Stayed at Kawaiahaʻo Female Seminary (summer 1891–1892). Acting principal at Kawaiahaʻo Female Seminary (1893) in absence of Miss Pope. Principal, Connecticut Agricultural College, Storrs (1893–1896). Employment bureau, YWCA, Brooklyn, New York. Died November 1, 1904, in Canistio, New York. Obituary in *Southern Workman* (1905, p. 61).

KEONAONA, Julia (1872–1937) Listed on the program for the closing exercises of Kawaiahaʻo Female Seminary at Kawaiahaʻo Church (June 4, 1890); recited "Rock of Ages." Does not appear on Miss Winter's list of students, so might have left the seminary in 1890. Married (1915) Stephen Langhern Deoha, Sr. (his fourth wife) and resided in Hilo. Listed in the 1920 and 1930 census. Died 1937 and buried in Homelani Memorial Park.

KING, James A. Minister of the interior, Provisional Government of Hawaiʻi

(1893–1898). *Directory and Handbook of the Kingdom of Hawai'i* (1890) lists him as captain, port superintendent, Wilder Steamship Co.

KINNEY, Helen Julia (1870–1960) Born August 4, 1870, in Honolulu, to John Russell Kinney and Sarah Capen Dimond Kinney. Attended Oberlin College (1887–1891) as a literary student. Oberlin College friend of Miss Winter, staying with her cousins, the Waterhouse family (1891). Married (1894) Joseph A. Simpson; three children, including paleontologist George Gaylord Simpson. Lived in Chicago, Cheyenne, Denver, and New York City. Member of Presbyterian Church. Died in Albuquerque, New Mexico.

KIWAHA, Keluia (1878–1916) Born to Kiwaha and Kalukimua of Hilo; of Hawaiian ancestry. Death certificate gives her parents as Samuel Kiwaha and Kahikimua. Student of Miss Winter at Kawaiaha'o Female Seminary. Entered (December 1894) Kamehameha School for Girls at age sixteen and graduated (1897). Education supported by Mrs. C. A. Brown; records note that she is from Honolulu. Married J. Lui of Hilo. Accompanied Mrs. Brown on a tour of the United States as her nurse. Hawai'i State Archives holds a marriage record of Keluia Kiwaha, who married (1901) George Kini. Death certificate states she died December 31, 1916, in Honolulu.

KNAPP, Alice E. Oswego Normal School (1889). Principal, Kamehameha Preparatory Department (1894–1909; 1910–1920). Riding acquaintance of Miss Winter; romantic interest of Mr. Anderson. Miss Alice E. Knapp joined the Central Union Church (April 1892).

KOFOID, Charles Atwood (1865–1947) Born October 11, 1865, in Granville, Illinois, to Nelson Kofoid (born Nels Kofoed) and his first wife, Janette Blake (1844–1865). A.B., Oberlin College (1890); A.M. (1892); Ph.D., zoology, Harvard University (1894). Married (June 30, 1894) Carrie Prudence Winter; no children. Instructor in invertebrate morphology, University of Michigan (1894–1895); superintendent, Illinois River Biological Survey; instructor, University of Illinois (1897–1903); professor (1903–1936) and chair (1910–1936), Department of Biology, University of California. Chief scientist and planktologist, Eastern Tropical Pacific Expedition on USFS *Albatross* with Alexander Agassiz (1904–1905). Assistant director, Scripps Institution for Biological Research (1903–1923). Major, U.S. Sanitary Corps, laboratory car Metchnikoff, Fort Sam Houston, Texas (1918). Died May 30, 1947, in Berkeley, California.

KU, Ellen Student of Miss Winter at Kawaiahaʻo Female Seminary (1891); resident at Waiāhole, Oʻahu. At Kawaiahaʻo Female Seminary when her name appeared on an invitation list for a party (June 4, 1892). Married (1894) and lived in Heʻeia.

KUAEA, Esther U. K. (1874–1944) Born to Moses Kuaea and Tamar Kuaea. Student at Kawaiahaʻo Female Seminary (1892) when her name appeared on an invitation list for a party (June 4, 1892). Hawaiian Evangelical Association (1878) lists Esther Kuaea as one of the daughters of missionaries and clergymen enrolled at Kawaiahaʻo Female Seminary (1878) whose expenses were partially paid by the HEA. Father commended by Rev. O. Gulick as one of the finest preachers in Hawaiian. Listed in the 1890 Honolulu directory as a student. The *Hawaiian Gazette* (December 17, 1895) commended her playing during services at Kaumakapili Church. Mentioned in the issue of August 26, 1896, as a student of Wray Taylor who was making great progress on the organ; described as a Hawaiian musician of great promise. Married (1896) Solomon David Koki; two children. Wedding described in the *Hawaiian Gazette* (December 11, 1896); reception held at Kawaiahaʻo Female Seminary. The 1900 census lists the family as living in Honolulu. Obituary appeared in the *Honolulu Advertiser* (September 4, 1944, p. 9) and gave her name as Mrs. Esther Kuala Koki, her date of death as September 2, and her age as sixty-nine.

LAHAINA, Emma Student of Miss Winter at Kawaiahaʻo Female Seminary beginning 1890; of Hawaiian ancestry. Student at Kawaiahaʻo Female Seminary when her name appeared on an invitation list for a party (June 4, 1892). Miss Winter annotated her name as "out Molokaʻi" on a list of students.

LANE, William Carey (1821–1895) Born in County Cork, Ireland. Arrived in Hawaiʻi about 1850. Married (c1853) Mary Kukeakalani Kahooilimoku. Lived near Hauʻula; had a large family of six sons and six daughters. Several of the sons, most prominently Lot Lane and John Lane, were imprisoned for participating in the 1895 effort to restore Queen Liliʻuokalani to the throne. It is not clear which of these handsome young men called Romeo by Miss Winter attended St. Louis School, a prominent school in Honolulu for Catholic boys.

LEAVITT, Mary Greenleaf Clement (1830–1912) Born in Hopkinton, New Hampshire, to Rev. Joshua Clement and Eliza Harvey Clement. Educated at Thetford Academy, Vermont, and Massachusetts State Normal School,

Framingham. Married Thomas H. Leavitt (divorced); one child. School-teacher, lecturer, feminist, and president of the Women's Christian Temperance Union (WCTU).

LELEO, Lucy M. (c1873–1945) Born on South Sea Island, according to census records, to Rev. G. Leleo, Hawaiian Evangelical Association missionary to the Gilbert Islands, and Elizabeth Leleo; sister of Willie Leleo. Obituary lists her birthplace as Tahiti. The *22nd Annual Report of the Hawaiian Evangelical Association June 1885* (p. 28) notes that HEA paid the fees of Lucy Leleo at Kawaiahaʻo Female Seminary. *43rd Annual Report of the Hawaiian Mission Children's Society* (1885) says that Lucy Leleo arrived Christmas day from Micronesia on the *Jennie Walker* and was one of four girls whose fees were paid at Kawaiahaʻo Female Seminary by HMCS. On June 4, 1890, and June 4, 1891, Lucy Leleo performed a piano duet during the closing exercises at Kawaiahaʻo Female Seminary. Her essay "The Work of the Christian Endeavor Is Progressing" is mentioned in the *Hawaiian Gazette* (January 26, 1897). Married (1900) Henry Vierra, Jr., who listed himself as a bookkeeper. Father's name is listed as Kaleihua Leleo on her License to Marry. Listed in census of 1910 and 1920 as living in Honolulu. E. L. Damon (1945, p. 127) recalls that Lucy Leleo, a student of Capt. Berger, was organist at Kawaiahaʻo Church and, as Mrs. Vierra, was organist at Kaumakapili Church for thirty years. Died November 3, 1945, at age seventy-one, according to the obituary in the *Honolulu Advertiser* (December 3, 1945, p. 5).

LEWERS, Catherine Rebecca Carter (b1844) Born February 24, 1844, in Honolulu, to Captain Joseph Oliver Carter and Hanna Truphant Lord Carter; sister of H. A. P. Carter, the Hawaiian minister to the United States. Married (1867) Robert Lewers, merchant and founder of Lewers & Cooke; two children.

LEWIS, Alice Kalahikiola (1870–1962) Born January 11, 1870, in Hawaiʻi to John G. Lewis and Amelie Kamahie Lewis; sister of Harriet. The family notes that the mother's name was Amelia Kalena and that Alice was called Hikiola by her mother. Mentioned in the *28th Annual Report of the HEA* (June 1891, p. 21) as a former student of the seminary who joined the faculty that year. Listed as a teacher in the *Daily Bulletin* (June 8, 1892) account of the annual public examination. Married (February 1, 1896) William F. Ordway; five children. Wedding described in the *Evening Bulletin* (February 3, 1896, p. 5) and the *Hawaiian Gazette* (February 4, 1896, p. 3). Family recalls that she attended the Pan American Exposition (Buffalo, New York, 1901) and worked as a representative in the Hawaiian village. The family moved to California (1910), and after her husband's death (1911), Alice Lewis Ordway raised her daughters alone, with a strong sense of pride in their Hawaiian heritage. She died September 17, 1962, in Aptos, Santa Cruz, California.

LEWIS, Harriet Kawaikapu (1874–1939) Born June 17, 1874, in Kohala, Hawai'i, to John G. Lewis and Amelie Kamahie (or Kalena) Lewis; sister of Alice. Student of Miss Winter at Kawaiaha'o Female Seminary (1890); of Hawaiian ancestry. Married twice: (February 16, 1893) Charles E. Blake, a graduate of Kamehameha, and accompanied him to a teaching position at Lāhaināluna (divorced 1903), five children; Fred Beringer, one child. Miss Appleton provides a long description of the first wedding her journal in the Oberlin College Archives, including the detail that Sanford B. Dole gave the bride away. Caroline Babb mentions her in a letter home dated July 7, 1893, and says that she was at Kawaiaha'o Female Seminary seven to eight years before her first marriage; also mentions the couple's experiences at Lāhaināluna. Died June 24, 1939, in Honolulu. Obituary appeared in the *Star Bulletin* (June 24, 1939, p. 5).

LILI'UOKALANI, Queen (1838–1917) Born September 2, 1838, in Honolulu to high chief Kapaakea and high chiefess Keohokalole; *hānai* to high chief Abner Paki and high chiefess Konia. Her full name was Lydia Lili'u Loloku Walania Wewehi Kamaka'eha Pākī-Dominis. Baptized with the Christian name Lydia and educated by missionaries at the High Chiefs School. Gifted singer and composer of songs, including "Aloha Oe." Married (1862) John Owen Dominis. Served as Princess Regent for King Kalākaua during his travels in 1881 and 1890. Reigned as Queen Lili'uokalani (January 29, 1891–January 17, 1893). Traveled widely in Hawai'i, interacting with people of all classes. Overthrown (1893) and imprisoned in 'Iolani Palace (1895). Died November 11, 1917, in Honolulu; buried in the Royal Mausoleum. Her papers are in the Hawai'i State Archives. Her memoirs were published as *Hawai'i's Story by Hawai'i's Queen.* Her biography appears in *Notable Women of Hawai'i.*

LIMA, Violet K. (d1915) Student of Miss Winter at Kawaiaha'o Female Seminary beginning 1890. Wrote an English essay, "My life as a school girl in

Honolulu." Fostered by two ladies who sent her to Kawaiahaʻo Female Seminary at age five. About fourteen years of age in 1892. Listed as reciting "A Fly's Cogitations" on the program for the closing exercises of Kawaiahaʻo Female Seminary at Kawaiahaʻo Church (June 4, 1890). Her name appeared on an invitation list for a party at Kawaiahaʻo Female Seminary (June 4, 1892). Newspapers praised her musical performances. Several programs listing her musical performances are in Miss Pope's *Memory Book*, (vol. 1) in the Kamehameha School Archives. The *Hawaiian Gazette* lists her as an assistant in the Miller Street Kindergarten (1896). *The Biennial Report of the President of the Bureau of Public Instruction to the Legislature of the Republic of Hawaiʻi 1896* (p. 86) lists V. Lima as a teacher at the Portuguese Kindergarten (September 1895). *The Report of the Minister of Public Instruction to the President of the Republic of Hawaiʻi for the Biennial Period Ending December 31, 1897* lists her as a teacher at the Chinese Kindergarten. She is mentioned in the *Honolulu Republican* (December 22, 1900) as second assistant at the Konawaena School. *Department of Public Instruction, Report of the Superintendent of Public Instruction to the Governor of the Territory of Hawaiʻi for the Year Ending December 31, 1900* (p. 138) lists Violet Lima, part Hawaiian, as a teacher with a kindergarten teaching certificate at Konawaena School in South Kona district November 1900. She is listed by the *Hawaiian Gazette* (May 3, 1907) as a teacher. Department of Education files show that she was a principal at Kalaheo School, Kōloa, Kauaʻi (1907–1908). Her correspondence from Kōloa can be found in the Hawaiʻi State Archives. Married (1908) Allan M. Boyle in Hilo; three children. Her husband was chief bookkeeper at Honokaa Sugar Company on the island of Hawaiʻi, where she died November 20, 1915, in childbirth.

LIMA, Zelie Piikea (b1883) Born in Honolulu to John Lima and Pa. Student of Miss Winter at Kawaiahaʻo Female Seminary (1893) from Honolulu. Zelie Lima is listed as a student at Kamehameha School for Girls (1902). She performed Bohn in a piano recital at Kamehameha, reported in the *Honolulu Republican* (January 17, 1902). License to Marry (July 5, 1905) issued for Zelie P. Lima, age twenty-one, and Herman K. Miller, age twenty-four, an American resident at the naval station is in the Hawaiʻi State Archives. The ceremony was performed by Rev. H. H. Parker.

LITTLE, Alice Cowles (1865–1958) Born May 9, 1865, in Janesville, Wisconsin, to Thomas Henry Little and Sarah Florella Cowles Little, both involved in missionary work. Completed Oberlin Academy (1881); A.B. in Literary Course, Oberlin College (1888). ABCFM Missionary in the Micronesian Islands (1888). Teacher at the mission school at Kusaie (1890–1893). Worked for the Women's Board of Missions (1897–1907), for whom she traveled to South Dakota, Oklahoma, Wisconsin, and Michigan. Secretary and then treasurer, Ohio Branch of American Missions Board. Moved to Oberlin, where she remained for the rest of her life. Wrote down the alphabets of archipelago languages. Attended the commissioning of the *Morning Star VI* in 1947. Died December 23, 1958. Her diaries in the Oberlin archives include maps that were useful to the U.S. Navy in 1944.

LONO, **Esther** Pupil of Miss Winter at Kawaiahaʻo Female Seminary. Listed in the *20th Annual Report of the Hawaiian Evangelical Association, June 1883* (p. 10) as one of the daughters of missionaries and clergymen enrolled at Kawaiahaʻo Female Seminary whose expenses were partially paid by the HEA. Rev. William Nehemiah Lono and his wife, Julia Lono, are listed as missionaries to the Gilbert Islands by the HEA; later affiliated with the Kaumakapili Church in Honolulu. Esther Lono's conduct in school is praised in the *Annual Report of the Hawaiian Mission Children's Society* (1885). Appears on the program for the closing exercises of Kawaiahaʻo Female Seminary at Kawaiahaʻo Church (June 4, 1890), playing a piano duet with Anna Rice.

LONOHIWA, **Kahaunani** On Miss Winter's list of students at Kawaiahaʻo Female Seminary in 1892. A homework assignment in Miss Winter's papers is signed Kahaunani. The *Hawaiian Gazette* (March 19, 1892) describes a school outing and lists "Kanoni Lunahiwa" as playing centerfield for Kawaiahaʻo Female Seminary in a baseball game in "The Scholars Outing—A Merry Time spent at Remond Grove Thursday."

LOVELL, **Julia** Born on Kauaʻi, friend of Victoria Ahoi and Emily Bartholomew, lived in Kauaʻi. The *Hawaiian Gazette* (June 8, 1894) commends her essay on Kapiʻolani and lists her as a graduate of the first class of Kamehameha School for Girls (1897). Assistant teacher at Kamehameha School for Girls at the time of her engagement to Capt. W. L. (Winfield Lane) Bowers of the Merchants Patrol. A newspaper clipping describing her wedding is in Miss Pope's *Memory Book* (vol. 1) at Kamehameha School Archives. Married twice: W. L. Bowers; Burke. In 1902 she resided at Beretania Street, Honolulu. According to her family, she retired to Maui. Her name appears periodically in *The Friend* as an officer of the Kawaiaha'o Female Seminary alumnae. Martha Warren Beckwith acknowledges the help of Mrs. Julia Bowers of Honolulu in her 1917 translation of *La'ieikawai.*

LOWREY, Alice Lovinna Moore (1827–1921) Born November 1, 1827, in Putney, Vermont. Married (1851) Frederick Canfield Lowrey; three children, including Ida Beatrice Lowrey and Nellie Moore Lowrey. Served afternoon tea to Miss Winter on January 4, 1893.

LOWREY, Nellie Moore (b1867) Born March 13, 1867, in Pittsfield, Massachusetts, to Frederick Canfield Lowrey and Alice Lovinia Moore Lowrey. Her sister, Ida Beatrice Lowrey, married William R. Castle. Married (1898) William Levi Moore, a physician, in Honolulu; three children.

LUCAS, Emelia Student at Kawaiaha'o Female Seminary.

LYMAN, Henry Joiner Kaleiokalani (1870–1932) Born December 18, 1879, in Hilo, to Rufus Anderson Lyman and Rebecca Hualuni Brickwood Lyman; grandson of missionaries David Belden Lyman and Sarah Joiner Lyman. Graduate of Kamehameha School. A.B., Oberlin College (1894); spent junior year at Cornell. Married twice: (1902) Grace Newman (died 1913); (1917) Frances Holland Thompson, one child. Deputy tax assessor and collector, Puna district Hawai'i (1896–1915); sugar planter and coffee planter, Puna; supervisor, Hawai'i County (1912–1915); postmaster and served on commissions; member, Territorial Legislature (1919–1921); delegate, Republican Convention, Chicago (1916). Died October 29, 1932, in Hilo.

LYMAN, Lillian Louisa Hanakahi (1866–1894) Born November 2, 1866, in Paauhau, Hawai'i, to Rufus Anderson Lyman and Rebecca Hualuni Brickwood Lyman; granddaughter of missionaries David Belden Lyman and Sarah Joiner Lyman. Teacher at Kamehameha Preparatory (1890). Died June 5, 1894, in Hilo.

LYONS, Albert Brown (1841–1926) Born April 1, 1841, in Waimea, Hawai'i, to missionary Lorenzo Lyons and his second wife, Lucia Smith Lyons. Educated at Punahou, Oahu College; graduated from Williams College (1865). Received an M.D. from the University of Michigan (1868). Married (1878) Edith Malvina Eddy; two children. Chemist at Detroit Medical College (1868–1881). Consulting chemist for Park Davis Co. in Detroit (1881–1889), when he became government chemist in Hawai'i and professor of chemistry at Oahu College. Deacon at the Central Union Church. Returned to Detroit (1897).

LYONS, **Edith Malvina Eddy** (1849–1929) Born February 4, 1849, in Mineral Point, Wisconsin, to Rev. Zachery Eddy and Malvina Cochran Eddy. Married (1878) Albert Brown Lyons; two children. Died December 4, 1929.

MCCULLY, **Ellen Harvey** (b1844) Born in Corinth, Maine, to Greenleaf P. Harvey and Abigail Lois Dexter Harvey. Married (1866) Lawrence McCully; one adopted child, Alice Lawrence McCully. Mrs. McCully was a volunteer at Kawaiahaʻo Female Seminary. Married (1895) Rev. John H. Higgins. Genealogical sources identify her as Eliza Ellen Harvey (b1842) and resided in Oakland, California, late in her life.

MCCULLY, **Lawrence** (1831–1892) Born May 28, 1831, in New York, to Charles McCully. Attended Yale College. Arrived Honolulu (December 1854). Married (1866) Ellen Harvey. Police justice, Hilo (1855–1857). Established orange grove, Kona. Admitted to the bar, Honolulu (1859). Elected to Hawaiʻi House of Representatives (1860), speaker. Interpreter, Supreme Court of Hawaiʻi (1860–1865). Clerk, Supreme Court. Deputy Attorney General. Associate Justice, Supreme Court of the Kingdom Hawaiʻi (1877–1892). Member of the Privy Council (1889). Died April 10, 1892, in Honolulu. Obituary appeared in the *Hawaiian Gazette* (April 12, 1892, p. 4).

MCLENNAN, **Martha Ellwood** (1859–1896) Born March 22, 1859, in Salineville, Ohio. Attended Oberlin Preparatory Department (1879); graduated from Oberlin College (1885). Friend of Miss Pope. Teacher, Salineville (1885–1889); principal, Makawao School (1890–1894). Her resignation as principal of Maunaʻolu Seminary in Makawao is announced in *Hawaiian Gazette* (January 30, 1894). Oberlin alumni records note that she died September 23, 1896, in Salineville as a "result of a breakdown" after her return from Hawaiʻi.

MCLEOD, **Katheryn Constance** School maʼam who joined Miss Winter on trip to Hawaiʻi (1892). According to Helen Pratt's *Story of the Mid-Pacific Institute,* Katherine McLeod came from Nova Scotia, Canada, and served as principal of Kawaiahaʻo Female Seminary (1902–1908). However, Kathryn Constance McLeod is the author of the annual reports of Kawaiahaʻo Female Seminary published by the Hawaiian Evangelical Association

(1895), and Katheryn C. McLeod is listed as principal of Kawaiahaʻo Female Seminary in Thrum's *Almanac and Annual 1900*. Margaret Brewer wrote Carrie Winter (December 9, 1893) that Miss McLeod's fiancé of long standing died (September 1893). Attended New York City Mission Training class (1895). The *61st Annual Report of the Hawaiian Mission Children's Society* (1913, p. 10) notes that Miss K. C. McLeod, formerly of Kawaiahaʻo Female Seminary was head of Okanagan College, Summerland, British Columbia.

MCVOY, Martin, Jr. (c1866–1949) Born in Minnesota to Martin McVoy Sr. and Mary McVoy. B.S., University of Michigan; B.L., Cornell (1892); attended Cornell Law School. Teacher at Kamehameha School (1890). Thompson (1941) describes him as a Cornell graduate from New York who convinced Principal Oleson to hire him at Kamehameha School for Boys. He is mentioned in *The Friend* (1906) as residing in New York. Associated with the Commercial Union Assurance Company of New York in 1894 and was president of Industrial Underwriters, Inc. at his death. Married Elsa Christen McVoy. Founder of the Locke Steel Belt Company of Bridgeport and other companies. Sportsman and trap shooter who chaired the committee that organized the U.S. Olympic trapshooting team in 1920. Left a bequest to Cornell University. Died January 8, 1949. Obituary appeared in the *New York Times* (January 9, 1949).

MCWAYNE, Albert (b1853) Born Geneva, Illinois, to Andrew McWayne. In Honolulu as early as 1878, entered partnership with Dr. Georges Trousseau. Physician attended students at Kawaiahaʻo Female Seminary. M.D. of homeopathic medicine, Hahnemannian Medical College, Philadephia (1883). Married (1878) Lucy Hannah Robinson; four children. Listed in Honolulu Directory: as coffee planter in Kona and district magistrate (1879); as physician of the Insane Asylum (1891); as a physician and surgeon (1900). Obituary appeared in the *Evening Bulletin* (November 18, 1899). His death was listed in *The Friend* (December 1, 1899, p. 1).

MAHELONA, Samuel (1861–1892) Born July 7, 1861, in Lāhainā, Maui, to S. W. Mahelona. Educated at the Royal School. Bookeeper, Allen & Robinson; treasurer, Kawaiahaʻo Church; member, Honolulu Road Board. Married (1882) Emma Kauikeolani Napoleon; four children. Their residence on King Street was right behind Kawaiahaʻo Female Seminary. Died May 24, 1892; buried at Kawaiahaʻo Church Cemetery. The Kawaiahaʻo Female

Seminary students sang at the funeral, which was attended by the Queen. Obituary appeared in the *Daily Bulletin* (May 25, 1892).

MAKAIMOKU, Lilian Listed as a student in the *1882 Circular of Kawaiahaʻo Seminary;* student of Miss Winter (1890). Of Hawaiian ancestry. She and her classmates presented a dialogue listed on the program for the closing exercises of Kawaiahaʻo Female Seminary at Kawaiahaʻo Church (June 4, 1890). Miss Winter annotates her name "dead" on list of former students.

MAKAIMOKU, Lydia Mother was a student at Kawaiahaʻo Female Seminary; she had a stepfather at the time of her death. Listed as a student in the *1882 Circular of Kawaiahaʻo Seminary;* student of Miss Winter (1890). Of Hawaiian ancestry. Sister of Mary Makaimoku. The transcribed diaries of Lilla Estelle Appleton, in the Oberlin College Archives, commend her essay on housekeeping as well received by her audience. Her composition "Hotchpotch" is listed on the program for the closing exercises of Kawaiahaʻo Female Seminary at Kawaiahaʻo Church (June 4, 1890). Her composition "Housekeeping" was delivered at the Kawaiahaʻo Female Seminary concert (June 9, 1892), praised by the *Hawaiian Gazette,* and mentioned in the *Daily Bulletin.*

MAKAIMOKU, Mary (d1891) Mother was a student at Kawaiahaʻo Female Seminary; she had a stepfather at the time of her death. Student at Kawaiahaʻo Female Seminary who died August 1891 after long illness. Sister of Lydia. There is a death certificate for Mary Makaimoku, age fourteen, who died August 5, 1891, and was buried at Kawaiahaʻo Cemetery.

MALONE, Nancy J. (b1850) Born November 9, 1850, in Akron, Ohio. Teacher, public school, Akron, Ohio for ten years; teacher (1878) and later associate principal (1886), Kawaiahaʻo Female Seminary; teacher and later principal, Kamehameha Preparatory (1887–1894). Margaret Brewer wrote (1890) that Miss Malone submitted the idea for the Industrial School for Hawaiian Girls to Cousin's Society for funding. *The Biennial Report of the President of the Bureau of Public Instruction to the Legislature of the Republic of Hawaiʻi 1896* (pp. 67, 69) lists Miss N. J. Malone as a teacher at the Government English School in Waiheʻe (September 1894). Listed on the staff of the Hawaiian Board of Public Instruction in Waiheʻe (1896). In 1901 listed as one of the founders of Alexander House Settlement, Wailuku, Maui; that same year, she established a kindergarten at Baldwin House in Lāhainā.

MARTIN, George Henry (1859–1944) Born March 31, 1859, in Lawrence, Massachusetts, to John M. Martin and Kate Currier Martin. Entered Boston University Homeopathic School of Medicine (1877) but left to accept a position as druggist at the National Soldiers' Home, first in Hampton, Virginia, then in Milwaukee, Wisconsin. Completed medical studies at Boston University (1881). Married (1891) Eleanor Frances Bowers. Practiced medicine in San Francisco, then Honolulu, where his patients included King Kalākaua. Accepted chair of clinical medicine, then mental and nervous diseases, Hahnemann Hospital College, San Francisco (1888–1897). Beginning 1890, he served as officer in the California State Homeopathic Medical Society and championed homeopathy in the state. Neurologist, Fabiola Hospital, Oakland. Author of medical books, including *Manual of Nervous Diseases and Their Homeopathic Treatment* (1896). Died December 16, 1944, in Pasadena, California.

MEAD, Helen Kingbury Castle (1860–1929) Born August 5, 1860, to Samuel Northrup Castle and Mary Tenney Castle. Attended Oberlin College as a literary student and conservatory (1877–1879, 1883–1884). Married (1891) philosopher George Herbert Mead; one child. Died December 25, 1929, in Chicago. Jane Addams eulogized her at funeral.

MEHEULA, Alice Student of Miss Winter at Kawaiahaʻo Female Seminary (1890); of Hawaiian ancestry.

MINNIE, Maria On Miss Winter's list of former students. Name spelled Minni in Miss Winter's teaching notebook.

MOE, Mary Student of Miss Winter at Kawaiahaʻo Female Seminary. Miss Pope wrote (January 1, 1894) that she married a young railroad engineer from Specklesville, Maui.

MOODY, Dwight Lyman (1837–1899) Born February 5, 1837, in Northfield, Massachusetts, to Edwin Moody and Betsy Holden Moody. Married (1862) Emma Ravell. Famous evangelist and founder of Northfield Academy, Northfield, Massachusetts, who hosted John Wise during his visit there (1890). Rev. Hyde translated some of Mr. Moody's sermons into Hawaiian. Died December 1899 in Northfield.

MORI, Mr. Japanese student first of Miss Harris, then Miss Winter. Worked at Bishop Bank as interpreter (English, Japanese, German).

MOSSMAN, William Riding companion of Miss Winter on Maui. Age nineteen in 1890. Graduate of Oakland High School. Caretaker of Haleakala Ranch. Two W. Mossmans listed in *Directory and Handbook of Honolulu and the Hawaiian Islands:* W. F., manager of Haiku Sugar Company Store; and W. L. with a post-office address.

MUSIN, Annie Louise Hodges (1857–1921) Born in Oshkosh, Wisconsin, to Alexander Phelps Hodges and Adelaide Felton Hodges. A soprano billed as "The American Nightingale" in her concert programs, she visited Honolulu with her husband, Ovide Musin.

MUSIN, Ovide (1854–1929) Born September 22, 1854, in Nandrin, Belgium. Studied at the Liege Conservatory. Violinist and composer who performed first in the United States (1883); organized the Ovide Musin Company, which toured Australia, New Zealand, and Mexico (1893), then performed in Honolulu en route to Asia. Established a violin school in New York (1908). Married (1891) soprano Annie Louise Hodges; no children. Died November 24, 1929, in Brooklyn, New York. Obituary appeared in the *New York Times* (November 25, 1929).

MYERS Family Mr. Emerson refers to the Myers as the richest family on Moloka'i. This may be the family of Rudolph Wilhelm Meyer, appointed surveyor of Moloka'i (1848). Married the Moloka'i high chiefess Kalama. Established the Meyer Sugar Mill (1878).

NAKAPUAHI, Carrie Keala (1876–1911) Born August 13, 1876, in Hilo, to George Nakapuahi (West) and Kalei Nakapuahi (later Mrs. Charles Moore). Student of Miss Winter at Kawaiaha'o Female Seminary (1893). Mentioned by Miss Appleton (January 10, 1893) in a letter to her mother that is available transcribed from Vermont Historical Society: "I have one new girl in class this term a pretty girl and one who has the name of being a good girl. Her name is Carrie Nakapuahi." The *Independent* (June 7, 1895) lists her essay "Ke Aloha"as being delivered at the closing ceremonies for Kawaiaha'o Female Seminary. The *Hawaiian Gazette* (December 3, 1895) lists her as a performer at a Kawaiaha'o Female Seminary concert. The *Hawaiian Gazette* (October 20, 1896) lists Miss Violet Lima and Carrie Nakapuahi as assistants at the Miller Street kindergarten. Listed as a bridesmaid at the wedding of her classmate Esther Kuaea in the *Hawaiian Gazette* (December 11, 1896). The *Independent* (January 8, 1898) reprinted an article that first appeared in the *Hilo Tribune* announcing the marriage of Carrie Nakapuahi, educated at Kawaiahaʻo Female Seminary, to Theophilus Metcalf Ikaia Rowland. They resided in Hilo in 1900 but lived in San Francisco in 1910. Died March 8, 1911, in San Francisco of complications following the birth of her sixth child.

NATHANIEL, Lizzie Born to Thomas Kainikawaha Nathaniel (d1904 in Kalaupapa) and Mary E. Kaanehu (d1900). Former student at Kawaiahaʻo Female Seminary. *The Friend* (April 1, 1885, p. 6) notes a vote made by the Fort Street Church to appropriate funds for the care of Lizzie Nathaniel at Kawaiahaʻo Female Seminary. Miss winter wrote her brother, Alpheus Winter (December 19, 1890) that "little Lizzie is at the receiving station outside the city and probably be sent to Molokaʻi." The Kawaiahaʻo students took up a collection for the lepers and offered to make clothing for Lizzie. There is no woman of this name listed in the indexes for the receiving stations at Molokaʻi or elsewhere at the Hawaiʻi State Archives. License to marry (September 25, 1900) issued in Kona, Oahu for Phillip HoʻOmanawanui Naone, Sr. and Lizzie Nathaniel, age nineteen, nationality Hawaiian; three children. Lizzie Makaneaela Naone was shot and killed by her husband at their home on Kawaiahaʻo Lane and South Street in Honolulu (October 8, 1904), a crime covered by all the Honolulu newspapers. The *Evening Bulletin* (May 16, 1905, p. 5) reported on the trial and noted that Lizzie's sister was Keahiloa Nalimu. Buried in Kawaiahaʻo Cemetery.

NEEDHAM, Nancy Richmand ("Nannie") (1867–1924) Born July 24, 1867, in Perry, Lake County, Ohio, to William G. Needham and Susan M. Cook. Married (1891) Rev. Harcourt William Peck; three children. Died May 9, 1924, in Rialto, San Bernadino, California. Buried Loma Linda Cemetery in Fullerton.

NEEDHAM, Susan M. Cook (b1834) Woman of Honolulu, wife of William G. Needham and mother of Nancy R. Needham. Mrs. William G. Needham is listed in the *Directory of the City of Honolulu* as a teacher at a Fort Street school.

OBED, Hannah Student of Miss Winter at Kawaiahaʻo Female Seminary (1893). Mentioned in letter from Helen Kalola Kahaleahu (July 18, 1893).

OKABE, Jiro Born in Japan. M.A., University of Chicago. Traveled to Hawaiʻi

(1880) and was affiliated with the Hawaiian Evangelical Association. In 1888, called to the Chapel of the Holy Cross, where he ministered to Japanese laborers. Ordained in 1890 at Central Union Church. In 1891, called as pastor to the first Japanese Church in Hilo. In 1892, moved to Honolulu. Traveled to Japan and recruited additional Christian ministers, who worked under him and later succeeded him in the parish. One of the founders of the Hawaiian Historical Society.

OLESON, **Abigail Jane Adams** ("Abby") (1850–1916) Born February 19, 1850, in Brookfield, Massachusetts, to John Adams and Marcia Bond Adams. B.L., Oberlin College (1881). Married (1882) William Brewster Oleson; seven children. Teacher, Marion, Ohio (1881–1882); teacher, Kamehameha (1882); corresponding secretary, Women's Board of the Pacific (1908–1915). Died June 3, 1916, in White Plains, New York.

OLESON, **William Brewster** (1851–1915) Born September 9, 1851, in Portland, Maine, to John Oleson and Matilda Prince Oleson. Graduated Theological Seminary, Oberlin (1877); B.D., University of Maine (1897); M.S. (1906). Arrived Hawaiʻi (1878). Married twice: Sophia Merwin Hall (died 1881); (1882) Abigail Jane Adams, seven children. Pastor, Gambier, Ohio (1877); principal, Hilo Boarding School (1878–1886); principal, Kamehameha School (1886–1893); pastor, Congregational churches in Massachusetts for fourteen years. Returned to Hawaiʻi as secretary of the Hawaiian Evangelical Association (1908–1915). Declined position as minister of foreign affairs, Kingdom of Hawaiʻi. Father was of Danish ancestry, and his mother a Massachusetts relative of the Brewsters. Died March 15, 1915, on a train in Seligman, Arizona. Obituary in 1915 *Annual Report of the Hawaiian Mission Children's Society.*

OPEKA, **Hannah Kailinaoa** (1876–1914) Born April 5, 1876, in Kōloa, Kauaʻi, to Benjamin Opeka and Ana Lanihau Koakanu. Student at Kawaiahaʻo Female Seminary; on Miss Winter's list of former students in her sewing class.

OPEKA, **Mary Kiliwehi** (1877–1909) Born in Kōloa, Kauaʻi, to Benjamin Opeka and Ana Lanihau Koakanu. Her name appears on Miss Winter's list of former students and on an invitation list for a party at Kawaiahaʻo Female Seminary (June 4, 1892). A letter by Mary Opeka dated October 2, 1894, is in the Sandwich Islands Mission Collection in the "Schools—Oahu—Kawaiahao

Seminary, 1866–1905" folder at Mission Houses Library, Honolulu. Mentioned in the *43rd Annual Report of the Hawaiian Mission Children's Society* (1895, p. 30) as one of four girls whose fees were paid at Kawaiahaʻo Female Seminary by the HMCS.

PAHAU, Robert Kolomoku (1869–?) Born August 20, 1869, in Honolulu. Graduated, Kamehameha School (1891). Neighbor of Kawaiahaʻo Female Seminary. Married (1894) Mary Ellen Bridges; two children. Engineer's assistant in Honolulu. Died before 1919.

PARKER, Samuel Palmer (1853–1920) Born May 7, 1853, in Kohala, Hawaiʻi, to Ebenezer Parker and Kilia Nahulanui Parker. Married (1871) Hattie Panana Kaiwaokalani Napela; nine children. Rancher, foreign minister, attorney general, and prime minister of Hawaiʻi (1891–1893) under Queen Liliʻuokalani. Member of the Privy Council.

PATCH, Susanne Ridgely (c1864–1944) Born about September 1864 in New Orleans, to William Young Patch and Clarissa Whitney Williams Patch. Her birth year varies in census records, and her obituary says she died in 1944 at age ninety-four. Music teacher at Kawaiahaʻo Female Seminary (1889–1892). A notice in *Daily Bulletin* (January 17, 1889, p. 6) announces, "Miss S. R. Patch of Kawaiahao Female Seminary, teacher of Voice and Piano is prepared to receive pupils." According to the *Hawaiian Gazette,* she sang "Nearer My God to Thee" with the choir of the Kawaiahaʻo Female Seminary on February 24, 1891, at the memorial service for King Kalākaua at Kaumakapili Church. Listed as a teacher of vocal music at Oahu College in Honolulu City Directory and *Handbook of Hawaiʻi* (1892); listed in the faculty directory of the college (1893–1894). Lydia Aholo recalls her music teacher in her oral history (1969) and notes that Miss Patch was a friend of the Queen until she was dethroned, and then was "the first one to go against the Queen." *Hawaiian Gazette* (June 26, 1896) includes a notice that she would resume her music teaching at the residence of Mrs. E. Wall in August. Her musical performances are mentioned in the *Hawaiian Gazette* until 1900, when she returned to San Francisco, where she is mentioned occasionally in the society pages as appearing in musical and theatrical performances. Listed in 1900 census as voice teacher resident in San Francisco. She was active in women's clubs and was an officer of the Daughters of the

American Revolution. The National Society of the DAR (1915, p. 255) lists her. Died March 9, 1944, in San Mateo, California. Her obituary appeared in *San Mateo and Daily News Leader* (March 10, 1944).

PECK, Harcourt William (1861–1934) Born March 16, 1861, in Lansdown, Ontario, Canada, to William A. Peck and Eliza Amelia Gowan Peck. Secretary of the YMCA in Honolulu (1891–1892). Married (1891) Nancy Richmand Needham; three children. Collector of snail shells on Moloka'i. Returned to Honolulu on mission work (1894) and became pastor of the Methodist Episcopal Church in Honolulu. In 1902, he is pastor of the Methodist Episcopal Church in Prescott, Arizona. Died June 27, 1934, in Anaheim, California.

PEPOON, Helen Abby (1856–1944) Born October 30, 1856, in Painesville, Ohio, to Benjamin Pepoon, a farmer who ran a station on the Underground Railroad, and Eliza Ann Hollister Pepoon. B.L., Oberlin College (1878); Ph.B. (1892); A.B. (1904); M.A. (Hon.), Whitman College. Teacher and then principal, Wisconsin Female College, Fox Lake, Wisconsin (1880–1888). Principal, Kawaiaha'o Female Seminary (1889–1891). Teacher, Grand River Institute, Austinburg, Ohio (1892–1893). Principal, then professor of Latin, Whitman College (1893–1921). Toured Europe and Asia on leave (1910–1912), and taught Latin to Chinese students at the ABCFM Mission at Foochow, China, where she survived the Boxer Rebellion. Sometimes listed as Helen C. Pepoon. Resided in Walla Walla near Whitman College for many years with her elder sister, Julia, then retired to Seattle, where she died on July 23, 1944. Whitman College Archives holds some of her letters and a biographical file.

PERKINS, Sarah Emmons (c1813–1893) Born in East Haddam, Connecticut, to Samuel Emmons. School teacher. Married (1832) Henry Augustus Perkins; three children. "Benefactress" to Miss Winter at Oberlin College. Died April 6, 1893, in Hartford, Connecticut. Obituary appeared in the *Hartford Courant* (April 7, 1893).

PETERSON, Arthur Porter (1858–1895) Born November 21, 1858, in New Bedford, Massachusetts, to Daniel Porter Peterson and Jerusha Clark Peterson. Attended Oahu College (1870–1875); University of Michigan law school. Served as deputy attorney general, then attorney general (June 1890–February 1891). Married (1883) Nettie Lincoln Brown; one child.

Named by Queen Liliʻuokalani to serve in her cabinet (January 13, 1893) as attorney general; served until the overthrow of the Queen on January 17. Participated in the 1895 counter-revolution that attempted to restore Queen Liliʻuokalani to the throne. Died March 16, 1895, in exile, buried in Honolulu. In his obituary in the *San Francisco Call* (March 17, 1895), his friends attributed his death to the rigors of imprisonment in Honolulu.

PIIKOI, Mary Kaimookalani Kamaolipua (1879–1946) Born January 14, 1879, in Waikīkī, to D. Piikoi Okuu. Also known as Mary Piikoi Okuu. On Miss Winter's list of former students at Kawaiahaʻo Female Seminary (1892). There are letters from Mary Piikoi dated October 2, 1894, and October 29, 1895, in the Sandwich Islands Mission Collection in "Schools—Oahu—Kawaiahao Seminary, 1866–1905" folder at Mission Houses Library, Honolulu. Kamehameha Schools lists Maria Piikoi as a graduate of Kamehameha School for Girls (1900) and lists her as a student in normal school. Mary Kaimookalani Kamaolipua Okuu Piikoi married (1899) Isaac Hakuole Harbottle; ten children. The *Independent* (December 22, 1899) described the wedding, which was held at Kawaiahaʻo Female Seminary. President, Kawaiahaʻo Alumnae; vice president, Hui Kaahumanu; custodian, Daughters of Hawaiʻi; member, Kapiolani Maternity Home Society. Died May 6, 1946, in Honolulu. Obituary and a sketch appear in the *Honolulu Advertiser* (May 7 and 8, 1946). A scholarship named in honor of the Harbottles supports education and Hawaiian culture.

PINDER, Susan E. Englishwoman who visited Hawaiʻi (1891–1892); traveled on the *Zealandia* with Emma Jordan and met Miss Winter on the ship. The Pinders were related by marriage to the Waterhouse family.

POGUE, William Fawcett (1856–1932) Born January 12, 1856, in Lāhainā, Maui, to missionary John Fawcell Pogue and Maria Kapule Whitney Pogue. Educated at Oahu College and Marietta College. Married (1880) Emma Victoria Saffrey; fourteen children. Manager, Haleakala Ranch Company; irrigation expert.

POND, Chauncey Northrup (1841–1920) Born October 23, 1841, in Medina County, Ohio, to farmer Henry Nelson Pond and Mary Jerusha Castle Pond. Stepfather was Caleb A. Bowen; half-brother was William A. Bowen of Honolulu. The family moved to Oberlin, Ohio (1858). A.B., Oberlin (1864); A.M. (1868); D.D. (1901). Married (1864) Harriet Permelia Perkins;

three children. Financial secretary, Oberlin Theological Seminary, for three years. Pastor in Berea, Kentucky (1873–1875); pastor, First Congregational Church, Wauseon, Ohio (1875–1878); corresponding secretary, Ohio Sunday School Association; superintendent, American Sunday School Union; president, Ohio Conference of Charities and Corrections; northern secretary, Industrial Missionary Association of Alabama; editor, *Plantation Missionary* magazine; editor of publications, America Home Missionary Society, for five years. Moved to Oberlin (1883) and died there June 12, 1920. His papers are at Oberlin College Archives.

PONIAWA, Miss. Student at Kawaiaha'o Female Seminary who died in 1890.

POPE, Ida May (1862–1914) Born July 30, 1862, in Crestline, Ohio, to manufacturer Dr. William Pope and Cornelia Rochester Waring Pope. Attended Bucyrus Union Schools and was privately tutored by F. M. Hamilton and Rev. J. K. Black. Lit., Oberlin College (1886). Teacher, Bucyrus, Ohio. Arrived Hawai'i (1890) to teach at Kawaiaha'o Female Seminary; principal (1891–1894); principal, Kamehameha School for Girls (1894–1914). Helped found Kaiulani Home for Girls and Kanakila Home for Working Girls. Member, Hawaiian Mission Children's Society. Died July 14, 1914, in Chicago; buried, Bucyrus, Ohio. May Atherton Richards established the Ida M. Pope scholarship to enable Hawaiian women to continue their education. Biography appears in *Notable Women of Hawai'i*. Her papers are in the Huntington Library, San Marino, California.

POPE, Katherine (b1865) Born in Ohio, to Dr. William Pope and Cornelia Rochester Waring Pope. Sister of Ida May Pope and Anne Pope. In 1891, she moved to Chicago with her family and worked as a journalist for the Western Newspaper Union. Went to Maui as governess to the Baldwin family, but became a teacher at Kamehameha School for Boys (1893). After several years in Hawai'i, homesteaded property in Northern Wisconsin, and then returned to Kamehameha School for Boys. Author of *Hawai'i, the Rainbow Land* (1924). According to 1930 federal census, lived in Chicago at that time.

POWERS, Emma (1871–?) Born June 1871 in Hawai'i, to Capt. A. R. Powers and Mary Francis Powers; sister of Margaret Powers. William O. Smith was her guardian after her father was lost at sea in 1877. Listed as a student in the *1882 Circular of Kawaiaha'o Seminary*. A leper at Moloka'i, residing with her husband, mother, and a baby born in Kalawao (1891). Mentioned in a letter from Miss Pope (May 3, 1891) in the collection at Huntington Library. Married twice: (1889) William J. Feary at Kalaupapa, two sons; (1904) Joseph Kamakawelewele, at Kalaupapa. Listed in 1900 federal census as resident with her husband, William J. Feary, first assistant superintendent in the Leper Settlement; infant son, Fred; and mother, Mary Powers. Mentioned in a letter to the editor of the *Independent* (June 13, 1901, p. 3) from "One of the Afflicted Ones"; it says she is an importer of *pa'i'ai*.

POWERS, Margaret (Maggie) (1873–1939) Born August 12, 1873, in Honolulu, to Capt. A. R. Powers and Mary Francis Powers. William O. Smith was her guardian after her father was lost at sea in 1877. Her mother and sister were lepers on Moloka'i. Her composition "Changes at the Kawaiaha'o Seminary" was presented at the closing exercises for Kawaiaha'o Female Seminary (June 4, 1891) and published in the *Hawaiian Gazette* (June 16, 1891). In it she notes that she arrived at Kawaiaha'o Female Seminary at five. Listed as a student in the *1882 Circular of Kawaiaha'o Seminary*. In 1892 appointed teacher at a government school on the island of Hawai'i with Helen Hoppin. Her departure is mentioned in the *Daily Bulletin* (September 20, 1892), which notes that her classmates saw her off to her new position as teacher at the Makapala English school in Kohala, singing "Auwe Aloha Ino Oe." *The Biennial Report of the President of the Bureau of Public Instruction to the Legislature of the Republic of Hawai'i 1896* (pp. 59, 61, 135) lists Margaret Powers, nationality P.H. [Part Hawaiian] holding a teaching certificate, second class, as a teacher at Makapala in Kohala District September 1892 and commends her as an able primary teacher. Teacher at Pohukaina School (1913–1938) and founder and director of the playground. *Hawaiian Gazette* notes the marriage (July 13, 1897) of Margaret Powers and Frederick Waldron in Kohala, Hawai'i; three children. The *Gazette* (August 6, 1897) notes resignation of Margaret Powers from Makapala School. *Report of the Superintendent of Public Instruction to the Governor of the Territory of Hawai'i from December 31, 1910 to December 31, 1912* (p. 208) lists Mrs. Margaret Waldron as a teacher at Pohukaina. In later life she was revered by her students, who knew her as Mother Waldron; a park in Honolulu is named in her honor. Bob Dye's *Hawai'i Chronicles* notes that Mother Waldron is mentioned frequently in the University of Hawai'i ethnic studies department's oral history "Remembering Kakaako

1910–1950." Obituaries in many Hawaiian papers noted her passing; the *Honolulu Star Bulletin* (May 8, 1936) called her "Friend of the Poor."

PRATT, **Sophia Hall Boyd** (1833–1911) According to genealogical sources, born August 28, 1833, in Jefferson County, New York, to Rev. James R. Boyd and Elizabeth Moseley Camp Boyd; sister of Agnes Hall Boyd Judd. Married (1859) James Hyde Pratt; four children.

PREVIER, **Tillie** Student of Miss Winter at Kawaiahaʻo Female Seminary beginning October 1890; of Hawaiian ancestry. Her name appears on an invitation list for a party at Kawaiahaʻo Female Seminary (June 4, 1892). The *Independent* (June 7, 1895) lists her recitation on the South Sea Islands delivered at the closing ceremonies for Kawaiahaʻo Female Seminary. The performance of Tillie Previere at the seminary is mentioned in the *Hawaiian Gazette* (December 2, 1895). Listed as the recipient of a normal certificate and a teacher in Waiawa District of ʻEwa (September 1898) in the *Report of the Minister of Public Instruction to the President of the Republic of Hawaiʻi for the Biennial Period Ending December 31, 1899* (pp. 95, 129, 150). In this report, her nationality is listed as Hawaiian. Tillie Previer, a schoolteacher born in May 1879, is listed in the 1900 census as resident in the family headed by William Kamana of Oʻahu. His twenty-two-year-old daughter is Esther Kamana.

PUNI, **Emma** Student of Miss Winter at Kawaiahaʻo Female Seminary (1890) who, Miss Winter notes, was out of the seminary in March 1891. Miss Winter implies Miss Puni is one of the girls she whipped for disobedience.

PUNI, **Eunice Kameeualani** (1875–1954) Born July 10, 1875, in Kōloa, Kauaʻi. One source lists her parents as John Puni and Eunice Kekumailani Koia. LDS sources give her last name as Manoi, and the names of her parents as Nahielua Manoi and Kealohamauloa Napovelua. Student of Miss Winter at Kawaiahaʻo Female Seminary (1890); of Hawaiian ancestry. Her name appears on a invitation list for a party (June 4, 1892). Her relationship with Henry Hartwell Kawahinehelelani Blake produced one child. Married twice: George Ahuai (d1896); William Rose (1906), three children. Her first marriage was described in the *Daily Bulletin* (August 14, 1893, p. 3). Met Carrie Winter Kofoid and her husband when they visited Honolulu (1930). Died March 29, 1954, in Honolulu. Obituary appeared in the *Honolulu Advertiser* (March 31, 1954, p. A9).

PUNI, Tamar Student of Miss Winter at Kawaiahaʻo Female Seminary beginning 1890; of Hawaiian ancestry. Student at Kawaiahaʻo Female Seminary (1892) when her name appeared on an invitation list for a party (June 4, 1892), but Miss Winter annotates in pencil that Tammar Puni is dead.

PUʻUOHAU, Anna Born to Rev. Thomas Puʻuohau of Honolulu and Priscilla Nohoanu Puʻuohau; elder sister of Koni and Maria Puʻuohau. Her grandfather lived in Waikīkī. Student at Kawaiahaʻo Female Seminary listed in the *1882 Circular of Kawaiahaʻo Seminary* and mentioned in the *Hawaiian Gazette* (June 4, 1886) and *Daily Bulletin* (June 4, 1886). Her school fees and those of her elder sister, Emma Puʻuohau, were paid by Hawaiian Mission Children's Society. Mentioned by Margaret Brewer (July 20, 1890) as one of the first students at the Industrial School for Hawaiian Girls in a letter addressed to Miss Appleton, transcribed and available at Vermont Historical Society.

PUʻUOHAU, Koni Born to Rev. Thomas Puʻuohau of Honolulu and Priscilla Nohoanu Puʻuohau; sister of Emma and Anna Puʻuohau and of Maria Puʻuohau Piltz. Her grandfather lived in Waikīkī. Listed as a student in the *1882 Circular of Kawaiahaʻo Seminary* and a student of Miss Winter in 1890. Left Kawaiahaʻo Female Seminary (1893) at urging of her grandfather and refused to return. Miss Pope writes in a letter to her family dated February 2, 1892, "She is so bright and mischievous—all the time up to some fun. She is not good, but she likes me just about as much as I do her. She is but fifteen and one of my most promising cherubs. She has not borne an angelic reputation, but she can be killed by kindness.... I have been quite partial to her, but poor child! She has never been appreciated, and was just pining to have some one love her. She had a regular fight with one of the teachers last year and tried to run away." First name variously spelled Koni, Konia, Koniae. Miss Winter says she is related to Queen Liliʻuokalani. Miss Appleton wrote in her diary that Koni ran away with a man. Miss Winter and later Miss Appleton visited her and tried to persuade her to return to the seminary. Miss Pope wrote January 31, 1894, "I saw Koni for the first time last week she looks ghastly and I do not believe she will live long."

PUʻUOHAU, Maria Kahopekaʻa (1877–1932) Born July 13, 1877, to Rev. Thomas Puʻuohau of Honolulu and Priscilla Nohoanu Puʻuohau. Student of Miss Winter at Kawaiahaʻo Female Seminary (1890–1892); of Hawaiian ancestry. Her English essay "My Journey from Honolulu to Constantinople" is commended by Miss Winter as best in her class in a letter of May 27, 1892. After the death of Maria's parents, Queen Lili'uokalani took over her care. The Queen insisted that she leave the seminary in June 1892 and Maria said she had no good home to go to. The Queen gave her land in Waikīkī. Married (1900) sea captain George H. Piltz; six children. Her License to Marry is in the Hawai'i State Archives. A short biographical essay on Maria Puuohau Piltz in Emma M. Phillips' *33 Women of the Restoration* (pp. 164–167) gives her birth and death dates, mentions her education at St. Andrew's Priory and Kawaiaha'o Female Seminary, and describes her conversion and long service to the Reconstructed Mormon Church. Died December 13, 1932.

RATHBURN, **William Kolo** (1868–1950) Born April 15, 1868, in Kōloa, Kaua'i, according to his obituary. Later moved to Moanalua, O'ahu. Graduated in the first class at Kamehameha School (1891). Married (December 24, 1891) Katherine Clarke. Employed by the Dillinghams. The Kamehameha directory of 1903 lists him as a resident of Punalu'u, Ko'olauloa. Kamehameha directory lists him as manager, Kahuku Ranch. Obituary states that he was manager of Kahuku Rancho Co. for forty years. Census (1900, 1930) lists William K. Rathburn and Katherine Clarke living in Ko'olauloa with four children. In 1922, appointed to the Hau'ula district court bench and served until 1943. In 1939, retired to Waiale'e. Died February 10, 1950, in Honolulu. Obituary appeared in the *Honolulu Star Bulletin* (February 11, 1950).

RICE, **Anna Opunui** Born March 1, 1873, in Līhu'e, Kaua'i, to William Opunui and Fanny Coggeshall. Annie Opunui is listed as a student in the *1882 Circular of Kawaiaha'o Seminary* and was a student of Miss Winter in 1891. Married (August 17, 1892) Koani in Līhu'e, Kaua'i (his name is also listed as John Hosea Jr. Koani); eight children.

RICE, **Mary Sophia Hyde** ("Mother Rice") (1816–1911) Born October 11, 1816, in Seneca Village, New York, to Rev. Jebez Backus Hyde and Jerusha Aiken Hyde. Educated in public schools and graduated from Fulton Seminary (1839). Married (1840) William Harrison Rice; five children. Served in Hana, Maui (1841–1844). She learned to speak Hawaiian fluently. In 1844, they were transferred to Honolulu, where her husband taught at

Punahou School until 1854. Moved to Līhuʻe, Kauaʻi, where her husband managed the Līhuʻe Sugar Plantation and she ran a Sabbath school for children. After his death, she served for a few years as matron at Mills Seminary in Benicia, California, then returned to Hawaiʻi, residing with her children. Donated funds to build the sewing house at Kawaiahaʻo Female Seminary. Died May 25, 1911, in Līhuʻe, Kauaʻi. Her biography appears in *Notable Women of Hawaiʻi.*

RICHARDS, Theodore (1867–1948) Born March 29, 1867, in Montclair, New Jersey, to Joseph H. Richards and Frances Baker Richards. Attended Adelphia Academy, Brooklyn; A.B. (1888), M.A. (1892), Wesleyan University; attended Columbia Law School. Married (1892) Mary ("May") Atherton, of Honolulu; four children. Music teacher at Kamehameha School (1889–1891); principal (1891–1893); field secretary, Hawaiian Board of Missions (1899–1900); treasurer, Mid-Pacific Institute (1900–?); first president, Anti-Saloon League, Honolulu. Died May 27, 1948; buried at Kawaiahaʻo Church.

ROBINSON, Mark Prever (1852–1915) Born July 4, 1852, in Honolulu, to James Robinson and Rebecca Prever Robinson. Entered the lumber and shipping business with S. C. Allen (1875–1882), later Allen & Robinson. A founder of First National Bank; trustee, Oahu Sugar Co. Elected minister of foreign affairs, Kingdom of Hawaiʻi (1892–1893). Married (1877) Sophia Louise Campbell; four children. Died in Honolulu.

RUEVSKY, Daniel Stoianoff (Stoyanoff) Born in Sistova, Bulgaria. B.S., Dartmouth College (1887); attended Boston Divinity School and Hartford Seminary. Took Mr. Richards' place as a teacher at Kamehameha School (1892–1894). Exploits as a baseball player were closely followed by the *Hawaiian Gazette.* Married in Sofia, Bulgaria, according to *Handicraft* (November 1897, p. 1). Served as Director of State Printing; teacher, Roberts College, Constantinople. Wrote a book in Bulgarian, *Hawaiian Islands,* published in Sofia (1900). A copy is in the Hawaiian Mission Children's Society Library in Honolulu.

SCHARF, Eduard Pianist accompanying Ovid Musin and wife in their concerts in Honolulu (1892).

SCOTT, Marion MacCarrell (1843–1922) Born August 21, 1843, in Fauquier,

Virginia, to John Scott and Margarte MacCarrell Scott. Attended Urania College and the University of Virginia. Principal, Washington Grammar School, California. Member of the faculty of the Imperial University of Japan; helped establish Tokyo Normal School, the first teacher training institution in Japan (1871–1874). Married Emma F. Brown; three children. Arrived in Honolulu (1881) and established the first public high school in Honolulu. Listed in the *Directory and Handbook of the Kingdom of Hawai'i* (1890): "Prof. M. M. Scott is principal at Fort St. School, government school for white children in Honolulu." The M. M. Scott Scholarship was established in his honor.

SEVERANCE, **Lucinda Maria Clark** (1843–1921) Born September 22, 1843, in Wailuku, Maui, to missionaries Rev. Ephraim Weston Clark and Mary Kittredge Clark. Educated at Punahou School. Joined Miss Winter on trip to Hilo (1892). Married (1866) Luther Severance; two children. Lived in Hilo, where her husband was appointed port master, and rendered devoted service to churches and good causes. Died July 10, 1921; eulogized in *The Friend*.

SMITH, **Flora** (Florence M. K.) (1877–?) Born in Kaua'i, to Antone Smith and Sarah Kala Nuuihiwa; sister was Clara Smith Lyman (Mrs. Eugene H. Lyman), of Hilo. Friend of Helen Kalola; student of Miss Winter at Kawaiaha'o Female Seminary (1891). Her name appears on an invitation list for a party at Kawaiaha'o Female Seminary (June 4, 1892). Left school and went to Kaua'i (1893). The *Hawaiian Gazette* reports in 1896 that Miss Smith is taking normal school training, and the *Independent* (January 4, 1897) reports Miss Flora Smith was appointed assistant at Waihoe school. *The Biennial Report of the President of the Bureau of Public Instruction to the Legislature of the Republic of Hawai'i 1896* (p. 86) lists Miss F. Smith as a teacher in the Hawaiian kindergarten (January 1895). *The Report of the Minister of Public Instruction to the President of the Republic of Hawai'i for the Biennial Period Ending December 31, 1897* lists her as a teacher at Waihe'e (January 1897). *The Friend* (February 1904, p. 11), reports that she married Mr. Campbell, manager of the Kapoho Plantation in Puna. Census records and the biography of her husband in *Men of Hawai'i* note Florence M. K. Smith Campbell married (1899) William H. C. Campbell, manager of Kapoho Sugar Plantation in 1900 and later president of Volcano Stables & Transportation Co. in Hilo; five children. In 1920, she is listed as a probation officer in Juvenile Courts, Hilo.

SMITH, Mary Abbey Hobron (1856–1930) Born April 10, 1856, in Honolulu, to Thomas Henry Hobron and Frances Elizabeth Gray. Married (1876) William Owen Smith; five children. Died November 30, 1930, in Honolulu.

SMITH, Sarah Louise (1865–1908) Born in Newton Center, Massachusetts. At age twenty-one went as missionary teacher to Micronesia. Married (1891) Capt. George F. Garland, master of the missionary steamer *Morning Star;* three children. She traveled on the vessel with her husband frequently, often from Honolulu to Micronesia. Upon retirement, Captain and Mrs. Garland took charge of the Missionary Home in Oberlin. Died May 1908 in Columbus, Ohio, according to *Missionary Herald* (1926, v. 122).

SMITH, William Owen (1848–1929) Born August 4, 1848, in Kaua'i, to missionaries Dr. James Owen Smith and Millicent Knapp Smith. Married (1876) Mary Abbey Hobron; five children. Attorney in Honolulu who invested Miss Winter's money; sheriff of Kaua'i, admitted to the bar 1875; law partner of Lorrin A. Thurston; member, legislature, Kingdom of Hawai'i (1878–1893); attorney general; member, legislature, Provisional Government of Hawai'i (1893–1899); member, Board of Kawaiaha'o Church; trustee, Kamehameha School (1884–1886, 1897–1929); member, Committee of Safety, which overthrew Queen Lili'uokalani (1893); trustee, Estate of Lili'uokalani. Died April 13, 1929, in Honolulu.

SNOW, Ella B. Friend of Margaret Brewer from Massachusetts. Teacher, Punahou Preparatory (1886–1891). Listed as Ella A. Snow in 1900 Honolulu City Directory. *The Report of the Minister of Public Instruction to the President of the Republic of Hawai'i for the Biennial Period Ending December 31, 1897* lists her as a teacher at Kaumakapili (September 1895). *Department of Public Instruction, Report of the Superintendent of Public Instruction to the Governor of the Territory of Hawai'i for the Year Ending December 31, 1900* (p. 143) lists Ella B. Snow, nationality American, as teacher in Honolulu.

SOARES, Antonio O. (1859–1930) Born February 10, 1859, in Sao Jorge, Azores, to Joao Victorino Soares and Maria Margareda de Bettencourt Soares. Emigrated to the United States at age fourteen. Arrived Hawai'i (September 1890). Ordained, Central Union Church (1891), according to *Hawaiian Gazette* (June 16, 1891, p. 7). Pastor, Central Union Church's Portuguese Mission, Honolulu (1891–1896); pastor, Portuguese Church, Honolulu (1896–?). Assisted at the Portuguese churches on Maui and in

Hilo. Married twice: Rachel Fernandez (d1895), two children; (1898) Arcenia Fernandez. Died March 19, 1930, in Honolulu.

SOARES, Rachel Fernandez (1862–1895) Born February 7, 1862, in Springfield, Illinois, to Portuguese Protestants John Ignatius and Mary Augusta Fernandez. Married (1883) Antonio O. Soares and accompanied him to Honolulu, where he became pastor of the Central Union Church's Portuguese Mission; one child. Active member, Women's Board of Missions for the Pacific Islands, whose annual reports mention her activities. Author of "Report of the Portuguese Mission," published in *The Friend* (August 1895, pp. 58–59). Died November 2, 1895, in Honolulu at age thirty-four. Obituary appears in the *33rd Annual Report of the Board of the HEA* (1896, p. 14). Death also mentioned in *Hawaiian Gazette* (November 5, 1895) in a report of the HMCS meeting. Eulogy by Rev. C. M. Hyde, "Mrs. Rachel F. Soares," published in *The Friend* (December 1895, pp. 91–92).

STEVENS, John Leavitt (1820–1895) Born August 1, 1820, in Mt. Vernon, Maine, to Capt. John Stevens and Charlotte Lyford Stevens. Attended Maine Wesleyan Seminary and was ordained a Unitarian minister. Married (1845) Mary Lowell Smith; four children. Purchased the *Kennebec Journal* in Augusta, Maine, with James G. Blaine (1854). Career diplomat for the United States with several posts around the world; U.S. minister to Hawaiʻi (1889). Advocate of annexation, Stevens conspired with Thurston and Dole in the coup d'état that ended the Hawaiian monarchy; then swiftly recognized the republic and advocated for annexation. Recalled and forcibly retired from federal service (1893) for his actions during the Hawaiian revolution. Died February 8, 1895, in Augusta, Maine.

STILES, Gertrude Ellen (1870–1906) Born September 4, 1870, in Manchester, Iowa, to Rev. Edmund Root Stiles and Angeline Amelia Bruce Stiles. A.B., Oberlin College (1896). Spent two years as missionary teacher at Makawao School on Maui with her sister Irene. Taught in Wilmington, Ohio (1900–1901). Married (August 20, 1901) Ralph L. Cheney; one child. Moved to Albany, New York (1901), then Niagara Falls (1903) with her husband, who worked for the YMCA. Member of Congregational Church. Died in Niagara Falls, New York.

STILES, Irene Rhoda (1869–1951) Born September 8, 1868, in Lowell, Michigan, to Rev. Edmund Root Stiles and Angeline Amelia Bruce Stiles. Ph.B.,

Oberlin College (1894). *Oberlin Review* notes she is at Makawao School, Maui, with her sister Gertrude (1891). Teacher, Denmark Academy in Iowa (1894–1897), Manchester, Iowa (1897–1900), Waterloo, Iowa (1900–1901). Married (August 20, 1901) Congregational minister Miles Bull Fisher in Oberlin; three children. Died July 21, 1951, in Claremont, California.

TAVARES, Antoine Ferreira (1875–1941) Born April 11, 1875, in Azores, to Antone Tavares and Maria Tavares; of Portuguese ancestry. Educated at Maui Grammar School. Admitted to the bar Wailuku, Maui (1898). Married twice: (1899) Julia M. Akana (died), ten children; (1920) Mathilda Silva, four children. Truant officer, postmaster, and deputy tax collector in Makawao, Maui. Elected to Territorial House of Representatives, Hawai'i (1911); served in government until 1920. Died 1941 on Maui.

TERRY, Casele (Cassie) Alda Reamer (1857–1944) Born April 24, 1857, in Smithville, Ohio, to Jacob Reamer and Sophia Fitzer Reamer. B.L., Oberlin College (1878); A.M., Hillsdale College (1884). Assistant principal, Massillon High School (1879–1883); dean of women, Hillsdale College (1883–1887); principal, Kamehameha Preparatory (1888–1890); principal, Hilo Boarding School for Boys (1890–1897); private teacher (1899); member, Women's Board of Missions for the Pacific Islands. Married (1890) Willard Stetson Terry. Died February 15, 1944, in Honolulu.

TERRY, Willard Stetson (1856–1925) Born December 16, 1856, in New Bedford, Massachusetts. Married (1890) Cassie Alda Reamer. Teacher, Kamehameha School; manager, Hilo Boarding School for Boys (1890–1897). In 1920 census, listed as manager of a coffee mill in Hilo. Willard S. Terry served on the Board of Inspectors, Hawai'i Prisons (1922–1925). Died in Hawai'i.

THOMPSON, Alice Haviland (1855–1945) Born in Brooklyn, New York, to Robert B. Haviland. Attended Oswego Normal School, 1878. Married (1882) Uldrick Thompson; four children, including Robbie and Uldrick.

THOMPSON, Captain Thomas (1853–1924) Born December 15, 1853, in Oslo, Norway. Began his career in the Pacific (1873). Master of the bark *C. O. Whitmore.* Master of the bark *S. C. Allen* from the time she was built (1889); it was this vessel on which Miss Winter returned to the mainland (1893). Married Rose Rasmusen; one child. The 1900 census lists sea captain Thomas Thompson, Rose Thompson, and daughter, Edna, residing in San Francisco. Died in Aberdeen, Washington.

THOMPSON, **Uldrick** (1849–1942) Born to Ambrose Thompson and Phoebe Reynolds Thompson. Orphaned at age four when parents died of tuberculosis; raised by his uncle, Uldrick Reynolds. Advanced diploma, Oswego Normal School (1879). Teacher, public schools in Peconic Bay (1881); teacher, Hoboken German Academy. Arrived (1889) in Honolulu at the invitation of Gen. Armstrong. Teacher, Kamehameha School (1889–1892, 1901–1922); principal (1898–1901). Married (1882) Alice Haviland; four children. His memoir, *Reminiscences of Old Hawai'i with Account of Early Life,* was published in Honolulu by Kamehameha School (1941).

THRUM, **Anna Laura Brown** (1845–1916) Born in New York. Married (1865) Thomas George Thrum, publisher and author; five children, including Frederick William Thrum. Lived in Mānoa. Her son, a surveyor, left (1892) to attend college in Ann Arbor.

THRUM, **Frederick William** (1870–1937) Born in Honolulu to Thomas George Thrum and Anna Laura Brown Thrum. B.S., University of Michigan at Ann Arbor (1896). Married (1897) Ellen Breston Nellie Sisson. Engineer, surveyor, and land agent in Hilo.

THRUM, **George Ernest Augustine** (1869–1902) Born in Honolulu to Thomas George Thrum and Anna Laura Brown Thrum. Worked at post office in Honolulu (1890). Listed in the *Directory and Handbook of the Kingdom of Hawai'i* (1890) as Clerk, T. G. Thrum. Married (1894) Rose Hight (divorced 1895). Died June 21, 1902, in Honolulu. His will is in the Hawai'i State Archives.

THURSTON, **Lorrin Andrews** (1858–1931) Born July 31,1858, in Honolulu, to Asa Goodale Tyerman Thurston and Sarah Andrews Thurston. Educated at Punahou School and Columbia University. Admitted to the bar, Honolulu (1878). Law partner of William O. Smith. Married twice: Margaret Clarissa Shipman, one child; Harriet Potter, two children. Elected to the House of Representatives Kingdom of Hawai'i (1886), then to House of Nobles (1892). Drafted the "Bayonet Constitution" (1887); one of the founders of the Hawaiian Patriotic League, which worked to restrict the power of Hawaiian monarchs. Delegate to United States sent by Provisional Government of Hawai'i (1893). Participant in the overthrow of Queen Lili'uokalani and leading proponent of annexation (1898). Became publisher of *Honolulu Advertiser* (1900).

TIMOTEO, Enoch Semaia (1847–1917) Born April 8, 1847, inWailuku, Maui, to Kikalaika Timoteo and Kahionamaka. Raised in Waialua; trained by Rev. C. M. Hyde at North Pacific Mission Institute. Ordained June 27, 1880. Married (1879) Mary Kealohapauole Timoteo. Pastor, native church at Waialua (1880–1897). *The Friend* (September 1893, p. 71) calls him a pastor "of great intelligence, and kind spirit. He has long been a personal friend of the ex-queen, and is still loyal to her in his politics." Pastor, Metropolitan Church of Kaumakapili Church. Traveling evangelist (1901–1910). Served at Napoopoo, Kona, Hawai'i. Pastor of Wainee Church in Lāhainā, Maui, when he died August 3, 1917. Active member of HEA; trustee of Kawaiaha'o Female Seminary (1887).

TROUSSEAU, Georges Philippe (1833–1894) Born May 1, 1833, in Paris, to Armand Trousseau. Educated at Ecole de Medicin, Paris. Arrived (1872) in Honolulu. Married Edna Vaunois (separated 1865); two children. Entered into a *punalua* relationship with Makanoe, the wife of Kaaepa; they had three children, a son Keoki (George) and two daughters educated at Kawaiaha'o Female Seminary. Served on the Board of Health in Hawai'i (1872–1887); served as port physician in Honolulu. Conducted research on leprosy. Appointed Medical Charge of the Insane Asylum at Kalihi (1873). Staff member, Queen's Hospital. Patients included King Lunalilo, King Kalākaua, and Queen Lili'uokalani. From 1875–1879, he operated a ranch in Kona. In 1890, he and his nephew established the Hawaiian Ostrich Farm, near Diamond Head. Supporter of the Hawaiian monarchy, Trousseau had a very low opinion of missionaries, especially the missionary party that overthrew Queen Lili'uokalani (1893). Died May 4, 1894, in Honolulu. Biography by Jean Greenwell appeared in the *Hawaiian Journal of History* 25 (1991, pp. 121–145).

TURNER, Charlotte Louisa (1853–1933) Born April 8, 1853, in Danvers, Massachusetts. Teacher, Ainakea Government School, North Kohala, Hawai'i (1881–1890); teacher, Chinese Mission Makapala, Kohala; teacher, Kamehameha Preparatory (1890–1891); teacher, Waihee School, Maui (1893). Took charge of the Chinese mission in Wailuku, Maui (1896). Closely associated with Nancy J. Malone at Kamehameha Preparatory and Waihee School; with her, founded Alexander House Settlement (1901). Author of *Twenty-Seven Years on Maui*. Died September 2, 1933. Her biography appears in *Notable Women of Hawai'i*.

VAN ANGLEN, Annie (1851–?) Born in Harrodsburg, Kentucky, to John Van Anglen. Listed in 1880 census as dressmaker. Head of the dressmaking department at Kawaiahaʻo Female Seminary (1891–1892). The *Hawaiian Gazette* (November 3, 1891) calls her Mrs. Van Anglen from San Francisco. The *Pratt Institute Monthly* (1898) lists Annie Van Anglen as receiving a certificate in normal school training. Women's Board of Missions for the Pacific Islands lists Miss Annie Van Anglen from Kentucky as a member (1892). The *Hopkinsville Kentuckian,* a newspaper, said (July 26, 1901) the Harrodsburg town librarian, Annie Van Anglen, was appointed to teach at a school in Honolulu.

VON GRAEVEMEYER, W. Listed as postmaster for Makawao in Hamoa, Hana district, Maui (1891–1895). Affiliated with Kaluanui Haiku Sugar Co.

WALKER, Elizabeth L. (c1844) Born in England. Married (1867) Captain F. D. Walker; four children. Accompanied her husband, captain of the American bark *Wandering Minstrel* when the family and crew were shipwrecked February 3, 1888, on Midway Island and rescued on March 17, 1889, by Captain C. Johnson and the crew of the British schooner *Norma.* An account of the events appeared in *Te Aroha News* (4 Haratua 1889, p. 6). Resided in Honolulu 1892; listed in the 1900 census as living on King Street.

WATERHOUSE, Eleanor ("Nellie") (1870–1938) Born January 31, 1870, in Honolulu, to Henry Waterhouse and Julia Hawkins Dimond Waterhouse. Attended Oberlin College as conservatory student (1887–1891). Teacher, Chinese Mission, Honolulu. Married (1893) Arthur Bacon Wood; one child. Active in YMCA and other philanthropic organizations in Hawaiʻi and California. Author of *Memoirs of the Waterhouse Family* (1930). Died June 21, 1938, in Honolulu.

WATERHOUSE, Eleanor Dickenson (1813–1891) Born February 14, 1813 in England. Married (1838) Rev. John Thomas Waterhouse; eight children. Died December 2, 1891, in Honolulu.

WATERHOUSE, Henry (1845–1904) Born April 16, 1845, in Hobart, Tasmania, to English missionaries John Thomas Waterhouse and Eleanor Dickenson Waterhouse. Arrived Honolulu (1851). Married twice: (1869) Julia Hawkins Dimond (died), five children; (1899) Ida Whan Sturgeon. Died February 20, 1904. Obituary appeared in the *Honolulu Gazette* (February 23, 1904, p. 3).

WATERHOUSE, John (1873–1945) Born November 20, 1873, in Honolulu, to John Thomas Waterhouse and Elizabeth Bourne Pinder Waterhouse. Educated at Punahou School; A.B., Princeton (1896). Married (1900) Martha M. Alexander, six children. In business in Honolulu with his father (1896–1899); Bishop & Co. bankers (1899–1901); Alexander & Baldwin, Ltd. (1901–?).

WATERHOUSE, Julia Hawkins Dimond (1844–1897) Born February 9, 1844, to Henry Dimond and Ann Maria Anner Dimond. Married (1869) Henry Waterhouse; five children. Died May 1, 1897, in Pearl City, according to *The Friend* (June 1897, p. 6).

WATERHOUSE, Mary Stangenwald ("May") (1871–1915) Born October 27, 1871, in Honolulu, to Henry Waterhouse and Julia Hawkins Dimond Waterhouse. Attended Oberlin College (1887–1891). Married (1894) David Watson Corbett. Died April 9, 1915, in New York.

WHITE, Maria (?–1892) Student at Kawaiaha'o Female Seminary; about twelve when she died from consumption.

WHITNEY, John Morgan (1838–1927) Born October 1, 1838, in Marlboro, Vermont, to Moses Allis Whitney and Ananda Morgan Whitney. Attended Oberlin College (1854–1859); studied dentistry with Dr. J. S. Siddall of Oberlin; D.D.S., Pennsylvania College of Dental Surgery (1868); Sterling Medical College (1874). Married (1869) Mary Sophronia Rice; three children. Arrived (1869) Honolulu and practiced as dentist (1874–). Deacon of Central Union Church for more than forty years. Charter member of Honolulu Social Science Association. Died November 17, 1927, in Honolulu.

WHITNEY, Mary Sophronia Rice (1837–1925) Born November 29, 1837, in Cleveland, Ohio, to Lewis J. Rice and Sarah Coleman Rice. Litt., Oberlin College (1859). Married (1869) dentist, John Morgan Whitney; three children. Classmate of G. F. Wright at Oberlin College. Instructor, Oahu College (1869–1871). Amateur botanist in Honolulu; president, WCTU in Honolulu (1884–1892); secretary, Associated Charities of Hawai'i; member, Central Union Church. Died February 22, 1925, in Honolulu.

WILCOX, Albert Spencer (1844–1919) Born May 24, 1844, in Hilo, to missionary Abner Wilcox and Lucy Eliza Hart Wilcox. Attended Punahou. Married (1898) Emma Kauikeolani Napoleon, widow of Samuel Mahelona.

Manager, Līhuʻe Plantation, Kauaʻi, and other plantations. Manager, Hana-maulu Plantation. President, C. Brewer Estate, Ltd.; director, Inter-Island Steam Navigation Co. and many other business interests. Member, House of Representatives, Kingdom of Hawaiʻi (1891–1892). Died July 7, 1919, in Līhuʻe, Kauaʻi. His obituary appears in the *68th Annual Report HMCS 1920* (pp. 82–83).

WILCOX, Helen Keoike (Kioki) A student of Miss Winter at Kawaiahaʻo Female Seminary from Hanamāʻulu, Kauaʻi, beginning in 1891. Ward of Albert S. Wilcox. She is listed in Kamehameha School for Girls records as Helen K. Keoiki, half-Chinese, age eighteen in October 1895, when she entered Kamehameha. Completed her studies there (1898). Listed as a laundress who took charge of the Kamehameha Laundry (February 1898). Listed in the Kamehameha Schools Register as matron's assistant (1902). Her musical performance at the annual public examination of Kawaiahaʻo Female Seminary is praised in the *Daily Bulletin* (June 8, 1892).

WILCOX, Robert William Kalanihiapo (1855–1903) Born February 15, 1855, in Kahalu, Honulaua, Maui, to William Slocum Wilcox and Kalua Makoleo-kalani, a descendant of chiefs of Maui. Attended Haleakalo Boys' Boarding School, Makawao. Supported King Kalākaua, who sent him to Royal Military Academy, Turin, Italy; lieutenant of artillery. Married twice: Baroness Maria Carolina Isabella Luigia Sobrero (divorced), one child; (1896) Princess Teresa Owana Kaohelelani Laanui, three children. Surveyor, San Francisco (1887–1889). Returned to Hawaiʻi and served in the legislature (1880, 1890, 1892). Formed the National Liberal Party (1891). Leader of the Hawaiian revolution (1889); tried for treason and acquitted. Founder and editor, the *Liberal/Ka Liberal.* Involved in Hawaiian rebellion (1895), the attempt to restore Liliʻuokalani to the throne, convicted, death sentence commuted to thirty-five years in prison, pardoned 1898. Delegate to U.S. Congress from the Territory of Hawaiʻi (1900–1903). Died October 23, 1903, in Honolulu.

WILDER, William Chauncey (1866–1926) Born July 12, 1866, in Geneva, Illinois, to William Chauncey Wilder and Eliza Scott Wilder. Arrived (1869) in Hawaiʻi. President, Wilder Steamship Company. Delegate to the United States sent by Provisional Government of Hawaiʻi (1893). Married (1917) Therese Adele Smith. Died November 26, 1925. Obituary appeared the next day in the *Honolulu Advertiser.*

WILLARD, Frances Elizabeth Caroline (1839–1898) Born September 28, 1839, in Churchville, New York, to Josiah Willard and Mary Thompson Hill Willard. Graduated from North Western Female College (1859). Teacher and president, Evanston College for Ladies (later merged with Northwestern University). Suffragist and one of the founders and second president of the Woman's Christian Temperance Union (WCTU). Died February 17, 1898, in New York City.

WILSON, Charles Burnette (1850–1926) Born July 4, 1850, aboard British brig *Diana* en route from Tahiti to Fanning Island to British sea captain of the same name and Tetaria, his Tahitian chiefess wife. Married twice: Eveline Townsend, one child; (1905) Mary Ahia. Arrived in Honolulu from Tahiti (1850s), entered business, and was elected to the fire department. Joined the Honolulu Rifles. As Superintendent of Water Works, became a trusted advisor to King Kalākaua and his successor, Queen Liliʻuokalani. Advanced to Marshal by the Queen and was greatly distrusted by the missionary party. Died September 12, 1926, in Honolulu. Obituary appeared in the *Honolulu Advertiser* (September 12, 1926).

WING, Mabel Rosamund (1864–1950) Born June 19, 1864, in Providence, Rhode Island. Instructor, Oahu College (1891–1893). Married (1892) Henry Northrup Castle. Died April 23, 1950, in Chicago.

WINTER, Alpheus (1838–1903) Born February 17, 1838, in Belchertown, Massachusetts, to Alpheus Winter and Prudence Kenfield Winter. Graduated Rock River Seminary, Mount Morris, Illinois, and studied theology with Rev. Samuel Foster in Onarga, Illinois; ordained Congregational minister (1863). Married Flora Damaris Thompson; six children, including Carrie P. Winter. Pastorates include Onarga, Illinois (1862–1864); South Coventry, Connecticut (1864–1868); North Congregational Church, New Hartford, Connecticut (1868–1869); North Greenwich, Connecticut (1874–1878); and Tryon, North Carolina (1894–1902). Secretary, Connecticut State Temperance Association (1870–1874). Died May 29, 1903, in Tryon, North Carolina. Buried Tryon City Cemetery.

WINTER, Carrie Prudence (1866–1942) Born August 24, 1866, in South Coventry, Connecticut, to Rev. Alpheus Winter and Flora Damaris Thompson. A.B., Oberlin College (1890); M.A., University of Illinois (1903). Married (1894) Charles Atwood Kofoid. Teacher, Kawaiahaʻo Female Seminary

(1890–1893). Author of a series of articles on Hawai'i for the *Hartford Courant* (1893). Operated private school for girls, Middlefield, Connecticut (1894). Member, Congregational Church of Berkeley, California; president, Women's Association of the Church; member, Missionary Committee of the Church; teacher at Church School. Resident, Michigan (1895), Illinois (1896–1903), Berkeley (1903–1942). Traveled extensively abroad with her husband. In Berkeley, member of Women's Faculty Club, Town and Gown Club, Mobilized Women of Berkeley, League of Women Voters. Died in November 4, 1942 in Berkeley, California.

WINTER, **Flora Damaris Thompson** (1835–1918) Born February 18, 1835. Married Rev. Alpheus Winter; six children, including Carrie P. Winter. Died May 30, 1918, in Tryon City, North Carolina.

WINTER, **Julia Flora** (1873–1908) Born in Middlefield, Connecticut, to Rev. Alpheus Winter and Flora Damaris Thompson Winter; sister of Carrie P. Winter. Graduate of Northfield Academy (1893); A.B., University of Illinois (1897). Married (1907) John Edgar Hatch; one child. Principal, Girl's Department, Mount Selinda School, Rhodesia, Africa. Assisted in the translation of the Bible into Ndan language. Died April 12, 1908, in Melsetter, Rhodesia, of blackwater fever after the birth of her son.

WINTER, **Mahlon Alpheus** (1863–1943) Born September 20, 1863, in Onarga, Illinois, to Rev. Alpheus and Flora Damaris Thompson Winter; brother of Carrie P. Winter. Married three times: Jessie, one child; (1891) Ermine Lois (Jo) (divorced); Ida Belle Creel. Resided in Richmond, Virginia, and Washington, D.C. Book publisher, writer, inventor, manufacturer, and chemist; president, M. A.Winter Company of Washington D.C.; first vice-president, United States Savings Bank of Washington D.C.; commander-in-chief, Minute Men, an independent military organization; member, Order of the Founders and Patriots of America, Sons of the American Revolution, Sons of the Revolution, and honorary member of the Society of the Mexican War Veterans and a Mason of the thirty-second degree. Died December 1943 in Washington, D.C.

WISE, **John Henry** (1869–1937) Born July 19, 1869, in Kohala, Hawai'i, to Julius A. Wise and Rebecca Nawaa. Graduate, Hilo Boarding School (1886); graduate, first class of Kamehameha School (1887). Worked for Wilder Steamship Company (1889). Departed Hawai'i (August 1890) on steamer

Australia. Visited Northfield Academy (1890) before entering the Oswego Training School and Oberlin College, where he attained fame as a football player. Graduated from Oberlin Theological Seminary (1897). Married (1897) Lois Kawai; ten children. Returned to Hawai'i and briefly worked at the Hawaiian Board of Missions in Honolulu but resigned because of his royalist sympathies and began a political career. Great friend of Prince Jonah Kuhio Kalaniana'ole and conspired with him and others to overthrow the Provisional Government in the counter-revolution (1895); sentenced to prison and fined. Later a political manager for Prince Kuhio. Became a carpenter (1898). In Kansas City as delegate to Democratic convention (1900). Served as interpreter for the House of Representatives (1901). Served as a legislative clerk for two sessions (1904 and 1907). Served as clerk of Senate (1913 and 1915). Served four years in Senate starting 1915. Kapiolani Park superintendent (1915). Credited with Hawaiian rehabilitation legislation. Appointed director of Prohibition for Hawai'i by President Coolidge (December 1923). Farmer (1925–1926); teacher (1926–1935). Translated a collection of Hawaiian legends and was considered an expert on Hawaiian language and folklore. Lifelong supporter of Native Hawaiian causes. Died August 12, 1937, in Honolulu.

WONG, Annie (1878–1903) Student of Miss Winter at Kawaiaha'o Female Seminary; of Chinese ancestry. Had a deformed arm or hand. Her mother sent her at age fourteen to Kawaiaha'o Female Seminary on the advice of F. W. Damon. Her essay "My life as a school girl in Honolulu" says that she is about seventeen (1891). This may be Annie Wong, born in England (September 1878) to Tet Yun Wong and How Lee Wong; sister of Fook Wong, listed in the 1900 federal census. The *Annual Report of the HEA* for 1899 to 1902 lists Annie Wong as a Mission Day School teacher at the Chinese Mission in Honolulu; also mentioned in the *Annual Report of the Women's Board of Missions for the Pacific Islands* (1899, p. 23) as instructing (Edith) Mable Sunter in Chinese. The *39th Annual Report of the HEA* (1902, p. 28) lists her as a teacher at the Mission Day School. The *Hawaiian Star* (November 6, 1903) carries this notice: "Wong Charles Ahfook petitions that he be appointed administrator of the estate of his deceased sister, Annie Wong, which is stated to have a value of $263.85." The *Evening Bulletin* (November 14, 1903) also includes a petition from Wong Charles Ahfook to be named administrator of the estate of Annie Wong, intestate. The hearing was set for December 7 under Judge De Boit. *Hawaiian Gazette* (November 14, 1904) notes that Mrs. Y. Ho Wong, heir at law of Annie Wong, deceased, has receipted matters to Wong Charles Ahfook, and the estate is near settlement (November 15, 1904). The *Hawaiian Gazette* (November 18, 1904) notes that Mrs. Y. Ho Wong is the heir of Annie Wong's estate.

WOOD, Arthur Bacon (1868–1931) Born December 10, 1868, in Sycamore, Illinois, to Thomas Harmon Wood and Catherine Allen Wood. Ph.B., Oberlin College (1892). Visited Honolulu (1890). Married (1893) Eleanor Waterhouse; one child. Member, Board of Education of the Republic of Hawai'i (1896 and 1897); member, Public Instruction Commission (1901–1905); editor, *The Friend* (1902); president, Middletown, New York, Red Cross; secretary, YMCA, Camp Dix; member, YMCA overseas office, New York; member, Congregational Church. Real estate/insurance business in Hawai'i (1895–1903). Settled in Berkeley, California. Died July 30, 1931, in Berkeley, California.

WOOD, Clifford Brown (1859–1939) Born in Cincinnati, to William Wood and Elizabeth Tait Wood. He attended the University of Michigan School of Pharmacy (1878–1878); graduated, University of Illinois at Chicago School of Medicine (1883); intern, Cook County Hospital (1883–1884). Married Genevieve J. Gilmore; three children. Arrived (1886) in Honolulu. City physician; surgeon, Kakaako Hospital; physician, Lunalilo Home; attending surgeon, Queen's Hospital (1890–1920). Physician who attended Miss Harris in Honolulu. Member of the Citizen's Guard and was a proponent of annexation. Member of the Board of Heath of Honolulu (1894–1905), including service during the plague epidemic that swept through Honolulu's Chinatown (1900). Member, Council of State (1895). In private practice with Dr. Francis Day (1899–1906). Member, Board of Medical Examiners (1903–1905); president, Hawaiian Territorial Medical Society (1898, 1925).

WRIGHT, Mrs. Edwin A passenger on the ship *Zealandia* with Miss Winter; called on her at Kawaiaha'o Female Seminary (September 1890).

Insufficient information was available to conclusively identify the following individuals listed in the letters: Miss Aden, Mr. Brenner, Mrs. Carter, Dr. Clark,

Mrs. Cole, Mr. Collins, Mr. Crocker, Lieutenant Field, Mr. Lyman, Mr. More, Miss Morris, Mr. Mossman, Mr. Nickol, Mrs. Oliver, Mr. and Mrs. Scott, Mr. Severance, Mr. Shipman, Miss Smith, Mrs. Smith, Mr. Staples, Mr. Tenney, Mr. Walsh, Mrs. Whittier, and Dr. Wiggins.

Credits

Frontispiece by artist Barron Storey.

Images on pages xvi, xxii, xxiii, xxvii, 17, 33, 41, 51, 59, 61, 66, 87, 97, 101, 116, 120, 129, 137, 149, 154, 160, 162, 175, 183, 185, 187, 192, 198, 200, 202, 228, 236, 238, 246, 248, 251, 254, 267, 276, 277, 280, 282, 288, 289, 296, 301, 303, 306, 307, 308 are all courtesy of the Scripps Institution of Oceanography Archives, University of California–San Diego Libraries.

Images on pages xxvii and 279 are courtesy of Mary Lois Ivey, Pope Family.

Images on pages xxix, 15, 45, 75, 88, 95, 102, 143, 204, 228, 247 are courtesy of Betsy Lang and Jim Evans, Appleton Family.

Images on pages 46, 69, 231 are courtesy of The Bancroft Library, University of California–Berkeley.

Image on page 138 was provided courtesy of the Whitman College and Northwest Archives, Walla Walla, Washington.

Image on cover was provided courtesy of Hawaiian Mission Children's Library, Mission Houses Museum, Honolulu, Hawai'i.

Image on page 14 was provided courtesy of Mid-Pacific Institute, Honolulu, Hawai'i.

Images on pages 44, 186, 240, 255 are courtesy of Kamehameha School Archives.

Selected Bibliography

Manuscripts

Aholo, L.K. 1969. Oral history interview conducted by Helena G. Allen. Kamehameha School Archives.

Alumni Office. 1833–1990. In *Records (Formers/Graduates)*, Oberlin College Archives, record group 3213, box 16, class files.

American Board of Commissioners for Foreign Missions Archives. Houghton Library, Harvard College Library, Harvard University. Folder 152, Emma Kane.

Appleton, L. E. 1880–1893. *Transcript of journal of Lilla Appleton dealing with Hawaii and its revolution, 1880–1893.* Oberlin College Archives, record group 30, subgroup 334, series 2, box 2. (The original journal remains in family hands.)

———. Papers. 1886–1893. In Vermont Historical Society, Berre, Vermont.

———. 1886–1937. In *Alumni File,* Oberlin College Archives, record group 28.

———. 1888. Kawaiahaʻo Seminary presentation to Hawaiian Mission Children's Society. In Lilla Estelle Appleton Papers. Student File. Oberlin College Archives, record group 30, subgroup 344, series 4, box 5.

Being prayed to death: A seminary sensation at Lahaina. The wife of a teacher the victim of a kahuna who is a deacon in a native Church. 1893. In *Babb Letters,* The Bancroft Library, University of California–Berkeley. (Undated newspaper clipping enclosed in a letter from Caroline Babb to her family dated July 7, 1893.)

Babb, G. and C. Letters. The Bancroft Library MSS 2000/62, University of California–Berkeley.

Bingham, E. 1868. Letter to N. G. Clark, April 20. In *Children of the Mission,* Hawaiian Mission Children's Society Collection, Mission Houses Museum Library, Honolulu.

Bishop, S. E. Letters (BSH 1–943). Huntington Library, San Marino, CA.

Chamberlain, M. A. 1889. Memoirs of the past, linked to scenes of the present in the history of Kawaiahaʻo Seminary. Typescript. In *Education Collection,* Hawaiian Mission Children's Society, Mission Houses Museum Library, Honolulu.

Hawaiʻi State Archives. Department of Education. Violet K. Lima Department of Education File 261–67–32.

——. Divorce Records. 4th Circuit, Page 3. Divorce 69 Pupulenui. A38. Thrum, G. (Rose H. Thrum vs. George E. Thrum, suit for divorce.)

——. Marriage Records.

——. Third Circuit, Page 2. Guardianship of Hanaike: Emma. (In regard to the matter of Emma Hanaike and Bennie Hanaike, minor heirs of Kaneualani w. of Hilo, Hawaiʻi, deceased intestate.)

——. 1877. Probate Records. First Circuit. P. 1125. Probate. A. R. Powers.

——. 1897. Probate Records. First Circuit. P. 3084. Probate. Anna M. Armstrong.

——. 1902. Probate Records. First Circuit. P. 3531. Will. George Earnest Augustine Thrum. Filed August 4.

Hawaiian Mission Children's Society Library. Folder: "Schools—Oahu—Kawaiahaʻo Seminary." This file includes "Beneficiaries of the HMCS at the Kawaiahaʻo Seminary" and other documents, reports, and photographs crucial to an understanding of the history of Kawaiahaʻo Female Seminary and the lives of its students.

Hawaiian Mission Children's Society Library, Mission Houses Museum, Honolulu, s.v. Photograph Collection s.v. "Schools—Kawaiahaʻo Seminary." (This includes a c1888 photograph of the students of Kawaiahaʻo Female Seminary standing outside the school. The print is labeled with the names of the children and their teachers.)

Kamehameha School Archives. Admissions ledger, A–K. Kamehameha School for Girls, Kamehameha School, Honolulu.

——. Commencement programs. Kamehameha School for Girls, Kamehameha School, Honolulu.

———. Kamehameha Class of 1897. Graduation photograph with identifications of each student. Kamehameha School, Honolulu. (This valuable photograph is also available electronically on the Kamehameha School Website.)

———. Register for 1902–1903. Kamehameha School, Honolulu.

Kofoid C. A. Papers. Scripps Institution of Oceanography Archives, University of California–San Diego Library.

Norton, H. S. 1881. Document dated February 8 that begins "$50 received from the Hawaiian Board," Hawaiian Mission Children's Society Library, Mission Houses Museum, Honolulu, s.v. "Oahu—Schools—Kawaiaha'o Seminary."

———. 1882. "To the members of the H.M.C. Society," Hawaiian Mission Children's Society Library, Mission Houses Museum, Honolulu, s.v. "Oahu—Schools—Kawaiaha'o Seminary, 1866–1905."

Penrose, S. B. L. Correspondence, 1906–1912, s.v. Pepoon, Helen A. Whitman College and Northwest Archives, Walla Walla, WA.

Photograph Files. 1886, 1900, etc. In *Class photograph collection*, Oberlin College Archives, record group 32/13.

Pope, I. M. 1891. Letter to Pope family, February 2. (This and other letters from Ida May Pope are in family hands.)

———. Memory Book I, 1894–1903, and Papers. Kamehameha School Archives, Kamehameha School, Honolulu.

———. Papers (HM 47008–47018). Letters to Lois (Pope) Prosser and others, 1897–1914. Huntington Library, San Marino, CA.

Whitman Alumnus, June 1921, page 9. (Untitled article on the retirement of Helen Pepoon.)

Whitman College Catalog. 1893. Whitman College and Northwest Archives, s.v. Helen Pepoon, Lady Principal and Professor of Latin, Walla Walla, WA.

Published Sources

Alexander, W. D. 1898. *Report of the Minister of Public Instruction.* Honolulu: Territory of Hawaii.

———. 1902. The development of education in Hawaii. *The Friend* 59, no. 12 (December): 22–24.

Alexander, W. D., and A. T. Atkinson. 1888. *An historical sketch of education in the Hawaiian Islands.* Honolulu: Board of Education of the Hawaiian Kingdom.

Allen, H. G. 1991. *The betrayal of Liliuokalani: Last queen of Hawaii 1838–1917.* Honolulu: Mutual Publishing.

Anderson, G. H., ed. 1999. *Biographical dictionary of the Christian missions.* Grand Rapids: Eerdmans Publishing Company.

Anderson, R. 1862. *Memorial volume of the first fifty years of the American Board of Commissions for Foreign Missions.* Boston: American Board of Commissions for Foreign Missions.

Appleton, L. E. 1891. "School-keeping among Indians," *The Friend* 49, no. 12 (December): 92–84.

Baker, A. S. 1945. Morning stars and missionary packet. Honolulu: The Friend for Hawaiian Evangelical Association.

Bandy, D. W. 1990. Bandmaster Henry Berger and the Royal Hawaiian Band. *Hawaiian Journal of History* 24: 69–91.

Benham, M. K. P. 1998. The voice "less" Hawaiian: An analysis of educational policymaking 1820–1960. *Hawaiian Journal of History* 32: 121–140.

Beyer, C. K. 2003. Female seminaries in America and Hawai'i in the 19th century. *Hawaiian Journal of History* 37: 91–118.

———. 2004. Manual and industrial education for Hawaiians during the 19th century. *Hawaiian Journal of History* 38: 1–34.

———. 2007. The connection of Samuel Chapman Armstrong as both borrower and architect of education in Hawai'i. *History of Education Quarterly* 47, no.1: 23–48.

———. 2010. Setting the record straight: Education of the mind and hands existed in the United States before the 1880s. *American Education History Journal* 37, no.1: 149–168.

Bishop, S. E. 1891. The Hawaiian queen and her kingdom. *Review of Reviews* 4: 146–153.

Burstall, S. A. 1971. *The education of girls in the United States.* New York: Arno Press.

Canivali, R. 1977. Hilo Boarding School: Hawaii's experiment in vocational education. *Hawaiian Journal of History* 11: 77–96.

Castle, A. L. 1989. Harriet Castle and the beginning of progressive kindergarten education in Hawaii 1894–1900. *Hawaiian Journal of History* 23: 119–136.

The Centennial Book: One hundred years of Christian civilization in Hawaii 1820–1920, A symposium. 1920. Honolulu: Central Committee of the Hawaiian Mission Centennial.

Circular of Kawaiahao Seminary. 1882. Honolulu: Hawaiian Gazette for Hawaiian Historical Society.

Clark, A. H., ed. 1902. *A national register of the society, Sons of the American Revolution.* New York: Louis H. Cornish. (Accessed http://books.google .com/books.)

Co-Education. 1891. *Hawaiian Gazette* 26, no. 28: 9. (Accessed from the Library of Congress site Chronicling America http://chroniclingamerica .loc.gov/.)

Coan, L. B. 1907. Early days at Kawaiaha'o Seminary. *The Friend* 64, no. 7 (July): 9.

Coan, T. 1840. *Progress: Hilo Girls' School.* Boston: American Board of Commissioners for Foreign Missions.

Coffman, T. 2008. *Nation within: The history of the American occupation of Hawai'i.* Revised edition. Kihei, Hawai'i: Koa Books.

Crunden, R. M. 1982. *Ministers of reform: The Progressives' achievement in American civilization 1889–1920.* New York: Basic Books.

Daily Bulletin. June 13, 1892. (Accessed from the Library of Congress site Chronicling America http://chroniclingamerica.loc.gov/.)

Damon, E. M. 1923. Hilo Boarding School. *The Friend* 93, no. 7 (July): 152–155, 168–170.

———. 1945. *The stone church at Kawaiahaʻo.* Honolulu: Honolulu Star Bulletin Press for Kawaiahaʻo Church.

Daughters of the American Revolution. 1908. *Directory of the National Society of the Daughters of the American Revolution.* Washington, DC: Daughters of the American Revolution.

Daws, G. 1967. The decline of Puritanism at Honolulu in the 19th century. *Hawaiian Journal of History* 1: 31–42.

———. 1968. *Shoal of time: A history of the Hawaiian Islands.* New York: Macmillan.

Delta Kappa Gamma Society. 1981. *Makers of destiny Hawaiian style: The lives of pioneer women educators in Hawaii.* Honolulu: Delta Kappa Gamma Society, International BetaBeta State.

Directory and handbook of the Kingdom of Hawaii. 1890. Honolulu: Pacific Press Publishing Company, 1890. (Accessed through Ancestry.com.)

Honolulu, Hawaii directory, 1890 (database on-line). Provo, UT: The Generations Network, Inc., 2000. Original data: *Honolulu, Hawaii, 1890.* Honolulu: The Pacific Press Publishing Company, 1890. http://search.ancestry.com/search/ (This directory can also searched through Ulukau, The Hawaiian Electronic Library.)

Directory and hand-book of Honolulu and the Hawaiian Islands. 1884–1892. San Francisco: F. L. Husted. (Called Polk-Husted directory. Accessed through Ancestry.com.) *Honolulu, Hawaii Directory, 1890* (database on-line). Provo, UT: The Generations Network, Inc., 2000. Original data: *Honolulu, Hawaii, 1890.* Honolulu: The Pacific Press Publishing Company, 1890. http://search.ancestry.com/search/ (The directories for 1890 and 1892 can also be searched through Ulukau, The Hawaiian Electronic Library.)

Directory of the city of Honolulu and island of Oahu. 1890. Honolulu. (Accessed through Ancestry.com.) *Honolulu, Hawaii Directory, 1890* (database on-line). Provo, UT: The Generations Network, Inc., 2000. Original data:

Honolulu, Hawaii, 1890. Honolulu: The Pacific Press Publishing Company, 1890. http://search.ancestry.com/search/.

Drills.—Fourth paper, The hoop drill. 1892. In *Delineator Magazine,* Charles Atwood Kofoid Papers, Scripps Institution of Oceanography, University of California–San Diego Library.

Emerson, N. B. 1884. The education of Hawaiian girls. In *Annual Reports of the Hawaiian Mission Children's Society.* Honolulu: Hawaiian Mission Children's Society.

Emerson, O. P. 1928. *Pioneer days in Hawaii.* Garden City, NY: Doubleday, Doran, and Company.

Extracts from the minutes of the general meeting of the Sandwich Islands Mission. 1836. Honolulu: Sandwich Islands Mission.

Female boarding school in foreign missions. 1866. Boston: Missionary House.

The Friend. 1889–1894. Volumes 48–52, Honolulu.

———. 1902–1905. Volumes 60–62, Honolulu. (Some later volumes of this periodical are available in digital form through http://books.google.com/books.)

Frear, M. D. 1918. Mid-Pacific. *The Friend* 77, no. 7 (July): 151–158. (This entire issue of *The Friend* is an appeal for support for the Mid-Pacific Institute; Frear's article presents the school's history. Accessed http://books.google.com/books.)

Frear, W. 1920. *A century of achievement.* Honolulu: Hawaiian Mission Association.

Fuchs, L. H. 1961. *Hawaii pono: A social history.* New York: Harcourt, Brace & World, Inc.

Garland, G. F. 1897. The voyage of the Morning Star, 1890–1891. In *In lands afar: A second series of mission stories of many lands,* edited by Elnathan Ellsworth Strong, 301–305. Boston: American Board of Commissioners for Foreign Missions.

———. 1897. The twelfth voyage of the Morning Star, 1894–1895. In *In lands afar: A second series of mission stories of many lands,* edited by Elnathan

Ellsworth Strong, 313–316. Boston: American Board of Commissioners for Foreign Missions.

Garland, Mrs. G. F. 1897. Dining with a king. In *In lands afar: A second series of mission stories of many lands,* edited by Elnathan Ellsworth Strong, 309–312. Boston: American Board of Commissioners for Foreign Missions.

———. 1897. The young people of Micronesia. In *In lands afar: A second series of mission stories of many lands,* edited by Elnathan Ellsworth Strong, 317–320. Boston: American Board of Commissioners for Foreign Missions.

General Council of the Congregational and Christian Churches. 1891. *The Congregational year book, 1891.* Boston: Congregational Sunday School and Publishing Society. (Accessed http://books.google.com/books.)

Grimshaw, P. 1989. *Paths of duty: American missionary wives in nineteenth-century Hawaii.* Honolulu: University of Hawai'i Press.

Gulick, A. 1932. *Evolutionist and missionary John Thomas Gulick.* Chicago: University of Chicago Press.

Hagar, E. B. 1973. *Continuing memoirs: Family, community, university.* Oral history interview conducted by Susan Reiss. Regional Oral History Office, The Bancroft Library, University of California–Berkeley.

Hawaii. Republic. Board of Education. 1896. *The biennial report of the president of the Bureau of Public Instruction to the legislature of the Republic of Hawaii 1896.* Honolulu: Hawaiian Gazette Company. (Title within varies: Board of Education. Biennial report of the Bureau of Public Instruction to the legislature of the Republic of Hawaii...for the period beginning April 1, 1894 and closing December 1, 1895. Accessed http://books.google.com/books.)

———. Department of Public Instruction. 1897. *The report of the Minister of Public Instruction to the President of the Republic of Hawaii for the biennial period ending December 31, 1897.* (Accessed http://books.google .com/books.)

———. Department of Public Instruction. 1900. *The report of the Minister of Public Instruction to the President of the Republic of Hawaii for the biennial period ending December 31, 1899.* Honolulu: Hawaiian Gazette Company Print. (Accessed http://books.google.com/books.)

Hawaii. Territory. Department of Public Instruction. 1901. *Report of the superintendent of Public Instruction to the governor of the Territory of Hawaii for the year ending December 31, 1900.* Honolulu: Hawaiian Gazette. (Accessed http://books.google.com/books.)

———. Department of Public Instruction. 1909. *Report of the superintendent of Public Instruction to the governor of the Territory of Hawaii from December 31, 1906 to December 31, 1908.* Honolulu: Bulletin Publishing Company. (Accessed http://books.google.com/books.)

———. Department of Public Instruction. 1913. *Report of the superintendent of Public Instruction to the governor of the Territory of Hawaii from December 31, 1910 to December 31, 1912.* Honolulu: Bulletin Publishing Company, Ltd. (Accessed http://books.google.com/books.)

Hawaiian Evangelical Association. 1878, 1884, 1887, 1895, 1896, 1900. *Annual report of the Hawaiian Evangelical Association.* Honolulu: Hawaiian Board. (Accessed http://books.google.com/books.)

Hawaiian Gazette. Accessed through Library of Congress site Chronicling America.

Hawaiian Mission Children's Society. 1906. Items from absent members of the Cousin's Society. *The Friend* 61, no. 2 (February): 10–11. (This article mentions the marriage of Flora (Smith) Campbell of Kawaiahaʻo Female Seminary. Accessed http://books.google.com/books.)

———. 1871. *Nineteenth annual report of the Hawaiian Mission Children's Society presented June 17, 1870.* Honolulu: Black & Auld.

———. 1882. *Annual report.* Honolulu: Hawaiian Mission Children's Society.

———. 1888, 1913. *Annual report of the Hawaiian Mission Children's Society.* Honolulu: Press Publishing Company. (The HMCS provided support for Kawaiahaʻo Female Seminary, and its annual reports included reports by the principal of the school. Volumes 36–43 [1888–1894] accessed http://books.google.com/books.)

Hyams, B. K. 1985. School teachers as agents of cultural imperialism in Territorial Hawaii. *Journal of Pacific History* 20, no. 4: 202–219.

In memoriam (Myra Davis). 1898. *Whitman College Quarterly* 2, no. 3: 38.

The Independent. (Accessed from the Library of Congress site Chronicling America http://chroniclingamerica.loc.gov/.)

Joseph Ballard Atherton (Obituary). 1903. *The Friend* 61, no. 6 (June): 5.

Kahuna work. 1891. *The Friend* 49, no. 10 (October): 79.

Kamehameha Girls School. 1894. *The Friend* 52, no. 10 (October): 77.

Kamehameha's memorial. 1895. *Paradise of the Pacific* (May): 69–70.

Kaplan, J. 1974. *Lincoln Steffens: A biography.* New York: Simon and Schuster.

Katsuki, B. 1981. Medical men who helped to shape Hawaii. *Hawaiian Medical Journal* 40, no. 10: 279–282.

Kaua'i Historical Society. 2011. *In honor of Na Wahine Kiekei Women of Distinction: In honor of chiefess Kamakahelai and Emma Kauikeolani Wilcox.* Līhu'e: Kaua'i Historical Society.

Kawaiaha'o Seminary. 1904. *The Friend* 41, no. 2 (February): 9.

Kawaiaha'o Seminary: At the close of the first twenty years of its history, with a brief history of other schools for Hawaiian girls. 1885. Honolulu: Hawaiian Children's Mission Society.

Kawaiaha'o Seminary: Twenty-fourth annual exercises at Kawaiaha'o Church. 1891. *Hawaiian Gazette* 26, no. 23: 5. (Accessed from the Library of Congress site Chronicling America http://chroniclingamerica.loc.gov/.)

Kellogg, V. 1914. Faces and races. *Journal of Heredity* 6, no. 6 (June 1914).

Kikuchi, W. K. and S. Remoaldo. 1992. *Cemeteries of Kaua'i.* Pahi, Kaua'i: Kaua'i Community College and University of Hawai'i.

Kleinberg, P. G. 1990. "Pieces of civilization: The Wailuku Female Seminary samples." Thesis, University of Hawai'i–Mānoa.

Kofoid, C. P. 1906. *Puritan influences in the formative years of Illinois history.* Springfield, IL: State Journal Company. (This is Carrie Prudence Winter's master's thesis in history from the University of Illinois.)

Kuykendall, R. S. 1966. *The Hawaiian Kingdom 1778–1854: Foundation and transformation.* Honolulu: University of Hawai'i Press.

Liliʻuokalani. 1964. *Hawaii's story by Hawaii's queen.* Rutland, Vermont, and Tokyo, Japan: Charles E. Tuttle Company, Inc. (Originally published in Boston by Lee and Shepard, 1898.)

Loebenstein, A. B. 1893. Hawaii (Oahu) Honolulu (City): Map of the lower part of the city of Honolulu and the Harbor front. (1:2,400) Library of Congress, Geography and Map Division.

Logan, D. 1903. *Hawaii: Its people, climate and resources.* Honolulu: Pioneer Advertising Company.

Loomis, A. 1976. *For whom are the stars?* Honolulu: University of Hawaiʻi Press.

Malo, D. 1951. *Hawaiian Antiquities: Moolelo Hawaii.* 2d ed. (N. B. Emerson, trans.) Honolulu: Bishop Museum Press.

Margaret Kenwill (Obituary). 1905. *Southern Workman* 34, no. 1: 61–62.

McClelland, A. E. 1992. *The education of women in the United States: A guide to theory, teaching, and research.* New York: Garland Publishing.

McKinzie, E. K. 1983, 1986. *Hawaiian genealogies: Extracted from Hawaiian language newspapers* (2 vols.), edited by Ismael W. Stagner. Lāʻie, HI: The Institute for Polynesian Studies, Brigham Young University (distributed by University of Hawaiʻi Press).

Mihesuah, D. A. 1998. *Cultivating the rosebuds: The education of women at the Cherokee Female Seminary, 1851–1909.* Urbana and Chicago: University of Illinois Press.

Missionary album: Portraits and biographical sketches of the American Protestant missionaries to the Hawaiian Islands. 1969. Honolulu: Hawaiian Mission Children's Society.

The Missionary Herald at home and abroad. 1890, 1891. Volumes 86, 87. (Accessed http://books.google.com/books. The full text of *The Missionary Herald* is accessible at http://www.archive.org/stream/missionaryheral21 missgoog/missionaryheral21missgoogdjvu.txt.)

Moblo, P. 1999. Leprosy, politics and the rise of Hawaii's Reform Party. *Journal of Pacific History* 34, no. 1: 75–89.

Morris, M. E. 1929. "Development of secondary education in Hawaii." Thesis, University of Hawai'i.

Mullin, P. C. 1973. Kofoid, Charles Atwood. *Dictionary of Scientific Biography* 7: 447.

Nellist, G. F., ed. 1930–1938. *Women of Hawaii.* 2 vols. Honolulu: E. A. Laangton-Boyle.

A noble craft, latest addition to the clipper fleet in the Hawaiian trade, the new American bark S.C. Allen. 1889. *Hawaiian Gazette* 24, no. 6: 5. (Accessed from the Library of Congress site Chronicling America http://chroniclingamerica.loc.gov/.)

Oberlin College. *General catalogue of Oberlin College 1833–1908. Including an account of the principal events in the history of the college with illustrations of the college buildings.* Oberlin: Oberlin College, 1909. (This important resource is available from several sites, including the Internet Archive http://www.archive.org/details/generalcatalogue00oberrich.)

Julia Charlotte Pepoon (Obituary) "57." 1909. *Oberlin Alumni Magazine* 5, no. 9: 378. (Julia Charlotte Pepoon was the eldest sister of Helen A. Pepoon. Accessed through http://books.google.com/books.)

Odgers, G. A. 1933. "Education in Hawaii, 1820–1893." Ph.D. diss., Stanford University.

Palmer, J. A., Jr. 1894. *Memories of Hawaii and Hawaiian correspondence.* Boston: Lee and Shepard.

Peterson, B. B. 1984. *Notable women of Hawaii.* Honolulu: University of Hawai'i Press.

Phillips, E. M. 1960. *33 women of the Restoration.* Independence, Missouri: Herald House.

Piercy, L. W. 1992. *Hawaii's missionary saga: Sacrifice and godliness in paradise.* Honolulu: Mutual Publishing.

Pope, A. 1914. Letter from Miss Anne Pope to the children of Miss Ida M. Pope. *The Friend* (September). (Copy available in Oberlin College Archives Alumnae/Former Student files, group 28, file 818, s.v. Pope, Ida May.)

Pope, K. 1924. *Hawaii, the rainbow land*. New York: Thomas Crowell Company.

Powers, M. 1891. Changes at the Kawaiahaʻo Seminary. *Hawaiian Gazette* 26, no. 24: 2. (Accessed through the Library of Congress site Chronicling America http://chroniclingamerica.loc.gov/.)

Pratt, H. G. 1939. *In Hawaii: A hundred years*. New York: Charles Scribner's Sons.

———. 1957. *The story of Mid-Pacific Institute*. Honolulu: Tongg Publishing Company, Ltd.

Punahou School. *Oahu College list of officers, instructors and students, historical sketch 1841–1906*. 1907. Honolulu: Hawaiian Gazette Company. (Includes a historical sketch of Oahu College by William DeWitt Alexander, and lists of trustees, presidents, instructors, matrons, librarians, superintendents of grounds, and students, 1841–1906. Accessed from http://books.google.com/books.)

Pyke, C. 2006. Mystery in the garden (Margaret Abernethy Brewer Fowler). *Scripps Magazine* (Summer). (Accessed http://www.scrippscollege.edu/media/magazine/category/2010-Spring/index.php.)

Robert, D. L. 1986. *American women in mission: A social history of their thought and practice*. Macon, GA: Mercer University Press.

The Sandwich Islands: Stereopticon lecture on "The geographical features and social conditions of the Hawaiian Islands." n.d. (A photocopy of this two-page pamphlet was received from the family of L. E. Appleton; the pamphlet describes Miss Appleton's images and lectures on Hawaiʻi.)

Shor, E. N. 1974. Kofoid, Charles Atwood. *Dictionary of Scientific Biography* Supplement 4 (1946–1950, 1974, 461–462). New York: Charles Scribner's Sons.

Siddall, J. W., ed. 1921. *Men of Hawaii: A biographical reference library. Complete and authentic of the men of note and substantial achievement in the Hawaiian Islands*. 2 Vols. Honolulu: Honolulu Star Bulletin, Limited.

Spiess, F. N. 2002. Charles Kofoid's role in establishing the Scripps Institution of Oceanography. In *Oceanographic history: The Pacific and beyond*, editors

Keith R. Benson and Philip F. Rehbock, 7–16. Seattle: University of Washington Press.

Strong, E. E. 1897. *In lands afar: A second series of mission stories of many lands; A book for young people.* Boston: Congregational House for ABCFM.

Sweet seminarians. 1892. *Daily Bulletin* (Honolulu) June 13. (A clipping of this article is in Carrie Prudence Winter's letters, but the article can be accessed through the Library of Congress site Chronicling America.)

Teachers' excursion to the volcano June 23–July 7 two full weeks $ fifty-five $. 1903. Honolulu. (A photocopy of this pamphlet was obtained from Kamehameha Archives, Kamehameha School.)

Thompson, U. 1941. *Reminiscences of old Hawaii with account of early life.* Dobbs Ferry, NY: Privately printed.

Thrum, T. G., comp. 1890. *All about Hawaii: Hawaiian almanac and annual for 1891, A handbook of information on interesting matters related to the Hawaiian Islands.* Honolulu: Press Publishing Company. (Accessed http://books.google.com/books.)

———. 1891. *All about Hawaii: Hawaiian almanac and annual for 1892, A handbook of information on interesting matters related to the Hawaiian Islands.* Honolulu: Press Publishing Company. (Accessed http://books.google.com/books.)

———. 1892. *All about Hawaii: Hawaiian almanac and annual for 1893,* Honolulu: Press Publishing Company. (Accessed http://books.google.com/books.)

To wear uniform. 1891. *Hawaiian Gazette* (September 15): 5. (Accessed through Library of Congress site Chronicling America http://chroniclingamerica.loc.gov/lccn/.)

Turner, C. L. 1929. *The story of Maunaolu Seminary.* Honolulu: The Friend.

The trustees of Kawaiahaʻo Seminary tender their resignations. 1894. *Hawaiian Gazette* (June 15): 3. (Accessed through Library of Congress site Chronicling America http://chroniclingamerica.loc.gov/lccn/.)

Wagner, S. E. 1986. "Sojourners among strangers: The first two companies of missionaries to the Sandwich Islands." Ph.D. diss., University of Hawai'i–Mānoa.

Welter, B. 1980. Cult of true womanhood: 1820–1860. In *Woman's experience in America: An historical analogy,* edited by Esther Katz and Anita Rapone. New Brunswick, NJ: Transaction Books.

Westervelt, W. D. 1911. *The first twenty years of education in the Hawaiian Islands.* Honolulu: Hawaiian Historical Society.

Wilcox, E. W. 1910. *The new Hawaiian girl; A play.* London: Gay & Hancock, Ltd. (Accessed from Internet Archive http://www.archive.org/stream/newhawaiian.)

Williams, R. M. 2000. Deaths and funerals of major Hawaiian ali'i. Honolulu: Rianna M. Williams.

Winter, C. P. 1892. An American girl in the Hawaiian Islands. *Southern Magazine* (November). (Obtained a copy from the Charles Atwood Kofoid Papers, box 69, which was stamped "William and Mary Library.")

———. 1893. Blount is very busy. *Hartford Courant* (May 29): page 7.

———. 1893. Carrie Winter's views. *Hartford Courant* (November 13): page 1.

———. 1893. Fine Hawaiian scenery. Precipitous cliffs and beautiful valleys. *Hartford Courant* (May 6): page 1.

———. 1893. Hawaii hears the news. Regret that annexation has been delayed. *Hartford Courant* (March 25): page 11.

———. 1893. Hawaii's crisis, story of a young woman student. Letter to the Courant. *Hartford Courant* (February 3): page 1.

———. 1893. The juicy sugar cane. *Hartford Courant* (May 13): page 11.

———. 1893. King Kalakaua's death: How the news was received at Honolulu. *Hartford Courant* (February 1893): page 1.

———. 1893. The land of vowels. Glorious scenes on Hawaiian soil. *Hartford Courant* (April 10): 8.

———. 1893. Latest from Hawaii. Decided stand taken by Japan. Escaped prisoner not returned. *Hartford Courant* (April 15): page 5.

Wisniewski, R. A. 1979. *The rise and fall of the Hawaiian Kingdom: A pictorial history*. Honolulu: Pacific Basin Enterprises.

Wist, B. O. 1937. "American foundations of public education in Hawaii: The socio-economic factors which were influential in the shaping of an American public school system in Hawaii." Ph.D. diss., Yale University.

———. 1940. *A century of public education in Hawaii*. Honolulu: Hawaiian Educational Review.

Wood, E. W. 1930. *Memoirs of the Waterhouse family*. Honolulu: Privately printed. (Photocopy obtained from Hawaiian Mission Children's Society, Mission Houses Museum Library.)

Women's Board of Missions for the Pacific Islands. 1899. Annual report.

Websites

Ancestry.com for access to census records, Honolulu city directories, and genealogical information.

Chronicling America, Library of Congress website: http://chronicling america.loc.gov/.

Hawaiian Roots. Genealogy for Hawaiians. Index of obituaries from Hawaiian newspapers: http://www.hawaiian-roots.com/hawaiiangazette.htm.

Kamehameha School Archives website: http://kapalama.ksbe.edu/archives/. All of the information on this website was useful, but especially relevant to our work was the material on Kamehameha School for Girls and the photographs of early classes.

Kekoolani Genealogy of the Descendants of the Ruling Chiefs of Hawaii: http://www.kekoolani.org/.

Mission Houses Museum website: http://www.missionhouses.org/. Everything on this site is useful to researchers, but the virtual collections are especially helpful to scholars searching for historical images.

Ulukau, The Hawaiian Electronic Library: http://ulukau.org/gsdl2.7/cgi-bin/algene.

Index

Page numbers in boldface type refer to illustrations.

Brewer & Company, 327, 328, 333, 346, 386;
Buddhism, 306;

California, 5, 6, 303, 305, 354, 358;
camping, xxxi, xxxii, 127, 128, 129, 130, 133, 135, 140, 179, 208, 210, 214;
Canada and Canadians, 317, 333, 363, 370;
canoes, outrigger, 12;
carriages, 12, 50, 68, 70-71, 79, 83, 166, 197, 206, 216, 217, 218, 243, 281;
Castle & Cooke, 244, 273, 317, 324, 328, 332, 333;
Catholicism and Catholics, 52, 117n3, 220, 221, 224, 306, 357;
Central Union Church, Honolulu, xxx, 36, 49, 53, 59, 81, 155, 159, 231, 245, 275, 281n1, 318, 321, 324, 327, 332, 334, 342, 345, 346, 355, 362, 368, 380, 386;
Charleston (ship), 32, 52, 54, 75, 77, 82, 83, 85, 87;
City of Pekin (ship), 190;
Chamber of Commerce, Honolulu, 226;
Chicago, 2, 3, 191, 294, 332, 334, 343, 355, 361, 365, 372, 373, 387;
Chiefs' Children's School, xi, 311, 318, 321, 322, 358, 364;
China, 7, 305, 334, 370;
Chinatown. *See* Honolulu—Chinatown, San Francisco—Chinatown;
Chinese in Hawai'i, xix, xx, 23, 34-35, 40n6, 58, 94, 96, 97, 131, 148, 155, 185-186, 193, 208, 209, 233, 276, 277, 289, 334, 338, 349, 382, 389;
cholera, 229, 232;
Christmas, 39, 56, 57, 59, 62, 63, 142, 151, 152, 155, 158, 245, 249, 251, 357;
Claudine (ship), 265, 266, 267, 270;
clergy, xvii, xxi, xxvii, 35, 199, 202, 204, 215, 216, 245, 287, 321, 383, 388;
Clifton Springs Sanatorium, 258, 283n2;
clothing, 7, 58, 109, 121, 167, 182, 186, 194, 195, 197;

Coco Head, 11;
coconut, 26, 34,150, 249, 276;
Coconut Island, Hawai'i (Moku-ola), 216;
Connecticut, xxi, 2, 3, 177, 210, 232, 291, 303, 330, 371, 388;
constitution, 32, 77, 165, 227, 264, 283n4;
Constitution of 1887, xiii, 336, 383;
consumption, xxvii, 103, 113, 309, 313, 334, 337, 382, 385;
cooking, xxx, 34, 62, 107, **137**, 144, 150, 153, 198, 256, 259, 276;
coral, 11, 111;
courts and trials, 190, 200, 203n2, 203n3, 284n19, 316, 335, 336, 341, 248, 322, 367, 376, 379, 387. *See also* Supreme Court
courtship and marriage, xii, xviii, xix, xxi, 23, 37, 90, 98, 100n11, 113, 140, 142, 156, 159, 172, 190, 203, 205, 228, 256, 257, 306. *See also* weddings
Crown lands, 82, 268;
curriculum, 70, 90, 254;

dancing and balls, 21, 71, 173, 214, 230, 233, 245, 270;
Darwinism, 161, 163, 269;
death and mourning, xviii, xxvii, 10, 75-77, 80-83, 87, 89, 95, 100n5, 100n10, 106, 107, 134, 135, 136n5, 169, 174, 184n2, 194, 307;
Diamond Head (Leahi), 11, **15**, 23, 61, 145, **228**, 230, 292, 383;
discipline and punishment. *See* Kawaiaha'o Seminary-discipline and punishment

Easter, 93, 95, 180, 285;
eggs, 74, 85;
England, 47, 85, 92, 179, 273, 276, 280, 282, 337;
English Language, xxx, 23, 41, 71, 90, 91, 104, 108, 140, 144, 154, 157, 198, 238, 254;
examinations, 59, 153, 154, 167, 195, 196, 198, 292;

transportation, xxiv, 33, **51**, 62, 86, 236, 306; shops, 37, 53, 62, 94, 193, 199; water, xxv, 106, 114, 289;

Honolulu Sailors' Home, 39;

ho'okupu, 85, 100n7;

Horner Bill, 227;

horseback riding, 49, 74, 85, 113, 124, 130, 131, 172, 188, 195, 214, 218, 235, 266, 273, 278, 288, 292, 297;

horses and mules, xxv, 49, 50, 56, 68, 70, 83, 85, 124, 125, 126, 127, 130, 134, 142, 146, 161, 172, 177, 181, 184, 187, 188, 207, 218, 257, 262, **279**, 294, 295;

hula, xxxi, 270;

hymns, xxx, 76, 87, 129, 170, 355;

hysteria, 252;

Illinois, 4, 304, 355, 388;

Indians, North American, 5, 312, 316, 345, 349, 354;

Independence Day (Hawaiian), 54;

Independent, 16, 309, 321, 367, 371, 373, 374, 378;

influenza, 109, 304;

insects, xxvi, 22, 28, 29, 56, 74, 108, 163, 287;

'Iolani Palace, xxix, **45**, 47, 48, **66**, 75-77, 80, 82, 87, 97, 176, 264, 359;

Iowa, 4, 334, 381;

Irenegard (ship), 297;

Japan, 273, 279, 280, 282, 286, 289, 378;

Japanese in Hawai'i, 27, 158, 207, 216, 217, 260, 271, 272, 273, 277, 279, 282, 284n11, 302, 342, 366, 368;

kahilis, 48, 76, 83, 87, 132, 195, 283n3;

Kahuku, 220;

kahunas, xiii, 113, 118n10, 160, 269, 289;

Kaliuwa'a, 221;

Kamehameha Preparatory School, xxxiii, 12n3, 32, 61, 107, 206, 232, 250, 309, 343, 344, 348, 355, 362, 365, 381, 384;

Kamehameha School for Boys, Honolulu, xxxiii, 15, 25, 32, 33, 36, 37, 49, 61,68, 145, 147, 169, 180, 305, 306, 333, 379; music, 170; students, 25, 30, 32, 33, 62, 88, 156, 180, 242, 250, 271, 309, 323, 330, 346, 352, 389; teachers, 37, 69, 74, 96, 110, 137, 138, 147, 155, 183, 201, 206, 223, 231, 232, 243, 245, 258, 260, 282, 315, 316, 320, 323, 327, 343, 361, 363, 368, 369, 376, 377, 382;

Kamehameha School for Girls, Honolulu, xix, xxxiii, 36, 174, 305, 310, 314, 341, 347, 348, 349, 350, 352, 354, 355, 360, 361, 371, 372, 386;

Kane'aukai, xxx, 220;

Kaua'i, 96, 305 316, 323, 377, 386; Kawaiaha'o students from, xxvii, 309, 310, 312, 318, 320, 341, 345, 348, 351, 353, 359, 361, 369, 374, 376, 378, 386;

Kaua'i Industrial School, 180, 352, 375;

Kaumakapili Church, Honolulu, xxx, **162**, 347, 353, 356, 357, 360, 369, 383;

Kawaiaha'o Alumnae Quartette, 354;

Kawaiaha'o Church, Honolulu, xxvi, xxx, 49, 58, 112, 140, **175**, 194, 202, 265, 277, 306, 321, 324, 353, 354, 357, 360, 364, 379;

Kawaiaha'o Female Seminary, xi, xxi, xxx, xxiv, 12, 18, 24, 30, 39, 81, 95, 98, 99, 100n12, 115, **116**, 120, 148, 153, 154, 173-174, **175**, 186, 196, 197, 202, 233, 239, 258,281, 254; buildings and facilities, 12, 16, 18-20, 58, 77, 185; curriculum, xxi, xxx, 18-20, 23, 70, 90, 120, 140, 157, 254; daily schedule, 22-23, 25, 27, 28, 120, 186, 238, 239; deaths, 89, 100n10, 169, 184n2, 364; discipline and punishment, xii, xxi, xxxi, 24, 25, 29, 30, 36, 37, 39, 44, 53, 54, 55, 56, 59, 60, 64, 68, 72, 73, 77, 85, 86, 90, 93, 94, 139, 141,168, 170, 173, 178, 181, 198, 233, 258, 285; enrollment, xxiv, xxvii, 19, 120, 139, 159, 185, 228; finances, xxvi, xxx, xxxiii, xxxiv, 81, 91, 99, 115, 122, 174,

Marshall Islands, 331;

Massachusetts, 2, 321, 329, 333, 335, 336, 337, 338, 344, 345, 346, 354, 357, 365, 366, 368, 371, 379, 384, 381, 388;

Maui, xxxi, 106, 117, 121, 122, 123, 126, 129, 146, 174, 210, 272, 313, 335, 339, 381, 383, 384; Kawaiahaʻo students from, 309, 310, 311, 342, 348, 350, 354;

Mauna Kea, 217;

Mauna Loa, 129, 320;

Maunaʻolu Seminary, xi, 123, 313, 341, 363;

McKinley Tariff Bill, 165, 166, 184n1, 267;

medicine, 31, 161, 182, 271, 275. *See also* physicians

Micronesia, xxvi, 155, 174, 245, 282, 322, 331, 340, 344, 352, 357, 360, 379, 384;

Mid-Pacific Institute, xxxiv, 324, 328, 377;

missionaries, ix, x, xi, xiii, xiv, xv, xvi, xxx, 1, 7, 97, 124, 155, 165, 167, 174, 282, 303, 304, 305, 306, 320, 322, 265, 338, 352, 360, 370, 379, 383;

missionary work, xxiii, 28, 210, 360, 370;

Missouri, 4;

Mohican (ship), 270;

Mokuola. *See* Coconut Island, Hawaiʻi;

Molokaʻi, 11, 15, 49, 59, 101-103, 105, 117n2, 126, 155, 158, 205, 256, 303, 321, 325, 326, 336, 350, 351, 366, 370;

Monowai (ship), 83, 145, 269;

Mormons, 320, 376;

Morning Star (ship), 22, 106, 110, 111, 118n8, 180, 199, 299, 322, 338, 379;

mosquitos, 22, 23, 24, 27, 57, 72, 147, 203. *See also* insects

Mount Holyoke Seminary, 337, 338;

music and musicians, 6, 11, 30, 48, 57, 60, 62, 76, 80, 82, 85, 99, 103, **116**, 153, 157, **162**, 170, **175**, 179, 191, **192**, 221, 285, 321, 327, 349, 356, 357, 366. *See also* Royal Hawaiian Band

musical instruments, 201, 221, **280**;

mythology, Hawaiian, 132, 389, 222;

Naniwa (ship), 279, 280, 282;

National Liberal Party, 327;

National Reform Party, 165, 166;

Native Americans. *See* indians, North American;

Nebraska, 4, 316;

New York, 2, 50, 72, 148, 223, 258, 292, 314, 327, 329, 336, 338, 339, 354;

New York Herald, 327, 345;

New Zealand, 6;

newspapers, 16, 76, 241, 266, 270, 276, 293, 317, 327, 353;

Nipsic (ship), 31;

Normal School, 167, 311, 348, 349, 352, 371, 378, 384;

Northfield Academy, 147, 366, 388;

Oʻahu, 15, 218, 219, 224, 224n6; Kawaiahaʻo students from, xxvii, 309, 314, 325, 330, 334, 335, 340, 341, 347, 353, 356;

Oahu College, 27, 92, 110, 171, 313, 317, 321, 329, 335, 337, 338, 345, 362, 369, 371, 372, 386, 387. *See also* Punahou School

Oahu Railway and Land Company, 184n6;

Oakland High School, 311, 324, 366;

Oberlin College, x, xv, xvii, xviii, xix, xxii, xxiii, xxxiii, 1, 12, 32, 36, 37, 62, 68, 79, 96, 104, 108, 118n11, 137, 138, 161, 206, 230, 261, 273, 310, 314, 316, 324, 328, 329, 332, 338, 342, 343, 344, 355, 360, 361, 362, 365, 368, 370, 371, 372, 381, 384, 386, 388, 389, 390; picnic, 16, **149**;

Occidental Hotel, 6, 294;

Oceanic (ship), 262;

Oceanic Steamship Company, **17**;

oceanography, 304, 356;

Olinda, 126, 320;

Opera House, Honolulu, **192**, 231;

opium, xiii, 191, 227, 262, 263, 267, 282;

organs and organists, **162**, 231, 250, 256, 290, 356, 357;

Ostrich Farm, Honolulu, 54, 65n5, 107, 383;

About the Editors

Dr. Sandra Bonura is a Southern California counselor educator whose long-standing love of Hawai'i and people's stories were immediately engaged by the discovery of Carrie's letters and the characters and events they brought to life. Her efforts to find the long-inaccessible reel-to-reel taped recollections of Lydia Ka'onohiponiponiokalani Aholo, the hānai daughter of Queen Lili'uokalani, and return them to the state are a permanent contribution to Hawaiian history. As someone who herself likes to disconnect from technology and reflect, Sandee believes that old-fashioned correspondence prove that the lost art of letter writing should be revived. She is busy on her second Hawaiian epistolary novel.

Deborah Day has a B.A. from the University of Massachusetts, Amherst and an MLS from Simmons College. She has a certificate from the NHPRC/University of Wisconsin, Madison/State Historical Society of Wisconsin Institute for the Editing of Historical Documents. She was archivist of Scripps Institution of Oceanography, UCSD Libraries until retirement. She lives in San Diego, California.